Confronting Ecological and Economic Collapse

From the first appearance of the term in law in the Clean Water Act of 1972 (US), ecological integrity has been debated by a wide range of researchers, including biologists, ecologists, philosophers, legal scholars, doctors and epidemiologists, whose joint interest was the study and understanding of ecological/biological integrity from various standpoints and disciplines. This volume discusses the need for ecological integrity as a major guiding principle in a variety of policy areas, to counter the present ecological and economic crises with their multiple effects on human rights.

The book celebrates the 20th anniversary of the Global Ecological Integrity Group and reassesses the basic concept of ecological integrity in order to show how a future beyond catastrophe and disaster is in fact possible, but only if civil society and ultimately legal regimes acknowledge the need to consider ecointegrity as a primary factor in decision making. This is key to the support of basic rights to clean air and water, for halting climate change, and also the basic rights of women and indigenous people. As the authors clearly show, all these rights ultimately depend upon accepting policies that acknowledge the pivotal role of ecological integrity.

Laura Westra is Professor Emerita (Philosophy) and Sessional Instructor, Faculty of Law, University of Windsor, Canada, and Sessional Instructor, Faculty of Law, University of Milano (Bicocca), Italy. She is the author, editor or co-editor of 29 books on ecological integrity, five of which are published by Earthscan/Routledge.

Prue Taylor is Deputy Director, New Zealand Centre for Environmental Law and Senior Lecturer, School of Architecture and Planning, University of Auckland, New Zealand.

Agnès Michelot is Maître de conférences HDR en droit public and co-director of the Center of Juridical and Political Studies (CEJEP) at the Université de La Rochelle, France.

Confronting Ecological and Economic Collapse

Ecological integrity for law, policy and human rights

Edited by Laura Westra, Prue Taylor and Agnès Michelot

Routledge
Taylor & Francis Group

LONDON AND NEW YORK

earthscan
from Routledge

First published 2013
By Routledge
2 Park Square, Milton Park, Abingdon, Oxon, OX14 4RN

Simultaneously published in the USA and Canada
by Routledge
711 Third Avenue, New York, NY 10017

First issued in paperback 2015

Routledge is an imprint of the Taylor & Francis Group, an informa business

British Library Cataloguing in Publication Data
A catalogue record for this book is available from the British Library

Library of Congress Cataloging-in-Publication Data
Confronting ecological and economic collapse : ecological integrity
for law, policy and human rights / Edited by Laura Westra, Prue
Taylor and Agnès Michelot.
pages cm.
Includes bibliographical references and index.
1. Environmental law, International. 2. Ecological integrity.
3. Climatic changes. 4. Financial crises. 5. Economic forecasting.
6. International economic relations. 7. Human beings–Effect of
climate on. I. Westra, Laura, editor of compilation. II. Taylor,
Prue, 1961- editor of compilation. III. Michelot, Agnès,
editor of compilation.
K3585.C6589 2013
344.04'6–dc23
2012050088

ISBN13: 978-0-415-73055-6 (pbk)
ISBN13: 978-0-415-82525-2 (hbk)

Typeset in Baskerville
by Fish Books Ltd.

Contents

Contributors

Klaus Bosselmann
Countries of affiliation: New Zealand, Germany
Professor of Law
University of Auckland NZ Centre for Environmental Law
IUCN World Commission on Environmental Law
Email: k.bosselmann@auckland.ac.nz
www.law.auckland.ac.nz/uoa/os-klaus-bosselmann

Donald A. Brown, JD, MA (Liberal Studies, Philosophy and Art)
Country of affiliation: USA
Scholar in Residence, Sustainability Ethics and Law
Widener University School of Law
Email: dabrown57@gmail.com
http://ethicsandclimate.org

Peter G. Brown, PhD (Columbia)
Country of affiliation: Canada
Professor
McGill University, School of Environment

Peter D. Burdon, BA, LLB (Hons), PhD
Country of affiliation: Australia
Senior Lecturer
Adelaide Law School, University of Adelaide
Email: peter.d.burdon@adelaide.edu.au
www.adelaide.edu.au/directory/peter.d.burdon

Noémie Candiago
Country of affiliation: France
PhD Student
University of La Rochelle
Email: ncandiago@gmail.com

Sheila D. Collins, PhD
Country of affiliation: USA
Professor Emerita (Political Science)
William Paterson University
Email: sheila.collins65@verizon.net
www.wpunj.edu/cohss/departments/pol_sci/faculty/collins/index.dot

Joseph W. Dellapenna, BBA (Michigan), JD (Detroit College of Law), LLM
(International and Comparative Law) (George Washington), LLM
(Environmental Law) (Columbia)
Country of affiliation: USA
Professor of Law
Villanova University School of Law
Email: dellapen@law.villanova.edu
www.law.villanova.edu/Our%20Faculty/Faculty%20Profiles/
Joseph%20W%20Dellapenna.aspx

Joan Gibb Engel, PhD
Country of affiliation: United States
Email: jgengel@comcast.net

Giovanni Ferri
Country of affiliation: Italy
Dept Economic and Political Sciences and Modern Languages
LUMSA – Holy Mary of the Assumption Free University
Email: gioferri@gmail.com or g.ferri@lumsa.it
Papers on SSRN at: http://ssrn.com/author=205760
Different cultures/disciplines meet at Saint Nicholas School
www.saintnicholas-school.com

Shaun Fluker, LLM
Country of affiliation: Canada
Associate Professor (Law)
University of Calgary Faculty of Law
Email: sfluker@ucalgary.ca

Michelle Gallant, PhD (Law) LLM
Country of affiliation: Canada
Associate Professor of Law
Faculty of Law, University of Manitoba
Email: gallant@ad.umanitoba.ca

Geoffrey Garver, LLM, JD, BS (Chem. Engineering)
Countries of affiliation: Canada, USA
PhD Candidate (Geography)
McGill University
Email: gginmont@sympatico.ca

Janice Gray, BA, LLB, (Grad) Dip Ed, (Grad) Dip Leg Practice, MA
Country of affiliation: Australia
Senior Lecturer
Faculty of Law, University of New South Wales, Sydney, Australia
Email: j.gray@unsw.edu.au

Vicky Karageorgou, LLM, PhD Law
Country of affiliation: Greece
Lecturer in European Administrative and European Environmental Law
Panteion University of Social and Political Sciences
Email: vkaragiorgou@yahoo.gr

Yuliya Lyamzina, MBA, PhD
Countries of affiliation: Czech Republic, Austria
PhD in Public Health and Epidemiology
Masaryk University,
Sessional Instructor, Medical Faculty
Brno, Czech Republic
Email: lyamzina@yahoo.com

Owen McIntyre, BA, LLB, PhD
Country of affiliation: Ireland
Senior Lecturer
Faculty of Law
University College Cork
National University of Ireland
Email: o.mcintyre@ucc.ie

Jack Manno, PhD
Country of affiliation: USA
Associate Professor of Environmental Studies
SUNY College of Environmental Science and Forestry
Email: jpmanno@esf.edu
www.esf.edu/es/manno/

Agnès Michelot
Country of affiliation: France
Maître de conferences, HDR, co-director of the Center
of Juridical and Political Studies (CEJEP)
University of La Rochelle
Email: agnes.michelot@univ-lr.fr

William E. Rees, PhD, FRSC
Country of affiliation: Canada
Professor Emeritus (human ecology, Planning)
University of British Columbia School of Community
and Regional Planning
Email: wrees@mail.ubc.ca

Tullio Scovazzi
Country of affiliation: Italy
Professor of International Law
University of Milano-Bicocca, Milan
Email: tullio.scovazzi@unimib.it

Prue Taylor, LLB, LLM, LLM
Country of affiliation: New Zealand
Deputy Director, New Zealand Centre for Environmental Law
School of Architecture and Planning, University of Auckland, NZ
Email: Prue.Taylor@auckland.ac.nz

János I. Tóth, PhD
Country of affiliation: Hungary
Associate Professor (Philosophy)
University of Szeged
Email: jtoth@philo.u-szeged.hu

Valentina Vadi, PhD (Law)
Countries of affiliation: Netherlands, Italy
Marie Curie Postdoctoral Fellow
Maastricht University
Email: v.vadi@maastrichtuniversity.nl

Laura Westra, PhD, PhD (Law)
Countries of affiliation: Canada, Italy
Professor Emerita (Philosophy)
University of Windsor
Sessional Instructor, Faculty of Law
www.ecointegrity.net
www.globalecointegrity.net

Foreword

Confronting Collapse

Peter G. Brown

> It's all a question of story. We are in trouble now because we do not have a good story. We are in between stories. The old story, the account of how the world came to be and how we fit into it, is no longer effective.
>
> (Thomas Berry, *The Dream of the Earth*)

The question of what it is to be human and a part of the Universe is an age-old question. Answers are framed in narratives. And the overarching narrative of our culture is leading us toward multiple collapses. Embedded in the core values and assumptions of all major modern-day institutions, be it economics, governance or finance, is a story about humans and nature based on faulty notions of humanity and what it means to be a human subject in the Universe. The dichotomy of humans versus nature, which was exalted during the late Western Enlightenment, is knit into these institutions; yet it has proven to be highly detrimental to intergenerational and interspecies flourishing of life on Earth. Humans and nature are seen as discrete and distinct entities, disconnected from one another and not interacting with each other. These faulty assumptions are the root of the reason why modern society is facing a time of collapse.

Today, we face multiple crises: lack of jobs, unmanageable debt, poverty, illegitimate and ineffective governments, and population growth. Most important, we are also in a severe ecological crisis; and as this unfolds the others will massively and tragically worsen. Ecological collapse is not something that may happen in the future: its leading edge is everywhere to be seen – in a destabilized climate, an acidified ocean, desertification, and loss of the life forms with which we share heritage and destiny. Everywhere to be seen, that is, except in most of the world's capital cities.

The gathering storm

The economic crisis

Globally hundreds of millions of people are unemployed or underemployed. The policy response has been to stimulate aggregate demand through changes in taxes and spending (fiscal policy) and expansion of credit (monetary policy). These increases, if successful, will contribute to an increase in economic activity and employment, resulting in more oil consumed and more greenhouse gases produced. This further destabilizes the climate, which adds to sea level rise, salt water penetration of aquifers, stronger storms, increased acidification of the oceans, and so on. If present trends of fossil fuel use continue, we will be committing the Earth to an eventual sea level rise of about 80 meters, a climate not felt for millions of years – and one with which the human and other species are not adapted.

The money crisis

One of the principal means employed in recent decades (especially since the early 1980s) is the expansion in the variety and magnitude of financial instruments and institutions. Only a very small amount of money is created in the form of coins and bills by governments. Banks can create money *ex nihilo* with little in the way of reserves. Credit purchases vastly increase purchasing power through the creation of credit by the company that issues the cards. Investment houses create financial instruments based on other financial instruments. The result is a cycle whereby large financial institutions have control over governance; undercutting effectiveness and legitimacy.

It is estimated that gross world product is around US$75 trillion; while the total amount of money is vastly larger, perhaps by several orders of magnitude. As John Fullerton has pointed out, this problem has two dimensions. On one hand, as this money is spent, it inevitably further destabilizes the Earth's life support systems. In a word, there is more money than there is Earth. On the other hand, much of the money that people think they have should not be spent. For example, any realistic response to the climate crisis will require leaving large amounts of oil, coal and natural gas in the Earth's crust. But it is unlikely that the holders of money are going to be happy about enormous write-downs on their balance sheets. Financial turmoil is already resulting – with negative effects felt both in the social realm (such as with employment and welfare) and with Earth's systems.

The poverty crisis

At the same time that some people have too much money, hundreds of millions have too little. Yet development efforts based on the Western model of consumption oriented societies pose unacceptable risks to the Earth's life support systems. To increase economic activity in one part of the world, we need to decrease it in another. This is one of the principal reasons why the 'degrowth' movement has developed in Europe and has begun to fledge in North America. But following this prescription seems completely unthinkable to some policy-makers (such as those in the United States and Canada).

The population crisis

To make matters worse, the countries where the poorest people live have the highest birth rates. UN population projections for 2050 estimate another 2 billion people on Earth, and the likelihood of 10 billion by the end of the century. These numbers, as sobering as they are, assume that rising levels of material and monetary wealth will be essential for the eventual stabilization of the population, hence adding to the ecological crisis.

We have entered a perfect storm. As we try to address one problem, we worsen the others. This is the most profound governance problem our species has ever faced. Because we lack a holistic framework, we do not see these problems as interconnected; or ourselves as seamlessly embedded in the Earth and the Universe. To address the multiple crises of our time we need to completely reground and redeploy our knowledge systems in these light of this understanding. And to do this we need a wholly new narrative about ourselves, our planet, and our place in the Universe. *Confronting Ecological and Economic Collapse* aims to help reconstruct our master narrative, and thereby envision a restored and flourishing future for life on Earth.

Introduction

Laura Westra

It has been twenty years from the inception of our multidisciplinary quest for an in depth understanding of biological and ecological integrity, starting in 1992 and fully funded by Social Sciences and Humanities Research Council of Canada (SSHRC) from 1992 to 1999, when I, as Principal Investigator, retired from the University of Windsor. Each of the meetings of the following years after 1992, added some strand to the understanding we were seeking. Some of those findings were reflected in my first book on environmental ethics, *The Principle of Integrity* (Westra, 1994), but the work of research continued to expand, adding new members to what eventually became the Global Ecological Integrity Group.

In 2000 our 'final' multi-authored definition of ecological integrity was published (Westra *et al.*, 2000), and from that time on, our meetings included other disciplines beyond the original group of scientists and philosophers, as the focus shifted to a consideration of the role of ecological integrity, now defined, in a variety of fields.

For the most part the new additions to the group were legal scholars and specialists in medicine and epidemiology, in line with the twin developments of our joint research trajectory, the focus of which was, increasingly, the interface between ecology and human rights. In December 1998, we held a meeting in Rome, at the offices of the World Health Organization (WHO), under the aegis of Dr Roberto Bertollini, together with member Colin Soskolne, who produced a document in 1999 that is still an important statement on the relation between ecological integrity and public health (Soskolne and Bertollini, 1999).

From that standpoint (i.e. from the intimate connection between ecological integrity and human rights to life/health), the second new trend (i.e. the legal interface between human rights and ecological integrity) represents a logical move. This move was also sustained by our newly established connection with the Earth Charter Organization and the IUCN, as well as my own return to school to pursue a second PhD, this time in jurisprudence, and the eventual publication of that thesis (Westra, 2004). The interface between human rights and ecological integrity has been perhaps the most important development of the group's interests and scholarship, as that was followed by work on related human rights, such as the rights to water, to safe healthy food and to unpolluted air, with particular focus on climate change and toxic exposures.

The WHO connection also led us to the first of two volumes celebrating twenty years of what started as the Global Ecological Integrity Project, and now is the Global Ecological Integrity Group (GEIG); that collection was entitled *Human Health and Ecological Integrity*. This collection was the result of a meeting at the School of Medicine at Charles University in Prague in 2011, and it showcases the centrality of public health to the interests and aims of the group.

This volume represents the second result of twenty years of work on the part of the GEIG, and the focus is now on the possibility of moving forward from a global state of the world reflecting multiple crises, from the economy to ecology and to governance itself, all of which reflect grave violations of human rights. Confronting collapse essentially starts from the premise that refusing to accept the centrality of ecological integrity for the protection of human rights on the part of lawmakers and governing bodies, both domestic and international, has contributed significantly to the multiple collapses the world is facing.

This is the basic thread that has been running through most of the collections published by GEIG, and it was especially evident in the fifteenth-anniversary collection (Westra *et al.*, 2008). At this time, this book has several questions it intends to answer: the first question is the obvious one: where should we go from here? The second one, once we identify a more desirable state for which to aim, is this: how, precisely, can we proceed towards that goal?

It is somewhat coincidental that our own meeting in 2012 coincided with the Rio + 20 meeting, and that occasion will be reported and critiqued in one of the last chapters of this volume. The book includes five parts, and the first part traces the history of the ecological integrity concept, starting with the 'historical' review by Jack Manno, of the main scholars who have had a strong impact on the group's work and on the new directions to which they pointed through their own research. That 'select' group included scientists, philosophers and legal scholars, and their varied background attests to the importance of ecological integrity in many fields.

In the second chapter, Shaun Fluker reports on the 'return' to ecological integrity as one of the main principles intended to govern the establishment and the operations of national parks in Canada. Not only is ecological integrity – at least on paper – foundational to national parks now, but the concept is also used to assist in cases where the rights of Canadian First Nations are under attack. Chapters 3 and 4 choose a particularly useful international legal instrument, one that may hold some promise to provide a possible new avenue through which to approach the present multiple collapses. Prue Taylor discusses the Common Heritage of Mankind principle in general, whereas Tullio Scovazzi discusses its use in regard to marine ecosystems.

In Chapter 5 Agnès Michelot brings Part I to a close, through an examination of our main theme – that is, the presence of ecological integrity in the legal regimes of the European Union – and the possible connection between that concept and environmental justice in that region.

Part II considers the interface between disintegrity and some of the basic rights violations involved. In Chapter 6, Don Brown discusses the connection between the human rights violations engendered by climate change and the ongoing corporate-funded disinformation campaigns regarding that issue. The following three chapters start with Vicky Karageorgou discussing environmental permits regarding water in Greece, followed by Owen McIntyre's analysis of EU environmental law and 'sustainable development', as sustainability is a concept that does not appear in EU law at this time, while Joseph Dellapenna considers international water law. In the final chapter of this part, Yuliya Lyamzina discusses the interface between UN law and gender-specific human rights.

Part III traces the impact of disintegrity in various forms through cases that show the possibility of improvement either through better local laws as reported in János Tóth's case study regarding Kolontar in Hungary; or through grass-roots public involvement in Australia in Janice Gray's chapter.

Part IV turns to the economic crisis that affects the whole world at this time, from the member states of the European Union, to countries in Asia, Africa and the United States. The first two chapters examine the problems that give rise to the present crisis, as Giovanni Ferri discusses the inadequacy of the present regulation of global finance, and Michelle Gallant proposes shifting some of the responsibility for global finance to credit unions, as institutions that present different priorities for their operations. Geoff Garver in turn reports on the latest thinking developed in contrast with globalized capitalist 'growth'; that is, the emerging of the 'degrowth paradigm'. This theme is continued by Noémie Candiago as she traces the relation between 'degrowth' and ecological debt. In Chapter 17, Valentina Vadi turns to international investment law and the conflict between the necessary control of the tobacco industry and trademark protection.

Part V proposes new approaches that might result in mitigating, if not eliminating the grave difficulties discussed in the previous chapters. J. Ron Engel provides an introduction to the topic, given his lengthy interaction with the IUCN and the Earth Charter, and his ongoing work on Earth Democracy. In Chapter 18 Peter Burdon reports on the present status of that ongoing project, originally launched by the IUCN in 2009 at the meeting of the GEIG in Florence, with some results published in 2010 in *Democracy, Ecological Integrity and International Law* (Engel *et al.*, 2010).

Burdon's approach attempts a dialogue with Marxism and bioregionalism, as the next step in that project. In Chapter 19, Joan Engel reviews one of the 'evolutionary narratives' that is proposed as basic to ensure a better way of relating to the Earth; that is, the *Journey of the Universe* (Brian Swimme and Mary Evelyn Tucker), a film that describes the history of evolution of the planet, intended to be the best guide for a future flourishing 'Earth community'. A completely different approach is found instead in the chapter by Sheila Collins. Her focus is the recently emerging Occupy Wall Street movement, which is spreading globally with a number of explicit goals. The movement demands in fact are such that, if met, they might represent a true step forward, of benefit to both crises we are facing.

In contrast with the Occupy movement, the Rio + 20 meeting, with its 'key themes' of 'green economy' and 'institutional reform', both of which represent the main concern of governing states (deflecting both attention and resources from the necessity for basic green concerns, including ecological sustainability), is examined by Klaus Bosselmann in Chapter 21.

The final chapter's title appears to run counter to the forward thrust, and the cautiously optimistic tone deliberately sought in this volume. William Rees has been awarded the Boulder Prize in Ecological Economics jointly with Mathis Wackernagel in 2012, at the meeting in Rio. His final chapter reiterates Rees's deep understanding of human nature and history, both of which indicate the necessity for radical changes, to move closer to the ethical, legal and social goals supported by the return to integrity, which is our main theme. The presence of ecological integrity supports sustainability, and is therefore compatible with the bioregional changes he invokes to replace the present practices fostered by globalization.

The Global Ecological Integrity Group has published a number of collections centred on the role that integrity can and should play in human life. In each case the joint effort was primarily either to elucidate the concept of integrity or its applications, but the central consideration was to demonstrate how life in all its aspect would benefit significantly from changes intended to place integrity in a central role.

Yet it was always clear that aside from the scholars belonging to this group, for the most part integrity was viewed as an interesting but quaint notion, whose value we needed to 'sell', given that it characterized natural systems that excluded the presence of modern human endeavours. Perhaps the title of the fifteenth-anniversary collection says it best: *Reconciling Human Existence with Ecological Integrity* (Westra *et al.*, 2008).

In contrast, the present volume attempts to show that our *de facto* separation from integrity has led to a series of multiple collapses in all sectors of human life, and the gravity of those collapses suggests the necessity for radical change, starting with the acceptance of integrity's centrality, in order to find solutions. The issues on which these chapters focus, the cases they relate and the avenues of change they propose are not meant to provide simple answers to the complex problems we face. But we are no longer 'pleading' for the consideration of integrity. We are now boldly stating that any and all answers we or others propose will fail at this time, unless integrity becomes the main ingredient in each proposal, so that the survival of life on Earth is given priority.

References

Engel, R. Westra, L. and Bosselmann, K. (eds) (2010) *Democracy, Ecological Integrity and International Law*. Newcastle-upon-Tyne: Cambridge Scholars.

Soskolne, C. and Bertollini, R. (1999) *Ecological Integrity and Sustainable Development: Cornerstones of Public Health*. Rome, Italy: World Health Organization.

Westra, L. (1994) *The Principle of Integrity*. Lanham, MD: Rowman Littlefield.

Westra, L. (2004) *Ecoviolence and the Law*. Ardsley, NY: Transnational Publishers.

Westra, L., Miller, P., Karr, J. R., Rees, W. E. and Ulanowicz, R. E. (2000) 'Ecological integrity and the aims of the Global Ecological Integrity Project', in D. Pimentel, L. Westra and R. Noss (eds) *Ecological Integrity: Integrating Environment, Conservation and Health*. Washington, DC: Island Press, pp. 19–41.

Westra, L. Bosselmann, K. and Westra, R. (eds) (2008) *Reconciling Human Existence with Ecological Integrity*. London: Earthscan.

Westra, L., Soskolne, C. L. and Spady, D. W. (2012) *Human Health and Ecological Integrity: Ethics, Law and Human Rights*. Abingdon: Earthscan.

Part I

The role and history of integrity (from grave problems to possible reversals)

Introduction

Laura Westra

This part sets the tone for the theme of the whole book: the vital importance of returning to ecological integrity or seeking to see it implemented in public policy and legal regimes. The first chapter by Jack Manno traces our work on ecological integrity from its inception, and his discussion demonstrates clearly that he is the best possible 'historian' not only of the activities of our group, but of the ongoing development of the use and the understanding of ecological integrity.

Many have attempted to define and explain the concept from various standpoints, even aside from the definition provided in 2000 by our group (Pimentel *et al.*, 2000). For instance, the concept was used in relation to sustainability (Bosselmann, 2008), public policy (Karr, 2008) and human rights (Taylor, 1998), among others, and I have used it myself with regard to ethics (Westra, 1994, 1998) and to law (Westra, 2004). But no one has traced its development and its multiple aspects better than Jack Manno and the numerous contributing scholars he cites.

In Chapter 2, Shaun Fluker looks forward, within the realm of law, rather than considering the concept's past history. Ecological integrity has been present in Canadian environmental law, especially in regard to National Parks, for a long time, without having been treated seriously enough to make a difference in either provincial or federal policy decisions. The recent turn to extend somewhat the reach of that concept to include it in legal decisions concerning treaty rights of Canadian First Nations indicates a turn to a possible increased use of ecological integrity, which is particularly significant because of its relation to the human rights of Indigenous peoples.

Chapters 3 and 4 consider international law as an important (if not often used) instrument, supporting the principle of the Common Heritage of Mankind. That principle defends the primacy of morality and human rights to their traditions and culture, as part of that global 'republique des arts et des sciences' (Scovazzi, 2011) that represents the basis of the brotherhood of all humanity, beyond procedural legality. Prue Taylor discusses the importance of that principle in relation to international ecological governance and emerging efforts to internationalize the public trust doctrine, while Tullio Scovazzi considers its application to issues regarding the seabed.

Agnès Michelot concludes with a chapter that sounds a negative though important note: rather than discussing ecological integrity in EU law, her research demonstrates that the concept is not represented at all in that body of legal regimes (at least, not explicitly as such). Her problem is similar to that encountered by Owen McIntyre in Chapter 8, as his discussion of 'sustainable development' in EU law omits any notion of the concept of sustainability (which is based on integrity, but which is absent altogether from that body of law). In contrast, there are several cognate expressions that are used to indicate the quest for better environmental quality. Michelot's work spearheads the journey of discovery for corresponding notions that might indicate a better way in the quest for a safer future.

References

Bosselmann, K. (2008) *The Principle of Sustainability*. Aldershot: Ashgate.

Karr, J. (2008) 'Attaining a Sustainable Society', in L.Westra, K. Bosselmann and R. Westra (eds), *Reconciling Human Existence with Ecological Integrity*. London: Earthscan, pp. 21–38.

Pimentel, D., Westra, L. and Noss, R. (2000) *Ecological Integrity: Integrating Environment, Conservation and Health*. Washington, DC: Island Press.

Scovazzi, T. (2011) 'Diviser c'est detruire: Ethical principles and legal rules in the field of return of cultural property', *Rivista di Diritto Inernazionale*, XCIV (2): 341–95.

Westra, L. (1994) *The Principle of Integrity*. Lanham, MD: Rowman Littlefield.

Westra, L. (1998) *Living in Integrity*, Lanham, MD: Rowman Littlefield.

Westra, L. (2004) *Ecoviolence and the Law*. The Netherlands: Brill, Leiden.

1 Why the Global Ecological Integrity Group? The rise, decline and rediscovery of a radical concept

Jack Manno

> Integrity is wholeness, the greatest beauty is
> Organic wholeness, the wholeness of life and things, the divine beauty
> of the universe. Love that, not man
> Apart from that, or else you will share man's pitiful confusions, or
> drown in despair when his days darken.
> (Robinson Jeffers, from the poem 'The Answer', 1938)

These lines appear on the cover of *Not Man Apart* (Brower, 1969), a coffee table book of Robinson Jeffers's poems and photos of spectacular vistas of California's Big Sur coast. Produced by the Sierra Club, the foremost environmental advocacy organization in 1965, it was one of the first 'nature books' with a message. It celebrates the ecological worldview of Jeffers's poetry, in which Big Sur is much more than the sum of its details. Neither man nor woman nor surf or seabird exists apart from its context, which includes the physical details in view and a larger experience of wholeness incorporating the photographer, the poet, the reader and the creative intelligence and awareness of each. At the time, ecology, that branch of biology that studies relations and interactions of living things in context, was coming into popular consciousness. Its message: the best and most interesting things in life are not *things* but relations, communities.

Rachel Carson, in her enormously influential book *Silent Spring*, had recently insisted that 'In nature nothing exists alone' (Carson, 1962: 51). We can't understand nature, nor can our political systems protect nature's threatened species and places without taking into account complex interdependencies in which all life exists. Carson indicted the petrochemical industry precisely for their failure to recognize complexity and acting out of a reductionist paradigm and a lust for profit when they manufactured hormonally and neurologically active chemical compounds and released them in large quantities into the environment. The silent spring of which Carson wrote was a saddening testimony to the widespread unravelling of ecosystems on which birdsong ultimately depends. The industry thought only of the intermediate products, the ones that performed economically valued tasks such as eliminating pests or preventing fire or cleaning metal.

But in nature nothing performs one task only. These chemicals would not, could not, do just one thing. Carson insisted that in a world of ecological relations a novel chemical, especially one designed precisely to act upon living organisms, would have ramifying repercussions. She pointed out that living organisms have evolved in a context that did not include chlorinated organic designer compounds. Humans and other contemporary non-human beings could not have evolved to safely metabolize chemistry that their ancestors had never encountered.

Ecosystems are made up of living organisms interacting in relationships structured by flows of energy and matter. These patterns, though variable, are emergent properties of the relationships and they are recognizable and meaningful enough so that people, experts and non-experts alike, can communicate with each other about ecosystems both as types and as unique individual expressions of a type. The many colleagues associated with the Global Ecological Integrity Group over the past twenty years have focused precisely on this ephemeral set of emergent properties that link humans in complex ecological relations that structure ecosystems. We have called it 'integrity', following Aldo Leopold and many others. This chapter presents a brief history of ecological integrity, the foundational concept on which the Global Ecological Integrity Project began as a transdisciplinary team of biologists, economists, regional planners, philosophers, legal scholars, social psychologists and others trying to give practical meaning and policy relevance to this ephemeral but essential concept.

Ecological integrity is a 'radical' concept, radical in the original sense of the word, meaning the root, the foundation of the stability that makes it possible for human minds and civilizations to plan and organize. Ecological integrity was being lost at a disturbing rate and much of our early work was about documenting these losses and examining the underlying, not always obvious reasons for them. In the early 1990s, when I first met Dr Laura Westra, the founder of the Global Ecological Integrity Group, we were both examining the effects of the loss of integrity of the Great Lakes of North America. For some time the Great Lakes had gone haywire from the bottom up and the top down. For one, overfishing, toxic chemical pollution and invasion of alien species had decimated native populations of salmon and trout, the top predators of the Great Lakes food web. The smaller bait fish on which salmon and trout once fed multiplied without check. Their numbers exploded and as they fed upon the tiny crustaceans and other zooplankton these tiny animals crashed, meaning nothing was left to consume the algae. That was the top down crisis. The bottom up crisis was the over fertilization of the lakes from the run-off of nutrients from agriculture and household and industrial use of phosphorus-containing detergents which triggered excessive algal growth. These top-down and bottom-up processes interacted to produce huge algal mats. The waves brought them to shore where they lay rotting along with the remains of sudden die-offs of alewives, herring-like fish whose numbers exploded from lack of predation pressures and then collapsed. As catastrophic as these ramifying processes were, they were just one of many that were affecting fundamental Great Lakes chemical, physical and biological systems. Residents and visitors experienced a depleted fishery, malodorous shore conditions, foul water quality and deformed and dying wildlife. These were the symptoms. They demanded action.

What was it that had been thrown so off balance? The lakes had always been variable. Storm-water had always carried nutrients into lakes and caused algal blooms. Long before industrialization and large cities, Lake Erie's shallow central basin would occasionally be depleted of oxygen. But these changes were temporary. The lakes bounced back. They were resilient to the environmental extremes for which the Lakes were known. Some quality brought the lake – or similarly a forest ecosystem, a prairie, a desert – back into balance after a disturbance. What is that *something* that represented the ability to bounce back, to reconnect, to continue to support healthy life in relatively predictable ways even after a major disturbance?

To this quality many ecologists gave the name 'integrity', and a new vocabulary joined the dictionary of environmental management in the Great Lakes and elsewhere. Ecological integrity was woven into the language of the Great Lakes Water Quality Agreement (GLWQA) between Canada and the US, which has as its stated purpose 'to restore and maintain the chemical, physical and biological integrity of the waters of the Great Lakes basin ecosystem'. Laura Westra and I had each grown interested in how to achieve this goal of 'integrity'. How would those responsible for implementing the agreement know when they had succeeded? Or even know when they were heading in the right direction?

At that time, the agreement was being widely heralded for its successes in reducing phosphorus loads that had caused dead zones in Lake Erie and fouled shorelines with abundant rotting algae. But as pollutant loads declined, new challenges arose. A steady flow of evidence linked a broad range of wildlife disorders and human health effects to toxic chemicals in the environment; polychlorinated biphenyl (PCB), dioxin and other chlorinated organic compounds either directly produced by or the by-products of Great Lakes industry and agriculture. Theo Colborn of the World Wildlife Fund was collecting threads of evidence from wildlife and human health studies and concluding that the evidence pointed to chemical disruption of endocrine functioning, the chemical messaging system. Arguably it was the very definition of a decline in biological integrity.

The Great Lakes Water Quality Agreement was only one of several efforts to get ecological integrity into environmental law and practice. Lynton Caldwell, a political scientist and member of the Great Lakes Science Advisory Board, had argued in 1970 for an ecological viewpoint that '*might be described*' as follows:

> Man is a part of his own environment and is in continuous interaction
> with it: this total environment exists in dynamic equilibrium governed
> by natural laws, which cannot be disregarded with impunity and which
> exemplify the order and reliability of the universe.
>
> (Caldwell, 1970: 209)

Even before integrity entered the Great Lakes agreement, the United States
Clean Water Act had referred to the 'The chemical, physical and biological
integrity of our Nation's waters'. Later, Canada's National Park Act required
that forests be managed to maintain their 'integrity', and more recently the
European Water Framework adopted integrated river basin management.
The rise of the concept of ecological integrity can be seen in many attempts
to apply systems approaches to both environmental problems and to
ecological theory. Yet despite the ecological language, the mainstream
end-of-pipe, chemical-by-chemical, innocent-until-proven-guilty, utility-maxi-
mizing approaches almost always prevailed. In the Great Lakes, for example,
Remedial Action Planning, a binational programme to identify and
remediate the most heavily polluted areas, turned away from linking local
sources to system-wide effects, becoming instead an accounting system of
'beneficial uses'. The US and Canadian governments abandoned the efforts
to develop ecosystem-based criteria to measure success and settled for a data
mining exercise disconnected from the goals of the Great Lakes Water
Quality agreement.

And yet the concept of ecological integrity has refused to disappear. It is
being rediscovered in the context of understanding the behaviour of systems
that operate at the global scale. For example, in 2012 the United Nations
Environment Programme issued the fifth edition of its annual Global
Environmental Outlook in preparation for the Rio + 20 conference. The
report warned that the Earth's environmental systems were being pushed
towards their biophysical limits, beyond which loom sudden, irreversible and
potentially catastrophic changes:

> As human pressures on the earth...accelerate, several critical global,
> regional and local thresholds are close or have been exceeded. Once
> these have been passed, abrupt and possibly irreversible changes to the
> life-support functions of the planet are likely to occur, with significant
> adverse implications for human well-being.
>
> (UNEP, 2012)

GEIG began by defining, measuring and modelling Ecological Integrity but
soon was asking what responsibilities governments have when they commit
to protecting and restoring ecological integrity. What laws, policies and
institutions will make it most likely to achieve the goal of restoring and
maintaining ecological integrity in ecosystems around the world? What's the
relation to such concepts of sustainability and resilience? How can we

determine progress? Is there a gradient of Integrity? Can there be more or less Integrity or is it only present or absent? What methods are best for reporting on Integrity? And most of all, what approaches in law, policy, ethics, economics and international negotiations are most consistent with the goal of integrity? What is and should be an ethics of integrity? The goal has been to get practical about ecological integrity while maintaining philosophical rigour.

The remainder of this chapter recalls the development of ecological integrity and some of the debates and discussions within the Global Ecological Integrity Group. Aldo Leopold – philosopher, ethicist and naturalist – is often credited with first applying the notion of integrity to biology in essays in his *Sand County Almanac* (Leopold, 1949). Leopold described a right relationship between human communities and the land – a land ethic, as he called it. History, he suggested, demonstrated that as civilizations advanced, the scope of what was considered subject to ethical considerations grew. Societies grew more complex and people depended on each other in a widening circle for exchanging goods, providing service and making life manageable and occasionally peaceful. Interdependence was the key to ethical awareness. 'All ethics', he wrote, 'rest upon a single premise: the individual was a member of a community of interdependent parts' (ibid.: 203). If that made sense, than it also made sense for people to recognize how dependent we are on the land. And just as we owe ethical consideration to those individuals who make up the whole of our communities, Leopold continued:

> We must realize the indivisibility of the earth – its soil, mountains, rivers, forest, climate, plants, animals, and respect it collectively not as a useful servant but as a living being…The land is one organism. Its parts, like our own parts, compete with each other and cooperate with each other. The competitions are as much a part of the inner workings as the cooperations…These creatures are members of the biotic community and if (as I believed) its stability depends on its integrity, they are entitled to continuance.
>
> (Ibid.)

Leopold's understanding of integrity foretold the science and analysis of self-organizing systems where the stability and continuance of emergent qualities, including life itself, depends on feedback loops and the exploitation and dissipation of energy flows and gradients. Leopold was a naturalist, an observer, popularizer and protector of special places, not a theoretical ecologist. But in reporting on his observations he named an elusive quality essential to understanding why protecting endangered animals and places would always require more (and in some ways, less) than set-asides, hunting restrictions, water discharge limits and the whole panoply of environmental regulation that would occupy environmentalists to this day.

Some forty years later ecologists began studying the structures of the networks of energy and material flows that made ecosystems more than just the sum of its component organisms and their environment. Certain dynamics operated in ecosystems of all types. There were common rules and coherent patterns resulting from nature's tendency to balance two evolutionary essentials: food and protection. This led to insights about the inherent conflict between nature's ecological striving for sustainability and the human economic penchant for maximizing production. E. P. Odum, one of the originators of systems ecology, explained that:

> the 'strategy' of succession as a short-term process is basically the same as the 'strategy' of long-term evolutionary development of the bio-sphere- namely, increased control of, or homeostasis with, the physical environment in the sense of achieving maximum protection from its perturbations…the strategy of 'maximum protection' (that is, trying to achieve maximum support of complex biomass structure) often conflicts with man's goal of 'maximum production' (trying to obtain the highest possible yield). Recognition of the ecological basis for this conflict is, I believe, a first step in establishing rational land-use policies.
>
> (Odum, 1969)

Maintaining ecological integrity would require humans to act as if integrity mattered.

Ecosystem-based policies began to appear via the efforts of, among others, Thomas Jorling one of the drafters of the US Clean Water Act. He has been credited as the person who inserted into the legislation the statement that 'The objective of the Act is to restore and maintain the chemical, physical and biological integrity of the nation's waters.' In 1976 he wrote:

> The intellectual roots of this perspective are found in the study of evolution. The objective of this concept is the maximum patterning of human communities after biogeochemical cycles with a minimum departure from the geological or background rates of change in the biosphere. Framed another way the objective is to move from linear pathways in the movement of matter and energy to circular pathways.
>
> (Jorling, 1976)

Following its appearance in the US Clean Water Act and the Great Lakes Water Quality Agreement it appeared that Integrity might become an important goal for environmental policies worldwide. It offered a goal consistent with a scientific understanding of what the real problem was. After all, clean water could be achieved with enough chlorine. But the Clean Water Act and the Great Lakes Water Quality Agreement were about protecting and restoring ecosystems and the statement of goal needed to be consistent with this task. It was at this point that the Global Ecological

Integrity Group came into being. Pointing to the need to implement integrity-based promises, Canada's National Science and Engineering Research Council funded a project proposed by Laura Westra to bring together a multi-disciplinary team of scientists and scholars to derive a definition, methodologies for quantification, measurement tools and an understanding of what percentage of Earth's major ecosystems would need to be retained in a state of ecological integrity to avoid global ecological collapse and the existential human crisis that might imply integrity.

As the team met, traded ideas and tested methodologies, GEIG's first book was written, titled *Ecological Integrity: Integrating Environment, Conservation, and Health* and published in 2000 by Island Press. In it Westra *et al.* (2000: 19) illustrated the concept of ecological integrity with reference to a barren Chilean desert that in 1997 burst into a 'wonderland of flowers and grasses' when an El Niño event triggered a rare abundance of rain. Though rarely seen, the potential had been there dormant. 'This burst of life occurred because anthropogenic stress was largely absent from the history of the desert…In essence, the desert retained its biological potential' (ibid.). That potential is particular and geographically and climatologically specific. Integrity does not exist in isolation in any particular organism but in mixed biotic and abiotic systems that are essential to life. *Ecosystems* as systems are what express ecological integrity, not individual seeds or plants. Does the desert bloom? Or is it the flowers? Perhaps El Niño blooms, or is it the rain that does the blooming? Systems with integrity have their own unique rhythms observable only over time; no snapshot can capture hidden potential until the moment that potential is actualized. Integrity is the outcome, of natural history, the narrative of place. The story is one of nested hierarchies, systems within systems where the origin story of one level is the story of the structured interactions at the level below even as the relations at that level are generating the emergent characteristics of the level above. The many layers of systems' stories are related hierarchically; processes at the higher levels of the regional and the global determine what happens locally. Integrity at the local and individual level requires integrity at regional and global scales. It is no surprise that the Global Ecological Integrity Group began mostly with ecological systems scientists and philosophers wanting to define and measure Integrity and came be populated by mostly law and policy scholars debating methods to protect and restore Integrity. This is how the story of GEIG has emerges with theoretical ecology and the laws of physics at its base and the Earth Charter and the rights of Mother Earth at its pinnacle.

How can complex ecological systems be described, modelled and quantified? Bob Ulanowicz at the University of Maryland's Chesapeake Biological Laboratory suggested one way. Applying mathematical tools developed by information theorists to the food webs that structure ecosystems, he developed a way of analysing system integrity using an index he calls 'ascendancy', which integrates measures of the strength of the connectedness of the system with measures of the degree of redundancy of the pathways through which matter and energy is exchanged, which is referred to as 'overhead'. As systems self-organize, the less efficient pathways are abandoned and the options for connectedness decline. Systems can become brittle, superefficient but vulnerable to collapse if one highway of connectedness breaks down. Thus there are always trade-offs between efficiency and resilience. There are optimum system states that correspond with integrity.

The search for measurable definitions of integrity drew in some of the world's top systems theorists. For example, the late James Kay argued that:

> Traditional ecological theory has attempted to describe ecosystems stress response using simple notions such as stability and resilience. In fact, stress response must be characterized by a richer set of concepts...Is the change along the original developmental pathway or a new one? Is the change organizing or disorganizing? Will the system flip to some new state in a catastrophic way? Is the change acceptable to humans?...The concept of integrity must be seen as multidimensional and encompassing a number of ecosystem behaviors.
>
> (Kay, 1990: 209)

Lance Gunderson and C. S. 'Buzz' Holling (2002) offered another way to look at the balance between change and persistence in natural systems. There is a complex directionality in systems, especially natural systems, which involve adaptive cycles of growth, overdevelopment, or restructuring and renewal. If ecosystems are prevented from restructuring and renewal because humans have grown to depend on their services, then the systems go brittle and rather than restructuring they may then instead collapse disastrously. For example, when people attempt to prevent all forest fires, the resulting build-up of broken branches and dried wood can lead to far hotter and more destructive fires; if water levels on rivers and streams are regulated to prevent the occasional flood or levels too low for navigation then wetlands become mucklands and seeds never see the sun. The result is monocultures of cattails or other hardy wetland plants, loss of biodiversity and clogged fish spawning sites. Unfortunately, for those who wished to dampen or control natural variability, the effort seemed certain to lead to greater extremes, more destruction. This then was another insight from the work on Ecological Integrity. The Integrity of air, water and soil seemed to depend on the cycle of structuring, growth, restructuring and renewal that Hollings and Gunderson named 'panarchy'.

The exchange of ideas about integrity faced its own optimization problem; how to balance the intellectual need for rigorous and coherent ecological theories with the need to make informed judgments about protecting and restoring Integrity in particular places and ecosystems. How could the GEIG fulfil its promise to inform the decision-making process about how to promote integrity? As important as theory is, we could not just settle for advancing ecosystem theories. We had to turn to the social, political and economic dynamics undermining ecological integrity systematically and without reprieve everywhere on Earth. As Willem Vanderburg, editor of the *Bulletin of Science, Technology and Society*, put it:

> The processes that contribute to a loss of integrality of the natural ecology are in fact identical to the ones occurring in the social ecology of any modern society…both are rooted in contemporary culture. By culture I mean the basis on which the members of a society interpret their experience and structure the relationships with one another and the world (past, present and future) into a coherent way of life.
>   (Willem Vanderburg quoted in Dickie *et al.*, 1990: 106)

Our modern industrial culture, its way of life, seems to be undermining integrity not accidentally but deliberately to serve its own defining values of economic growth through consumption. Tragically, the way we see the world is mistaken in a particularly destructive way. Societies are social systems and, like ecosystems, are structured by networks of flows and exchanges of matter and energy. Over time, as the most efficient pathways, those structured by market relations, grow in volume and power and those pathways structured by community and ecological relations become underdeveloped or disappear entirely, societies grow in a pattern that could be called maldevelopment and they lose social system integrity. The energetic and material networks of industrial production and consumption overwhelm networks of community connectedness and ecosystem connectedness. This concentration of power happens at the expense of diversity and resilience. As societies advance in their abilities to concentrate power, its members grow increasingly dependent on smaller numbers of more powerful networks of energy and material flows to deliver the goods. As a result people become more vulnerable to the impacts of system change (restructuring). As with ecosystems, social and economic system integrity is threatened with overdevelopment and collapse. As reggae singer Jimmy Cliff would have it, 'The harder they come, the harder they fall, one and all'.

Bill Rees, the originator (with Mathias Wackernagel), of ecological footprint accounting and analysis, and a long-time colleague in the Global Ecological Integrity Group, took a lead role in explaining the relation between ecosystemic and social dynamics. He explained:

> the mere existence of people in a given habitat implies significant effects on local ecosystems' structure and function. This is the consequence of two simple biological realities: first, human beings are big animals with correspondingly large individual energy and material requirements; and second, humans are social beings who live in extended groups. The invasion of any previously 'stable' ecosystem by people therefore

invariably produced changes in established energy and material pathways. There will be a reallocation of resources among species in the system to the benefit of some and the detriment of others. To this extent at least, people invariably perturb or 'disturb' the systems of which they are a part.

(Rees, 2000: 142)

Rees insisted that 'the global ecological crisis is an all-but-inevitable consequence of unique qualities of human ecology and behavior. The solution, however, must be sociopolitical. Can we deconstruct the consumer society and replace it with something gentler, both more humane and more ecocentric' (ibid.: 153). My own work on commoditization at the GEIG meetings has focused on those economic system dynamics that result in individual and social welfare being tied increasingly to high levels of energy and material consumption (Manno, 2000). Commoditization is a structuring process through which marketable goods and services (i.e. commodities) are systematically privileged over non-commodity, non-commercial means of satisfying human means and wants. As a result of this powerful unnatural selection process the economy of market goods and services becomes overdeveloped and grows exponentially until it exceeds the capacity of earth's resources to maintain both global ecological integrity and meet the demands of the growing economy. At such a time (arguably the present), the economy enters a debt-based crisis that threatens the integrity of global socioeconomic systems in tandem with the decline in integrity of the world's ecosystems. Since each dollar represents a claim on future energy and material resources (to be embedded into future goods or services) a massive expansion of debt guarantees massive future claims on the Earth at exactly the time that all the insights from the GEIG research suggests that we needs to significantly reduce the current pressures on the Earth from human economic activities.

The answer has to be a restructuring of dominant socioeconomic systems. Perhaps, the most important tool for restructuring is the Law. It is no surprise that GEIG's founder and leader, Laura Westra, chose to earn a second doctorate, in law, to supplement her PhD in philosophy, in which she had developed a rich philosophical case for ecological integrity. Prue Taylor, author of the international law text *An Ecological Approach to International Law: Responding to the Challenges of Climate Change* (Taylor, 1998), also joined GEIG. Prue argued that:

ecological integrity could be implemented in law, using the tool of ecological human rights…This ecological context acknowledges human need to use natural resources, but goes further to recognize that humanity is an integral part of ecological systems…A sense of moral responsibility towards nature will be an essential component of this endeavor. In recognition of this, ecological human rights give legal

effect to moral obligations by expressing them in terms of responsibilities to protect and enhance ecological systems, in acknowledgement
of a range of values.

(Ibid.: 106)

It was inevitable that GEIG would turn its attention to new principles for
guiding how we relate to earth's ecosystems. In the late 1990s GEIG joined
forces with the Earth Charter Initiative to promote a new global Charter
of Rights and Responsibilities. The initiative had emerged from the failure
to achieve global agreement on an Earth Charter at the 1992 United
Nations Conference on Environment and Development in Rio. Some of
those who had written and circulated drafts in advance of Rio left there
with a plan for a global campaign to ask communities, organizations and
individuals to become signatories to the Earth Charter. The environmental theologian J. Ron Engel, one of the drafters of the Earth Charter,
joined GEIG. He wrote: 'Our best hope for reconciling human existence
and ecological integrity lies in the peoples of the world undergoing a
transformation of consciousness that is religious in quality and committing themselves to the all-embracing covenant of life' (Engel, 2008). He
explained perhaps the origins of this chapter when he wrote, 'If my fellow
members of GEIG frequently assume the prophetic voice in their speaking
and writing, it is because they believe everything hangs on human
adherence to the moral demands of the covenant of life' (ibid.: 282).
Principle Five of the Earth Charter is particularly relevant, as it obligates
signatories to 'Protect and restore the integrity of Earth's ecological
systems, with special concern for biological diversity and the natural
processes that sustain life' (see www.earthcharterinaction.org/
content/pages/Read-the-Charter.html).

As GEIG enters its third decade of intellectual engagement with the
concept of ecological integrity, many of us have learned to listen to the
prophetic voices of Indigenous teachers who have warned countless times
that what we do to the Earth we do to ourselves, and that the Earth does not,
and cannot, belong to us; it is we who belong to Her. Returning to Indigenous understandings of right relations between people and nature is not
and cannot be a move toward the past, but instead a commitment to building
a future in which Earth's ecosystems and human communities self-organize
interdependently as resilient communities of integrity.

References

Brower, D. (1969) *Not Man Apart: Lines from Robinson Jeffers*. San Francisco, CA: Sierra
    Club.
Caldwell, L. (1970) *Environment: A Challenge to Modern Society*. Boston, MA: Natural
    History Press.
Carson, R. (1962) *Silent Spring*. New York: Houghton Mifflin.

Dickie, L. M. and Bandurski, B. L. (1990) 'Integrity and surprise in the Great Lakes Basin ecosystem: implications for theory and testing', in C. J. Edwards and H. A. Regier (eds) *An Ecosystem Approach to the Integrity of the Great Lakes in Turbulent Times*, Special Publication 90-4. Ann Arbor, MI: Great Lakes Fishery Commission, pp. 105–18.

Engel, R. (2008) 'What Covenant Sustains Us?' in L. Westra, K. Bosselmann and R. Westra (eds), *Reconciling Human Existence with Ecological Integrity*. London: Earthscan, pp. 277–92

Gunderson, L. and Holling, H. (eds) (2002) *Panarchy: Understanding Transformations in Human and Natural Systems*. Washington, DC: Island Press.

Jorling, T. (1976) 'Incorporating ecological principles into public policy', *Environmental Policy and Law*, 2: 140–55.

Kay, J. (1990) 'A nonequilibrium thermodynamic framework for discussing ecosystem integrity', in E. Clayton and H. Regier (eds) *An Ecosystem Approach to the Integrity of the Great Lakes in Turbulent Times*, Special Publication 90-4. Ann Arbor, MI: Great Lakes Fishery Commission, pp. 209–38.

Leopold, A. (1949) *A Sand County Almanac: with Other Essays on Conservation from Round River*. New York: Oxford University Press.

Manno, J. P. (2000) 'Commodity potential: an approach to understanding the ecological consequences of markets', in Pimentel, D., Westra, L. and Noss, R. (eds) *Ecological Integrity: Integrating Environment, Conservation and Health*. Washington, DC: Island Press, pp. 336–51.

Odum, E. P. (1969) 'The strategy of ecosystem development', *Science*, new series, 164 (3877) (18 April), pp. 262–70.

Rees, W. (2000) 'Patch disturbance, ecofootprints, and biological integrity: revisiting the limit to growth (or why industrial society is inherently unsustainable)', in D. Pimentel, L. Westra and R. Noss (eds) *Ecological Integrity: Integrating Environment, Conservation and Health*. Washington, DC: Island Press, pp. 122–39.

Taylor, P. (2008) 'Ecological integrity and human rights', in L. Westra, K. Bosselmann and R. Westra (eds), *Reconciling Human Existence with Ecological Integrity*. London: Earthscan, pp. 89–108.

UNEP (2012) *Global Environmental Outlook 5*, United Nations Environment Programme, Nairobi, Kenya, available at www.unep.org/geo/pdfs/geo5/ GEO5_report_full_en.pdf

Westra, L., Miller, P., Karr, J. R., Rees, W. and Ulanowicz, R. (2000) 'Ecological Integrity and the Aims of the Global Integrity Project,' in D. Pimentel, L. Westra and R. Noss (eds), *Ecological Integrity: Integrating Environment, Conservation and Health*. Washington, DC: Island Press, pp. 19–41.

2 Environmental norms in the courtroom

The case of ecological integrity in Canada's National Parks

Shaun Fluker

Introduction

Modern environmentalism has left a profound mark on moral philosophy by extending the reach of traditional norms and expanding the roster of ethics available to guide our behaviour. Non-anthropocentric theorists extend moral agency beyond today's human population by applying norms such as justice, fairness, liberty, equity and respect to non-human animals, future generations, other species and ecosystems generally. Environmentalism also provides the basis for new norms such as sustainability, integrity, and precaution, which seek to guide us towards a better world in which the environmental impacts of industrial society are fully considered.

Law features prominently in discussions relating to environmental ethics. Law tends to reflect favoured norms and thereby reinforces their dominance as our guide. The common law governing ownership of land, for example, reflects and reinforces the view that land ought to be valued only in relation to how it contributes to human ends. Thus land which is not put to direct human use is thought to serve no purpose (Freyfogle, 1993). Law is a means by which to enforce norms. Legal rules assign liability and prohibit acts, and the law backstops these commands with the threat of sanction for those who fail to adhere. Law also provides a forum, either a legislature or a courtroom, wherein competing norms confront each other and battle for our attention.

In the legal implementation of environmental norms, the courtroom takes a backseat to the legislature. In some jurisdictions this is expressly the case. Lord Goff wrote in a 1994 UK House of Lords decision that the prevalence of statutory laws governing environmental protection may actually render the development of common law undesirable in this area.[1] In a more recent comparative study of environmental law in 19 countries, the dominance of legislation over the common law in this area is striking (Kotze and Paterson, 2009).

This dominance of the legislature over the courtroom has its roots in the beginning of the industrial age in the nineteenth century. Lawmakers at the time embraced legislation as the more effective tool to address collective concerns over industrial pollution (Coyle and Morrow, 2004). Indeed the common law has traditionally been reluctant to recognize collective rights or interests. So when environmental norms such as sustainability or integrity gained popular appeal in the mid-twentieth century, advocates were predisposed towards international treaties or domestic legislation as the means by which to enforce them. Thus legal reference to such norms is almost exclusively in codified instruments, and the interpretation thereof, rather than as a principle of common law. As one example, Tollefson (2012) observes that legal consideration of the precautionary principle worldwide is almost exclusively a matter of statutory interpretation.

This chapter uses the study of a proposed road construction in Wood Buffalo National Park, one of Canada's largest and more remote national parks, to explore some implications that arise when environmental norms attain legal force by virtue of legislative process rather than judicial reasoning. Or, to put it another way, when the norm is implemented as a statutory rule or principle rather than a common law rule or principle. One implication is that environmental issues are seen more as a matter of politics than ethics or law, and thus decision-makers simply place environmental norms into the mix of political discussion to be balanced against other interests. Another implication is that there is a measure of formalism in environmental law that constrains the ability or even willingness of the judiciary to seriously grapple with environmental norms. The judiciary simply tinkers at the margin of environmental disputes and largely defers to the legislature when it comes to putting environmental norms to work. The result is that legal implementation of environmental norms does not benefit from the ongoing deliberations of an independent judiciary. The result is that environmental norms remain very much in the background of human governance, seemingly unable to displace the existing thought patterns that value economic growth above all else.

Ecological integrity as a priority in legislation and policy

In 1949 Aldo Leopold famously wrote: 'A thing is right when it tends to preserve the integrity, stability and beauty of the biotic community. It is wrong when it tends otherwise.' With these words, Aldo Leopold gave ecological integrity popular recognition as a norm to guide human activity in relation to the rest of the biotic community. As Jack Manno describes in Chapter 1 of this volume, the latter half of the twentieth century saw extensive growth in the literature describing the science and ethics of ecological integrity (see also Fluker, 2010). The norm is contested and difficult to understand, encompassing notions of ecosystem resilience and optimum capacity (Westra, 1994). Some commentators even question whether the norm can inform decision-making (Schrader-Frechette, 1995). Others suggest the norm is contested precisely because ecological integrity forms the bedrock of a challenge to entrenched modes of thought. Bruce Morito (2002) describes ecological integrity the basis for a new paradigm of decision-making that relies on attunement rather than detachment. Most commentators associate ecological integrity with an ecological state free of human disturbance. On this view, human activity necessarily impairs ecological integrity and thus paradigm ecological integrity is found in ecosystems protected from human disturbance. These commentators tend to advocate for the preservation of core protected areas wherein humans have little or no presence. It thus comes as little surprise that the norm of ecological integrity figures prominently in the management of Canada's national parks and, given the contested nature of ecological integrity, that its implementation has been a challenge.

The struggle between advocates of 'parks for people' and 'parks for preservation' defines the modern history of Canada's national parks (Campbell, 2011). Historians and other scholars generally agree that Canada designated its early national parks to fulfil the public policy objective of nation-building and to generate economic returns. At the forefront of any identifiable parks purpose was the satisfaction of recreational, economic or spiritual interests of Canadians. Since the late 1960s preservationists have battled the parks for people ideology governing Canada's national parks, applying pressure on the federal government to assert the preservation of nature for its own sake as the primary purpose in the parks. Ecological integrity has become the centrepiece for this advocacy.

Ecological integrity was first expressed in Canadian national parks policy in 1979, and several years later Canada amended its National Parks Act to state the maintenance of ecological integrity is the first priority in national park zoning and visitor use management.[2] While this statutory provision was subsequently cited in several judicial decisions, it was not the focus of litigation and its meaning was never thoroughly considered.[3] While not having much legal significance, this enactment did symbolize a strengthening of the ecological integrity mandate in national parks decision-making.

In 1998 the Minister of Canadian Heritage appointed a panel of scientists to assess the ecological integrity of the national parks. In 2000 the panel provided the Minister with its conclusion that the ecological integrity of most national parks was in peril (Parks Canada, 2000). The panel concluded from its field visits that human activity was largely responsible for an overall ecological decline in the parks (Parks Canada, 2000: 1-11–1-17). In order to help restore the ecological integrity in the parks, the panel recommended new parks legislation to place the maintenance or restoration of ecological integrity as the *overriding* priority in national parks management. The consensus among panel members was that a stronger legal mandate was necessary to provide authority for Parks Canada to say 'no' to what the panel viewed as excessive human activity in the parks.

Canada responded in February 2001 by legislating an expanded ecological integrity mandate in the *Canada National Parks Act*[4] with the following additions to sections 2 and 8 in the legislation:

Section 2(1) – Definitions
'ecological integrity' means, with respect to a park, a condition that is
determined to be characteristic of its natural region and likely to persist,
including abiotic components and the composition and abundance of
native species and biological communities, rates of change and
supporting processes.

Section 8(2) – Ecological Integrity
Maintenance or restoration of ecological integrity, through the
protection of natural resources and natural processes, shall be the first
priority of the Minister when considering all aspects of the management
of parks.

These ecological integrity provisions sit alongside section 4(1) which
dedicates the parks to the use and enjoyment of Canadians:

Section 4(1) – Parks dedicated to public
The national parks of Canada are hereby dedicated to the people of
Canada for their benefit, education and enjoyment, subject to this Act
and the regulations, and the parks shall be maintained and made use of
so as to leave them unimpaired for the enjoyment of future generations.

The categorical priority in section 8(2) afforded to the maintenance or
restoration of ecological integrity in the national parks combined with the
emphasis on natural conditions and native species in the legislated definition
make a convincing case that these legislative provisions require national
parks to be managed as places where the preservation of nature for its own
sake is the first priority with human interests of secondary concern. In its
literal terms, section 8(2) requires that national parks be managed as core
preservation areas with little human presence or influence. In other words,
the legislation purports to implement the norm of ecological integrity. Yet,
this legislative priority for ecological preservation in national parks decision-
making has curiously not produced any discernible change from the parks
for people ideology that has dominated parks governance for a century.
Indeed, recent evidence suggests economic and recreational interests are
actually becoming more rather than less influential in management
decisions for certain parks (Gailus, 2011).

Ecological integrity in Wood Buffalo National Park

The Federal Court of Canada has directly considered the ecological integrity
rule in the Canada National Parks Act in two cases, and has referred to the
rule in several others. All judicial consideration has resulted from an
application for judicial review of a Parks Canada decision concerning parks
management. The first consideration of section 8(2) was provided by Justice

Gibson of the Federal Court Trial Division in a 2001 judicial review of the Parks Canada decision to approve the construction of a road in Wood Buffalo National Park.[5] In 2003, Justice Gibson's interpretation of section 8(2) was upheld by Justice Evans in the Federal Court of Appeal.[6] These two decisions remain the leading authority on the meaning and scope of the section 8(2) ecological integrity mandate for Parks Canada.

Wood Buffalo National Park straddles the northeast corner in the province of Alberta and southern edge of the Northwest Territories, covering approximately 45,000 square kilometres. Canada established the park in 1922 to protect declining populations of wood buffalo (Foster, 1978). In 1983 the park received international recognition as a United Nations World Heritage Site as habitat for threatened wood buffalo and whooping crane species, as well as being recognized for protecting one of the world's largest inland freshwater deltas.

In 1998 the municipality of Fort Smith, located on the northern boundary of the park in the Northwest Territories, submitted an application to Parks Canada seeking approval to construct and operate a road crossing the park from east to west along the Peace River. Parks Canada commissioned an environmental assessment which concluded that a new road would have some environmental impact on the park, but taking into account mitigation measures this impact was not likely to be significant. Parks Canada acknowledged on the record of this case that the proposed road did not serve a park purpose. In May 2001 Parks Canada (as the Minister's delegate) approved construction of the road, but did so without any reference to ecological integrity in its written decision.

The Canadian Parks and Wilderness Society (CPAWS) viewed these facts as the ideal case to test the new ecological integrity provisions which had recently been enacted by Canada in the Canada National Parks Act.[7] CPAWS is a national environmental organization with a long history of advocating for preservation in Canada's national parks. CPAWS was also an active contributor to the policy work that led to the 2001 ecological integrity legislative amendments. Accordingly, CPAWS has a genuine interest in how the ecological integrity norm is implemented by the parks legislation. CPAWS applied to the Federal Court in June 2001 seeking judicial review of the road approval on the basis that these facts made for a clear violation of the new ecological integrity rule set out in section 8(2) of the Canada National Parks Act.

Justice Gibson ruled that Parks Canada has the statutory authority to approve the road, and he was not convinced by the evidence on environmental impacts or the fact that Parks Canada failed to mention ecological integrity in its decision.[8] In dismissing the CPAWS application, Justice Gibson described the new statutory provisions as non-substantial changes to the legislation and went on to provide a remarkable interpretation of the section 8(2) ecological integrity mandate and its relationship to section 4(1):

Further, I agree with counsel for the respondents that the record, when read in its totality, is consistent with the Minister and her delegates according first priority to ecological integrity in arriving at the decision under review. That the decision is clearly not consistent with treating ecological integrity as the Minister's *sole* priority is clear. However, that is not the test. I reiterate: subsection 4(1) of the new *Act* requires a delicate balancing of conflicting interests which include the benefit and enjoyment of those living in, and in close proximity to, Wood Buffalo National Park. This is particularly so when that Park is as remote from services and facilities as is in fact the case and as is likely to remain the case for some time. In the circumstances, while Wood Buffalo National Park, like other National Parks, is dedicated to the people of Canada as a whole, it is not unreasonable to give special consideration to the limited number of people of Canada who are by far most directly affected by management or development decisions affecting the Park. I am satisfied that it was reasonably open to the Minister and her delegates to conclude that the interests of those people overrode the first priority given to ecological integrity where impairment of such integrity can be minimized to a degree that the Minister concludes is consistent with the maintenance of the Park for the enjoyment of future generations.

...Subsection 8(2) of the *Act* does not require that ecological integrity be the 'determinative factor' in a decision such as that under review. Rather, it simply requires that ecological integrity be the Minister's 'first' priority and, as indicated immediately above, I am satisfied on the totality of the evidence before the Court that it was her first priority in reaching the decision here under review. I acknowledge that the record before me does not disclose that the Minister and her delegates used the phrase 'ecological integrity' in their decision making process, or, in fact, in the decision that is under review itself. That reality does not lead inexorably to a conclusion that ecological integrity was not considered or was not given a first priority. I am satisfied on the record that it is clear that ecological integrity was taken into account by the Minister and her delegates. I am further satisfied that it was, as well, given first priority notwithstanding that it was not found to be the determinative factor in all of the circumstances.[9]

This reading of section 8(2) differs significantly from its literal wording. Not only does Justice Gibson employ utilitarian logic to read down the ecological integrity priority as just another factor for Parks Canada to weigh in carrying out its section 4(1) mandate to balance human use with environmental preservation, he concludes that a parks decision can promote the interests of people over the maintenance of ecological integrity and still comply with section 8(2).

CPAWS arguably fared worse at the Federal Court of Appeal. Justice Evans ruled the Court owes significant deference to Parks Canada in the exercise of its statutory authority to manage the national parks, and accordingly he stated the Court will not revisit how Parks Canada weighs ecological integrity and other factors in its management decisions.[10] Moreover, in dismissing the CPAWS appeal Justice Evans placed the onus on CPAWS to establish what components of restoring or maintaining ecological integrity were missing in the Parks Canada road approval or, alternatively, to submit evidence on how the road construction would impair the park's ecological integrity.[11] Justice Evans places the evidentiary burden on CPAWS, despite the wording of section 8(2) which assigns the obligation on the Minister, and Parks Canada as her delegate, to implement the ecological integrity norm.

These two Wood Buffalo National Park decisions of the Federal Court provide Parks Canada with the legal authority to consider the maintenance or restoration of ecological integrity as just another factor in parks decision-making. Even worse from the perspective of the ecological integrity norm, these decisions suggest ecological integrity is a factor which can be overridden by human commercial or economic interests.[12] Judicial interpretation of section 8(2) has significantly undermined the priority afforded to preservation which the Canada National Parks Act purports to implement.

While these decisions offer plenty to consider on their own, this case is particularly illustrative here because the road proposal was concurrently challenged in separate legal proceedings at the same Court. The Mikisew Cree First Nation also applied to the Federal Court for judicial review of the Parks Canada road approval in Wood Buffalo National Park, filing their application in June 2001 just one week after the CPAWS application was filed with the Court. The Mikisew application asserted the decision by Parks Canada was an unlawful infringement of aboriginal rights under section 35 of the Constitution Act.[13]

Madam Justice Hansen ruled the road approval infringed upon Mikisew legal rights to hunt and carry on their traditional lifestyle in Wood Buffalo National Park. Accordingly, she quashed the Parks Canada road approval.[14] The reasoning of Justice Hansen in the Mikisew application provides an interesting contrast to that of Justice Gibson and Justice Evans in the CPAWS application.

Parks Canada led evidence on environmental impacts of hunting to oppose the Mikisew application. It is hard to miss the irony of Parks Canada asserting that hunting is incompatible with maintaining the ecological integrity of Wood Buffalo National Park, while at almost the same time asserting the road is compatible with ecological integrity in the CPAWS application. Justice Hansen had little difficulty in rejecting this argument by giving significant weight to the evidence on the proposed road's environmental impacts and emphasizing that aboriginal hunting is intertwined with the ecology of the park.[15] Indeed, Justice Hansen relied on evidence of adverse environmental impacts from the proposed road, including wildlife habitat fragmentation, to support her ruling that Parks Canada infringed Mikisew legal rights.[16] As she concluded:

> Subsistence hunting and trapping by traditional users of the Park's resources has been in decline for many years. Opening up this remote wilderness to vehicle traffic could potentially exacerbate the challenges facing First Nations struggling to maintain their culture. For example, if the moose population is adversely affected by increased poaching or predation pressures caused by the road, Mikisew will be forced to change their hunting strategies. This may simply be one more incentive to abandon a traditional lifestyle and turn to other modes of living. Further, Mikisew argues that keeping the land around the reserve in its natural condition and maintaining their hunting and trapping traditions is important to their ability to pass their skills on to the next generation of Mikisew.[17]

The Mikisew application was ultimately heard by the Supreme Court of Canada. It is noteworthy for present purposes that a unanimous Supreme Court agreed with Justice Hansen that the Mikisew legal rights were infringed by the adverse environmental impacts of the proposed road.[18]

The remoteness and wild nature of Wood Buffalo National Park seems to inform judicial reasoning on the lawfulness of the proposed road in the Mikisew application. The ecological integrity of Wood Buffalo National Park, in terms of its natural condition and biological communities, is given an emphasis here that is absent in the reasoning of either Justice Gibson or Justice Evans in the CPAWS application, despite a statutory rule that purports to make ecological integrity a priority. Some would suggest the presence of a constitutional or aboriginal rights argument in the Mikisew application explains its different outcome. Perhaps this is so, but I argue below that the statutory nature of the CPAWS application also provides an explanation for the difference. In other words, the fact that parks legislation is not under consideration in the Mikisew application explains why the ecological integrity norm figures more prominently in the Court's reasoning.

The Court views the CPAWS application as a request to arbitrate between competing interests. The law is seen as a forum to balance interests, and in this case that balance is between the socio-economics of a new transportation route and the preservation of a diminishing wilderness. In the mind of the Court the dispute at issue in the CPAWS application is largely one of politics rather than principle. This emphasis is not apparent in the Mikisew application, where the Court seems focused on rights (and obligations) based on tradition, culture and ecology.

Legal scholars note a strong correlation between statutory rules and utilitarian logic (Coyle and Morrow, 2004). The general argument is that statutory rules characterize law in polycentric terms. The categorical assertion of obligation in a statute, such as that set out by section 8(2) in the

Canada National Parks Act, is inextricably linked to the policy debate that underlies its enactment. This linkage renders a categorical statutory rule that should produce deliberation on rights and obligations into an assessment of competing interests. This is an unfortunate result for the prospect of norms such as ecological integrity whose implementation challenges entrenched worldviews. In order to even be considered for legal implementation, the norm must be significantly tempered. This is precisely what occurs in the CPAWS application. More critically, one might suggest the rhetoric of balancing competing interests is used to mask a preference for economic interests over ecological integrity; that in fact there is no balancing exercise in the reasoning process, it is simply a choice between alternative courses. One side will necessarily be marginalized by the decision, and here it is ecological integrity. There are exceptional cases where the categorical assertion of environmental obligation in a statutory rule has prevailed over competing interests in judicial consideration, but these really are exceptions.[19]

The statutory nature of the CPAWS application also injects formalism into the Court's legal reasoning. The Court views its function as applying a rule enacted by the legislature. This application requires the Court to engage in statutory interpretation and judicial review. These two doctrines constrain the judicial role into deciphering the intention of the legislature and deferring to the authority of its delegates. The effect is to stifle creativity and imagination in the courtroom. Legal reasoning in the CPAWS application, and presumably the arguments of the parties before the Court, focuses on dissecting the wording of section 8(2) in the Canada National Parks Act to decipher what 'first priority' was intended to mean. Does it mean the preservation of ecological integrity is the determinative factor in parks decision-making? Or is it just the first of many priorities? The doctrine of judicial review instructs the Court to defer to the authority of Parks Canada to decide how to implement the ecological integrity norm. In this policy of curial deference to legislative authority, the Court has a lesser role in developing rules enacted by statute. Parks Canada is the authoritative voice on ecological integrity for national parks. In the Mikisew application, by contrast, the Court engages with ecological integrity by considering the socio-ecological history of the park, its natural character, and the potential impacts of the proposed road on the area. The Mikisew application may still leave much to be desired in relation to implementing the ecological integrity norm, but it is at least an attempt by the judiciary. Which is more than can be said for the CPAWS application.

Conclusion

I have attempted to demonstrate that the statutory character of environmental law impedes the implementation of environmental norms; moreover, that these impediments are systemic and unlikely to be overcome. The case of ecological integrity in Wood Buffalo National Park offers a particularly illustrative study because it is a rare instance of parallel legal proceedings concerning the same subject-matter, with legislation applicable in one set of proceedings but not the other. The essential observation in the CPAWS application is the unwilling Court who not only refuses to engage with the ecological integrity norm, but arguably subverts it by allowing economic interests to trump preservation in the park. The Mikisew application provides an illustrative contrast of a more ecologically engaged Court, but in using it here I am not suggesting the common law is a panacea for all that ills the implementation of environmental norms such as ecological integrity. Indeed, the critics persuasively argue that the common law is simply politics dressed in new clothes. Nonetheless, the statutory nature of environmental law injects a certain logic and formalism into legal reasoning that impedes the development and implementation of environmental norms.

Notes

1   *Cambridge Water Co v. Eastern Counties Leather* [1994] 1 All ER 53 at 76.
2   *National Parks Act,* RSC 1985, c N-14, s 5(1.2).
3   See e.g. *Sunshine Village Corp v. Canada (Minister of Environment and Minister of Canadian Heritage)* (1996), 44 Admin LR (2d) 201, 202 NR 132.
4   *Canada National Parks Act,* SC 2000, c 32.
5   *Canadian Parks and Wilderness Society v. Canada (Minister of Canadian Heritage),* 2001 FCT 1123.
6   *Canadian Parks and Wilderness Society v. Canada (Minister of Canadian Heritage),* 2003 FCA 197.
7   Taken from interview notes on file with the author.
8   *Canadian Parks and Wilderness Society v. Canada (Minister of Canadian Heritage),* 2001 FCT 1123 at para 47.
9   *Canadian Parks and Wilderness Society v. Canada (Minister of Canadian Heritage),* 2001 FCT 1123 at paras 52–53.
10 *Canadian Parks and Wilderness Society v. Canada (Minister of Canadian Heritage),* 2003 FCA 197 at paras 68–99.
11 *Canadian Parks and Wilderness Society v. Canada (Minister of Canadian Heritage),* 2003 FCA 197 at paras 89, 101–105.
12 This conclusion is reinforced by the second case involving the consideration of section 8(2) wherein the Federal Court dismissed an application by the Mountain Parks Watershed Association for judicial review of a Parks Canada water permit renewal issued to Chateau Lake Louise (*Mountain Parks Watershed Assn. v. Canada (Minister of Canadian Heritage),* 2004 FC 1222).
13 *Constitution Act, 1982,* being Schedule B to the *Canada Act,* 1982 (UK), 1982, c 11. Section 35(1) reads: 'The existing aboriginal and treaty rights of the aboriginal peoples of Canada are hereby recognized and affirmed.'
14 *Mikisew Cree First Nation v. Canada (Minister of Canadian Heritage),* 2001 FCT 1426.
15 *Mikisew Cree First Nation v. Canada (Minister of Canadian Heritage),* 2001 FCT 1426 at paras 67–74, 87–98.
16 *Mikisew Cree First Nation v. Canada (Minister of Canadian Heritage),* 2001 FCT 1426 at paras 87–98. This evidence came from both the environmental assessment report and cross-examination of the Wood Buffalo National Park Superintendent who admitted that the road construction would adversely impact wildlife habitat in the Park.

17 *Mikisew Cree First Nation v. Canada (Minister of Canadian Heritage)*, 2001 FCT 1426 at para 98.
18 *Mikisew Cree First Nation v. Canada (Minister of Canadian Heritage)*, 2005 SCC 69 at para 44.
19 The paradigmatic example of categorical reasoning in the application of statutory environmental law is perhaps the 1978 decision of the United States Supreme Court in *Tennessee Valley Authority v. Hill*, 437 US 153 (1978).

References

Campbell, C. (2011) *A Century of Parks Canada*. Calgary, Canada: University of Calgary Press.
Coyle, S. and Morrow, K. (2004) *The Philosophical Foundations of Environmental Law*. Portland, OR: Hart Publishing.
Fluker, S. (2010) 'Ecological integrity in Canada's national parks: the false promise of law', *Windsor Review of Legal and Social Issues*, 29, pp. 89–123.
Foster, J. (1978) *Working for Wildlife: The Beginning of Preservation in Canada*. Toronto, Canada: University of Toronto Press.
Freyfogle, E. (1993) 'Ownership and ecology', *Case Western Reserve Law Review*, 43, 1269–97.
Gailus, J. (2011) 'All sizzle, no stake', *Alternatives*, available at www.alternativesjournal.ca/articles/all-sizzle-no-stake (accessed 25 October 2012).
Kotze, L. J. and Paterson, A. R. (2009) *The Role of the Judiciary in Environmental Governance*. Dordrecht, The Netherlands: Kluwer.
Leopold, A. (1949) *A Sand County Almanac*. New York: Oxford University Press.
Morito, B. (2002) *Thinking Ecologically: Environmental Thought, Values and Policy*. Halifax, Canada: Fernwood.
Parks Canada (2000) *Unimpaired for Future Generations? Conserving Ecological Integrity with Canada's National Parks*. Ottawa, Canada: Panel on the Ecological Integrity of Canada's National Parks.
Schrader-Frechette, K. (1995) 'Hard ecology, soft ecology, and ecosystem integrity', in L. Westra and J. Lemons (eds), *Perspectives on Ecological Integrity*. Dordrecht, The Netherlands: Kluwer, pp. 125–45.
Tollefson, C. (2012) 'A precautionary tale: trials and tribulations of the precautionary principle', available at www.cirl.ca/system/files/Chris_Tollefson-EN.pdf (accessed 25 October 2012).
Westra, L. (1994) *An Environmental Proposal for Ethics: The Principle of Integrity*. Lanham, MD: Rowman & Littlefield.

3 The future of the common heritage of mankind

Intersections with the public trust doctrine

Prue Taylor

Introduction

The 'common heritage of mankind' (CH) is a controversial principle or concept of international law. Properly understood, it has the potential to overcome some of the grave deficits of state-centric international (environmental) law. In particular: the tragedy of the commons (in terms of both its use and abuse and its enclosure or privatization); democratic deficits; growing inequality (accumulation of wealth by some states, corporations and elites); and the absence of ecological responsibility (Baslar, 1997; Taylor, 2012). Despite its promise (or perhaps *because* of it), CH has often been marginalized as a political principle. Thus is has been described as utopian or (politically) divisive, because of its implications for property, territorial sovereignty and distributive justice (Baslar, 2007).

One way to advance the argument for the continued relevance of CH, despite the efforts of many states to dismiss it, is to more clearly articulate the philosophical foundations of CH, particularly as these relate to 'natural law' as a legitimate source of international legal obligations. The person closest to this task was the philosopher and theologian, Father Peter Serrecino Inglott (1936–2012), an expert on the philosophy of Thomas Aquinas, a follower of de Chardin and a Catholic priest. His ethical orientation was very consistent with the ethical fundaments of ecological integrity (Westra, 1998). Father Peter, together with Elizabeth Mann Borgese, worked on elucidating the essence of CH. Jurist Arvid Pardo translated it into hard legal principles, which saw CH become 'soul' of the law of sea convention and the basis for a revolutionary resource management regime (Baslar, 1997).

In recent years, there has been a noticeable resurgence in academic interest in CH. A bibliography lists over 500 academic articles, published in fourteen languages (Taylor and Stroud, 2012). That this is so, despite *realpolitik*, is partly attributable to its power to generate moral solidarity about human-nature relations and the need to transform global environmental governance. The resurgence in interest in CH is also linked to three inter-related discussions that are gaining renewed prominence, governance of the commons (Bollier and Helfrich, 2012), the role of natural law and the public trust doctrine. The focus of this chapter will be on the intersection between a 'reinvigorated' or 'renewed' understanding of the public trust doctrine (PTD), and CH. The basic question asked is – what does this mean for the future of CH? Will it be helpful or potentially harmful?

This chapter uses a recent initiative to internationalize PTD as an opportunity to raise and explore a number of legal and ethical issues. The legal issues are core to translating the metaphor of 'international environmental trusteeship' from metaphor to operative legal concept (Sand, 2004). International environmental trusteeship is central to PTD, but is also key to CH. CH has been described as one of the most advanced examples of trusteeship, in international law (Birnie and Boyle, 2002: 144). Responses to these issues will need to be found to advance PTD, but they will also be relevant (in varying degrees) to the future use of CH. The chapter then returns to ethical issues and asks whether the normative foundations of PTD are sufficiently clear and understood, in comparison with CH. It also raises questions with respect to property and commons management. It concludes by making some observations on what international PTD initiatives might mean for the future of CH.

Public trust doctrine – renewed or reinvigorated

Peter Sand has described the revival and innovation of PTD as one of the most successful innovations in US environmental law over the last four decades (Sand, 2007: 521). He was referring to PTD as a doctrine that has been extended beyond its historical understanding in US law, as a limited doctrine of public access and ownership of navigable rivers and tidelands (Turnipseed *et al.*, 2010). Since the seminal work of Joseph Sax (1970), PTD has been understood (in some US jurisdictions) as a more flexible principle. The essence is that 'certain gifts of nature – pure air, clean water, a stable climate, and healthy ecosystems – belong to everyone and cannot be appropriated for exclusively private use' (Turnipseed *et al.*, 2010: 8). Significantly, this modern environmental understanding of PTD imposed a legal obligation on states to protect the 'gifts of nature' for the benefit of the general public. Some US states have recognized PTD as applicable to protect against ecological degradation. It may have a common law, statutory or constitutional basis, depending on the legal framework in particular states. Most significantly, it imposes a legally enforceable duty on the state, in respect of federal or state land and resources, to conserve and protect, for the benefit of current and future generations. Citizens have legal standing to enforce this obligation. In the Mono Lake case (for example) the state of California was required to balance the ecological needs and uses of Lake Mono against Los Angeles's need to consume water. The California Supreme Court affirmed the duty of the state to 'protect the people's common heritage of streams, lakes, marshlands and tidelands' (Turnipseed *et al.*,

2010: 8). The application of PTD lead to the restoration of the lake's ecosystem and significant changes to California's water management regime (ibid.: 8).

In simplified terms, the PTD as applied to natural resource management, has been described as meaning that:

(a) certain natural resources – regardless of their allocation to public or private uses – are defined as part of the 'inalienable public trust';
(b) certain authorities are designated as 'public trustees' to guard these resources; and
(c) every citizen, as beneficiary of the trust, may invoke its terms to hold the trustees accountable and to obtain judicial protection against encroachments or deterioration.

(Sand, 2007: 521)

Public trust doctrine Rio + 20 Proposal

In recent years, some legal scholars have begun to collectively advocate for the PTD doctrine (Turnipseed *et al.*, 2010). In 2012, for example, a group of predominantly US lawyers took a proposal for the internationalization of the PTD, to the Rio + 20 conference (Turnipseed *et al.*, 2012).[1] Although the PTD is best known in the US legal context, aspects of public trust responsibilities have been applied in other legal systems including India, Pakistan, South Africa, Sri Lanka and Tanzania. In national law, it is mostly found in legal systems based on Anglo-Saxon common law (Blumm and Guthrie, 2012). A more general notion of public trust is also found in some international treaties, namely the 1972 UNESCO Convention for the Protection of the World Cultural Heritage, the 2001 FAO International Treaty of Plant Genetic Resources for Food and Agriculture, and the 1982 Law of the Sea Convention (LOS), in which the International Seabed Authority is created as trustee, in respect of the deep seabed, for the benefit of mankind (Sand, 2007; Taylor, 2012).

The intention of the Rio + 20 PTD proposal was to bring the notion of public trusteeship to the global conversation about sustainable development. Specifically, to use the notion of public trust to frame the conversation about managing natural resources for current and future generations (intergenerational equity) and the governance of international common resources. (Turnipseed *et al.*, 2012: 3). The proposal takes the best possible formulation of PTD and (by way of example) applies it to governance of 'living ocean resources in marine areas beyond national jurisdiction' (ibid.: 5). This is an area of international oceans governance that raises significant issues given claims to extended continental shelves (particularly in respect of the Arctic) and uncertainty regarding management of marine genetic resources in areas beyond national jurisdiction. In both instances, there is critical lack of clarity regarding international (i.e. state and institutional) responsibility to protect the water column and ecological systems, and with respect to the sharing of benefits. Thus, PTD is being proposed as a legal concept that clarifies the role of states as 'public trustees'.

Embracing resource stewardship, legal accountability and intergenerational equity, the essential elements of PTD could include:

• international areas and common natural resources, including the high seas and wildlife therein, are held within a Public Trust;
• States are trustees and specified international institutions (e.g., UN General Assembly) oversee the execution of the Trust by (trustee) states;
• all of the world's citizens (both present and future) are beneficiaries of the Trust;
• States and beneficiaries are entitled to information about the status of the Trust resources, to participate in management decisions and enforce performance of the Trust.

(Turnipseed *et al.*, 2012: 6)

Although the particular focus of the PTD Rio + 20 proposal was on governance of living ocean resources in marine areas beyond national jurisdiction, it was hoped that the proposal would also make a contribution to broader global governance issues. Specifically, because of its focus on intergenerational equity and greater (legal) accountability for the decisions of governments, 'the PTD could supply a strong legal basis to the proposed establishment of an "Ombudsperson, or High Commissioner for Future Generations," as well as underlie "steps to give further effect to Rio Principle 10 at the global, regional and national level"' (Turnipseed *et al.*, 2012: 4; see also The Future We Want document[2]). Principle 10 of the Rio Declaration emphasizes the importance of accountability for achieving sustainable development, referring to public participation, information sharing and access to judicial remedies. Thus the PTD Rio + 20 Proposal was intended to contribute to both international and national legal development.

While the final decision of the Rio +20 conference did not provide unanimous support for an Ombudsperson or High Commissioner for Future Generations, the door remains ajar. The final document records agreement to establish a 'high-level political forum' to follow up on sustainable development. As part of the process to establish this forum, states have agreed to 'consider the need for promoting intergenerational solidarity for the achievement of sustainable development, taking into account the needs of future generations, including by inviting the Secretary-General to present a report on this issue' (The Future We Want, para. 86). While this is positive, states were far less explicit on efforts to improve state accountability, referring primarily to the limited mechanisms of reporting and exchange of information (The Future We Want, para. 78).

For the purposes of this chapter, what is particularly important about the PTD Rio + 20 proposal is that it is advocated as a legal doctrine that could (potentially) have the same application as CH, but that it is a trusteeship model that would 'bridge the divide between the common heritage and common property principles' (Turnipseed *et al.*, 2012: 6). Although not explicitly stated, the implication seems to be that PTD would be more acceptable to states than CH. Two examples illustrate the intention of the advocates to use PTD instead of (or in place of) CH. First, as already noted, PTD is applied to marine living resources beyond national jurisdiction. The current international negotiations on this very issue involve some states and academics advocating that those resources are currently, or ought to be, treated as the CH. Other states and academics reject CH in this context (Scovazzi, 2007; Oude Elferink, 2007). The second example involves efforts to re-establish the UN Trusteeship Council. The objective was that this Council be reconstituted to act as 'guardian and supervisor of the common heritage of mankind in the twenty-first century' (Salib, 1998). This initiative is mentioned, but it is not expressly linked to its origins and history as a means to popularize and institutionalize CH, so that it be used more widely in law and forums for the management of the Earth's natural environment (ibid.). Rather, it is generally cited as an example of an effort to internationalize public trusteeship for global resources both outside (and potentially within) national jurisdiction (Turnipseed *et al.*, 2012: 5).

While PTD appears to be favoured over CH, the exact basis of this is not made clear. One can only speculate that reasons might include: the politically divisive history of CH as evidenced by states' refusal to use it as the basis for the UN Conventions on biological diversity and climate change; the accusation that CH socializes natural resources and prevents their utilization by commercial investors; and the fear that CH threatens state sovereignty over globally significant resources within national jurisdiction (Baslar, 1997). In short, the ecological ethic of CH has become obscured by controversial property and equity notions, associating CH with profit-sharing and exploitation (ibid.).

Later in this chapter I will look in more detail at the issue of using PTD to replace CH. However, before doing so, some of the specific legal issues associated with any use of international environmental trusteeship are considered.

International environmental trusteeship – beyond metaphor

Peter Sand (2004) notes that the 'metaphor' of international environmental trusteeship (or stewardship/guardianship) generally creates a bilateral relationship between present generations of humanity (as trustees) and future generations (as beneficiaries). In contrast, the legal structure of international environmental trusteeship creates a trilateral relationship between the community (as trustor/settlor), states (as trustees) and people (as beneficiaries; ibid., 55).

Out of this trilateral legal relationship, some of the core legal issues include (*inter alia*):

- Who is the settlor, in the case of ecological systems beyond national jurisdiction, or in the case of case of ecological systems within national jurisdiction? Is it nation states and citizens? How is their consent obtained?
- Who or what are the trustees? Nation states? International agencies controlled by states, or that operate independently of states? Should the trustees be or include representatives of civil society and/or NGOs? How can the identification and appointment of trustees reflect a legitimate mandate and prevent capture?
- Who or what is the object/or corpus of the trust? Spaces and resources beyond national jurisdiction (international commons), or globally significant ecological systems, or whole of the planetary system, or designated parts of national jurisdictions?
- How will the interests of present and future generations of humanity be defined and represented? Present and future generations of other life – how will their interests be defined and represented?
- Is third party oversight of trustees necessary? If so, who would provide oversight and what would the competences be?
- What are the terms of the trust? Clear statements of the interests of the beneficiaries and the terms of the trust would be needed. For example, should priority be given to ecological responsibility to manage the corpus? How can this be achieved? An active duty to protect ecological integrity? Emphasis on fiduciary obligations of trustees rather than legal ownership, via clarity over the terms of the trust and the interests of beneficiaries? Do beneficiaries have rights to contribute to or collaborate in decision-making? Clear criteria for establishing account-ability? What economic tools are consistent with the terms of the trust? Resource rentals for the benefit of corpus management and all benefi-ciaries versus equitable benefit sharing?
- What mechanisms are needed to maximize international oversight of domestic action and (conversely) domestic oversight of international action? What rights, institutions, legal standing, causes of action and representatives would be required?
- What meaningful sanctions exist or need to be developed?

The above list of legal issues is not exhaustive. Rather it is a preliminary effort to add to the growing body of literature that explores the legal contours of the international environmental trusteeship concept. It is a truism to say that the devil will be in the details – although in the case of international environmental governance there is a general tendency to avoid details by resorting to vague and lengthy generalities. However, in fleshing out the legal details of environmental trusteeship, several factors will be useful to guide efforts. These have been identified by Elinor Ostrom (1990) as significant for determining the eventual success of governance regimes for common pool resources:

- the capacity to communicate;
- the capacity to develop trust;
- a sense of common future;
- (the absence of) power individuals blocking efforts to change the rules;
- (the absence of) perverse incentive systems resulting from government policy.

Public trust doctrine and the future of the common heritage of mankind

As suggested above, PTD has been put forward as an alternative to CH. It has, in common with CH, concern for ecological protection, future genera-tional equity and the obligation of responsibility, as key features. It is capable of a similar reach as CH. For example, it could be applied to ecological systems that are part of the international commons – either because they are beyond the limits of national jurisdiction or because they are shared global resources (concern for them transcends the national interests of individual states). However, unlike CH, PTD has not yet become politicized (and polarizing) within the international arena.

PTD is not the first concept to be put forward in an effort to side step objections to CH. The notion of 'common concern', for example, developed for this very reason. It was a compromise that arose out of developing states' rejection of the use of CH in the UN Climate Change and the Biological Diversity conventions. Developing states were concerned that the reach of CH, to natural resources within their territory, would become the justification for the assertion of external control and the assertion of intellectual property rights to biological resources, in particular. 'Common concern' was viewed as a much more benign notion implying the need for some element of environmental protection but preserving territorial sovereignty over natural resources (UNEP Group, 1990; Trindade and Attard, 1991). It is not the intention of this chapter to discuss the details of 'common concern', its evolution and exact relation-ship with CH. It is sufficient to observe that it generally highlights the global importance of certain resources and activities within the borders of states, either because of their importance (rainforests and fertile soils) or because of their shared and interconnected nature (atmosphere and watersheds). While this is very important in challenging reductionist state-centric worldviews, 'common concern' has not yet been successfully translated into legal form. It has remained declaratory. As a result, it has diverted attention away from CH and perhaps even created elements of confusion. Either way, the opportunity to continue to develop and clarify

CH beyond its historical application in the LOS was significantly diminished by the introduction of 'common concern'. In particular, the urgent need to transform state sovereignty, as exercised both *externally* and *internally*, in respect of shared ecological systems, has not yet been met. The blatant pursuit of national self-interests during nearly 30 years of climate change negotiations, is a salient case in point.

To avoid a similar mistake with PTD (i.e. throwing the baby out with the bath water), a thorough comparative analysis of CH and PTD is necessary. In the paragraphs that follow, an indicative selection of issues relevant to such a comparative analysis, are broadly outlined.[3]

Philosophical foundations

No matter what legal concept we are discussing or advocating, the law alone will not create the fundamental ethical shift needed to transform human-nature relationships. Nevertheless, law can and should play a critical supporting role in this societal transformation. For this reason, the ethical or normative foundations of legal concepts need to be carefully elucidated and examined. Failure to do this can result in legal concepts becoming distorted either intentionally or unintentionally, over time. In particular, there is a general tendency for economic values to trump, subsume or qualify, non-economic values. The precautionary principle, for example, is deeply rooted in the moral philosophy of Hans Jonas and his articulation of a moral theory to underpin human responsibility toward nature (Jonas, 1984). In stark contrast, international legal instruments have reduced it to the 'precautionary approach', and added a vital economic qualifier. Principle 15 of the Rio Declaration, for example, states:

> In order to protect the environment, the precautionary approach shall be widely applied by States according to their capabilities. Where there are threats of serious or irreversible damage, lack of full scientific certainty shall not be used as a reason for postponing *cost-effective measures to prevent environmental degradation.*

The economic qualifier of 'cost-effective measures' has been used to devastating effect as a justification to avoid taking meaningful measures to mitigate greenhouse gas emissions. Many measures needed to transition from fossil fuels to clean energy sources are blocked on the grounds that they will slow economic growth (i.e. they cost too much; Brown, 2012).

What then are the philosophical foundations of PTD? It is suggested here that this question merits much greater analysis that it has so far received. A number of writers and judges have explored the historical basis of PTD but its origins and ethical foundations remain controversial. This is not to suggest that further research will resolve all controversy, but it may usefully clarify the grounds of disagreement and make debate more transparent.

Along these lines, a recent article provided an overview of some claims to PTD's historical origins and concluded that:

> Despite the murky origins of the PTD, it has been invoked in legislation, in court rulings, and in constitutions for many of the things, such as environmental protection, ascribed to its partially fictitious history. So while its history remains controversial, to assess how the PTD may affect natural resources management now and in the future, we need to understand what the PTD is now, rather than what it was not then.
>
> (Sagarin and Turnipseed, 2012: 483)

While this conclusion is consistent with general theories about the flexibility and evolving nature of common law doctrines, this 'pragmatism' must negotiate potentially hazardous terrain. The same article went on to note that PTD potentially challenges conservative notions of private property rights. As a consequence, the positive development of an ecological PTD, over the last 40 years of US jurisprudence, was a trajectory that may not continue. Rather there were 'troubling signs' of regression in the form of pro-business group lobbying of judicial appointments to 'fill seats with judges who will rule in favour of strong private property rights' (Sagarin and Turnipseed, 2012: 485).

In modern (neo)liberal societies, with positivist common law legal systems, there is a general tendency for capitalism to create dominant legal rights in favour of resource exploitation, to create wealth for the minority. In the face of greater ecological stress or collapse, it is not unthinkable that these tendencies will strengthen and accelerate. These significant challenges to ecological values need to be responded to by employing the power of ethical and legal principles.

What then are the philosophical foundations of CH? Are they any better articulated than those of PTD? While much more work needs to be done in articulating these foundations, those closest to the concept describe it as a very old moral concept. At its core is the notion of sustaining the basis or foundations of life, for the benefit of all. This is a moral 'good' common to many cultures, religions and spiritual traditions. It expresses concern and responsibility for the 'other' which encompasses both human interactions and the human-nature relationship. The 'other' encompasses both present and future generations of humans and other life forms. The basic premise is the unity of all life and the place of humanity within that unity (Borgese, 1986: 125). But it also includes key elements of social equity in acknowledgement of the reality that ecological degradation and social inequity are intertwined.

One of the first known uses of CH in international law was in 1830, when it was suggested that things that could not be held by any nation, without affecting the interests of other nations, were the 'indivisible common patrimony'. Subsequent reference to and use of CH, particularly in the context of the 1982 LOS, has led some commentators to conclude that it has attained the highest degree of social legitimacy – as a type of non-derogable (or irrevocable) legal norm, similar to a *jus cogens* norm (Wolfrum, 2008). CH's expression of what are seen as universal communitarian values, links it to natural law and to renewed interest in cosmopolitanism and global constitutionalism.

Despite what might be a more developed philosophical foundation, CH has (on occasion) been misconstrued or misunderstood as a common property concept (Baslar, 2007; Tuerk, 2010). Efforts to interpret it in this way have limited its acceptance in treaty law. However, it is contended that properly understood – CH generates moral solidarity about the need to share and care for ecological commons, as a precious heritage or gift, between and across generations. CH evokes responsibility (for the ecological commons) over rights.

Property concepts?

A related issue that needs further clarification is whether, and (if so) in what sense, PTD is a property concept. For some commentators, PTD is essentially a property concept (Turnipseed *et al.*, 2010; Sax, 2008). Does it, for example, create the basis for better ecological management, by the state, of *publicly owned* resources? What is its relationship with private property rights? Does it interfere or conflict with the (supposedly) exclusive nature of private property rights? Alternatively, does it create a legal basis for an accommodation (or balance) between trust resources and individual property rights (Sagarin and Turnipseed, 2012)? If the latter, then is PTD capable of reshaping societal and legal notions of private property to include responsibility for ecological protection, in balance with use rights (Grinlinton and Taylor, 2011)?

These are important and complex issues, the resolution of which is important to creating conceptual clarity. This clarity is needed both for its own sake and as a bulwark against the slide to ownership and the tendency for economic utilization to dominate over ecological responsibility (environmental stewardship). In the context of ocean resources, Sand describes trusteeship as potentially helpful to re-asserting a distinction between *imperium* and *dominium* (Sand, 2007: 528). Furthermore, clarity about the 'character' of PTD will be significant to its chances for internationalization. As Peter Sand notes, the relative absence of international debate about trusteeship maybe due to the fact that there is no direct equivalent in contemporary civil law.[3] PTD, as it has emerged in US environmental law, therefore tends to be ignored or misunderstood by lawyers outside the Anglo-American legal tradition, as an inappropriate 'private law' concept (ibid.: 522). Sand, and others, contend that PTD is a 'public law' concept – a part of modern American constitutional law – because of its implications for State rights over natural resources (ibid.: 523).

The relationship between CH and property concepts is also highly significant for CH. As noted above, it has (on occasion) been misconstrued or misunderstood as a common property concept or, in the case of the deep seabed, as internationalizing (even socializing) the ownership of resources. In the first case this has led to undue emphasis on the potential to acquire intellectual property rights over genetic resources; in the second case, to undue emphasis on equitable utilization and benefit sharing. In short, states have focused on the supposed 'property' elements of CH for their own purposes and consistent with their own economic paradigms. These interpretations have left CH vulnerable to the criticism that it is of limited use when the priority needs to be respectful treatment of ecological systems, long-term protection and restoration – that is, protection of ecological integrity.

What has been forgotten or conveniently overlooked is that CH was intended as a *non*-property concept. In 1970 Arvid Pardo explained that the word property (in the case of CH) was avoided because it implies the right of use and misuse. 'Property implies and gives excessive emphasis to just one aspect: resource exploitation and benefit therefrom' (Borgese, 2000: xxvii). The consequences of CH as a non-property concept are highly significant (i.e. belonging to all, owned by none). First, it prevents any form of appropriation (or enclosure) either by states or private entities. This can range from territorialization, to privatization, to creeping 'green jurisdiction' – in the name of environmental conservation (Sand, 2007: 529). If the CH belongs to all humanity, it can be used by all but owned by none. Second, it puts emphasis on careful common management to facilitate long-term use by all humanity (not exclusively states). Economic value from use is an element, but value is primarily expressed in non-monetary terms (i.e. in a shared and relational context, in which use is morally, socially and ecologically bounded). In other words, the priority is long-term shared use value for all, not short-term exchange value for a few. Third, it does not conflict with state sovereignty, in respect of shared spaces and ecological systems within a state's national jurisdiction. States would still have the legal power to control and regulate, but this would be subject to limitations designed to protect the interests of all. This casts states in the role of trustees with fiduciary obligations to protect ecological systems for the common good of all. In this way, CH redefines state sovereignty rather than conflicts with it. In the view of Peter Sand, sovereignty bounded in this way potentially enhances the democratic legitimacy of the nation state.(Sand, 2004: 58–59).

As a non-property concept, CH is capable of articulating a subtle distinction that has significant consequences in both theory and practice. It embraces a positive vision of ecological systems belonging to everyone, giving rise to responsibilities as well as rights. This contrasts with a rather negative vision of ecological systems as belonging to *no one* and therefore left vulnerable to the tragedy of the commons or hidden agendas to enclose or propertize.

Public governance of public goods or commons management?

As noted above, the PTD Rio + 20 proposal clarifies the role of states as 'public trustees' of marine living resources beyond national jurisdiction. In legal terms, PTD has the capacity to ensure that the actions of states, are consistent with the interests of present and future generations of the world's citizens. These beneficiaries can hold the trustees legally accountable, for any failure. The risk to be avoided is that PTD becomes a legal vehicle for the type of 'public governance' of 'public goods' (and 'global public goods') that no longer 'signifies a community's authority to manage its…resources and express its own social or ecological demands' (Quilligan, 2012: 75). As James Quilligan argues, since the 1980s and the dominance of neoliberalism, states have principally concerned themselves with increasing the rights of private property, free markets and free trade: 'In a mystifying sleight of hand, the resources we use in common are identified as public goods and then deregulated and turned over to the private sphere for production and distribution' (ibid.). He notes that:

> The strong epistemological frame of reference that once linked the 'public sector' to our collective potential for governing and valuing our own resources and asserting a countervailing authority to private markets, has virtually disappeared. In theory, public still means people; in practice, public means government (as captured by elite interests who regularly impede the people's political rights and capacity to control their common goods).
>
> (Ibid.)

Preventing the sleight of hand that sees common goods become 'public' in name only, needs to be directly and explicitly addressed by PTD. It is suggested here that this will require more rigorous mechanisms than legal accountability of the trustees. The current neoliberal commitment of States calls into question whether and in what circumstances, they can be trustworthy trustees.

This issue is not restricted to PTD; it is also a valid issue for determining the details of any CH regime. The notion of commons management, for the benefit of all humanity, must not conflagrate CH *with* state governance and management, on behalf of humanity. For this reason, the institutional elements of a CH regime are critical. As noted elsewhere, to prevent states from subjugating the common good of all, to their own interests or those of the powerful elites, beneficiaries must be given a direct voice in management (Taylor, 2012). Even this may not be sufficient. Quilligan, for example, argues that we will need more evolved concepts of 'global civil society' (as a third sector beyond the market and the state) *and* of 'global citizenship' enabling people to reclaim their sovereign rights to protect, access, produce, manage and use common goods (Quilligan, 2012, 79).

Conclusion

This chapter has outlined the PTD Rio + Proposal, which is an effort to internationalize the PTD, as it has emerged in US environmental law and in some common law jurisdictions. As CH is also considered to be a form of trusteeship or fiduciary relationship, a comparative analysis of the two concepts will be helpful to move both concepts beyond the metaphor of international environmental trusteeship to legal implementation. However, this chapter has suggested that PTD should not be advocated as a concept to replace CH without much more careful comparative analysis of a number of key issues such as the philosophical foundations of each, and their relationship to notions of property and commons management. The advocacy of PTD in the absence of such an analysis, puts the progress made by the CH concept, over the last 40 years, at risk. With the benefit of a comparative analysis, the discourse on CH and PTD could be pursued in a mutually supportive manner. Ultimately, both seek to give legal form to advanced notions of ecological governance for the common good.

Notes

1   See also the work of Mary Christina Wood (Atmospheric Trust; see http://law.lclark.edu/law_reviews/environmental_law/past_issues/volume_39/39_1.php) and Peter Barnes (Sky Trust; e.g. Barnes, 2001). See also the work of Peter G. Brown (e.g. Brown and Garver, 2009).
2   The Future We Want, 'Zero Draft', Bureau of the UNCSD, Prepcom, 10 January 2012; outcome document adopted at Rio + 20 available at www.uncsd2012.org/content/documents/727The%20Future%20We%20Want%2019%20June%201230pm.pdf (accessed 28 November 2012).
3   The work of Peter H Sand (University of Munich, Germany) provides a sound basis for further comparative work. He has expertise in international law, civil and common law.

References

Barnes, P. (2001) *Who Owns the Sky?* Washington, DC: Island Press.
Baslar, K. (1997) *The Concept of the Common Heritage of Mankind in International Law.* The Hague, The Netherlands: Kluwer Law International.
Birnie, B. and Boyle, A. (2002) *International Law and the Environment.* Oxford: Oxford University Press.
Blumm, M.C. and Guthrie. (2012) 'Internationalising the Public Trust Doctrine: natural law and constitutional and statutory approaches to fulfilling the Saxion vision', *University of California Davis Law Review*, vol 44, available at http://papers.ssrn.com/sol3/papers.cfm?abstract_id=1816628
Bollier, D. and Helfrich, S. (2012) *The Wealth of the Commons: A World Beyond Market and State.* Florence, MA: Levellers Press.
Borgese, E. M. (1986) *The Future of the Oceans: A Report to the Club of Rome.* Montreal, Canada: Harvest House.

Borgese, E. M. (2000) 'The oceanic circle', in E. M. Borgese, A. Chirpot, M. L. McConnell and J. R (eds) *Ocean Yearbook 14*. Malta: International Ocean Institute, pp. 1–5.

Brown, D. (2012) *Climate Change Ethics: Navigating the Perfect Moral Storm*. Abingdon: Routledge.

Brown, P. G. and Garver, G. (2009) *Right Relationship: Building a Whole Earth Economy*. San Francisco, CA: Berrett-Koehler Pub.

Grinlinton, D. and Taylor, P. (eds) (2011) *Property Rights and Sustainability*. Boston, MA: Martinus Nijhoff.

Jonas, H. (1984) *The Imperative of Responsibility: In Search of an Ethics for the Technological Age*. Chicago, IL: University of Chicago Press.

Ostrom, E. (1990) *Governing the Commons: The Evolution of Institutions for Collective Action*. Cambridge: Cambridge University Press.

Oude Elferink, A. G. (2007) 'The regime of the area: delineating the scope of application of the common heritage principle and freedom of the high seas', *International Journal of Marine and Coastal Law*, 22 (1): 143.

Quilligan, J. B. (2012) 'Why distinguish common goods from public goods', in D. Bollier and S. Helfrich, *The Wealth of the Commons: A World Beyond Market and State*. Florence, MA: Levellers Press.

Sagarin, R. D. and Turnipseed, M. (2012) 'The public trust doctrine: where ecology meets natural resources management', *Annual Review of Environmental Resources*, 37, 473–96.

Sand, P. H. (2004) 'Sovereignty Bounded: Public Trusteeship for Common Pool Resources?' *Global Environmental Politics*, 4, 47–71.

Sand, P. H. (2007) 'Public trusteeship for the oceans', in T. M. Ndiaye and R. Wolfrum (eds), *Law of the Sea, Environmental Law and Settlement of Disputes*. Leiden, Netherlands: Koninklijke Brill, pp. 521–44.

Sax, J. L. (1970) 'The public trust doctrine in natural resource law: effective judicial intervention', *Michigan Law Review*, 68, 471.

Sax J. L. (2008) 'Unfinished agenda of environmental law', *Hastings West-Northwest Journal of Environmental Law and Policy*, 14, 1.

Scovazzi, T. (2007) 'The concept of common heritage of mankind and the genetic resources of the seabed beyond the limits of national jurisdiction', *Agenda Internacional*, 14 (25): 11.

Salib (1998) 'Oceans and the Law of the Sea United Nations Reform: Measures and Proposals', UNGA A/52/795, Fifty-Second Session Agenda, Items 39 and 157, 18 February.

Taylor, P. (2012) 'The common heritage principle and public health: honouring our legacy', in L. Westra, C. L. Solskolne and D. W. Spady (eds), *Human Health and Ecological Integrity: Ethics, Law and Human Rights*. Abingdon: Routledge, pp. 43–55.

Taylor, P. and Stroud, L. (eds) (2012) *Common Heritage of Mankind: A Bibliography of Legal Writing*. Malta: Fondation de Malte.

Trindade, A. C and Attard, D. J. (1991) 'The Implication of the "common concern of mankind" concept', in T. Iwama (ed.), *Policies and Laws On Global Warming: International and Comparative Analysis*. Tokyo, Japan: Environmental Research Centre.

Tuerk, H. (2010) 'The idea of common heritage of mankind', in N. A. M. Gutiérrez (ed.), *Serving the Rule of International Maritime Law*. Abingdon: Routledge, pp. 157–75.

Turnipseed, M., Sagarin R., Barnes, P., Blumm, M. C., Parenteau, P., and Sand, P. H. (2010) 'Reinvigorating the public trust doctrine: expert opinion on the potential of a public trust mandate in US and international environmental law', *Environment: Science and Policy for Sustainable Development*, 52, 5–14.

Turnipseed, M. *et al.* (2012) 'The Public Trust Doctrine and Rio + 20 (February), unpublished paper available from the author of this chapter.

UNEP Group (1990) *The Meeting of the Group of Legal Experts to Examine the Concept of The Common Concern of Mankind in Relation to Global Environmental Issues*, D. J. Attard (ed.). Nairobi, Kenya: United Nations Environment Programme.

Westra, L. (1998) *Living in Integrity: A Global Ethic to Restore a Fragmented Earth.* Lanham, MD: Rowman & Littlefield.

Wolfrum, R. (2008) 'Common heritage of mankind', *Max Planck Encyclopedia of Public International Law*, available at www.mpepil.com (accessed 25 November 2012).

4 The exploitation of genetic resources in areas beyond national jurisdictionion

Tullio Scovazzi

Introduction

New challenges are facing States as regards the subject of conservation and sustainable use of marine biodiversity in areas beyond national jurisdiction, especially as regards genetic resources. This paper will focus on the legal aspects of the subject. It will elaborate on how the present regime, as embodied in the United Nations Convention on the Law of the Sea (UNCLOS, Montego Bay, 1982), could evolve to address new challenges. The considerations made hereunder are based on the assumption that the essence of law is not conservation, but development and change, especially where new needs arise and are to be addressed.

The relevant aspects of the present UNCLOS regime

Two basic components of the present international law of the sea are particularly relevant for the subject of conservation and sustainable use of marine biodiversity in areas beyond national jurisdiction, namely the regime of the high seas and the regime of common heritage of mankind.

The high seas

Art. 86 UNCLOS refers to the high seas as to 'all parts of the sea that are not included in the exclusive economic zone, in the territorial sea or in the internal waters of a State, or in the archipelagic waters of an archipelagic State'.

The basic aspect of the high seas regime is freedom. According to Art. 87 UNCLOS:

> 1. The high seas are open to all States, whether coastal or land-locked. Freedom of the high seas is exercised under the conditions laid down by this Convention and by other rules of international law. It comprises, inter alia, both for coastal and land-locked States:
>   (a) freedom of navigation;

    (b) freedom of overflight;

    (c) freedom to lay submarine cables and pipelines, subject to Part VI;

    (d) freedom to construct artificial islands and other installations permitted under international law, subject to Part VI;

    (e) freedom of fishing, subject to the conditions laid down in section 2;

    (f) freedom of scientific research, subject to Parts VI and XIII.

2.   These freedoms shall be exercised by all States with due regard for the interests of other States in their exercise of the freedom of the high seas, and also with due regard for the rights under this Convention with respect to activities in the Area'.

As it can be clearly inferred from Art. 87, para. 2, the freedom of the high seas is not absolute, but is subject to a number of conditions, as specified by the relevant rules of international law. Also freedom of the sea must today be understood in its appropriate context.

When, in the seventeenth century, the principle of freedom of the sea was elaborated by Grotius[1] and his followers, nobody had in mind the problems posed by supertankers, nuclear-propelled vessels, off-shore drilling, mining for polymetallic nodules, fishing with driftnets and many other activities which take place in the marine environment today. This obvious consideration leads to an equally obvious consequence. We cannot today evoke the same concepts that Grotius used and give them the same intellectual and legal strength that Grotius gave them.

To rely in an absolute way on the principle of freedom of the sea was perhaps justified in the circumstances existing in the past. But this is no longer true. Today it cannot be sustained that a State has the right to engage in specific marine activities simply because it enjoys freedom of the sea, without giving any further explanations and without being ready to consider the opposite positions, if any, of the other interested States. Also the concept of freedom of the sea is to be understood in the context of the present range of marine activities and in relation to the other potentially conflicting uses and interests.

The needs of navigation and of other activities falling under the regime of freedom of the sea are important elements to be taken into consideration. But they have to be balanced with other interests, in particular those which have a collective character, such as the protection of the marine environment and the sustainable use of marine resources, as they concern the international community as a whole. Far from being an immutable theological dogma, the principle of freedom of the sea is to be understood not in an abstract way, but in the light of the peculiar circumstances under which it should apply.

The concept of common heritage of mankind

Under Art. 136 UNCLOS, the 'Area', that is the sea-bed and ocean floor and subsoil thereof, beyond the limits of national jurisdiction, and its resources, are the common heritage of mankind. This is the main innovating aspect of the UNCLOS with respect to the previous law of the sea regime. While other important innovations, such as the exclusive economic zone, may be considered as the result of a foreseeable evolution in international law of the sea, the concept of common heritage of mankind has a revolutionary character. It presupposes a third kind of regime which is completely different from both the traditional concepts of sovereignty, which applies in the territorial sea, and of freedom, which applies on the high seas.

The idea of the common heritage of mankind was launched in a memorable speech made at the United Nations General Assembly on 1 November 1967 by the representative of Malta, Mr Arvid Pardo.[2] The practical opportunity for proposing a new regime came from the techno-logical developments which were expected to lead in a relatively short time to the commercial exploitation of polymetallic nodules lying on the surface of the deep seabed and containing various minerals of appreciable economic value, such as manganese, nickel, cobalt and copper.

The application of the scheme of sovereignty was likely to lead to a series of competitive extensions of the limits of national jurisdiction on the sea bed. The application of the scheme of freedom was likely to lead to a rush towards the exploitation of economically and strategically valuable minerals falling under the regime of freedom of the high seas. According to Mr Pardo's speech, the consequences of both possible scenarios would have been equally undesirable. They would have encompassed political tension, economic injustice and risks of pollution. In a few words, 'the strong would get stronger, the rich richer'.[3]

The basic elements of the regime of common heritage of mankind,[4] applying to the seabed beyond the limits of national jurisdiction, are the prohibition of national appropriation, the destination of the Area for peaceful purposes, the use of the Area and its resources for the benefit of mankind as a whole with particular consideration for the interests and needs of developing countries, as well as the establishment of an international organization entitled to act on behalf of mankind in the exercise of rights over the resources.[5]

The proposal by Malta led to Resolution 2749 (XXV), adopted on 17 December 1970, whereby by the United Nations General Assembly solemnly declared that 'the sea-bed and the ocean floor, and the subsoil thereof, beyond the limits of national jurisdiction...as well as the resources of the area, are the common heritage of mankind' (Art. 1).

All the basic elements of the concept of common heritage of mankind can be found in Part XI of UNCLOS. The Area and its resources are the common heritage of mankind (Art. 136). No State can claim or exercise sovereignty over any part of the Area, nor can any State or natural or juridical person appropriate any part thereof (Art. 137, para. 1). The Area can be used exclusively for peaceful purposes (Art. 141). All rights over the resources of the Area are vested in mankind as a whole, on whose behalf the International Sea-Bed Authority (ISBA), which is the international organization created by the UNCLOS (Art. 137, para. 2), is entitled to act. Activities in the Area are carried out for the benefit of mankind as a whole, irrespective of the geographical location of States, whether coastal or land-locked, and taking into particular consideration the interests and needs of developing States (Art. 140, para. 1). The ISBA provides for the equitable sharing of financial and other economic benefits derived from activities in the Area through an appropriate mechanism (Art. 140, para. 2).

For the first time in the historical development of international law of the sea a world regime based on the management of resources by an international organization was included in a treaty of codification. The common heritage of mankind is a third conceptual option (*tertium genus*) which applies to a particular kind of resources located in a specific marine space. It does not eliminate the traditional notions of freedom or sovereignty applying in the other marine spaces. But it provides for a different and much more equitable approach.

As it is well known, the text of the UNCLOS was not adopted by consensus. It was submitted to vote after all efforts to reach consensus had been exhausted. It received 130 votes in favour, 4 against and 17 abstentions. Many developed States were among those which cast a negative vote or abstained. The main criticisms were addressed to the regime of the Area. According to the developed States, the UNCLOS regime would have discouraged mining activities by individual States and private concerns, would have unduly favoured the monopoly of activities by the ISBA, would have burdened the contractors with excessive financial and other obligations relating also to the field of transfer of technology and would have disregarded the interests of industrialized countries in the decision-making procedures of the Council, the executive organ of the ISBA.

In 1994 it was clear that the UNCLOS was expected to formally enter into force without the participation of many developed countries, that is without the participation of the limited number of States having the command of the technological and financial capability required to engage in deep seabed mining activities. To avoid the practical failure of a regime based on the principle of common heritage of mankind, the United Nations promoted a new negotiation on Part XI of the UNCLOS. It resulted in the Agreement Relating to the Implementation of Part XI of the UNCLOS, which was annexed to Resolution 48/263, adopted by the General Assembly on 17 August 1994. This resolution, while reaffirming that the Area and its resources are the common heritage of mankind, recognizes that 'political and economic changes, including in particular a growing reliance on market principles, have necessitated the re-evaluation of some aspects of the regime for the Area and its resources'.

The provisions of the 1994 Implementation Agreement and those of Part XI of the UNCLOS 'shall be interpreted and applied together as a single instrument' (Art. 2). However, in the event of any inconsistency between the 1994 Implementation Agreement and Part XI, the provisions of the former shall prevail. In fact, the label of 'implementation agreement' is a diplomatic device that covers the evident reality that in 1994 the UNCLOS was amended[6] and several aspects of the original concept of common heritage of mankind were substantively changed.[7]

Following the adoption of the 1994 Implementation Agreement, the UNCLOS has achieved an almost universal participation (with some notable exceptions). Although modified under the 1994 Implementation Agreement, the original spirit of the UNCLOS is not betrayed. The principle of common heritage of mankind still applies and remains a major source of inspiration for a treaty that achieves the codification and the progressive development of international law.

Since several years the ISBA has been working on the subject of exploration of the different mineral resources of the Area. In 2000 the ISBA Assembly approved the Regulations on Prospecting and Exploration for Polymetallic Nodules in the Area (the so-called mining code).[8] This has enabled the ISBA to sign contracts for exploration with eight investors. In 2010 and 2012 the ISBA Assembly approved, respectively, the Regulations on Prospecting and Exploration for Polymetallic Sulphides in the Area and the Regulations on Prospecting and Exploration for Cobalt-rich Ferromanganese Crusts in the Area. Unlike polymetallic nodules, which are found partially buried in areas of the deep seabed, sulphides[9] and crusts[10] are localized in their deposits. Concentrations of methane hydrates[11] are also found in the Area and may fall in the future under the regulatory powers of the ISBA.

However, the prospects coming from the mineral resources in the Area remain uncertain. A number of factors have inhibited progress towards commercial exploitation of mineral resources. These factors include the hostile environment in which exploration and mining will take place both as regards the open-ocean surface environment and the great depths at which deposits occur, the high costs involved in research and development of mining technology and the fact that, under current economic conditions, deep seabed mining remains uncompetitive compared to land-based mining.

In his report for 2010 the ISBA Secretary-General, Mr Odunton, remarked, *inter alia*, that the pace at which commercial mining in the Area is progressing continues to be slow. The efforts of the current eight contractors are primarily directed at long-term geological and environmental studies, financed through government funding by sponsoring or participating States, rather than at commercially driven research and development. Investment in mineral exploitation technology remains at a very preliminary stage and it appears unlikely that any of the contractors will move to commercial exploitation in the near future.[12]

Yet the concept of common heritage of mankind, that is a third and more equitable scheme departing from both the schemes of freedom or sovereignty, has actually been put in place under an international regime and an international organization has been established to manage marine mineral resources falling under this regime. But what seems now to be missing is the possibility to exploit in the short or medium term the resources to which the regime is intended to apply.

The question of genetic resources

The prospects for the exploitation of genetic resources in the deep seabed

While the prospects for commercial mining in the deep seabed are uncertain, the exploitation of commercially valuable genetic resources may in the near future become a promising activity taking place beyond the limits of national jurisdiction.

The deep seabed is not a desert, despite extreme conditions of cold, complete darkness and high pressure. It is the habitat of diverse forms of life associated with typical features, such as hydrothermal vents, cold water seeps, seamounts or deep water coral reefs. In particular, it supports biological communities that present unique genetic characteristics. For instance, some animal communities live in the complete absence of sunlight where warm water springs from tectonically active areas (so-called hydro-thermal vents).[13] Several species of microorganisms, fish, crustaceans, polychaetes, echinoderms, coelenterates and molluscs have been found in hydrothermal vent areas. Many of them were new to science. These communities, which do not depend on plant photosynthesis for their survival, rely on specially adapted micro-organisms able to synthesize organic compounds from the hydrothermal fluid of the vents (chemosynthesis).[14] The ability of some deep-seabed organisms to survive extreme temperatures (thermophiles and hyperthermophiles), high pressure (barophiles) and other extreme conditions (extremophiles) makes their genes of great interest to science and industry.[15]

But what is the international regime applying to genetic resources in areas beyond national jurisdiction?[16] In fact, neither the UNCLOS nor the 1992 Convention on Biological Diversity (CBD) provide any specific legal frame-work in this regard. The factual implications of the question are pointed out in a document issued in 2005 by the Subsidiary Body on Scientific, Technical and Technological Advice (SBSTTA) established under the CBD.[17]

First, only few States and private entities have access to the financial means and sophisticated technologies needed to reach the deep seabed:

Reaching deep seabed extreme environments and maintaining alive the sampled organisms, as well as culturing them, requires sophisticated and expensive technologies....Typically, the technology associated with research on deep seabed genetic resources involves: oceanographic vessels equipped with sonar technology, manned or unmanned submersible vehicles; in situ sampling tools; technology related to culture methods; molecular biology technology and techniques; and technology associated with the different steps of the commercialization process of derivates of deep seabed genetic resources. With the exception of basic molecular biology techniques, most of the technology necessary for accessing the deep seabed and studying and isolating its organisms is owned by research institutions, both public and private. To date, only very few countries have access to these technologies.[18]

Second, the prospects for commercial applications of bioprospecting activities seem promising:

Deep seabed resources hold enormous potential for many types of commercial applications, including in the health sector, for industrial processes or bioremediation. A brief search of Patent Office Databases revealed that compounds from deep seabed organisms have been used as basis for potent cancer fighting drugs, commercial skin protection products providing higher resistance to ultraviolet and heat exposure, and for preventing skin inflammation, detoxification agents for snake venom, anti-viral compounds, anti-allergy agents and anti-coagulant agents, as well as industrial applications for reducing viscosity.[19]

The commercial importance of marine genetic resources is demonstrated by the fact that all major pharmaceutical firms have marine biology departments. The high cost of marine scientific research, and the slim odds of success (only one to two percent of pre-clinical candidates become commercially produced) is offset by the potential profits. Estimates put worldwide sales of all marine biotechnology-related products at US$100 billion for the year 2000.[20]

Last, but not least, another important element to take into consideration is that the patent legislation of several States does not compel the applicant to disclose the origin of the genetic materials used:

Assessing the types and levels of current uses of genetic resources from the deep seabed proves relatively difficult for several reasons. First, patents do not necessarily provide detailed information about practical applications, though they do indicate potential uses. Moreover, information regarding the origin of the samples used is not always included in patent descriptions.[21]

More recently, the 2011 report of the United Nations Secretary-General on 'Oceans and the law of the sea' provided the following information on the relevant commercial developments:

> Recent work has focused in discerning the degree to which genetic resources from areas beyond national jurisdiction have contributed to commercial developments, such as patents applied for and granted. To date, it appears that a very small number of patents have originated from the seabed beyond national jurisdiction (generally related to deep-sea bacteria), while a great number have been used on genetic resources from the high seas (primarily micro-organisms, floating sargassum weed, fish and krill). Of concern are applications with potentially large environmental consequences, such as the proposed use of sargassum weed for biofuels.[22]

Common heritage of mankind versus freedom of the high seas

In 2006 the subject of the international regime for the genetic resources in the deep seabed was discussed within the Ad Hoc Open-ended Informal Working Group to Study Issues Relating to the Conservation and Sustainable Use of Marine Biological Diversity beyond Areas of National Jurisdiction,[23] established under United Nations General Assembly Resolution 60/30 of 29 November 2005. Opposite views were put forward by the States concerned.

Some States took the position that the UNCLOS principle of common heritage of mankind and the mandate of the ISBA should be extended to cover also genetic resources:

> Several delegations reiterated their understanding that the marine genetic resources beyond areas of national jurisdiction constituted the common heritage of mankind and recalled article 140 of the Convention, which provides that the activities in the Area shall be carried out for the benefit of mankind and that particular consideration should be given to the interest and needs of developing States, including the need for these resources to be used for the benefit of present generations and to be preserved for future generations....A number of delegations mentioned that the International Seabed Authority constituted an existing mechanism in this area and that consideration should accordingly be given to the possibility of broadening its mandate.[24]

Other States relied on the UNCLOS principle of freedom of the high seas, which would imply a right of freedom of access to, and unrestricted exploitation of, deep seabed genetic resources:

> Other delegations reiterated that any measures that may be taken in relation to genetic resources in areas beyond national jurisdiction must

be consistent with international law, including freedom of navigation. In their view, these resources were covered by the regime of the high seas, which provided the legal framework for all activities relating to them, in particular marine scientific research. These delegations did not agree that there was a need for a new regime to address the exploitation of marine genetic resources in areas beyond national jurisdiction or to expand the mandate of the International Seabed Authority.[25]

The Working Group held a second meeting in 2008.[26] Again, very different views were expressed as regards the regime to be applied to marine genetic resources, repeating what had already taken place in 2006:

> In that regard, divergent views were expressed on the relevant legal regime on marine genetic resources beyond areas of national jurisdiction, in particular whether those marine genetic resources were part of the common heritage of mankind and therefore fell under the regime of the Area, or were part of the regime for the high seas.[27]

The same different positions were manifested during the 2010 meeting of the Working Group.[28] This basic disagreement on the international regime of genetic resources leaves a sentiment of dissatisfaction. In fact, both the divergent positions move from the same starting point: 'The United Nations Convention on the Law of the Sea was recognized as the legal framework for all activities in the oceans and seas, including in respect of genetic resources beyond areas of national jurisdiction.'[29]

Why do two groups of States, moving from the same assumption, namely that the UNCLOS is the legal framework for all activities taking place in the sea, reach two completely opposite conclusions as regards the matter in question? A possible answer to the question is that there is some elaboration to make on the very starting point.[30]

A banality and its consequences

There is no doubt that the UNCLOS is a cornerstone in the field of codification of international law. It has been rightly qualified as a 'constitution for the oceans', 'a monumental achievement in the international community', 'the first comprehensive treaty dealing with practically every aspect of the uses and resources of the seas and the oceans', an instrument which 'has successfully accommodated the competing interests of all nations'.[31]

Nevertheless, the UNCLOS, as any legal text, is linked to the time when it was negotiated and adopted (from 1973 to 1982 in the specific case). Being itself a product of time, the UNCLOS cannot stop the passing of time. While it provides a solid basis for the regulation of many matters, it would be illusory to think that the UNCLOS is the end of legal regulation. International law of the sea is subject to a process of natural evolution and progressive development which is linked to States' practice and involves also the UNCLOS. Due to limits of space, it is not possible to elaborate here on the instances where changes with respect to the original UNCLOS regime have been integrated into the UNCLOS itself (evolution by integration); where different interpretations of the relevant UNCLOS provisions are in principle admissible and State practice may be important in making one interpretation prevail (evolution by interpretation); where the UNCLOS does not provide any clearly defined regime and the relevant legal regime is to be inferred only from State practice (evolution in another context); or where, due to the fact that the UNCLOS regime is clearly unsatisfactory (it happens very seldom, but it may happen), a new instrument of universal scope has been drafted to avoid the risk of undesirable consequences (evolution by further codification).[32]

What follows from the assumption that the UNCLOS is linked to the time when it has been negotiated goes close to a banality, but has the great strength of banalities. It is a matter of fact that the UNCLOS cannot make miracles. In particular, the UNCLOS cannot regulate those activities that its drafters did not intend to regulate for the simple reason that they were not foreseeable in the period when this treaty was being negotiated. At this time, very little was known about the genetic qualities of deep seabed organisms. For evident chronological reasons, the potential economic value of the units of heredity of this kind of organisms was not considered by the UNCLOS negotiators. When dealing with the special regime of the Area and its resources, the UNCLOS drafters had only mineral resources in mind.

This is fully evident form the plain text of the UNCLOS. The term 'activities' in the Area is defined as 'all activities of exploration for, and exploitation of the resources of the Area' (Art. 1, para. 1). Art. 133a defines the 'resources' of the Area to 'all solid, liquid or gaseous mineral resources *in-situ* in the Area at or beneath the sea-bed, including polymetallic nodules'.[33] The UNCLOS regime of common heritage of mankind does not include the non-mineral resources of the Area. However, for the same chronological reasons, the regime of freedom of the high seas does not apply to genetic resources either. While including provisions to living and mineral resources in areas beyond national jurisdiction, the UNCLOS does not provide any specific regime for the exploitation of marine genetic resources. The words 'genetic resources' or 'bioprospecting' do not appear anywhere in the UNCLOS. A legal gap exists in this regard. Sooner or later it should be filled (better sooner than later) through a regime which, to be consistent, should encompass under the same legal framework the genetic resources of both the Area and the superjacent waters.

However, not all of the UNCLOS should be left aside when envisaging a future regime for marine genetic resources beyond national jurisdiction. The scope of the regime of the Area is already broader than it may be believed at first sight. Under the UNCLOS, the legal condition of the Area has an influence also on the regulation of activities that, although different from minerals and mining activities, are also located in that space. The regime of the Area already encompasses subjects which are more or less directly related to mining activities, such as marine scientific research,[34] the preservation of the marine environment[35] and the protection of underwater cultural heritage.[36] As far as the first two subjects are concerned, it is difficult to draw a clear-cut distinction between what takes place on the seabed and what in the superjacent waters.

While a specific regime for exploitation of genetic resources is lacking, the aim of sharing the benefits among all States, which was the main aspect of the seminal proposal made by Arvid Pardo, can still be seen as a basic objective embodied in a treaty designed to 'contribute to the realization of a just and equitable international economic order which takes into account the interests and needs of mankind as a whole and, in particular the special interests and needs of developing countries, whether coastal or land-locked' (UNCLOS preamble). Also in the field of genetic resources, the application of the principle of freedom of the sea (that is the 'first come, first served' approach) leads to inequitable and hardly acceptable consequences.[37] New cooperative schemes, based on provisions on access and sharing of benefits, should be envisaged in a future agreement on genetic resources beyond the limits of national jurisdiction. This is also in full conformity with the principle of fair and equitable sharing of the benefits arising out of the utilization of genetic resources set forth by Art. 1 of the CBD and, more recently, by Art. 10 of the Protocol on Access to Genetic Resources and the Fair and Equitable Sharing of Benefits Arising from their Utilization (Nagoya, 2010).[38]

Moreover, bioprospecting, that is what is currently understood as the search for commercially valuable genetic resources of the deep seabed, can already be considered as falling under the UNCLOS regime of marine scientific research. The UNCLOS does not provide any definition of 'marine scientific research'. However, Art. 246, which applies to the exclusive economic zone and the continental shelf, makes a distinction between two kinds of marine scientific research projects, namely those carried out 'to increase scientific knowledge of the marine environment for the benefit of all mankind' (para. 3) and those 'of direct significance for the exploration and exploitation of natural resources, whether living or non-living' (para. 5a). This distinction supports the conclusion that, under the UNCLOS logic, also research activities of direct significance for the purpose of exploration and exploitation of genetic resources fall under the general label of 'marine scientific research'.[39] Also bioprospecting is consequently covered by Art. 143, para. 1, of the UNCLOS, which sets forth the principle that 'marine scientific research in the Area shall be carried out exclusively for peaceful purposes and for the benefit of the mankind as a whole'.[40] This provision refers to any kind of marine scientific research and is not limited to research on mineral resources. Yet the reading of Art. 143 in combination with Art. 246 contradicts the assumption that there is an absolute freedom to carry out bioprospecting in the Area.[41] States which are active in bioprospecting in this space are already bound to contribute to the benefit of mankind as a whole.[42]

Possible future developments

New prospects have emerged at the 2011 meeting of the Working Group.[43] A number of States, both developed and developing, proposed the commencement of a negotiation process towards a new implementation agreement of the UNCLOS that could fill the gaps in the present regime of conservation and sustainable use of marine biological diversity in areas beyond national jurisdiction.[44] While a general consensus on this proposal has not yet been achieved, commonalities are being developed among a number of States that were previously putting forward divergent positions. The States participating to the 2011 meeting of the Working Group recommended that:

(a) A process by initiated by the General Assembly, with a view to ensuring that the legal framework for the conservation and sustainable use of marine biodiversity in areas beyond national jurisdiction effectively addresses those issues by identifying gaps and ways forward, including through the implementation of existing instruments and the possible development of a multilateral agreement under the United Nations Convention on the Law of the Sea.

(b) This process would address the conservation and sustainable use of marine biodiversity in areas beyond national jurisdiction, in particular, together and as a whole, marine genetic resources, including questions on the sharing of benefits, measures such as area-based management tools, including marine protected areas, and environmental impact assessments, capacity-building and transfer of marine technology.

(c) This process would take place: (i) in the existing Working Group; and (ii) in the format of intersessional workshops aimed at improving understanding of the issues and clarifying key questions as an input to the Work of the working Group.[45]

At its 2012 meeting, the Working Group requested the United Nations Secretary-General to convene in 2013 two intersessional workshops on the topics of 'marine genetic resources' and 'conservation and management tools, including area-based management and environmental impact assessment'. The workshops are intended to improve understanding of the issues and clarify key questions in order to enable the United Nations General Assembly to make progress on ways to fulfil its mandate.[46]

The possibility of a third UNCLOS implementation agreement is envisaged as a possible way to move forward, as far as the existing instruments cannot fill the present governance and regulatory gaps and cannot provide the required specific regime. What is needed for the time being is the consolidation of a general understanding on a number of 'commonalities' that could become the key elements in the 'package' for a future global regime for the conservation and sustainable use of marine biodiversity in areas beyond national jurisdiction. This package could include a network of marine protected areas, environmental impact assessment, marine genetic resources, including access to and sharing of benefits from them, as well as capacity-building and technology transfer.

Notes

1   Anonymous (the author's name Grotius appeared for the first time in a Dutch translation published in 1614), *Mare liberum sive de jure, quod Batavis competit ad Indicana commercia, dissertatio*, Lugduni Batavorum, 1609.
2   A notable precedent can be found in a proposal made in 1927 by the Argentine jurist José León Suárez. He was entrusted by the League of Nations Experts Committee for the Progressive Codification of International Law with the drafting of a report on the international rules relating to the exploitation of marine living resources. Mr Suárez proposed that the living resources of the sea, and whales in particular, should be considered a heritage of mankind: 'Les richesses de la mer, en particulier les richesses immenses de la région antarctique, constituent un patrimoine de l'humanité, et notre Commission, constituée par la Société des Nations, est tout indiquée pour proposer au Gouvernement un moyen d'action avant qu'il ne soit trop tard' (Société des Nations, *Comité d'experts pour la codification progressive du droit international, Rapport au Conseil de la Société des Nations*, Geneva, 1927, p123).
3   'The known resources of the seabed and of the ocean floor are far greater than the resources known to exist on dry land. The seabed and ocean floor are also of vital and increasing strategic importance. Present and clearly foreseeable technology also permits their effective exploration for military or economic purposes. Some countries may therefore be tempted to use their technical competence to achieve near-unbreakable world dominance through predominant control over the seabed and the ocean floor. This, even more than the search for wealth, will impel countries with the requisite technical competence competitively to extend their jurisdiction over selected areas of the ocean floor. The process has already started and will lead to a competitive scramble for sovereign rights over the land underlying the world's seas and oceans, surpassing in magnitude and in its implications last century's colonial scramble for territory in Asia and Africa. The consequences will be very grave: at the very least a dramatic escalation of the arms race and sharply increasing world tensions, also caused by the intolerable injustice that would reserve the plurality of the world's resources for the exclusive benefit of less than a handful of nations. The strong would get stronger, the rich richer, and among the rich themselves there would arise an increasing and insuperable differentiation between two or three and the remainder. Between the very few dominant powers, suspicions and tensions would reach unprecedented levels. Traditional activities on the high seas would be curtailed and, at the same time, the world would face the growing danger of permanent damage to the marine environment through radioactive and other pollution: this is a virtually inevitable consequence of the present situation' (Pardo, *The Common Heritage – Selected Papers on Oceans and World Order*, Valletta, 1975, p31).

4   The word 'heritage' itself, which renders the idea of the sound management of a resource to be transmitted to the heritors, was preferred to the word 'property', as the latter could have recalled the *jus utendi et abutendi* (right to use and misuse) that private Roman law gave to the owner ('Introduction' by E. Mann Borgese to Pardo, ibid., pX).

5   A fifth element is the protection and preservation of the marine environment, which however relates to any kind of marine spaces.

6   'The 1994 Implementation Agreement is a curious creature. The 1982 LOSC does not permit reservations (arts. 309, 310) and the procedures for its amendment are both protracted and open only to State parties (arts. 311–317). Neither route was suitable for modifications of the Convention sought by the industrialized States that remained outside the Convention. Instead, the 1994 Implementation Agreement was made, its title disingenuously implying that it was concerned to put into effect the 1982 provisions rather than to change them. In fact, it stipulates that several provisions of Part XI of the LOSC 'shall not apply' and modifies the effect of others' (Churchill and Lowe, *The Law of the Sea*, 3rd edn, Manchester, 1999, p20).

7   For instance, the obligation of State Parties to finance the deep seabed mining operations of the Enterprise, that is the organ of the ISBA which carries out mining activities in the Area directly, is abrogated and the independent activities by the Enterprise are delayed until it is able to conduct mining operations through joint-ventures. A contractor which has contributed a particular area to the ISBA as a reserved area has the right of first refusal to enter into a joint-venture arrangement with the Enterprise for exploration and exploitation of that area. If the Enterprise does not submit an application for a plan of work for activities with respect to a reserved area within fifteen years, the contractor which contributed the area is entitled to apply for a plan of work for that area, provided that it offers in good faith to include the Enterprise as a joint-venture partner. The Enterprise and developing States wishing to obtain technology for deep seabed mining shall seek to obtain it on fair and reasonable commercial terms and conditions on the open market or through joint-venture arrangements. The decision-making procedure by the Council is modified by the introduction of the rule that, if all efforts to reach consensus have been exhausted, decisions on questions of substance are taken by a two-thirds majority, provided that such decisions are not opposed by a majority in any one of the chambers. This means that any of the five chambers of States established under Part XI of the UNCLOS (for example, the chamber composed of four of the major consumer or importer States) can veto the taking of decisions by the Council.

8   'Polymetallic nodules are lumps of metallic ore, between golf ball and soccer ball in size, scattered loosely in expansive fields on abyssal plains. Their quantity in a given area can be assessed simply by photographing the ocean bottom. They can be scooped up by mechanical harvesters with little physical damage to the seabed' (ISBA, *Press Release*, SB/9/1 of 23 July 2003, p2).

9   'Hydrothermal polymetallic massive sulphides occur typically in chimney-like structures, called smokers, surrounding undersea hot-spring vents. Their minerals come mainly from magma, the mass of molten rock deep beneath the earth's crust, where it breaches the ocean bottom in volcanic regions along the margins of ocean basins. Individual deposits are small and scattered. Mining would require the destruction of the smokers, with potentially catastrophic consequences for the exotic animal communities that live in the superheated, oxygen-deprived water and cannot exist in a normal environment dependent on sunlight' (Ibid.).

10 'Cobalt-rich ferromanganese crusts, derived like the nodules from metals precip-
    itated out of seawater, are fused to the seabed in layers up to tens of centimetres
    thick, often buried beneath other seabed deposits. They are found on the flanks
    and ridges of globe-encircling, mid-ocean mountain range. Assessment of their
    occurrence and metal content and their eventual exploitation will require
    digging or drilling the ores out of a solid rock bed' (Ibid.).

11 They are ice-like materials that occur in abundance in marine sediments and
    store immense quantities of methane.

12 However, the ISBA Secretary-General points out that the private sector
    investment in research on and prospecting for marine mineral deposits
    continues, both in the seabed under national jurisdiction and in the Area,
    indicating a strong interest in seabed minerals as a future source of metals. This
    suggests that the private sector is developing confidence in the legal regime for
    the orderly development of the resources of the Area that has been put in place
    within the ISBA framework and that there is a potential for a marine mineral
    mining industry to emerge as an alternative to land-based mining (see doc.
    ISBA/16/A/2 of 8 March 2010, paras 128 and 129).

13 Hydrothermal vents may be found both in the Area and on the seabed falling
    within the limits of national jurisdiction, according to the definition of
    continental shelf given by Art. 76 UNCLOS.

14 The discovery of hydrothermal vent ecosystems has given rise to a new theory as
    to how life began on Earth. It could have originated and evolved in association
    with hydrothermal vents in the primeval ocean during the early Archaean period
    (about 4,000 million years ago).

15 See Arrieta, Arnaud-Haond and Duarte, 'What lies underneath: conserving the
    oceans' living resources', *Science*, 25 March 2011.

16 On this question see Glowka, 'The deepest of ironies: genetic resources, marine
    scientific research, and the area', in *Ocean Yearbook*, 1996, p156; Scovazzi, 'Mining,
    protection of the environment, scientific research and bioprospecting: some
    considerations on the role of the International Sea-Bed Authority', in *Interna-
    tional Journal of Marine and Coastal Law*, 2004, p383; Arico and Salpin, *Bioprospecting
    of Genetic Resources in the Deep Seabed: Scientific, Legal and Policy Aspects*, Yokohama,
    2005; Leary, *International Law and Genetic Resources of the Deep Sea*, Leiden, 2006;
    Oude Elferink, 'The regime of the area: delineating the scope of application of
    the common heritage principle and freedom of the high seas', *International
    Journal of Marine and Coastal Law*, 2007, p143; Millicay, 'A legal regime for the
    biodiversity in the area', in Nordquist, Long, Heider and Moore (eds), *Law,
    Science and Ocean Management*, Leiden, 2007, p739; De la Fayette, 'A new regime
    for the conservation and sustainable use of marine biodiversity and genetic
    resources beyond the limits of national jurisdiction', *International Law of Marine
    and Coastal Law*, 2009, p221; Armas-Pfirter, 'How can life in the deep seabed be
    protected?', *International Law of Marine and Coastal Law*, 2009, p281; Ridgeway,
    'Marine genetic resources: outcomes of the united nations informal consultative
    process', *International Law of Marine and Coastal Law*, 2009, p309; Barnes,
    'Entitlement to marine living resources in areas beyond national jurisdiction', in
    Oude Elferink and Molenaar, *The International Legal Regime of Areas beyond National
    Jurisdiction: Current and Future Developments*, Leiden, 2010, p83; Scovazzi, 'The
    seabed beyond the limits of national jurisdiction: general and institutional
    aspects', in Oude Elferink and Molenaar, *The International Legal Regime of Areas
    beyond National Jurisdiction: Current and Future Developments*, Leiden, 2010, p43.

17 *Status and Trends of, and Threats to, Deep Seabed Genetic Resources beyond National
    Jurisdiction, and Identification of Technical Options for their Conservation and
    Sustainable Use*, doc. UNEP/CBD/SBSTTA/11/11 of 22 July 2005.

18 Ibid., paras 12 and 13. 'A limited number of institutions worldwide own or operate vehicles that are able to reach areas deeper than 1,000 meters below the oceans' surface, and can therefore be actively involved in deep seabed research' (Ibid., para. 16).
19 Ibid., para. 21.
20 Ibid., para. 22.
21 Ibid., para. 22.
22 Doc. A/66/70 of 22 March 2011, para. 63.
23 Hereinafter: the Working Group.
24 *Report of the Ad Hoc Open-ended Working Group to Study Issues Relating to their Conservation and Sustainable Use of Marine Biological Diversity beyond Areas of National Jurisdiction*, doc. A/61/65 of 20 March 2006, para. 71.
25 Ibid., para. 72.
26 Also the United Nations Open-Ended Informal Consultative Process on Oceans and the Law of the Sea addressed the subject of marine genetic resources at its 2007 meeting. However, the meeting was unable to reach overall agreement on the elements to be suggested to the UN General Assembly as regards the legal regime of such resources. See the co-chairpersons' possible elements to be suggested in the annex to UN doc. A/62/169 of 30 July 2007.
27 *Joint Statement of the Co-Chairpersons of the Working Group*, doc. A/63/79 of 16 May 2008, para. 32.
28 See *Letter Dated 16 March 2010 from the Co-Chairpersons of the Ad Hoc Open-ended Informal Working Group to the President of the General Assembly*, doc. A/65/68 of 17 March 2010, paras. 70–72.
29 Doc. quoted *supra* at note 27, para. 36. The statement is repeated in the resolutions on 'Oceans and the Law of the Sea' yearly adopted by the UN General Assembly. See, for instance, the preamble of Resolution 65/37, adopted on 7 December 2010, which emphasizes that the UNCLOS 'sets out the legal framework within which all activities in the oceans and seas must be carried out and is of strategic importance as the basis for national, regional and global action and cooperation in the marine sector, and that its integrity needs to be maintained'.
30 See Scovazzi, 'Is the UN Convention on the Law of the Sea the legal framework for all activities in the sea? The case of bioprospecting', in Vidas (ed.), *Law, Technology and Science for Oceans in Globalisation*, Leiden, 2009, p309.
31 Koh, 'A constitution for the oceans', in UN, *The Law of the Sea - Official Text of the United Nations Convention on the Law of the Sea with Annexes and Index*, New York, 1983, pxxiii.
32 See Scovazzi, 'The evolution of international law of the sea: new issues, new challenges', in Hague Academy of International Law, *Recueil des cours*, vol 286, 2001, p39.
33 In so providing, the UNCLOS narrows the term 'resources' that was used in a more abstract and broad sense in Art. 1 of UN General Assembly Resolution 2749 (XXV) (see *supra*, para. 2.B).
34 Art. 143 UNCLOS.
35 See Art. 145 UNCLOS.
36 See Art. 149 UNCLOS.
37 See *supra*, para. 2.B.
38 'Parties shall consider the need for and the modalities of a global multilateral benefit-sharing mechanism to address the fair and equitable sharing of benefits derived from the utilization of genetic resources and traditional knowledge associated with genetic resources that occur in transboundary situations or for which it is not possible to grant or obtain prior informed consent. The benefits

shared by users of genetic resources and traditional knowledge associated with genetic resources through this mechanism shall be used to support the conservation of biological diversity and the sustainable use of its components globally.' While the Nagoya Protocol does not apply to areas beyond national jurisdiction, it could become a source of inspiration. As stated in the 2011 report of the UN Secretary-General on 'Oceans and the law of the Sea', the adoption and implementation of the Nagoya Protocol 'may provide further opportunities to inform and advance the discussions on marine genetic resources, including by providing examples of how the sharing of benefits from the utilization of resources from areas within national jurisdiction may be addressed in a multilateral context' (doc. cit. *supra* at note 22, para. 256). Another source of inspiration could be the International Treaty on Plant Genetic Resources for Food and Agriculture, concluded in 2001 under the auspices of the Food and Agriculture Organization (FAO).

39 There is an inextricable factual link between marine scientific research (either pure or applied) and bioprospecting. A research endeavour organized with the intent to increase human knowledge may well result in the discovery of commercially valuable information on genetic resources.

40 Art. 241 UNCLOS is also relevant in a discussion on the legal condition of the genetic resources of the deep seabed. It provides that 'marine scientific research activities shall not constitute the legal basis for any claim to any part of the marine environment or its resources'.

41 Art. 143, para. 3, grants to the States the right to carry out scientific research in the Area, but binds them to co-operate with other States and the ISBA in various fields, including dissemination of results. Also this provision refers to any kind of marine scientific research in the Area. Yet, the mandate of ISBA deserves close scrutiny, especially if it is to be understood not only as an entity involved in marine mining activities in competition with others, but as the international organization which bears the main responsibility to realize a just and equitable economic order of the oceans and seas. Nothing prevents States from expanding the mining focus of the ISBA and granting to it some broader management competences in the field of genetic resources.

42 'The principle of common heritage in its substantive aspect is, like any norm of international law, capable of being applied in a decentralized manner by states. Even in the absence of *ad hoc* institutions every state is under an obligation to respect and fulfil the principle of the common heritage by ensuring that subjects within its jurisdiction do not act contrary to its object and purpose. This would be the case if a state authorised or negligently failed to prevent biotechnological activities in common spaces that had the effect of causing severe and irreversible damage to the unique biodiversity of that space. Similarly, a state would fail the common heritage if it authorised exclusive appropriation of genetic resources without requiring equitable sharing of pertinent scientific knowledge and without ensuring that a fair portion of economic benefits accruing from their exploitation be devoted to the conservation and sustainable development of such common resources'; Francioni, 'Genetic resources, biotechnology and human rights: the international legal framework', in Francioni (ed.), *Biotechnologies and International Human Rights*, Oxford, 2007, p14.

43 Resolution 65/37, adopted by the UN General Assembly on 7 December 2010, encouraged the Working Group, in view of its 2011 meeting, 'to improve progress on all outstanding issues on its agenda' (para. 164).

44 A new implementation agreement was already envisaged by certain States during the 2008 meeting of the Working Group: 'Several delegations considered that an implementation agreement under the United Nations Convention on the Law

of the Sea was the most effective way to establish an integrated regime and address the multiplicity of challenges facing the protection and sustainable use of marine biodiversity in areas beyond national jurisdiction. These delegations suggested that such an instrument was necessary to fill the governance and regulatory gaps that prevented the international community from adequately protecting marine biodiversity in the areas beyond national jurisdiction. It was proposed that such an instrument would address currently unregulated activities, ensure consistent application of modern ocean governance principles in sectoral management regimes and provide for enhanced international cooperation' (doc. quoted *supra* at note 27, para. 47).

45   See doc. A/66/119 of 30 June 2011, para. 1 of the annex.
46   See doc. A/67/95 of 13 June 2012, para. 1 and appendix.

5   Ecological integrity in European law?

Agnès Michelot

Europe could certainly be described as a proactive actor in developing environmental law and as a great supporter of ecological awareness. Many of the European nations are engaged in earnest efforts to develop sustainable practices in land use, consumption of natural resources and to maintain a rich level of biodiversity. The grassroots of this ecological awareness could be found in the history of environmental activism in Europe from the late nineteenth-century conservation and naturalist movements. Although some distinctions could be made between countries and regions, the role of Europe in ecological political awareness cannot be denied: northern Europe has traditionally defended the idea that humans hold a responsibility toward natural environment and that global environmental issues should be a highest preoccupation for international community; in eastern Europe, activism arose in the late 1980s linked to the issue of environmental degradation and human health; in southern Europe, political movements were created around local issues and campaigns (Hillstrom and Collier Hillstrom, 2003: 223–42). Today, most European countries participate actively in important international environmental instruments and play a dynamic role to elaborate innovative tools to conserve Europe's natural heritage (Romi, 2004).

At the same time Europe is responsible for a high level of environmental degradation in its own territories, as well as in other foreign territories, if we consider from a historical perspective the frightening environmental impact of its economic model of development (Fritz, 1997; Diamond, 1997). The viability of wilderness habitat is threatened by exploitation of forest and water courses, and by the diffusion of toxic pollutants into the air and water, while numerous habitat areas continue to be converted to support urbanization or agricultural operations.

The old continent is facing its own paradoxes through the development of a complex institutional network. To consider ecological integrity in European law, we are going to study how legal European instruments adopted by regional organizations refer to or use the concept. Of course, if there is a lack of direct reference to the concept, how could we determine if European organizations take it into account in one way or another, and by what means? Is there a specific concept of ecological integrity emerging from European environmental law and, if so, what is it, or what should it be?

From the right to destroy to respect for nature: the (difficult) reintegration of man into nature

Without attempting the ambitious effort of Philippe Descolas in his famous book *Par-delà nature et culture* ('towards nature and culture'), presenting how the dualism between nature and culture appears in European culture (Descolas, 2005: 108), we can at least underline the European tradition of juridical anthropocentrism that has delayed the adoption of any regulation referring to ecological integrity or to any ecosystem approach. Far from a voluntary recognition of the intrinsic value of ecosystems and from the protection of self-creative capacities of life to evolve over time (Westra, 2005), Europe made progress in building environmental law under pressure, facing imminent risks of irreversible ecological damages in different areas. Many European countries have suffered environmental disasters due to the lack of control of human activities, such as the Torrey Canyon oil slick (1967), touching England and French coasts; the Seveso accident in Italy (1976), with the contamination of 37,000 persons by a dioxyne cloud; the nuclear accident at Chernobyl in Ukraine (1988), with more than 20,000 people involved in the process of decontamination; and the major atmospheric pollution from Sandoz, near French border (1986).

But the 'old Europe' is also the continent that has demonstrated its capacity to organize a common response to critical situations in different areas through international cooperation and regulation. From experiencing disintegrity (or biotic impoverishment; Karr, 1993) to the right to environment, what are European legal instruments in the field of ecological integrity?

The multiplicity of organizations, the lack of reference to ecological integrity

Europe certainly has the most extensive body of regional rules of international environmental law in the world due to the construction of the European Union (today 27 states) and due to the very important role played by the Council of Europe (47 states) for ensuring respect of human rights, democracy and the rule of law. Europe is also quite active in developing international environmental through the UN Economic Commission for Europe created in 1947 – the only European organization regrouping all European countries – and through OECD, which supports European countries in the evaluation of environmental impact of economic activities, and facilitates environmental international cooperation and regulation.

European Union: from the priority of economic development to the interest for the quality of environment

From the Treaty of Rome on 25 March 1957 until the entry into force of the Treaty of Lisbon on the 1 December 2009, and on to the present day, the European Union (EU) has adopted a broad spectrum of legislation aimed at protecting and restoring the environment and improving the living standards of its citizens (Thieffry, 2011). The sources of European Commission (EC) law include secondary legislation creating rights and obligations which can in certain circumstances be relied on by natural and legal persons before the courts of Member States. Since the 1972 Stockholm Conference, the EC has also developed a series of environmental action programmes, which have systematically broadened the scope of environmental issues addressed.

But although sustainable development was made an EU objective with the principle of a high level of environmental protection in the Amsterdam Treaty of 1997, no reference seems to appear on the concept of ecological integrity, neither in the primary law (treaties) nor in the secondary law (unilateral acts, conventions and agreements), even if it is quite difficult to evaluate the hundreds of environmental legal instruments adopted by the EU. The reason for this lack appears quite evident if you consider that historically the EU has been built with the main objective of establishing a common market, an economic and monetary union to promote economic activities, a high level of employment, a high degree of competitiveness – and, later, a high level of protection and improvement of the quality of the environment. As Geert Van Calster wrote:

> Importantly, the inclusion of sustainable development in the highest hierarchy of Treaty objectives, at least does away with one impression: that in the event of discrepancies between environmental protection and economic development, the latter should automatically be given priority over the former.
>
> (Van Calster, 2002: 474)

This idea appeared reinforced considering the 'greening' of EU policies (Lenschow, 2002: 3–21) and the efforts displayed to implement the principle of environmental policy integration. In this perspective, the 6th Environment Action Programme (EAP), called 'Environment 2010: Our future, Our choice', made the integration of environmental concerns into other policies a strategic action in the continuity with previous EAPs.

Some environmental areas show the special preoccupation of the EU to achieve a 'good ecological status', as in the Directive 2000/60/EC of the European Parliament and of the Council of 23 October 2000 establishing a framework for Community action in the field of water policy. This framework directive highlighted the need for Community legislation covering ecological quality. The term of 'ecological status' is defined as 'an expression of the quality of the structure and functioning of aquatic ecosystems associated with surface waters' (article 2, §21). But even if one of the aims of the legislation is to protect aquatic and terrestrial ecosystems, there is no disposal referring to ecological integrity. The same consideration could be made with the Directive 2008/50/EC of the European Parliament and of the Council of 21 May 2008 on ambient air quality and cleaner air for Europe that is fully oriented to support existing air quality objectives. No reference is made to ecological integrity, but links between pollutants and human health are clearly expressed and the use of the concept of 'critical levels' shows the interest for the protection of living organisms *per se*. Indeed, following the 2008 Directive's definition, it is 'a level fixed on the basis of scientific knowledge, above which direct adverse effects may occur on some receptors, such as trees, other plants or natural ecosystems but not on humans' (article 2, §6). Also, the conception of environment 'as a whole' is used (i.e. in Directive 2008/1/EC of the European Parliament and of the Council of 15 January 2008) concerning integrated pollution prevention and control that intends 'to achieve the highest practicable level of protection for the environment as a whole' (Preamble, §15).

Council of Europe: principles to fight the disruption of integrity without referring to ecological integrity

The Council of Europe has, for a long time, devoted a part of its efforts to the conservation of natural habitats and has formulated many fundamental principles related to environment through various recommendations. The 1967 European Water Charter, later replaced by the 2001 European Charter on Water Resources, expresses links between ecological function of water and human societies but never refers directly to the concept of ecological integrity: 'Water is not only of vital importance for all forms of life, and thus for the protection of the environment; its availability in sufficient quantity and quality is also a prerequisite for the development of human societies' (article 2).

Later, the European Soil Charter adopted in 1972 recognized that soil is 'an entity in itself…a living and dynamic medium which supports plant and animal living. It is vital to man's existence as a source of food and raw materials' (article 1) and, once more, the ecological integrity never appeared. At least, the Charter refers to 'ecological principles' that need to be taken in consideration (Preamble), but without detailing them.

One of the most significant instruments concluded under the auspices of the Council of Europe is the 1979 Bern Convention on the Conservation of European Wildlife and Natural Habitats. Dedicated to the conservation of wild flora and fauna, especially endangered and vulnerable species, its brief preamble only refers to the recognition of 'the essential role played by wild flora and fauna in maintaining biological balances'. Providing appendices listing strictly protected plant and animal species and prohibited methods of hunting and other exploitation, the Bern Convention appears as a very classic instrument of biodiversity protection, unable to refer to ecological processes, and then to ecological integrity as a principle of action. Fortunately, the implementation of the Convention is kept under review by a Standing committee which may address recommendation to Parties and who played an important role to recognize biological interconnections (Recommendation no. 25 on Conservation of Natural Areas Outside Protected Areas, 1991).

Three other environment-related conventions within the framework of the Council of Europe demonstrate the involvement of this organization in environmental policy development: the Convention on Civil Liability for Damage Resulting from Activities Dangerous to the Environment (Lugano, 21 June 1993); the Convention on the Protection of the Environment through Criminal Law (Strasbourg, 4 November 1998); and European Landscape Convention (Florence, 20 October 2000). None of these conventions refer to ecological integrity; on the contrary, references to the environment are mostly linked to the defence of property and people's quality of life. The definition of environment adopted in the Lugano Convention is quite enlightening:

> environment includes:
> - Natural resources both abiotic and biotic, such as air, water, soil, fauna and flora and the interaction between the same factors
> - Property which forms part of the cultural heritage; and
> - The characteristic aspects of the landscape.

Environment is mainly presented as a provider of resources, property and heritage, and never as a sum of physical, chemical and biological integrity (Westra, 2005, referring to Karr's definition), nor from the perspective of ecosystem processes, even it is referring to 'interaction between factors'.

The right to nature: far from the concept of human ecological rights?

Most European texts in the field of environment express a very clear \anthropocentric approach to environment through dominant concepts such as 'natural and cultural heritage' and the right to protection of health and environment. Considering the 'right to destroy' (Rémond-Gouilloud, 1989) that denies any respect for nature, what place is there for ecological integrity?

Heritage perspective: meeting cultural and natural values

Clearly a patrimonial approach of environment in all its forms is developed in European legal instruments such as the Bern convention,[1] the European landscape convention and most of EU environmental legislation. As an example, the most comprehensive instrument for nature conservation, the Council Directive 92/43/EEC of 21 May 1992 on the Conservation of Natural Habitats and of Wild Fauna and Flora refers to 'the Community's natural heritage'.

But, of course, the most significant European instrument to understand the perception of relationship between nature and culture is the 'Landscape Convention'.[2] Landscape 'is a basic component of the European natural and cultural heritage' (Preamble) and 'an essential component of people's surroundings' (article 5). This text presents landscape as a political subject of general interest tightly linked to human well-being and European identity; it reintroduces a democratic dimension in all decisions in this field, considering that people do not have to undergo landscape changes without expressing their opinion. In this way it should be recognized as introducing elements of environmental justice. However, it remains silent on ecological integrity, and reaffirms that landscape constitutes a resource favourable to economic activity and whose management can contribute to job creation (Preamble).

Human rights and the environment

The Council of Europe has played a significant role in protecting the environment through the implementation of the European Convention on Human Rights and the European Social Charter. Its influence has been reinforced by the accession of the EU with the Lisbon treaty. Neither the convention not the Charter are designed to provide a general protection of the environment as such and, of course, no reference is made to ecological integrity. These texts do not guarantee a right to a sound, quiet and healthy environment, but they offer a certain degree of protection with regard to environmental matters, as demonstrated by the evolving case law of the court and decisions of the Committee on Social Rights in this field (Marguenaud, 2003; Garcia San José, 2005).[3]

The European Union is more or less in the same position within its own legal order. The Charter of Fundamental Rights of the EU (2010/C 83/02; Official Journal of the EU C83/399, 30.3. 2010) defends the right to life as a right for 'everyone' related to the condemnation of death penalty (article 1) and to the right to the integrity of the person (article 2). The reference to environmental protection appeared much further in article 37 and not expressly as a right. This disposal reaffirmed the principle of integration, but does not go any further in affirming a right to environment.

Health and environment

Defining ecological integrity, Laura Westra underlined the connection between health and integrity:

because of the global connection between health and integrity, and the right to life and to living…a true understanding of ecological integrity reconnects human life with the wild, and the rights to the latter with those of the former.

(Westra, 2005)

Is there a crucial effort to connect respect for the integrity of natural systems with human matters in European law? This is an interesting question. Some European initiatives definitely show some interest in establishing a connection between health and environment. With this purpose, the 1989 European Charter on Environment and Health,[4] in collaboration with the World Health Organization, expresses some priorities, but remains linked to a 'right/responsibility approach'.[5] In its preamble at least, it emphasizes 'the dependence of human health on a wide range of crucial environmental factors' and 'the vital importance of preventing health hazards by protecting the environment'. Another interesting aspect is its open view to environmental justice in insisting on the protection of vulnerable, disadvantaged and high risk groups (§3, 'Principles for Public Policy').

Some similar consideration of social environmental justice can be found in the EU Environment and Health Strategy (11 June 2003), with the ultimate objective to reduce the disease burden caused by environmental factors in the EU, especially for children. From the Single European Act of 1986, European Community has a legal basis to develop environmental law 'to contribute towards protecting health' and express the preoccupation to protect human's health from the degradation of environmental factors. Directive 2004/35/CE of the European Parliament and of the Council of 21 April 2004 on environmental liability with regard to the prevention and remedying of environmental damage confirms the permanent links between health and environmental risks, but also the classic approach commonly used within European environmental law restricted to 'polluter pays' and sustainable development principles. This directive is also the first European legal instrument referring to 'ecological services', and then expressing a deep utilitarian perspective on nature, far from the intrinsic value (Doussan, 2009). Later, the EU will develop its conception of ecosystem services related to biodiversity, clearly affirming the reference to an economic assessment.[6]

It appears quite obvious that European approach is far from recognizing a moral concern for non-human life and affirming human dependence upon ecological processes, as is required by the ecological integrity approach on the GEIG definition.

Towards nature and culture: experiencing ecological integrity in Europe?

European organizations have demonstrated their ability to adopt policies to fight environmental degradation and their preoccupation to join a high level of environmental quality, but most of the time environment appeared as the 'background of people' giving them well-being and quality of life. The minimum influence from human society to natural process is not pursued as an objective.

Traditionally, the history of legal instruments dedicated to conservation does not refer to ecological integrity but in the last period EU and Council of Europe demonstrate their will to develop international cooperation to create new scales of management and decision making with ecosystems at the centre.

From ecological networks to ecosystem approach: a way to ecological integrity?

The most complete work made on the ecological integrity concept produced by the GEIG is *Ecological Integrity: Integrating Environment, Conservation, and Health* (Pimentel *et al.*, 2000). This study concludes in its synthesis chapter that the ecosystem approach should be distinguished from ecological integrity and biodiversity concepts (ibid.: 387), and we do think that this distinction is quite essential.

Ecological integrity tends to preserve 'ecosystems' undiminished ability to continue their natural path of evolution, their normal transition over time, and their successional recovery from perturbation' (Westra, 2005). European environmental policies certainly intend to reach this general objective, as far as it is possible in the special ecological context of Europe, where density of population and level of urbanization are very high. EU has especially developed policies that require a movement from sectorally based to more ecosystem-based management, and the Council of Europe's initiatives help to create international cooperation in conservation linked to a new vision on spatial development of the European continent.[7]

Fighting fragmentation, developing ecological corridors and networks

European organizations have developed a huge concern for protected area networks from the 1970s. The Council of Europe set up the European Network of Biogenetic Reserves in 1976 with the objective of conserving representative samples of natural areas and critical habitats of endangered species, promoting scientific research and helping to raise public awareness in conservation. Another programme, called European Diploma, was implemented in 1965 to recognize the exceptional importance for Europe of some identified areas (protected areas, natural or semi-natural sites, elements of landscape) that are managed in an exemplary way. Also, the implementation of the Convention on the Conservation of European Wildlife and Natural Habitats entered into force on 1 June 1982 and has played an important role in developing ecological networks. The Standing Committee in 1996 has recommended the establishment of an 'Emerald

Network' of areas of special interest outside the EU, with a view to supplementing the Natura 2000 Network, on a similar basis, in non-Community countries, based on the highest possible methodological synergy. As the European Union is also a Contracting Party to the Bern Convention, the Natura 2000 Network is considered to be the EU contribution to the Emerald Network. Also, this network is linked to the Pan-European Ecological Network initiated by the Pan European Biological and Landscape Diversity Strategy (PEBLDS) in 1995, a significant regional initiative endorsed by the environment ministers of 55 countries, for building cross-sectoral and interagency partnerships for biodiversity conservation throughout Europe.

The PEBLDS is certainly one of the most interesting instruments concerning ecological integrity, because it aims in particular to substantially reduce or eliminate current threats to European biological and landscape diversity, increase the resilience of biodiversity and strengthen the ecological coherence of Europe as a whole (chapter 1, §1.4). The strategy addresses all biological and landscape initiatives under one European approach, and promotes the integration of biological diversity considerations into social and economic factors (Preamble). But the most interesting aspect about PEBLDS concerns the recognition of the principle of ecological integrity as a strategic principle, meaning that 'the ecological processes responsible for survival of species should be protected and the habitats on which their survival depends maintained' (chapter 2, §2.4). The other principles are also interesting: careful decision-making, avoidance, translocation, restoration and showing a new vision towards biodiversity conservation in Europe.

At the EU level, the 1979 Birds Directive, with a network of Special Protected Areas later completed by the 1992 Habitat Directive providing a Community-wide network of Special Areas of Conservation, constitute a coherent European ecological network to be called Natura 2000. Following their designations of sites as part of this network, member states must take measures to avoid the deterioration of the protected habitats or disturbance to protected species, and must make provision for environmental impact assessments of any project liable to have a significant effect on the site (article 6.3). Unfortunately, the report on the Conservation statute of habitat types and species from the Commission (13 July 2009) reveals that favourable conservation status has not been achieved for many habitats and species listed under the Habitat Directive.

In 1999, the European Spatial Development Perspective (ESDP) adopted in Postdam – an important step towards European integration on common objectives and concepts for the future development of the territory of the European Union – expressed the importance of including management of natural zones in spatial development strategy. Later the European Parliament resolution of 21 February 2008 on the follow-up of the Territorial Agenda and the Leipzig Charter: Towards a European Action Programme for Spatial Development and Territorial Cohesion (2007/2190(INI); 2009/C 184 E/15) reiterated that Natura 2000 is an important instrument for European spatial development. Indeed, the EAP 'insists that the requirements of Natura 2000 be fully implemented and that landscape corridors and open space networks between protected areas be created so that flora can disperse and fauna can move freely, thus preserving biodiversity'.

Moving to the ecosystem approach

If ecological networks in Europe have played a significant role to develop international cooperation in conservation areas, the influence of the Biodiversity Convention has been significant to move forward an ecosystem approach.

First, the EU has adopted several directives, strategies, recommendations and agreements that require a movement from sectorally based to more ecosystem-based, holistic environmental management. The Water Framework Directive protects and enhances the status of aquatic systems, as well as the terrestrial ecosystems and wetland linked to them. The EU intends to achieve good ecological status for its waters, measured against a reference derived from the natural unmodified conditions for water body. There is also a similar movement to extend the ecosystem approach to coastal zones through the adoption for the European Integrated Maritime Policy, the Marine Strategy Framework Directive and by measures under the common fisheries policy. The Integrated Coastal Zone Management recommendation calls for improving coordination of the actions between all authorities concerned both at seas and on land in managing the sea–land interaction.

Another specific European initiative – which is not an EU initiative – that could help to demonstrate the evolution to an ecosystem approach is the Convention on the Protection of the Alps (Salzburg, 7 November 1991),[8] the first instrument to focus on environmental protection of mountainous regions. Due to the recognition of the important ecological values and needs of soil to the European Alpine area, a protocol for the protection of soils (ACSPP) was adopted in 1998. It became the only specific binding instrument for soil in the world, and contains many of essential ecological concepts. The ACSPP is based on an ecosystem perspective and recognizes the highly sensitive ecological systems whose functional capacity must be preserved. It set out the functions of soil including natural functions, cultural functions and land use functions emphasizing the necessity to maintain an ecological balance in the region.

It should also be noticed that European countries are important actors in international environmental law-making and participate to develop international ecological cooperation through the UNESCO biosphere reserve network (MAB Programme), the Ramsar Convention on Wetlands, the Convention on Migratory Species and of course through the implementation of the Convention on Biological Diversity.

Fighting disintegrity: is there a European approach of ecological integrity?

Through dynamic regional institutions, real implication in international environmental law and a huge capacity to develop environmental policy, Europe has produced interesting instruments to fight disintegrity in all its forms (pollution, toxic wastes, wildlife destruction). In a way, analysing the content of these texts, we could conclude that ecological integrity is everywhere and nowhere (except in the Pan-European Strategy, which is not a binding instrument). In fact there are different discourses on ecological integrity. Due to GEIG work, we did refer to ecological integrity in a systemic–normative discourse, with the main objective being to preserve the capacity of life to organize, reproduce, adapt, sustain and evolve. The study of European environmental legal tools shows that, even with the progress of the ecosystem management, this approach does not correspond to European values and political and ethical choices. It appears that another discourse on ecological integrity could be more adapted to European ethical and scientist perspective.

Considering Council of Europe instruments, the transpersonal–collaborative discourse could be seen as the closest option followed by this organization. Ecological integrity could be accepted as a metaphor for understanding ecological, social and individual co-evolution. Environmental crisis demands a deep change in the way we interact with nature (Manuel Navarrete *et al.*, 2004: 221), assuming that ecosystems should be considered as part of human. This view could be perceived through the concept of natural heritage. Integrity is not clearly a foundational value.

Concerning EU discourse on ecological integrity, or more precisely the silence of the EU on the concept, it could lead to some various interpretations, but from a general perspective we can consider that regulations are based on the recognition of reciprocal interconnections between ecosystems and human systems. The role of scientists and the mechanisms of quality assessment are quite high, considering the main objective to improve or/and maintain the quality of environment. Therefore, in 2009 the EU created the European Environment Agency and the European Environment Information and Observation Network.[9] Directive 2011/92/EU, known as the Environmental Impact Assessment (EIA) Directive, and Directive 2001/42/EC, known as the Strategic Environmental Assessment (SEA) Directive, demonstrate the EU's capacity to collect data and to prevent project with significant effects on the environment through environmental assessment. Consultation with the public is also a key feature of environmental assessment procedures; connected to the implementation of the Aarhus Convention (to which the EU is a party), it leads to developing a democratic decision-making process .

To make environmental legislation more efficient, the EU tends to impose criminal penalties on certain behaviour that is seriously detrimental to the environment (Directive 2008/99/EC of the European Parliament and of the

Council of 19 November 2008 on the Protection of the Environment through Criminal Law). Member states should also ensure that inciting, aiding and abetting the committing of criminal acts will lead to effective, proportionate and dissuasive sanctions (Comte and Kramer, 2004).

Conclusion

European organizations have recently developed new concepts and instruments related to ecological integrity objectives, but the dominant orientation remains protection of European natural heritage and access to a high quality of environment, related to avoiding degradation of 'environmental factors'. The preoccupation to preserve future generations' interest is also sometimes expressed.

Environmental legislation is mainly based on a utilitarian approach that has been reinforced with the interest for ecological services at the detriment of the more interesting concept of ecological functions, which is closer to the ecological integrity philosophy. If environmental regulations reflect 'the way we look at the world' and determine our behaviour towards nature, we can certainly be worried about the future opportunity to see an emerging reference to ecological integrity in Europe (such as is expressed by GEIG), in a way that allows the development of a concrete and real ecological citizenship.

Notes

1   The Bern Convention recognizes that 'wild flora and fauna constitute a natural heritage of aesthetic, scientific, cultural, recreational, economic and intrinsic value that needs to be preserved and handed on to future generations' (Preamble).
2   The definition of landscape given by the European Landscape Convention is of special interest: '"Landscape" means an area, as perceived by people, whose character is the result of the action and interaction of natural and/or human factors' (article 1).
3   A number of cases raising environmental issues have come before the Court on issues such as noise levels from airports, industrial pollution or town planning.
4   See www.euro.who.int/__data/assets/pdf_file/0019/114085/ICP_RUD_113.pdf.
5   For an analysis of the jurisprudence of European convention on human rights, see Winisdoerffer (2009).
6   See, for example, Communication from the Commission – Halting the Loss of Biodiversity by 2010 – and Beyond – Sustaining Ecosystem Services for Human Well-being, COM/2006/0216 final: 'For many, the loss of species and natural habitats matters because they take an ethical view that we do not have the right to decide the fate of nature. More tangibly nature is valued for the pleasure and inspiration it provides...From an economic perspective, biodiversity provides benefits for present and future generations by way of ecosystem services.'
7   'Networks for sustainable spatial development of the European continent: bridges over Europe', developed by the 14th session of the European Conference of Ministers responsible for Spatial/Regional Planning (CEMAT), Council of Europe.

8   The Parties to the Alpine Convention are Austria, France, Germany, Italy, Liecht-
    enstein, Monaco, Slovenia, Switzerland and the European Community.
9   See Regulation (EC) no. 401/2009 of the European Parliament and of the
    Council of 23 April 2009.

References

Comte, F. and Kramer, L. (eds) (2004) *Environmental Crime in Europe*. Groningen, The
    Netherlands: Europa Law Publishing.

Descolas, P. (2005) *Par delà nature et culture*. Paris, France: Gallimard.

Diamond, J. (1997) *De l'inégalité parmi les sociétés – Essai sur l'homme et l'environnement
    dans l'histoire*. Paris, France: Gallimard.

Doussan, I. (2009), 'Les services écologiques: un nouveau concept pour le droit de
    l'environnement?' In C. Cans (ed.), *La responsabilité environnementale, prévention,
    imputation, réparation, préface de G.Viney*. Paris, France: Dalloz, pp. 125–41.

Fritz, J.-C. (1997) 'Le développement comme système de domination de la nature et
    des hommes', in C. Apostolidis, G. Fritz and J.-C. Fritz (eds), *L'humanité face à la
    mondialisation – Droit des peuples et environnement*. Paris, France: L'Harmattan,
    pp. 87–111.

Garcia San José, D. (2005), *La protection de l'environnement et la convention européenne
    des droits de l'homme*. Strasbourg, France: Editions du Conseil de l'Europe.

Hillstrom, K. and Collier Hillstrom, L. (2003) *The World's Environments – Europe: A
    Continental Overview of Environmental Issues*. Santa Barbara, CA: ABC-CLIO.

Karr, J. (1993) 'Protecting ecological integrity: an urgent societal goal', *Yale Journal
    of International Law*, 18 (1): 297–306.

Lenschow, A. (2002), 'Greening the European Union: An introduction', in A.
    Lenschow (ed.), *Environmental Policy Integration: Greening Sectoral Policies in Europe*.
    London: Earthscan.

Marguenaud, J.-P. (2003) *Droit de l'homme à l'environnement et cour européenne des droits
    de l'homme*, *RJE numéro spécial*, pp. 15–21.

Pimentel, D., Westra, L. and Noss, R. F. (eds) (2000) *Ecological Integrity: Integrating
    Environment, Conservation and Health*. Washington, DC: Island Press.

Rémond-Gouilloud, M. (1989) *Du droit de détruire*. Paris, France: Presses universitaires
    de France.

Romi, R. (2004) *L'Europe et la protection juridique de l'environnement*. France: PUF.

Thieffry, P. (2011) *Droit de l'Union européenne*. Brussels, Belgium: Bruylant.

Van Calster, G. (2002) 'Public environmental law in the European Union', in R. J. G.
    H Seerden, M. A. Heldeweg and K. R Deketelaere (eds), *Public Environmental Law
    in European Union and the United States*. Dordrecht, The Netherlands: Kluwer Law
    International, pp. 465–515.

Westra, L. (2005) 'Ecological integrity', in C. Mitcham (ed.), *Encyclopedia of Science,
    Technology and Ethics*, 2. Detroit, MI: Macmillan, pp. 574–8.

Winisdoerffer, Y. (2009) 'Environnement et santé dans la jurisprudence de la
    Convention européenne des Droits del'homme: un droit individuel à un environ-
    nement salubre', in P. Billet, M. Durousseau, G. Martin and I. Trinquelle (eds),
    Droit de l'environnement et protection de la santé. , Paris, France: L'Harmattan,
    pp. 131–43.

Part II

Ecological integrity and basic rights

The interface

Introduction

Agnès Michelot

The development of the work of the GEIG has aimed at the identification of ecological integrity and the definition of the role it should play in public policy. The erosion of life-support systems deeply interferes with the main objective to attaining a sustainable society in which natural services are protected and basic rights respected.

The chapters in Part II address the connection between ecological integrity and basic rights in many dimensions (ethical, social, legal), referring to specific experiences or to general experiments at international, regional (EU) or national level (US). Each chapter presents the difficulty of expressing some human and ecological right from an institutional or material approach.

Through the topic of the lessons learned from the disinformation campaign, Don Brown (Chapter 6) analyses the difficulty of accessing environmental information and the role of responsible skepticism in providing guidance to policy-makers in the context where technology gives the human race the power to seriously damage ecological systems (and, as a consequence, human health). He demonstrates that scientific uncertainty can be manipulated in a way that threatens environment and reaffirm the necessity to firmly implement some norms based on ethics. From the US experience of the climate change disinformation campaign, Brown explores the necessity to develop the right to information as a basic right related to ecological integrity.

Chapter 7 concentrates on public participation and judicial control from the European perspective, which gives a complementary approach on the necessity to examine in advance the environmental consequences of human activities through a transparent process. Vicky Karageorgou expresses the preoccupation to ensure the effective enforcement of environmental law and the need for a more holistic approach to environmental questions at the EU level. In this perspective the environmental impact assessment provides a useful legal basis to ensure that some potentially harmful projects are made in accordance with a requirement for development consent and an assessment of their effects.

Owen McIntyre (Chapter 8) also explores EU legal instruments to integrate environmental considerations into EU policies and activities. The principle of environmental integration – a principle that reflects the interdependence of social, economic, financial, environmental and human rights aspects – clearly has an impact on EU law. Elevated as a general principle in the European legal order, it participates to extend the limits of the Union's legal competences and to ensure that the different policies work towards the objective of a high level of protection and an improvement of the quality of the environment. Demonstrating the crucial role it could play on the road to ecological integrity, it is only with respect to this principle that the Charter of Fundamental Rights requires its objectives to be pursued in accordance with the fundamental objective of sustainable development.

Joseph Dellapenna, in Chapter 9, addresses the difficulty for the international community to develop governance strategies to respond efficiently to the emerging global water crises. The right to water is, of course, closely linked to the right to life, and the author presents the major gaps between all the recommendations produced by various institutions competing for leadership on water issues with no legal binding effects, and the enormous collective expectation.

In Chapter 10 Yuliya Lyamzina develops the same preoccupation to evaluate the capacity of international institutions to face crucial needs of the world. Her chapter focuses on gender to consider UN agencies' contribution. Lyamzina elucidates the question of violence against women and girls with effects on their health, a question that has previously not received much attention from the international community. The author explores the importance of close links between ecological integrity and the recognition of human dignity in fighting discrimination.

Ecological integrity cannot be disassociated from respect for all forms of life, expressed in all possible ways. It is necessary to defend all basic rights in all legal contexts, but it also needs efficient binding instruments and operational institutions, which are very often lacking.

6 Lessons learned from the climate change disinformation campaign about responsible scientific skepticism

Donald A. Brown

Introduction

Human technology relentlessly gives the human race increasing power both to prevent harm through such things as the conquering of disease, and to damage human health and the environment due to increasing impacts on ecological systems. Because of the complexity of ecological systems, the power of technology for harm as well as good, and the increasing speed of potential adverse impacts on human health and the environment, policy-makers are frequently confronted with the need to make decisions in the face of scientific uncertainty about issues that have potentially huge and sometimes catastrophic impacts. Frequently decisions on these issues will affect the economic interests of those who profit from the activities that threaten human health and the environment. These interests invariably pressure policy-makers not to restrict the activities in question unless there are high levels of scientific proof that the activities will actually cause great harm.

There are some human activities about which time or economic resource constraints prevent resolving scientific controversies about harm, and yet these activities greatly threaten human health and the environment. What should policy-makers do about these activities?

As we shall see, on climate change, a well-organized disinformation campaign financed by corporations and others whose economic interests are threatened by government policies that would restrict greenhouse gas emissions has relentlessly and vigorously sought to prevent government action to reduce greenhouse gas emissions. This chapter examines lessons that can be learned from climate change disinformation campaign about how not to discourage responsible scientific skepticism while being very critical of disingenuous claims that exaggerate scientific uncertainty about grave threats to human health and the environment.

The climate change disinformation campaign

For over 30 years, a debate about climate change has been waged that most Americans are at least dimly aware of. In this debate, media coverage of this debate have often characterized those opposed to action on climate change on the basis of scientific uncertainty as climate 'skeptics'.

Skepticism is the oxygen and catalyst of science, and should be encouraged. Yet most Americans are completely unaware that a well-financed, well-organized climate change disinformation campaign has been operating for over two decades, and that it has used tactics which cannot be classified as responsible skepticism. In fact, this campaign has often been engaged in tactics that are deeply ethically abhorrent.

To the extent that the US mainstream press has covered this controversy, it has reported on disputes between mainstream climate scientists and what are referred to as scientific 'skeptics' and in so doing ignored the ethically abhorrent tactics of the disinformation campaign discussed in this article. At the same time, the press coverage of scientific disputes about climate change has given opposition to climate change policy legitimacy that the disinformation campaign does not deserve because its tactics cannot be understood as responsible skepticism.

This disinformation campaign has largely been responsible for the United States failure to enact comprehensive climate change policies. Given the enormity, harshness and destructiveness of climate change impacts, the duties that high-emitting countries like the United States have to not harm hundreds of millions of people around the world who are vulnerable to climate change, and the fact that the world has now lost several decades in finding a solution to climate change at a time when the world may be running out of time to prevent dangerous climate change, the failure of the US media to report on the nature of this campaign to the American people is a grave, tragic and profound failure. The failure of the US press on this issue may be attributed at least in part, to the media's inability to distinguish between responsible scientific skepticism and bogus claims about scientific uncertainty.

There is a growing peer-reviewed sociological literature on the disinformation campaign which describes this phenomenon as a counter-movement (see, for example, McCright and Dunlap, 2000: 559). A counter-movement is a social movement that has formed in reaction to another movement (ibid.: 504). The climate change disinformation campaign can be understood to be a continuation of the counter-movements that arose among US political conservatives in reaction to the environmental, civil rights, women's rights and anti-war movements that arose in the 1960s in the United States. And so, the climate change disinformation campaign's methods and processes can be understood to be an extension of strategies that had already been developed among some, although not all, conservatives to counter the environmental movement that had developed in the late 1960s and 1970s around other environmental issues such as air and water pollution, safe disposal of waste and toxic substances, and protection of wetlands and endangered species.

Yet the emergence of global warming as an issue in the 1980s, with its potential for large-scale social change needed to ameliorate its threat, was seen as more threatening to conservatives in regard to industry, prosperity, lifestyle and the entire American way of life than were traditional pollution problems (McCright and Dunlap, 2000: 503). In other words, climate change directly threatened the central values of the US conservative movement even more than other environmental problems (ibid.: 505). As a result climate change has become the key environmental focus of the US conservative movement.

In addition, there have been some American industries whose welfare depends upon fossil fuel use have also participated in the disinformation campaign by funding this effort. The climate change disinformation movement can be understood to be comprised of many organizations and participants including conservative think tanks, front groups, Astroturf groups, conservative media, and individuals. This disinformation campaign frequently has used certain tactics to convince people and politicians that the science supporting climate change policies is flawed. The central claims of the climate change disinformation movement have been:

- There is no warming.
- It is not caused by humans.
- Reducing greenhouse gas emissions will cause more harm than good.
  (McCright and Dunlap, 2010: 111)

To support these claims, the climate denial machine frequently has made claims such as the following:

- mainstream climate scientists are corrupt or liars;
- descriptions of adverse climate change impacts are made by 'alarmists';
- scientific journals that publish climate related research are biased against skeptics; and
- mainstream climate science is 'junk' science.

The climate change disinformation machine also has made frequent ad hominem attacks on those who produce climate change science and sometimes has cyber-bullied both climate scientists and journalists. In summary, the climate change disinformation campaign has engaged in tactics that may not be classified as responsible skepticism, yet the US media has covered this campaign as if it was the output of reasonable scientific skepticism.

The climate change disinformation campaign began in the 1980s when some of the same scientists and organizations that fought government regulation of tobacco began to apply the tactics perfected in their war on the regulation of tobacco to climate change (Oreskes and Conway, 2010: 169–215). According to Pooley, the disinformation campaign began 'spinning around 1988 in response to the increasingly outspoken scientific community' (Pooley, 2010: 39). For almost 25 years this campaign has been waged to undermine support for regulation of greenhouse gases by most frequently making claims about the lack of scientific evidence on climate change.

To say that the campaign has been 'waged' is not to claim that it has been a tightly organized, completely coordinated effort by a few groups or individuals or that all participants have the same motives. In fact different participants may have radically different motives including the fact that some may be sincere, some appear to be motivated by protecting free markets without government intervention, and many appear to believe that no restriction on fossil fuel use can be justified without very high levels of proof of harms. Yet since the 1990s these different participants, according to *Newsweek*, have for the most part acted in a well-coordinated campaign among contrarian scientists, free-market think tanks and industry to create a fog of doubt around climate change (Begley, 2007). They have accomplished this through the production of advertisements, op-eds, lobbying, books, media attention, and quotations from skeptical scientists often associated with conservative think tanks. They have argued first that the world is not warming, measurements that indicate otherwise are flawed, any warming is natural, that is not caused by human activities, and if warming does occur it will be minuscule and harmless (ibid.).

Different groups created this counter-movement often acting independently of each other, yet connected through the internet to create a denial machine that has effectively responded to any public pronouncement by scientists or journalists that have asserted that human-induced climate change is a serious problem (ibid.). Conservative activists wrote hundreds of documents (including policy briefs, books, press releases and op-eds), held numerous policy forums and press conferences, appeared regularly on television and radio programs, and testified at congressional hearings on global warming (Dunlap and McCright, 2008).

As a result of the internet communication between participants in this campaign, charges by one of the participants have been quickly transmitted to others creating an echo chamber of counter-claims made in opposition to the mainstream scientific view of climate change.

The disinformation campaign's most important participants have been conservative think tanks according to the sociological literature (Jacques *et al.*, 2008). As we shall see, these think tanks developed the ideas, communications and media strategies, literature and press releases that have been widely deployed in rhetorical strategies to defend conservative interests by creating doubt about mainstream climate change scientific claims.

Initially most of the funding for this disinformation campaign came from fossil fuel interests and corporations whose products produce high levels of greenhouse gas emissions. On 21October 2010, John Broder of the *New York Times* reported that 'the fossil fuel industries have for decades waged a concerted campaign to raise doubts about the science of global warming and to undermine policies devised to address it' (Broder, 2010). According to Broder, the fossil fuel industry has:

created and lavishly financed institutes to produce anti-global-warming studies, paid for rallies and Web sites to question the science, and generated scores of economic analyses that purport to show that policies to reduce emissions of climate-altering gases will have a devastating effect on jobs and the overall economy.

(Ibid.)

Not surprisingly, the fossil fuel industry funded many of the initial efforts to prevent adoption of climate change policies. Both individual corporations such as ExxonMobil and Peabody Coal, as well as industry associations such as American Petroleum Institute, Western Fuels Associations and Edison Electric Institute, provided funding for individual contrarian scientists, conservative think tanks active in climate change denial, and a host of front groups that we will discuss below (Dunlap and McCright, 2011: 148).

Although the initial funding in the campaign may have come from certain corporations, Dunlap and McCright argue that conservative, free-market, and anti-regulatory ideology and organizations have recently been the main forces fuelling the denial machine first and foremost (ibid.: 144).

According to Dunlap and McCright, the glue that holds the elements of the climate disinformation campaign together is a shared hatred for government regulation of private industry, and so a staunch commitment to free markets and a disdain for government regulation are the ideas that most unite the climate denial community (ibid.).

The mainstream conservative movement, embodied in conservative foundations and think tanks, quickly joined forces with the fossil fuel industry (which recognized very early the threat posed by recognition of global warming and the role of carbon emissions) and wider sectors of corporate America to oppose the threat of global warming, not as an ecological problem, but as a problem for unbridled economic growth (ibid.). And so the disinformation campaign has been a movement that has been waged both by conservative organizations and some corporations.

To use the word 'campaign' is not meant to connote an organized conspiracy led by one or a few entities who coordinate all actors, but rather a social movement that creates widespread, predictable, and strong opposition to climate change policy and that consistently uses scientific uncertainty arguments as the basis of its opposition. This movement is a campaign in the sense that it is a systematic response of aggressive actions to defeat proposals to limit greenhouse gas emissions even though no one organization is coordinating all other organizations or individuals that participate in responses. And although some of the actors may be sincere, the tactics discussed in this article are, as we shall see, ethically reprehensible.

Those engaged in this disinformation campaign can be distinguished from responsible climate skeptics because the climate change denial campaign is a collective social movement run by professional advocacy working to discredit climate change' (Hoffman, 2011: 5). As such, this movement is not engaged in reasonable scientific skepticism but advocacy that stresses scientific uncertainty. In fact, McCright and Dunlap summarize the disinformation machine as having been engaged on misrepresenting, manipulating, and suppressing climate change research results (McCright and Dunlap, 2010: 111).

The original organizations that sought to undermine public support on climate policies by exaggerating scientific uncertainty have expanded to include ideological think tanks, front groups, 'astroturf' groups (i.e. groups organized by industry that pretend to be a legitimate grassroots organization) and campaigns led by PR firms (Oreskes and Conway, 2010: 169–215).

The tactics used by the climate change disinformation campaign have included the following ethically abhorrent tactics:

- lying or reckless disregard for the truth;
- cherry-picking the science;
- cyber-bullying and ad hominem attacks on scientists and journalists;
- manufacturing bogus, non-peer-reviewed science in fake conferences and publications;
- the use of ideological think tanks;
- the use of front groups that hide the real parties in interest;
- the use of fake grass-roots organizations known as astroturf groups; and
- specious claims about 'bad science' that are based upon the dubious assumption that no conclusions in science can be made until everything is proven with high levels of certainty.

Although the mainstream US media has sometimes (but infrequently) covered the disinformation campaign, missing from their coverage has been:

- A stronger sense of the strength of the consensus view on climate change. Every academy of science in the world supports the consensus view; over a hundred scientific organizations whose members have relevant scientific expertise support the consensus view; much of the science that should have been the basis for US action on climate change was settled 150 years ago, and there are clear qualitative differences between peer-reviewed science and the manufactured, non-peer-reviewed science usually relied upon by the disinformation campaign.
- A description of the tactics of the disinformation campaign, which cannot be understood as responsible skepticism, such as those listed above.
- The fact that it already too late to prevent grave suffering caused by climate change for some people in some parts of the world, and that the world has lost over twenty years during which action could have been taken to reduce the now enormous threat.
- The fact that hundreds of millions of people around the world who are most vulnerable to climate change's worst threats have never consented to be put at risk while the United States waits for absolute certainty.

- The fact that for each year the United States has waited to take action, the problem has become worse.

Given what is at stake from climate change, the failure of the US media to cover the disinformation campaign is a tragic, profound, and grave error. The mainstream US media has not only failed to cover this campaign, it has treated it as if it was reasonable scientific skepticism giving it a legitimacy that has increased its influence.

Norms to guide responsible climate skepticism

The experience from the climate change disinformation campaign suggests certain norms that should be followed in dealing with grave threats to human health and ecological systems that recognize the positive value of scientific skepticism but guard against exaggerations or out and out distortions about scientific uncertainty.

The duty of skeptics to subject their conclusions to peer review

Frequently, some skeptics have attacked the assumptions of mainstream scientists by offering their own non-peer reviewed claims about global warming. A strong ethical case can be made that climate skeptics should publish their scientific conclusions in peer-reviewed scientific journals before claiming that the science that they rely upon demonstrates that the consensus view is in error. There are several reasons for this.

- First, scientific claims usually are not entitled to respect by the scientific community until they withstand the scrutiny of peer review. Peer review in science is the process designed to weed out bogus scientific claims. If climate change skeptics are offering their scientific conclusions as evidence that the mainstream scientific view is in error and have not subjected their claims to the scrutiny of peer review, they may be misleading the public that climate change is not a threat. Because climate change harms could be catastrophic to many vulnerable people around the world if the main stream scientific view is correct, inaccurate scientific claims made to prevent policy has potential significant harmful consequences. Therefore, peer review of skeptical claims is ethically mandatory because people have a partic- ularly strong duty to not mislead people if the misinformation could lead to great harm.
- Second, given that the consensus view of climate change is based upon a voluminous amount of peer-reviewed science and has been examined by almost all scientific organizations with expertise over climate change science, the conclusion that business-as-usual releases of greenhouse gases will greatly harm some of the poorest people in the world is

entitled to respect until credible, peer-reviewed evidence establishes a basis for overturning the mainstream scientific view. Without peer review, the skeptical scientists have no basis for concluding that the science they rely on is truthful. If skeptics make claims not based upon peer-reviewed science, they simply have not fulfilled their duty to be careful about scientific claims.

For these reasons, climate change skeptics should subject their skeptical claims to peer review.

The duty of skeptics to subject any broad claims to review by organizations that have appropriate expertise

The science of climate change is comprised of an extraordinarily interdisciplinary mix of scientific disciplines and a huge body of scientific literature. According to one internet source there were around 21,000 chiefly peer-reviewed studies quoted by IPCC in its 2007 assessment (Manpollo Project, 2010). In other words, there are numerous scientific studies on which the consensus view is based.

Some skeptics have made claims that specific individual scientific studies demonstrate that climate change is not a great threat to human flourishing or the environment in cases where, at best, the scientific study only raises questions with one line of evidence on which the consensus view rests. Yet many conclusions reached by mainstream scientific organizations that have issued statements in support of the consensus view rely on multiple lines of evidence often from different disciplines. For instance, the conclusion that the Earth is warming is not only based upon the surface temperature measurements but also ocean and atmospheric temperature changes, the disappearance of ice and snow cover, the movement of plants and animals, the early flowering of plant species, the increased intensity of storms, the appearance of droughts in places that are expected to become drier as the planet warms, and rising sea levels. In other words, conclusions that Earth is warming is based upon multiple lines of evidence.

Because there are often multiple lines of evidence that support mainstream scientific conclusions about climate change, only claims that are considered in relationship to the entire body of robust lines of evidence that have formed the basis of mainstream scientific conclusions are entitled to respect. For this reason, before making general claims about climate change skeptics should subject studies that they want to rely on to review by institutions that have the breadth of scientific expertise to competently evaluate these studies in the context of the larger scientific literature. Skeptics should not only subject their claims about climate change science to the scrutiny of peer review, they should also refrain from making claims about the nature of the overall threats from human-induced climate change until their claims are evaluated by an organization or group of experts with the breadth of scientific expertise relevant to the claim before drawing ultimate conclusions about the meaning of individual studies.

The duty to not overstate conclusions that can be inferred from any individual or a limited number of studies

Frequently some ideologically driven skeptics have made claims that the consensus science position that humans are causing global warming has been completely debunked. In supporting this claim some skeptics will often point to one study or fact about climate change such as the claim that Antarctic snows have increased. They make this claim in either wilful or inadvertent ignorance of the fingerprinting and attribution of studies that are the basis for the consensus position that human activities are the likely cause of the undeniable warming that the Earth is experiencing. And so these skeptics are making claims that go far beyond what any one scientific study could prove even if the science on which they are relying is sound. To properly understand what's happening to our climate, scientists must consider the full body of evidence.

Some ideological skeptics frequently cherry-pick the climate science. 'Cherry-picking' means picking out of a lot of possible facts only those facts that support a predetermined conclusion while ignoring other facts. Most arguments that support climate skepticism, according to the website Skepti-calscience.com, have one thing in common – they neglect the full body of evidence and cherry-pick just the select pieces of data that support a particular point of view (Skeptical Science, 2010). In so doing these skeptics are overstating the potential significance of the scientific fact or study on which they rely. For this reason, climate change skeptics have a strong ethical duty to limit any claims they make about the meaning of any one study or fact to only those inferences that can be made from the study or fact on which they choose to rely.

The duty to restrict claims to those that have adequate evidentiary support

Particularly troubling from an ethical point of view is the behaviour of some of the ideologically driven skeptics, who make claims such as that the science of climate change is a complete fraud and a hoax, and try to convince others of this. They swat down the unprecedented and widely respected expertise that has weighed in on climate change, such as the world's Academies of Sciences, and most major scientific organizations that have expertise over climate change by claiming that the scientists that work for these organi-zations are corrupt without identifying evidence of the widespread corruption that would be needed to support such a sweeping claim. Such wild behaviour would be ethically problematic on any public policy controversy, but in the case of climate change, a threat that could cause great potential harm to the most vulnerable around the world, claims that there is no scientific support for human-induced climate change are ethically reprehensible. It is too absurd on its face to think that any reasonable observer can seriously conclude that climate change science is a hoax or a fraud, for it to be true, thousands of scientists who work with the most prestigious scientific institutions in the world would have to be corrupt. To support the claim that those thousands of scientists who support the mainstream view of science are corrupt, no evidence is offered other than wild speculation.

And so, as a matter of ethics, skeptics must not generalize from single issue controversies to make broad comprehensive conclusions about mainstream climate change views. Skeptics must limit conclusions about climate change science to those that are supported by specific evidence under consideration. This is a moral imperative. There is too much at stake not to do otherwise.

The duty to acknowledge that it is not 'bad' science to rely on less than fully proven scientific claims

One of the tactics deployed by those engaged in the disinformation campaign is to claim that scientific conclusions that are not based upon high levels of scientific proof are 'bad' science. Yet when stakes are high and decisions are urgent, waiting until all the proof is in may make catastrophic harm inevitable. To not act in such circumstances may have serious practical consequences. Therefore, in such circumstances, there may be a duty to act before high levels of proof have been demonstrated. For this reason, scientists must often make policy related recommendations using tests for the reliability of the scientific claims that are based upon criteria such as 'the balance of the evidence,' criteria on the quantity of proof necessary to satisfy a burden of proof that may be less stringent that scientists should expect in other kinds of research such as 95 per cent confidence levels. Ethics would require different criteria for establishing the quantity of proof necessary to satisfy the burden of proof depending on such issues such as what is at stake, can uncertainties be resolved before the harm is experienced, have the victims of the potential harm agreed to be threatened by the risk, does waiting for the uncertainties to be resolved make the potential problem worse. Therefore, it is not 'bad' science to make recommendations on lower than ideal levels of proof. Scientific skeptics, therefore, should openly acknowledge that there are some problems that require protective action despite scientific uncertainty.

Conclusion

The norms discussed in this paper will allow responsible skepticism about threats from human activities that threaten human health and the environment to proceed while limiting irresponsible claims made about scientific uncertainty. Given the potential magnitude of harms to human health and environment from human activities that will more than likely increase due to the increasing power of human technologies for good or harm coupled with the growing increase in human populations, finding ways of implementing the norms discussed in this paper is arguably a goal worthy of widespread and urgent support.

References

Begley, S. (2007) 'Global warming deniers: a well-funded machine', *Newsweek*, 13 August, available at http://msl1.mit.edu/furdlog/docs/2007-08-13_newsweek_global_warming_denyers.pdf (accessed 7 November 2012).

Broder, J. (2010) 'Climate change doubt is a tea party article of faith', *New York Times*, 21 October, http://community.nytimes.com/comments/www.nytimes.com/2010/10/21/us/politics/21climate.html?sort=newest&offset=2 (accessed 7 November 2012).

Dunlap, R. E. and McCright, A. M. (2008) 'A widening gap: Republican and Democratic views on climate change', *Environment*, September/October, pp. 26–35.

Dunlap, R. E. and McCright, A. M. (2011) 'Climate change denial: sources, actors and strategies', in C. Lever-Tracy (ed.), *Routledge Handbook of Climate Change and Society London*. London: Routledge, pp. 240–59.

Hoffman, A. J. (2011) 'Talking past each other? Cultural framing of skeptical and convinced logics in the climate change debate', *Organization and Environment*, 24, 3–33.

Jacques, P., Dunlap, R. E. and Freeman, M. (2008) 'The organization of denial: conservative think tanks and environmental skepticism', *Environmental Politics*, 17, 349–85.

Manpollo Project (2010) 'Number of papers cited by IPCC', forum discussion, Manpollo Project website, available at www.manpollo.org/forums/showthread.php?t=440 (accessed 9 November 2012).

McCright, A. M. and Dunlap, R. E. (2000) 'Challenging global warming as a social problem: an analysis of the conservative movement's counter-claims', *Social Problems*, 47, 499–522.

McCright, A. M. and Dunlap, R. E. (2010) 'Anti-reflexivity: the American conservative movement's success in undermining climate science and policy', *Theory, Culture and Society*, 26, 100–33.

Oreskes, N. and Conway, E. (2010) *Merchants of Doubt: How a Handful of Scientists Obscured the Truth on Issues from Tobacco Smoke to Global Warming*. New York: Bloomsbury Press.

Pooley, E. (2010) *Climate Wars, True Believers, Power Brokers and the Fight to Save the Earth*. New York: Hyperion.

Skeptical Science (2010) '3 levels of cherry picking in one argument', *Skeptical Science*, 21 July, available at www.skepticalscience.com/3-levels-of-cherry-picking-in-a-single-argument.html (accessed 9 November 2012).

7 Granting development consent by specific legislative act

Choice to circumvent public participation and judicial control? The European perspective

Vicky Karageorgou

Introduction

The environmental impact assessment (EIA) is a legal instrument recognized worldwide aiming at examining in advance the environmental consequences of certain development projects through a systematic and transparent process.[1] At the European Union level, the EIA Directive[2] is one of the cornerstones of the European Environmental law. An exception to the administrative procedure set in the Directive, is established in art. 1, para. 5, renumbered as art. 1, para.4 in its codified version (Directive 2011/92/EU).

Three separate but closely inter-related questions arise. The first question relates to the *rationale* of the exception and the requirements that have to be fulfilled for its application. The second one is whether this provision in its current form leaves enough room to the Member States (MS) to circumvent public participation requirements and to avoid the legality control by the administrative courts. The third question relates to the extent, to which the deviation from the ordinary administrative procedure can be regarded as compatible with the spirit of the Aarhus Convention and to whether there is a need for its modification. The scope of this paper is to take certain steps towards answering these questions. To this end, the first part of the analysis focuses on the public participation and the means for judicial review as important features of the EIA regime, while in the second part analysis is devoted to the requirements for the application of the exception as developed by the jurisprudence. Furthermore, the application of the exception by the Greek authorities is presented as an example of its systematic misuse being viewed as the result of its vague wording in conjunction with weak governance structures. Finally, certain conclusions are drawn concerning the 'drafting' of the exception, its compatibility with regulatory concept of the EU Environmental Law and the need for its reform.

EIA as an important instrument of European environmental law

General remarks

The primary purpose of the EIA Directive, as expressed in art. 2, para.1, is to ensure that those projects (public or private), which are likely to have significant effects on the environment, by virtue, *inter alia*, of their nature, size and location, are made subject to a requirement for a development consent and assessment of their effects. The systematic process set in the Directive can be described as a multi-stage administrative process. This process includes, *inter alia*, the preparation of a study identifying the effects of the proposed project on the environment, including the examination of alternatives, the provision of information to the competent authority and the public, the consultation with the public and the obligation that the information gathered should be taken into consideration in the development consent procedure.[3] The Directive is thus characterized by the emphasis on the procedural approach in terms of laying down minimum procedural requirements,[4] while the quality control in EIA is largely left to the national competent authorities. Certain procedural elements, such as the introduction of a clear cut obligation for an extensive examination of the reasonable alternatives[5] and the monitoring of the predicted impacts that can contribute to a 'dynamic' environmental protection, have not yet been introduced.

Public participation as an important feature of the EIA procedure

Public participation within the framework of the EIA Directive, also under the influence of the Aarhus Convention, is regarded as an element that can be meaningful in many ways. It can assist the decision-makers to identify the potential impacts of the proposed project and integrate ecological considerations into the final decision. It can also increase the legitimacy and acceptability of the decisions taken, thereby leading to less litigation.[6] From another point of view, though, it has been criticized as costly, time-consuming and obstructive.[7]

The revised EIA Directive, which requires public participation for all projects subject to an EIA, has transposed, mostly literally and with only one exception,[8] the relevant provisions of the Aarhus Convention (art. 6). The Directive emphasizes the importance of the environmental NGOs, as it recognizes *ipso jure* their interest to participate in the EIA procedure as a part of the 'public concerned',[9] once they meet the requirements set by the national law.

The Directive and to a lesser extent the Aarhus Convention leave enough room to the Member States (MS) to define the details of public participation. For example, both the requirements of 'an early and effective participation for the public concerned' (art. 6, para. 4) and for setting 'reasonable timeframes for public consultation'(art. 6, para. 6) give significant leeway to the MS in terms of organizing public participation procedures. This discretion has led to significant shortcomings concerning the context of the provisions that were adopted. For example, certain national laws do not provide the right of the public to participate in the scoping procedure, while others set time-frames, which are too short to guarantee an effective public consultation and disproportional to the complexity of the project in question.[10] In any future reform of the directive, it should thus be examined whether the introduction of new provisions limiting the discretion of the MS in this field is necessary for ensuring effective public participation.

Review procedures as an important feature of the EIA Directive

Another important feature of the amended EIA Directive relates to the obligation of the MS to provide judicial remedies where the right of participation is not respected and to establish review procedures in order to ensure the right of the 'public concerned' to challenge decisions relating to the EIA process. Article 10a of the Directive requires that MS must ensure that, in accordance with the national legal system, the public concerned (a) having a sufficient interest, or, alternatively, (b) maintaining the impairment of a right, where administrative procedural law requires this as precondition, have access to a review procedure before a court of law or other body established by law to challenge the substantive and procedural legality of the decisions, acts and omissions subject to public participation provisions. Article 10a respects the principle of the procedural autonomy of the Member States[11] and leaves them significant discretion in terms of determining what constitutes an 'impairment of a right' and of setting the conditions for the admissibility of the judicial means to challenge any relevant administrative act or omission. This discretion, though, comes in opposition to the limit that the national provisions must ensure wide access to justice and render effective the provisions of the EIA Directive on judicial remedies.[12] Furthermore, the respect for the different legal systems does not undermine the significance of this provision (art. 10a) as an important breakthrough for the European environmental law, because it sets a clear obligation to the MS to allow environmental NGOs to have access before the Courts in certain constellations concerning the impairment of EU environmental law.[13] Undoubtedly, this legal development sets national legal systems that are based on the 'doctrine of infringement of subjective rights', in front of significant challenges for reform.[14]

The exception from the ordinary EIA procedure

Article 1, para. 5, renumbered as art. 1, para. 4 in the codified version of the EIA Directive (Directive 2011/92/EU), provides that the Directive is not to apply to 'projects the details of which are adopted by a specific act of national legislation, since the objectives of the Directive, including that of supplying information, are achieved through the legislative process'.[15] In the search for the *rationale* of the exception and of the requirements for its application, it is necessary to examine the relevant jurisprudence of the Court of Justice of the European Union (CJEU).[16] This can be divided into two phases, namely the jurisprudence developed before the accession of the EU to the Aarhus Convention and that developed afterwards.

The jurisprudence before the Aarhus Convention

The European Court of Justice (ECJ) adopted a restrictive approach concerning the application of the exception from the very first case (C-435/97, *WWF and others*),[17] in which it was called to interpret art. 1, para. 5. The Court set two closely inter-related conditions: (i) the legislative act must be specific and display the same characteristics as the development consent (para. 58), and (ii) the objectives of the Directive must be achieved through the legislative process in the sense that the law includes all the elements necessary to assess the environmental impact of the project (para. 59). No reference was made to the *rationale* ('why') concerning the adoption of this exception. In the second case (C-287/98, *Linster*) that the Court was called to interpret art. 1, para. 5, it upheld its position about the fulfilment of the conditions identified in its *WWF and others* judgement for the application of the exception.[18] It also went a step forward, because it explained more extensively the relationship between the fundamental objective of the EIA process and the level of information that the legislator must possess for taking the decision (paras 54 and 59). The Court also tried to provide an explanation for the exception (para. 51) in the sense that when the objectives are achieved though the legislative process, there is no need to apply the Directive.[19] This seems to be a logical but not a documented explanation, because it does not focus on the reasons that justify the deviation from the ordinary administrative procedure and subsequently limit public participation and judicial control.

The jurisprudence under the influence of the Aarhus Convention

The CJEU was called to interpret art. 1, para. 5 of the EIA Directive in the light of the relevant provisions of the Aarhus Convention in the jointed cases *Boxus and* others.[20] The relevant judgement is significant in terms of setting limits to the practice of granting development consents for significant projects by law in many aspects. First of all, the Court has further specified the conditions set by its previous jurisprudence for the application of art. 1, para.5 (renumbered as art. 1, para. 4 in the codified version of the EIA Directive), by requiring that the national courts should take into account the entire legislative process which led to the adoption of the specific legislative act, and in particular the preparatory documents and the parliamentary debates, in order to decide whether this condition is fulfilled (para. 47). It is worth noting that the Advocate General Sharpston has specified even more clearly than the Court the characteristics that the legislative process must possess, in order to achieve the objectives of the Directive, by proposing a threefold functionality test.[21] Furthermore, the Court ruled in a strict manner that a legislative act 'which does no more than simply 'ratify' a pre-existing administrative act, by merely referring to overriding reasons in the general interest without a substantive legislative process enabling those conditions to be fulfilled having first commenced, cannot be regarded as a specific legislative act for the purposes of art. 1 para. 5 of the Directive' (para. 48).[22] Finally, the Court has contributed substantially to strengthening the legal protection provided by the national Courts by ruling that it must be amenable to judicial review either by a court of law or by an independent and impartial body established by law whether a specific legislative act granting development consent satisfies the conditions for the application of art. 1, para. 5 (para. 54) and moreover that if no review procedure in respect of the specific act of national legislation is provided, any national Court before which an action falling within its jurisdiction is brought, would have the task of carrying out the review concerning the fulfilment of the requirements of art. 1, para. 5 (para. 55).

The Court followed the same line of reasoning in its Solvay judgement too, which had an identical subject with the *Boxus and others* case, but related to the questions on the interpretation of the provisions of the Aarhus Convention that the Cour Constitutionelle referred to the CJEU for a preliminary ruling.[23] It is interesting to note that the Court ruled quite clearly but not persuasively enough that the interpretation arrived at in the *Boxus and others* case in relation to art. 1, para. 5 of the EIA Directive may be applied to art. 2, para. 2 of the Aarhus Convention.[24] Furthermore, as in its judgement in *the Boxus and others* case, the Court did not provide any justification for the introduction of the exception.

In conclusion, the above-mentioned judgements constitute characteristic examples of the recent jurisprudence of the CJEU, which, despite its limitations, contributes to restricting the discretion of the Member States to exclude certain environmental-related acts from judicial control and to set unreasonable hurdles to access to justice in environmental matters. The influence of the Aarhus Convention is evident.

Leeway for the systematic misuse of the exception: the case of Greece

Greece constitutes a characteristic example, where the legislator, by claiming harmonization with art.1, para. 5 of the EIA Directive, introduced a provision (art. 7 of Law 2338/1995) which stipulated that the development consent for big infrastructural projects having significant impact on the national economy is granted by law.[25] The Conseil d'Etat was called to rule on the validity of this provision both from a constitutional and from a European law perspective in a series of cases, where development consents for big infrastructural projects, falling within the scope of the EIA Directive, were granted by law. In this first wave of its relevant jurisprudence,[26] the Court held that art. 7 of Law 2338/1995, which constituted the basis for the legislative acts granting development consent, was compatible both with the relevant constitutional provisions and with the EIA Directive.[27]

The second wave of the relevant jurisprudence of the Conseil d'Etat is marked by a change in its stance. In particular, the Court both in section (Decision 1567/2005) and in plenary formation (Decision 1847/2008) ruled that the practice of granting planning, environmental and work consents by a single legislative provision could be acceptable from a constitutional and a European Union law perspective, only when the following conditions are satisfied: (i) it is applied in exceptional cases, and (ii) no individual rights, constitutional provisions and definitions of the EU law are violated. The Court ruled that these requirements were not fulfilled in that case and rendered this legislative provision invalid because it violated the constitutional principle of the separation of powers and the right to judicial review. It is worth noting that, while the Section decision made an explicit reference to the requirements for the application of art.1, para. 5 of the EIA Directive and ruled that the relevant legislative act did not satisfy these requirements, the plenary decision restricted this to a mere reference, according to which the EIA Directive explicitly allows granting development consent by law without presupposing the existence of reasons of overriding public interest.

In the second case in which the Conseil d'Etat was called to judge the conformity of a legislative provision granting planning, environmental and work consents with the Greek constitution and the EIA Directive, the Court in Section formation maintained the same line of reasoning followed in the above decisions concerning the conditions that have to be satisfied for this legislative practice to be exceptionally accepted. While the satisfaction of the conditions set by the CJEU for the application of art. 1, para. 5 was of secondary importance here, the central issue related to whether the principle of effective judicial protection derived both from art. 10a of the EIA Directive and from the relevant constitutional right (Article 20 of the Greek Constitution) could justify an extension of the jurisdiction of the Court on legislative acts that introduce individual regulations.[28] As there were divergent views among the members of the Court,[29] the section (Decision 391/2008) referred the issue to the plenary. The plenary decided that all these issues are closely related to the interpretation of art. 1, para. 5 and art. 10a of the EIA Directive (Decision 1047/2010). It did not, though, request a preliminary ruling, but decided to wait the decision of the CJEU in the case *Boxus and others*. Almost one year after the ruling of CJEU, the Court in its plenary formation has not yet reached a decision.

In conclusion, the change in Court's stance reflects the regulatory content of the Aarhus Convention and the modified EIA Directive in terms of providing effective legal protection. Furthermore, how the Court will respond to the relevant decisions of the CJEU on the preliminary rulings and whether it will set further limits to the practice of granting development consent by law with the aim to avoid judicial control, remains to be seen.

Concluding remarks

The analysis of the regulatory context of the exception set in art.1, para. 4 (art. 1, para. 5 in the previous version) and of the practical experience gained by its application in conjunction with the analysis of two important features of the EIA Directive (public participation and judicial review) led to the following conclusions concerning the questions raised about its *rationale*, its compatibility with the philosophy of the Aarhus Convention and the need for its reform:

(i)   The exception from the ordinary EIA procedure is drafted in a vague manner, so that its grammatical interpretation is not enlightening. The provision, in its current form, has, thus, left too much leeway to the Member States to apply it as they see fit, which in some cases has resulted in its systematic misuse, especially in countries with weak governance structures such as Greece.

(ii) The exception seems to be compatible only to a limited extent with the philosophy of the Aarhus Convention and the whole concept of the European environmental law, which place strong emphasis on public participation and access to justice on environmental matters. In a broader sense, it is also almost compatible with the principle of prevention and the sustainability principle which require an in-depth prior assessment of the environmental impacts of large-scale projects. This is due to the fact that it is questionable whether this fundamental objective can be achieved effectively through the legislative process.

(iii) The contribution of the jurisprudence of the CJEU has been very crucial in terms of clarifying the conditions of the application of Art. 1 para. 4 and of ensuring effective judicial protection as regards the fulfillment of these conditions. In particular, the latest jurisprudence, under the influence of the Aarhus Convention, has set significant limits to the discretion of the Member States to use these practices in order to avoid judicial control.

(iv) The relevant jurisprudence does not shed, though, enough light on the reasons that justify the use of the legislative process in exceptional cases. *Such a justification could be important not only for defining precisely the scope of the exception, but also for legitimizing in a broader sense its introduction by making visible its raison d'être.*

(v)   As the limits set by the jurisprudence cannot be effective in cases where the adoption of this practice does not become subject to judicial review or even when the national courts do not take the relevant jurisprudence of the CJEU sufficiently into account, a new legislative provision setting an exception from the EIA procedure has to be introduced. This legislative provision should lay down with precision the requirements that have to be fulfilled and also specify the reasons (of overriding public interest) that justify the deviation from the ordinary administrative procedure. In this context, it is to mention that the Proposal of the European Commission for a revision of the EIA Directive (released on 26 October 2012) narrowed, at least to some extent, the relevant exception ('the Directive shall not apply to projects the details of which are adopted by a specific act of national legislation, provided that the objectives of the Directive are achieved through the legislative process'), as, in contrast to the current version, it cannot be induced from the proposed wording that the objectives of the Directive are achieved *ex lege* through the legislative process. Furthermore, the obligation foreseen in the proposed provision, according to which Member States (MS) have to inform the Commission every two years of any application which they have made of the exception, can indirectly limit their discretion concerning its application.

(vi) Finally, ensuring effective judicial protection as that required by the Aarhus Convention is the most important guarantee for setting limits to choices that contravene significant environmental norms and for ensuring the effective enforcement of the environmental law in general. Although the recent jurisprudence of the CJEU has made significant steps in terms of providing citizens with effective remedies, there is still a need for a more holistic approach at the EU level by setting minimum harmonized standards to access to justice on environmental matters. Last but not least, judicial protection in all environment-related cases and especially in cases of 'arbitrary' legislative interventions such as those described earlier, should not lead to 'academic' victories in the sense that judicial decisions come too late to save anything.

Notes

1   See Glasson *et al.* (2005, p4).
2   The EIA Directive was amended three subsequent times. The initial Directive (85/337/EEC) and its three amendments (97/11, 2003/35 and 2009/31/EC) have been codified by Directive 2011/92/EU.
3   See Holder and Lee (2007, pp572–590).
4   The dominance of the procedural aspect in the EIA Directive can be justified in many ways. First of all, the development of the European environmental law responds to the necessity of setting a framework for the procedural coordination as regards the application of the fragmented quality provisions. Furthermore, it

reflects the regulatory philosophy, which recognizes procedure as a means of achieving the legitimacy of the decisions taken. Such an approach is of specific relevance in complex decision-making procedures, such as those granting development consent, because the legislator can set only 'weak' material standards. See Meßerschmidt (2011, p523).

5   The relevant provision of the EIA Directive (art. 5, para. 3, lit. 4) is criticized by Meßerschmidt (2011, p541) as weak because it does not introduce an obligatory assessment of the reasonable alternatives, but only an obligation to submit a report about the alternatives that have been studied. It seems to be more compatible with the purpose of the Directive that an obligation is established for the developer, according to which he has to present all reasonable alternatives, compare their environmental impacts and provide a specific justification, if he does not choose the most environmentally friendly option.

6   See Holder and Lee (2007, p548; 'triumph of the participatory democracy over the technocratic roots of environmental assessment').

7   See Verschnuren (2004, p39), presenting the arguments about the negative consequences of public participation.

8   There is only one significant aspect in which the Directive is not in line with the Convention. In particular, while art. 6, para. 7 of the Aarhus Convention grants to all members of the public the opportunity to participate in the decision-making process by submitting written comments, the Directive (art. 6, para.4) restricts this opportunity only to the public concerned. See Verschnuren (2004, p35).

9   Art. 1, para. 2 lit.e of the EIA Directive defines 'public concerned' as the public affected or likely to be affected by, or having an interest in, the environmental decision-making processes referred to in art. 2, para. 2. NGOs promoting environmental protection and meeting any requirements under national law shall be deemed to have an interest.

10 See Report from the Commission on the application and the effectiveness of the EIA Directive, as amended, Brussels, 23 July 2009, COM (2009), 538 final, p7.

11 The principle of the procedural autonomy, developed by the European Court of Justice (Case 33/76, *Rewe*, 1976, European Court Reports (ECR) 1989) can be understood as the freedom of the Member States to introduce the institutional and procedural arrangements, including judicial remedies, which are necessary for the application of EU law, in the absence of EU procedural rules pre-empting this discretion. The Court of Justice has identified two essential limits to the application of the principle: (i) the equivalence criterion, according to which the national rules set for the application of the EU law cannot be less favourable than those relating to similar situations of domestic nature; and (ii) the effectiveness criterion, according to which the national procedural rules chosen for the application of the EU law should not make virtually impossible or excessively difficult the exercise of the rights conferred by the European legal order. See Galetta (2010).

12 See CJEU, C-263/08, Case Djürgärden, 2009, ECR I-09967, paras 42–52. The Aarhus Compliance Committee has also taken a similar position, as it held that Contracting Parties are not allowed to introduce or maintain such strict criteria that they effectively bar all or almost all environmental organizations from challenging acts or omissions that contravene national law relating to the environment. See Aarhus Compliance Committee, Compliance by Belgium, ACCC/C/2005/11.

13 See CJEU, C-115/09, Case Bund für Umwelt und Naturschutz Deutschland, Judgement of the Court of 12 Mai 2011, paras 44–46. See also Ponchelet (2012, p287).

14 See Schwerdfeger (2007).
15 The exception was introduced after intense pressure by Denmark, which did not want the construction of the bridge of Oeserund to be a subject of an EIA procedure. See Krämer (2007, p131ff).
16 After the entry into force of the Lisbon Treaty, the European Court of Justice (ECJ) was renamed as Court of Justice of the European Union (CJEU).
17 See ECJ, C-435/97, Case WWF and others, 1999, ECR I-05613.
18 See ECJ, C-287/98, Case Linster, 2000, ECR I-6967.
19 For this interpretation see the Opinion of the Advocate General Sharpston delivered on 11 May 2011, Joined Cases C-128/09, C-129/09, C-130/09, C-131/09, C-134/09 C-135/09, para. 67.
20 The joined cases C-128/09, C-129/09, C-130/09, C-131/09, C-134/09 and C-135/09 concerned a raft of challenges to planning, environmental and work consents regarding the development of airports and railway projects in the Wallon Region (Belgium). The applicants brought actions against these consents before the Conseil d'Etat and while those actions were pending before the Court, the Parliament of Wallon adopted a decree ratifying those consents. The Court decided to refer some questions both to the Cour Constitutionelle and the CJEU. The questions referred to the CJEU for a preliminary ruling, related, *inter alia*, to the conditions for the application of art. 1 para. 5 and to the obligations for the MS arising from10a of EIA Directive to be interpreted in the light of art. 9, para. 2 of the Aarhus Convention. See Judgement of the CJEU of 18 October 2011.
21 The Advocate General Sharpston (Opinion delivered on 11 May 2011, para. 84) proposed that the national court will need to examine the following aspects, in order to decide as regards the achievement of the objectives of the Directive through the concrete legislative procedure: (i) the input which relates to whether sufficient information was placed before the legislator in order to evaluate the possible impact; (ii) the process which relates to whether the appropriate procedure was respected; (iii) the output which relates to whether the legislative measure is clear in terms of what is being authorized.
22 Such an approach is also in line with the position adopted by the Aarhus Compliance Committee ('When determining how to categorize a decision under the Aarhus, its label in the domestic law of the Party is not decisive'). See Aarhus Compliance Committee (ECE/MP.PP/C.1/2006/4/Add.2, para. 29).
23 See CJEU C- 182/10, Case Solvay and others, Judgement of the Court of 16 February 2012.
24 Under art. 2, para. 2 of the Aarhus Convention, the definition of 'public authorities' does not include bodies or institutions acting in legislative capacity. The Court held that this provision has substantially the same content as art. 1, para. 5 (renumbered as art. 1 para. 4 in the codified EIA Directive) and that there is nothing that could be deduced from the object or the scope of the Aarhus Convention that would preclude the Court from applying, for the interpretation of the provisions of that Convention, the similar provisions of the EIA Directive. This position of the Court raises certain doubts about its acceptability for a variety of reasons. First, the content of art. 2, para. 2 of the Aarhus Convention seems to be more general in comparison to art. 1, para. 4 of the EIA Directive, which is much more specific in terms of introducing an exception from the ordinary EIA administrative procedure. Furthermore, where the drafters of the Aarhus Convention wanted to provide the possibility for an exception from the EIA procedure, they introduced a specific exception, such as that concerning projects serving national defence purposes (art. 6, para. 1, lit. c). Finally, the application of the interpretation of art. 1, para. 5 (renumbered

as art. 1, para. 4) of the EIA Directive to art. 2, para.2 of the Aarhus Convention seems questionable too because the Aarhus Convention reflects a radically different philosophy in terms of ensuring public participation and judicial review in comparison to the initial version of the EIA Directive, in which the exception was introduced.

25 This provision was heavily criticized by the legal theory as a norm, which comes in contradiction with art. 1, para. 5 of the EIA Directive, first because it introduced a general exception for a category of projects and second because it did not set any conditions for its application, such as that required by art.1, para. 5. See Efstratiou (1999, p524ff).

26 See Conseil d' Etat Decision 6066/1996 (Plenary), concerning the environmental authorization of the Eleftherios Venizelos Airport, Decision 3824/1997 (Plenary) concerning the environmental authorization of the Rion-Antirion Bridge and Decision 2157/1998 (Plenary) as regards the environmental authorization of the Elefsina-Stavros and Spata Avenue.

27 In all these judgements there was, though, a strong minority opinion, according to which this practice contradicted the principle of the separation of powers (Art. 26 of the Constitution) and the right to judicial review (art. 20, para.1), because it constituted an act of intervention in pending trials. In the minority opinion of the decision 2597/1998, it was also argued that granting development consent by a legislative provision contradicts art. 1, para. 5 of the EIA Directive, because this provision cannot be applied to cases where the administrative procedure was chosen first and led to the issuance of an administrative act. See Christou (2010, pp110–111).

28 According to Article 95 of the Greek Constitution, which provides the foundation for the jurisdiction of the Conseil d' Etat, the Court has a general jurisdiction on petitions for the annulment of administrative acts.

29 The most radical one was that the petition for annulment can be exercised admissibly against legislative acts that introduce individual regulations, because no other judicial remedy can provide such an effective judicial protection as that.

References

Christou, V. (2010) *From the Ratification to the Issuance of Administrative Acts by Formal Law.* Athens-Thessaloniki, Greece: Sakkoulas Publications (in Greek).

Efstratiou, P.-M. (1999) 'Ratification of environmental permits by law and the protection of the environment', *Environment and Law,* 3 (4), 544ff (in Greek)

Galetta, D. U. (2010) *Procedural Autonomy of EU Member States: Paradise Lost? A Study on the 'Functionalized Procedural Competence' of EU Member States.* Berlin, Germany: Springer Verlag.

Glasson, J., Therivel, R. and Chadwick, A. (2005) *Introduction to Environmental Impact Assessment.* London: Routledge.

Holder, J. and Lee, M. (2007) *Environmental Law and Policy: Texts and Policy.* Cambridge: Cambridge University Press.

Meßerschmidt, K. (2011) *Europäisches Umweltrecht.* Munich, Germany: Beck Verlag.

Ponchelet, C. (2012) 'Access to justice in environmental matters: does the European Union comply with its obligations?', *Journal for Environmental Law,* 24 (2): 287–309.

Krämer, L. (2007) 'The development of environmental assessments at level of the European Union', in Holder and J. McGillivray, D. (eds), *Taking Stock of Environmental Assessment: Law, Policy and Practice.* London: Routledge Cavendish, pp. 131–48.

Schwerdfeger, A. (2007) 'Schutznormentheorie and Aarhus Convention-Consequences for the German Law', *Journal for European Environmental and Planning Law*, April, pp. 270–7.

Verschnuren, J. (2004) 'Public participation regarding the elaboration and approval of projects in the EU after the Aarhus Convention', *Yearbook of European Environmental Law*, 4. Oxford: Oxford University Press, pp. 29–48.

8 The principle of "integration" in international law relating to sustainable development

Sobering lessons for European Union law

Owen McIntyre

Introduction

The principle of environmental integration has long been regarded as an essential mechanism of international law for the effective implementation of sustainable development (Rieu-Clarke, 2005: 84–91). For example, the New Delhi Declaration of Principles of International Law Relating to Sustainable Development, adopted by the International Law Association in 2002, notes that:

> the principle of integration reflects the interdependence of social, economic, financial, environmental and human rights aspects of principles and rules of international law relating to sustainable development as well as the interdependence of the needs of current and future generations of human kind.

The 1995 Report of the Expert Group on Identification of Principles of International Law for Sustainable Development, convened by the UN Commission on Sustainable Development, concluded that 'the principle of interrelationship and integration forms the backbone of sustainable development'. Similar conclusions on the role and significance of the principle of integration have been articulated in the Legal Principles on Environmental Protection and Sustainable Development adopted by the World Commission on Environment and Development (1987) and the 2000 IUCN Draft Covenant on Environment and Development.

It is quite clear that the requirement for environmental considerations to be integrated into the planning and implementation of development activities can be regarded as a binding legal obligation, which has been included in the key environmental conventions associated with the 1992 UNCED process at Rio – the very process which first adopted, by means of the Rio Declaration, sustainable development as the overarching objective of States in reconciling the frequently conflicting imperatives of protection of the natural environment and promotion of economic and social development. Article 3(4) of the 1992 Climate Change Convention and Article 6 of the 1992 Biodiversity Convention respectively require States parties to integrate 'policies and measures to protect the climate system against human-induced change' and 'the conservation and sustainable use of biological diversity' into relevant development plans, programmes and policies, as does Article 4(2)(a) of the 1994 Desertification Convention (Rieu-Clarke, 2005: 85). Indeed, the need to integrate environment and development can be traced back to the 1968 African Conservation Convention and the 1972 Stockholm Declaration. In his influential Separate Opinion in the 1997 *Gab íkovo-Nagymaros (Hungary v. Slovakia)* case, International Court of Justice Judge Christopher Weeramantry expressly recognized that the integration of environmental and developmental issues is now a fundamental issue in international law.

However, long-standing international consensus about the role and significance of the principle of environmental integration doesn't necessarily mean that there exists a satisfactory working example of its implementation in practice. The experience of the European Union (EU) legal order, which exerts an incomparably greater measure of legal compulsion over its Member States than any other regime established under international law, and which has long incorporated environmental integration as a principle of its founding constitutional treaty, clearly illustrates the problem of giving meaningful effect to the principle. Despite the fact that the principle of environmental integration was first introduced into the EU legal order 30 years ago, by means of the 1983 Third Environmental Action Programme (EAP), its precise normative character and substantive content remain unclear. In common with the other guiding principles which are meant to provide a basis for EU action on the environment, the impact and justiciability of the stipulation that environmental requirements must be integrated into the definition and implementation of other EU policies and activities remains fraught with uncertainty. Following the failure of the so-called 'Cardiff process', by means of which the Union institutions attempted to formalize procedures and institutional mechanisms for the practical implementation of the principle in the context of EU decision-making, and the introduction into the post-Lisbon Treaty on the Functioning of the European Union (TFEU) of a host of new 'integration' principles requiring consideration of a range of additional policy objectives and requirements in general EU policy-making, this uncertainty has been exacerbated.

Origins of the principle of environmental integration in EU law

Though it may be possible to trace the origins of the EU principle of environmental integration to the very first attempts to formulate a Union environmental policy in the First EAP of 1973, it is more commonly associated with the Third EAP, adopted in 1983. As the Third EAP, covering the period 1982-1986, was largely concerned with the introduction of the EU's internal market (which was due to be completed by 1992) and with the role of environmental policies in that process, it is hardly surprising that it should have first set out the principle of integration of 'concern for the environment into the policy and development of certain economic activities...thus promot[ing] the creation of an overall strategy making environmental policy a part of economic and social development'. This formulation of the principle of integration now appears prescient in light of the subsequent emergence of the concept of sustainable development, and reminds us how central to the latter concept the integration of potentially conflicting policy objectives remains. Indeed, it is no coincidence that the original 1985 EU Environmental Impact Assessment (EIA) Directive was adopted during the life of the Third EAP, as the requirements inherent to this Directive can be regarded as an example of the practical application of the principle of integration. However, progress on the realization of the approach required under the integration principle was otherwise very modest and, despite the express inclusion of the principle in the Third EAP and the adoption of the EIA Directive during the term of the Programme, 'the fact remains that the bulk of Community environmental legislation continued to address environmental problems in the traditional vertical pattern of adopting measures with regard to a specific medium *e.g.* air, water, sea, noise, *etc.*' (Syngellakis, 1993: 64).

It was under the changes to the EC Treaty introduced by the 1986 Single European Act (SEA) that the principle of integration was elevated to the status of a legally binding requirement under EU law. The SEA added a Title VII to the EC Treaty, consisting of Article 130r, s and t, which for the first time conferred an express competence upon the EU institutions to act for the protection of the environment. In addition to listing the original objectives of EU environmental policy, Article 130r also set down the basic principles which were henceforth to guide EU environmental policy-making, including the unequivocal requirement that 'environmental protection requirements shall be a component of the Community's other policies'. Though this new Treaty stipulation, in combination with Article 162 of the Treaty of Rome which required the Commission to adopt its rules and procedures so as to ensure that it operated in accordance with the provisions of the Treaty, clearly required the Commission to adopt a procedure for consideration of the environmental implications of each proposal for EU legislation that it drafted, for some years the Commission's rules of procedure did not provide specific means to this effect (Baldock *et al.*, 1992: 26). Indeed, it was not until June 1993 that the Commission announced a number of internal procedural mechanisms, under the auspices of the Fifth EAP (1992–2000), for taking account of environmental considerations at an early stage of preparation of Commission measures. From 1993, each Commission Directorate General (DG) was required to assess the environmental impact of measures or programmes and, where the impact was expected to be significant, to have an environmental impact study prepared (Stokke and Forster, 1999: 340).

The Fourth EAP, which coincided with the adoption of the Single European Act and ran from 1987–1992, emphasized the need for integration even more clearly than the Third EAP. It discussed the concept at length and highlighted the principal policy areas for which the integration of environmental policy objectives would be necessary, including agriculture, competition, social policy, energy, tourism, transport, regional policy development and cooperation. However, it might be regarded as 'a vivid illustration of the deficit in implementing the pronouncements on environmental policy integration' that the Community institutions omitted to address the environmental implications of the internal market as an integral part of the 1985 White Paper on Completing the Internal Market and the subsequent 1992 legislative programme (Syngellakis, 1993: 66). This omission led to the setting up by the Commission in 1988 of a Task Force on the Environment and the Internal Market whose 1989 report provided an 'unequivocal endorsement of the integration of environmental protection into the restructuring and modernization of the Community, anticipated through the Internal Market programme' (ibid.: 66).

The amendments to the Treaty of Rome introduced by the Maastricht Treaty (TEU) in 1992 further enhanced the imperative character of the principle of environmental integration (Wilkinson, 1992), by introducing into the revised Environment Title XVI a new formulation of Article 130r that required that environmental protection requirements must be 'integrated into the definition and implementation of other Community policies'. In addition, the TEU introduced the principle of sustainable development into both the European Union and European Community legal orders and thereby placed considerable emphasis upon a concept that inevitably relies upon the integration of environmental considerations into other policy areas as a means of giving it practical effect. This renewed emphasis reflects the policy position taken under the Fifth EAP, which ran from 1992 to 2000 and identified the 'integration of environmental protection into the activities of critical actors and economic sectors as...the key mechanism in the realization of the programme' (Syngellakis, 1993: 69). In this regard it identified industry, energy, transport, agriculture and tourism as the targeted priority policy sectors. By the early 1990s some of the institutional machinery of environmental integration had been established, with environmental units having been set up in Commission DGs concerned with such policy areas as agriculture, transport, energy and fisheries, while a number of integrative consultation documents had been issued in relation to such policy areas (Syngellakis, 1993: 71).

However, it was arguably not until the amendments to the EC Treaty introduced in 1997 by the Treaty of Amsterdam that the principle of environmental integration was placed on an appropriate legal footing. The key change in respect of environmental policy brought about by this Treaty was the elevation of the integration principle, which had been contained in the former Article 130r, to Article 6 in Part I of the revised Treaty of Rome

(Macrory, 1999). It was entirely correct that it should have been moved from the environmental provisions of the Treaty, to which it had no useful application, to where it could apply to the various areas of Community policy covered by the Treaty and into the definition and implementation of which environmental protection requirements had now to be integrated. Thus, the Amsterdam amendments 'exported' the integration principle from the environmental provisions of the Treaty and promoted it to the status of a 'general principle' applicable to the entire EC Treaty (Jans, 2010: 1537–1538; Kingston, 2012, p107). The revised Article 6 expressly linked environmental integration to the principle of sustainable development, the constitutional significance of which was now made abundantly clear by means of its inclusion as one of the primary aims of the Community under Article 2. Revised Article 6 was considerably more explicit about the remit of the principle's application, expressly applying it to all the activities and policies listed in Article 3 of the revised EC Treaty. Article 3 contained a long list of such activities and policies, including measures relating to the common commercial policy, the internal market, the free movement of persons, agriculture and fisheries, transport, employment, economic and social policy, environment, industry, research and technology, health protection, culture, development cooperation, international trade, consumer protection, energy, civil protection, tourism, and equality. Thus, the Amsterdam Treaty amendments put it beyond doubt that sustainable development was now one of the overarching objectives of the EC Treaty and that a broadly applicable principle of environmental integration was one of the essential means for achieving this objective.

The period following the adoption of the Amsterdam Treaty witnessed frenetic developments relating to practical implementation of the integration principle. The Commission reviewed its 1993 internal communication and suggested a range of new measures in a 1997 communication which, however, also highlighted the inherent difficulties in implementing the principle. Specifically, this communication concludes that the various administrative arrangements intended to ensure integration of environmental requirements, including 'Environmental Evaluations' of all Commission activities, 'Environmental Impact' assessments of new legislative proposals, the use of so-called 'Green Stars' by DGs to identify proposals which may have significant environmental consequences, and the appointment of 'Integration Correspondents' within each DG, tended to operate in an informal, unsystematic and uncritical manner (Krämer, 2012). Therefore, the 1997 Luxembourg European Council tasked the Commission with development of a strategy on environmental integration, which was adopted by the 1998 Cardiff European Council, thus giving rise to the socalled 'Cardiff process'. This ongoing process had resulted in the development of practical requirements for the European Commission and for the Council of Ministers. In particular, relevant formations of the Council were invited to establish strategies for achieving environmental integration within their own policy areas, starting with the Transport, Energy and Agriculture Councils, before moving on to the Development, Internal Market, Industry, General Affairs, Economy and Finance, and Fisheries Councils. However, even though the Commission elaborated policy documents for each of these Council formations setting out a strategy on how to integrate environmental requirements into their respective areas of policy, Krämer points out that 'these documents were discussed once in the Council – and then the whole procedure stopped' (Krämer, 2012). Indeed, Krämer's conclusions about 'the failure of the EU approach, which was linked to the so-called Cardiff process' are echoed by the Commission's own 2004 stocktaking exercise on the implementation of the principle of environmental integration (European Commission, 2004: 31).

Article 11 of the newly adopted Treaty on the Functioning of the European Union (TFEU), the principal treaty currently providing for the operation of the Union institutions, reproduces almost identical wording to that of Article 6 of the revised EC Treaty, and states that 'Environmental protection requirements must be integrated into the definition and implementation of the Union's policies and activities, in particular with a view to promoting sustainable development.'

However, whereas 'on each occasion that the EEC Treaty was amended, the integration principle was strengthened' as 'each round of revisions enhanced the profile and its impact', Jans argues that 'the Lisbon Treaty brought an end to that pattern' (Jans, 2010: 1538, 1547). Indeed, the context in which it is placed in the TFEU has resulted in even greater uncertainty in respect of its true legal status and implications. For example, the proliferation of integration principles under Articles 7–10 and 12–13 of the Lisbon Treaty requiring that a wide range of policy objectives, additional to those relating to the environment, are to be taken into account in defining and implementing European Union policies generally, has raised new uncertainties about the priority accorded to and justiciability of the principle of environmental integration.

A slightly different articulation of the environmental integration principle was included in Article 37 of the 2000 Charter of Fundamental Rights of the European Union, which provides that 'A high level of environmental protection and the improvement of the quality of the environment must be integrated into the policies of the Union and ensured in accordance with the principle of sustainable development.' While the Charter was non-binding upon the Community institutions at the time of its adoption, the new Article 6 of the post-Lisbon TEU now provides that the Charter 'shall have the same legal value as the Treaties', thus conferring upon Article 37 of the Charter the same legal status as that enjoyed by Article 11 of the TFEU. Both now clearly bind the Union institutions, though the principle is set out differently in each and, arguably, somewhat more narrowly under the Charter (Jans, 2010: 1544).

Legal nature and implications of the principle of environmental integration

One key question which arises is that of which 'environmental protection requirements' must be integrated into the definition and implementation of the Union's policies and activities. It seems reasonable to conclude that the objectives of environmental policy set out under Article 191(1) TFEU must be taken into account in related sectoral policy measures, although these objectives appear quite general and normatively indeterminate and non-imperative in nature, requiring that:

> Union policy on the environment shall contribute to pursuit of the following objectives:
>
> • preserving, protecting and improving the quality of the environment,
> • protecting human health,
> • prudent and rational utilization of natural resources,
> • promoting measures at international level to deal with regional or worldwide environmental problems, and in particular combating climate change.

More significantly, it seems clear that the principles set out under Article 191(2), on which Union environmental policy is to be based, are to apply to other policy areas. The first paragraph of Article 191(2) provides that:

> Union policy on the environment shall aim at a high level of protection taking into account the diversity of situations in the various regions of the Union. It shall be based on the precautionary principle and on the principles that preventive action should be taken, that environmental damage should as a priority be rectified at source and that the polluter should pay.

While we have a somewhat clearer understanding of the practical means available for implementing these principles, at least in the context of environmental measures, examples of their inclusion in non-environmental measures remain relatively few. By referring to 'a high level of environmental protection and the improvement of the quality of the environment', both objectives expressly listed under Articles 191(1) and (2) TFEU, the wording of Article 37 of the Charter of Fundamental Rights might be taken to suggest that each of the aims and principles set out under these provisions are to apply to all EU policies. Further, the principle of 'coherence' or 'consistency' of EU law would appear to confirm that the general aims of Articles 191(1) and (2) come within the scope of the 'environmental protection requirements' alluded to in Article 11 TFEU (Franklin, 2011; Lenaerts and Corthaut, 2008; Von Bogdandy, 2010). In addition, it would appear that 'the policy aspects referred to in Article 191(3) TFEU should not a priori be excluded' from other sectoral policy measures, though they only provide broad policy guidance and might even be regarded as justifying derogations from the foregoing requirements set out under Articles 191(1) and (2) (Jans, 2010: 1533). Also, Article 191(3) itself merely requires that these factors should be taken into account, providing that:

> In preparing its policy on the environment, the Union shall take account of:
>
> • available scientific and technical data,
> • environmental conditions in the various regions of the Union,
> • the potential benefits and costs of action or lack of action,
> • the economic and social development of the Union as a whole and the balanced development of its regions.

As regards the question of *who* must integrate environmental protection requirements, Krämer (2012) points out that the TFEU is silent on the issue, but notes that

> as the TEU imposes obligations on EU institutions and on Member States, it can be safely stated that the EU institutions have to integrate environmental requirements. When EU Member States implement EU policies and activities, they might also have to respect Article 11.

Hession and Macrory (1998: 575), writing at the time of the Amsterdam Treaty amendments to the EC Treaty, also conclude that the principle of environmental integration applies to 'all relevant Community institutions and Member States in so far as they are charged with implementing Community policies'. As regards Community institutions, they further suggest that 'these would encompass at the very least all those Community bodies involved in defining or implementing community policy, including the Council of Ministers, the European Investment Bank and the European Parliament' (ibid.). As regards Member States, Hession and Macrory conclude that they are bound by the principle when acting within the Council of Ministers and involved in the 'design' of policy, as well as when taking responsibility for the 'implementation' of such policy, though in this latter role 'much would depend on the level of discretion granted at national level, and the extent to which a failure at national level to integrate an environmental dimension could frustrate the effect' of the principle (ibid.). They provide the example of a national body given responsibility for the distribution of Union funds. Though this conclusion is undoubtedly sound in principle, the applicability of the principle of environmental integration to Member State measures for the implementation of EU policy is effectively undermined by the severely limited utility of the principle as grounds for judicial review of such actions.

While there can be little doubt that the integration principle is firmly established as a solemn legal requirement set out under the founding Treaties of the European Union, doubts linger as to its precise normative character and significance. In fact, the principle of environmental integration can be understood as having an impact on EU law and policy-making in several distinct ways. First of all is its so-called 'enabling function', whereby it extends the limits of the Union's legal competences as governed by the Treaties. Under the so-called 'principle of conferral' or 'specific powers doctrine' set out in Article 5(1) of the post-Lisbon TEU, 'the Union shall act only within the limits of the competences conferred upon it by the Member States in the Treaties to attain the objectives set out therein'. However, in light of the principle of environmental integration, the Union institutions enjoy competence to take additional legal measures to ensure protection of the environment whenever they are acting in furtherance of a wide range of EU policies, including agriculture, transport, energy, development aid, trade and external relations, internal market and competition policy, commercial policy and regional policy. The ECJ has supported this function of the principle in cases such as Case C-513/99 *Concordia Bus Finland* [2002] ECR I-7213, where it confirmed that environmental objectives may be pursued in the context of public procurement. Essentially, in this role, 'the environmental integration principle broadens the objectives of the other powers laid down in the TFEU and thus limits the role of the specific powers doctrine in environmental policy' (Jans, 2010: 1541).

In addition, the principle may perform a 'guidance function', whereby 'European law may – and indeed must – be interpreted in the light of the environmental objectives of the TFEU, even with respect to areas outside the environmental field' (ibid.). Several of the other guiding principles of EU environmental policy, first incorporated into the EC Treaty by means of the Single European Act and Maastricht Treaty amendments, have been applied by the ECJ as aids to the interpretation of secondary legislation on the environment. For example, in Case C-127/02 *Waddenzee* [2004] ECR I-7405, the requirement to conduct an appropriate assessment of the likely ecological impacts of plans or projects under Article 6(3) of the 1992 Habitats Directive was interpreted in light of the precautionary principle, while the definition of waste under the Waste Framework Directive was extended having regard to the polluter pays principle and preventive and precautionary principles in Case C-1/03 *Van de Walle* [2004] ECR I-7613, although in this case the implications proved quite unwelcome (McIntyre, 2005). The principle of environmental integration itself played an important role in justifying the application of the precautionary principle, a guiding principle of EU environmental policy, to the protection of public health in the *Artegodan* case, [2002] ECR II4945 (Jans, 2010: 1541). Jans, citing Case C-379/98 *PreussenElektra AG v. Schhleswag AG* [2001] ECR I-2099, also argues that the principle has played a key role 'in justifying recourse to the *Cassis de Dijon* mandatory requirements, which now include environmental protection, to justify a directly discriminatory barrier to trade' (ibid.). Though the principle of environmental integration has now been elevated to the status of a general principle of EU law, its function as an aid to the interpretation of the rules of EU law remains closely connected to the guiding principles of EU environmental law set out under Article 191(2) TFEU. For the purposes of legislative interpretation, the principle possesses no inherent substantive values, but extends the relevance of the Article 191(2) principles beyond the narrow confines of EU environmental policy.

Finally, as one might reasonably expect, the principle of environmental integration can serve as a ground for reviewing the validity of an EU measure adopted in respect of a policy sector with the potential to impact upon the environment, where that measure may have failed to comply with, or at least take full account of, the essential environmental requirements of EU environmental policy. However, it would appear that the usefulness of such a general principle for the judicial review of measures taken by the Union institutions in the exercise of their significant legislative discretion is very severely limited. In Case C-341/95 *Bettati v. Safety Hi-Tech Srl* [1998] ECR I-4355, which involved a challenge to the validity of Ozone Regulation 3093/94, the Court, while accepting that the environmental objectives, principles and criteria of the former Article 130r must be respected by the Community legislature in implementing environmental policy, nevertheless found that:

> in view of the need to strike a balance between certain of the objectives and principles mentioned in Article 130r and of the complexity of the implementation of those criteria, *review by the Court must necessarily be limited* to the question whether the Council, by adopting the Regulation, committed *a manifest error of appraisal* regarding the conditions for the application of Article 130r of the Treaty. (*Emphasis added*)

If the scope for judicial review of environmental measures on the basis of the environmental requirements set out under the Treaty is limited, it stands to reason that the scope for judicial review on these grounds of measures which are not primarily environmental is even more limited. Though the *Bettati* case did not concern review for compliance with the integration principle, which has since been elevated to the status of a general principle and articulated in an unequivocally imperative manner, the principle inevitably involves the extended application of the requirements of Articles 191(1) and (2). If, as confirmed in *Bettati*, each Union institution enjoys 'a wide discretion regarding the measures it chooses to adopt in order to implement the environmental policy', it necessarily enjoys an even broader discretion in respect of measures adopted in other policy sectors where environmental requirements are only one of a number of issues to be considered, especially in light of the 'proliferation' of integration principles under the post-Lisbon TFEU, requiring integration of a wide range of EU policy objectives additional to environmental requirements.

The principle of environmental integration post-Lisbon

Uncertainty regarding the normative implications of the principle has only been exacerbated by the new Treaty regime ushered in post-Lisbon. For instance, it is of great significance that the principle of environmental integration is now but one integration principle among many included under the TFEU. Article 8 TFEU requires that the Union 'in all its activities…shall aim to eliminate inequalities, and to promote equality, between men and women', effectively a principle of gender equality integration. Rather more generally, Article 9 TFEU requires the integration of considerations arising under a number of economic and social rights, each in itself quite nebulous and uncertain. Article 10 TFEU in turn provides that, 'in defining and implementing its policies and activities, the Union shall aim to combat discrimination based on sex, racial or ethnic origin, religion or belief, disability, age or sexual orientation' – a principle of non-discrimination integration. Under Article 12 TFEU, 'consumer protection requirements shall be taken into account in defining and implementing other Union policies and activities' – a principle of consumer protection integration, while Article 13 TFEU introduces a principle of animal welfare integration. In addition to the specific sectoral integration principles listed above, Article 7 TFEU introduces a broad requirement that 'the Union shall ensure consistency between its policies and activities, taking all of its objectives into account in accordance with the principle of conferral of powers'. This principle of 'consistency' would appear to amount to a principle of 'general' or 'universal' integration of policy objectives, bringing all policy requirements listed under the TFEU into play and requiring that each must be considered in the adoption of every measure to which it might be relevant. Understood strictly, it would make redundant all of the specific sectoral integration principles listed above.

In terms of legal clarity, it does not help that each of the new, post-Lisbon sectoral integration principles is articulated somewhat differently, ranging from stipulations that the Union institutions 'shall aim' to meet, 'shall take into account' or 'shall ensure consistency between' certain sectoral policy objectives, to one requiring that the Union *and Member States* 'shall pay full regard' to certain sectoral requirements. While the principle of environmental integration is stated in the most imperative manner of all the post-Lisbon sectoral integration principles, with Article 11 TFEU requiring that 'environmental protection requirements *must* be integrated', there can be no doubting the conclusion that the 'true proliferation of integration principles' under the Lisbon Treaty (Jans, 2010: 1544–1545) has resulted in a significant downgrading of environmental integration. Obviously, a dramatic increase in the range and number of interests to be accommodated in the policy-making process makes that process of accommodation very much more complex and markedly reduces the relative weight to be accorded to any one type of interest. Of course, it might yet prove significant that the version of environmental integration set out under Article 37 of the Charter of Fundamental Rights of the European Union, itself now enjoying the status of a treaty provision, would appear to be rather narrower in scope than Article 11 TFEU, only requiring integration of a 'high level of environmental protection and the improvement of the quality of the environment...into the policies of the Union'. As it does not mention the 'activities' of the Union, nor require integration as regards the 'definition and implementation' of Union policies, Article 37 might be understood to be less relevant to specific measures and decisions and to the practical application of EU law and, thus, to be less justiciable. Jans expresses concern that 'an interpretation of Article 11 TFEU in line with the Charter may result in a further downgrading' (Jans, 2010: 1544).

On the other hand, Krämer stresses the close relationship between the principle of environmental integration, as articulated under both Article 11 TFEU and Article 37 of Charter of Fundamental Rights, and the fundamental Union objective of promoting sustainable development. Article 3(3) of the TEU includes sustainable development as one of the fundamental, overarching objectives of the European Union and Krämer suggests that the connection between Articles 11 TFEU and 3(3) TEU 'appears to mean that in order for sustainable development to be achieved, environmental requirements must be integrated into other EU policies'. Regarding the proliferation of integration principles to include the objectives of other areas of sectoral policy, he further points out that:

> Not only is the wording of the integration requirement in [Articles 8,9, 10 and 12 TFEU] less decisive, they do not refer to sustainable development. Nor does Article 3 TEU state that sustainable development is based on gender equality, social protection, consumer protection or absence of discrimination.
>
> (Krämer, 2012: 88)

On this basis, Krämer re-interprets the significance of the principle of 'consistency' set down under Article 7 TFEU so that it cannot be understood 'as meaning that the environmental objectives mentioned shall be considered as other, additional objectives of the transport, agricultural, fisheries, etc. policies and be treated as such' (ibid.: 90). Instead, remembering that Article 11 TFEU and Article 37 of the Charter both refer to one of the fundamental objectives of the Union, he concludes that 'there is a *particular obligation* for the EU institutions in the context of Article 7 TFEU to ensure that the different policies and activities take into account and work towards the objective of a high level of protection and an improvement of the quality of the environment' (emphasis added). In addition, he points out that 'there is no obligation comparable to Article 37 [of the Charter] placed on the EU institutions in the transport, agriculture, fisheries or competition areas…[so that]…the environmental sector stands out with regard to all other sectors of EU policy'. Though social and consumer policy are mentioned in the Charter, it is only in respect of the principle of environmental integration that the Charter requires its objectives to be pursued in accordance with the fundamental objective of sustainable development.

However, it is obvious that the political 'voice' previously afforded to the environment by the principle of environmental integration is now in danger of being drowned out by the din of all the other policy objectives which are required to be integrated into general EU policy making. Jans refers to this phenomenon as the 'minestrone effect', whereby, 'like the mixture of ingredients in minestrone, decision-making on the basis of multiple integration principles could result in measures where the component elements are still visible, but not as sharply and clearly as before' (Jans, 2010: 1546–1547). He expresses concern over the possibility that certain environmental standards might be diluted or offset through a process he calls 'reversed integration', that is 'a process by which certain environmental standards, such as environmental quality standards or emission standards, are lowered as a consequence of the requirement that other than environmental interests are to be taken into account' (ibid.).

In addition, the proliferation of sectoral integration principles is likely to limit the justiciability of the principle of environmental integration in quite specific ways. The requirement of Union institutions to take account of and balance a broad range of policy objectives and requirements inevitably strengthens and extends the discretionary powers of these institutions and makes it rather less likely that the ECJ would find that such discretion has been exceeded. Jans predicts that 'the ECJ will show even more deference to the EU's political institutions than before in this balancing act and will become even more reluctant to reach the conclusion that the European legislator committed 'a manifest error of appraisal' (Jans, 2010: 1546).

Also, under the specific powers doctrine, or the so-called 'principle of conferral', the key brake on creeping Union competence under the Treaties, the multiplicity of integration principles clearly extends the competence of the Union institutions to take legally binding measures to ensure that myriad sectoral policy objectives are pursued, or at least taken into account, when decisions are being taken in almost any area of EU policy-making. In addition to making EU measures more difficult to review, this effect 'makes it more difficult to draw a clear line between Union and Member State competences' (Jans, 2010: 1546, 1540). Indeed, recognizing the implications of the principle of consistency in terms of the extension of Union competence, Article 7 TFEU makes express, if somewhat weak and uncertain, reference to the principle of conferral of powers.

Normative content of the integration obligation

It only remains to examine what exactly the obligation to integrate environmental requirements, to the extent that it is enforceable or justiciable,
requires of EU policy-makers in practical terms. Hession and Macrory
summarize the obligatory policy requirements envisaged under the EU
principle of environmental integration as follows:

- a contribution towards the objectives of preserving, protecting and
  improving the quality of the environment, protecting human health,
  and the prudent and rational utilization of natural resources;
- a high level of protection;
- adherence to the four principles of precaution, prevention, rectifi-
  cation at source, and polluter pays; and
- the need to take into account certain additional factors including
  the diversity of situations within various regions of the community,
  available scientific and technical data, and the potential costs and
  benefits of action or inaction.

(Hession and Macrory, 1998: 578–9)

However, this general account leaves certain key questions unanswered.
Notably, it remains unclear whether the principle requires compliance by
policy-makers engaged in related sectoral policy areas with any and all
standards set down under EU environmental directives and regulations. In
many cases such standards may be contained in environmental directives
which are addressed to Member States rather than the relevant Union
institutions.

In this regard, Krämer focuses on the right of access to information, which
he regards as absolutely central to the practical implementation of the
principle of environmental integration. Specifically, considering the fundamental right of the public of access to environmental information, set out in
the 1998 Aarhus Convention and in EU secondary legislation, together with
Article 37 of the Charter and Article 296(2) TFEU, requiring that 'legal acts
shall state the reasons on which they are based', he concludes that:

> This means that the EU institutions are obliged to inform, when they
> make proposals for legislation, adopt legislative or other acts, or take
> decisions which are capable of affecting the environment, how they
> complied with the obligation to ensure a high level of protection or to
> improve the quality of the environment. Otherwise, the rights and
> guarantees which flow for citizens from Article 37 of the Charter are in
> fact empty.

(Krämer, 2012: 92)

However, he proceeds to list recent illustrative examples of EU initiatives relating to access to EU institution documents and to the transport and fisheries policy areas, where the Commission has failed to comply with this principle of 'good EU governance'. This understanding of the normative content of the obligation of environmental integration corresponds with that of Hession and Macrory, who suggest that 'the duty to integrate environmental requirements is suggestive of procedural rather than substantive protection' (Hession and Macrory, 1998: 579–580). They note that 'a familiar requirement often imposed on administrative bodies is to "take into consideration" certain factors, implying that once taken on board they may be rejected if they conflict with other goals' (ibid.), though they caution that it does have some substantive normative significance by reminding us that 'the terminology of the integration duty implies more than this; conflict with other areas does not entitle environmental requirements to be dismissed' (ibid.). In fact, Krämer lists the measures previously suggested by the Commission in the context of the Cardiff process, all now abandoned, to give practical effect to the principle.

Conclusion

This chapter attempts briefly to outline the problems experienced in the EU legal order in giving effect to environmental integration which, according to Krämer, 'is probably the most important environmental provision in the whole Lisbon Treaty, [yet] raises considerable implementation problems, for lawyers, policy-makers and administrations' (Krämer, 2012: 83). Given the advantages which the EU legal order enjoys over other regimes created under international law, in terms of mechanisms for the generation of environmental rules which are binding upon the Member States, as well as for their effective enforcement, these problems do not augur well for the prospects of achieving meaningful environmental integration in international law. Given the centrality of the latter principle for the realization of sustainable development, it is high time these problems were given due consideration by academic commentators and policy-makers involved in the elaboration of international environmental law and policy.

References

Baldock, D., Beaufoy, G. and Haigh, N. (1992) *The Integration of Environmental Protection Requirements into the Definition and Implementation of Other EC Policies.* London: Institute for European Environmental Policy.
European Commission (2004) *Integrating Environmental Considerations into Other Policy Areas: A Stocktaking of the Cardiff Process*, COM (2004) 394 final, 1, June, European Commission.
Franklin, C. N. K. (2011) 'The burgeoning principle of consistency in EU law', *Yearbook of European Law*, 30, 42–85.

Hession, M. and Macrory, R. (1998) 'The legal duty of environmental integration: commitment and obligation or enforceable right', in T. O'Riordan and H. Voisey (eds), *The European Union and Sustainable Development*. London: Frank Cass, pp. 100–12 (reproduced in R. Macrory, 2010, *Regulation, Enforcement and Governance in Environmental Law*. Oxford: Hart Publishing, pp. 567–83).

Jans, J. H. (2010) 'Stop the integration principle?' *Fordham International Law Journal*, 33, 1533.

Kingston, S. (2012) *Greening EU Competition Law and Policy*. Cambridge: Cambridge University Press.

Krämer, L. (2012) 'Giving a voice to the environment by challenging the practice of integrating environmental requirements into other EU policies', in S. Kingston (ed.), *European Perspectives on Environmental Law and Governance*. Abingdon: Routledge, p. 83.

Lenaerts, K. and Corthaut, T. (2008) 'Towards an internally consistent doctrine on invoking norms of EU law', in S. Prechal and B. van Roermund (eds), *The Coherence of EU Law*. Oxford: Oxford University Press, p. 495.

Macrory, R. (1999) 'The Amsterdam Treaty: an environmental perspective', in D. O'Keeffe and P. Twomey (eds), *Legal Issues of the Amsterdam Treaty*. Oxford: Hart Publishing, p. 171.

McIntyre, O. (2005) 'The all-consuming definition of "waste" and the end of the "contaminated land" debate? Case C-1/03: *Van de Walle*', *Journal of Environmental Law*, 17, 109.

Rieu-Clarke, A. (2005) *International Law and Sustainable Development: Lessons from the Law of International Watercourses*. London: IWA Publishing.

Stokke, O. and Forster, J. (1999) *Policy Coherence in Development Cooperation*. London: Frank Cass Publishers.

Syngellakis, A. (1993) 'The concept of sustainable development in European community law and policy', *Cambrian Law Review*, 24, 59.

Von Bogdandy, A. (2010), 'Founding principles of EU law: a theoretical and doctrinal sketch', *European Law Journal*, 16, 95.

Wilkinson, D. (1992) 'Maastricht and the environment: the implications for the EC's environment policy of the Treaty on European Union', *Journal of Environmental Law*, 4 (2): 221.

9 Thinking about the future of global water governance

Joseph W. Dellapenna

Introduction

Existing water institutional structures are either failing to address water challenges or are poorly equipped to cope with increasing pressure on water resources and the governance systems handling these resources. Different institutions are competing for leadership on water governance issues, which may already lead to duplications, contradictions and inefficiencies. In this chapter, I undertake an inquiry into the relation between global water institutional structures, with particular emphasis on the UN, and possible outcomes in terms of addressing impending water crises. I first discuss the key problems for global-level water governance and outline the trends in that governance, with a particular focus on the role that UN organs can play. I then present stories of what the world of water and water governance are likely to look like in 40 years and through this seek to identify the common challenges to water governance that could be suitably addressed at the global level and the possible institutional and legal responses to these challenges. I then analyse and compare these possible responses with a particular view to their compatibility with achieving one or another of the possible futures. This chapter is not an attempt to argue for any particular strategy or outcome. It merely attempts to highlight the connections between the two and to suggest therefore that water managers and water policy experts consider both in deciding on strategies for the future, selecting the strategy that seems to offer the best opportunity for achieving the most desirable future.

Stories of possible water futures

No one can predict with certainty what the water future of the planet will be. While climate disruption certainly is occurring, what its effects will be – how fast it will proceed, what will be its effects on specific regions of the planet, and how effectively nations and communities will mitigate or adapt to climate disruption – remain uncertain (Parry *et al.*, 2007). As a result of these uncertainties, the Millennium Ecosystem Assessment (MEA, 2005), the

Intergovernmental Panel on Climate Change (IPCC, 2007) and the Fourth Global Environment Outlook (UNEP, 2007) have developed different scenarios. The IPCC defined scenarios as 'plausible descriptions, without ascribed likelihoods, of possible future states of the world', while storylines are 'qualitative, internally consistent narratives of how the future may evolve, which often underpin quantitative projections of future change that, together with the storyline, constitute the scenario' (Parry *et al.*, 2007: 32). A brief look at these scenarios will explain the challenges likely facing humankind over the next 50 years.

Storylines in scenarios of reactions to climate disruption

The Intergovernmental Panel on Climate Change has developed a series of scenarios setting out possible water futures and scenarios for possible futures for other resources. Recognizing that major impacts are already occurring on the water resources and ecosystems of the planet (Parry *et al.*, 2007: 35–48), the Panel's 2007 report on the likely impacts, necessary adaptations, and expected vulnerabilities of climate disruption set forth four scenarios, named A1, A2, B1 and B2 (p22 endbox 3: 146–147). The storyline of the A1 scenario focuses on a future with rapid economic growth, and rapid introduction of technologies. It assumes that the global population will peak in the middle of the century and that there will be an increase in cultural and social interactions among people leading to convergence among regions. The A1 scenario is further subdivided along three paths depending on what energy sources predominate. The A2 scenario visualizes a hetero-geneous world where countries and people focus on self-reliance and local identities. Regions develop differently and more slowly. In the B1 world, global population peaks as in the A1 scenario, but the regions converge towards a service and information society, there is a reduction in material intensity with a strong focus on environmental impacts and governance that promotes sustainability and equity. The B2 scenario focuses on decentralized solutions emphasizing local routes to sustainable and equitable societies. It is a world with continuously but slowly increasing global population, intermediate levels of economic development, and less rapid and more diverse technological change.

The Millennium Ecosystem Assessment (MEA, 2005) also identifies four scenarios, named 'Global Orchestration' (which focuses both on sustainable development and fair trade with enhancement of global public goods and global education), 'Order from Strength' (which focuses on conservation efforts such as reserves, regional trade blocks, security and protection and is highly regional in character), 'Adapting Mosaic' (which focuses on local regional co-management and linking local communities to global communities) and 'Techno Garden' (which emphasizes green technology, tradable rights, free movement of goods, technical expertise, etc.). The current Global Environment Outlook (UNEP, 2007) also explores four scenarios. These are 'Policy First' (where governments, with active private and civic sector support, initiate and implement strong policies to improve the environment and human well-being, while still emphasizing economic development), 'Sustainability First' (where governments, civil societies, and the private sector work collaboratively to improve the environment and human well-being, with a strong emphasis on equity), 'Security First' (where the governmental and the private sectors compete for control in efforts to improve, or at least maintain, human well-being for mainly the rich and powerful in society) and 'Markets First' (where the private sector, with active government support, pursues maximum economic growth as the best path to improve the environment and human well-being).

Regional climate changes are affecting many physical and biological systems, which in turn have already begun to affect some human systems, impacts that are only likely to grow larger (Parry *et al.* 2007:35–64, 79–117). This is particularly true of hydrology and water resources (ibid.: 173–210; UNEP, 2007, ch. 4). Yet each of these possible scenarios posits a future of increasing stress on water resources, with or without dramatic and continuing population increase. Each of the major storylines features a need to respond to growing water crises. In a sense, the problems are not as serious as the foregoing statements make it appear for the current strains on freshwater are in large part due to human activities (Parry *et al.*, 2007: 48–50, 52–5, 71 box TS.7, 73, 75; UNEP, 2007: 119–22, 129–40). Constant changes in farming techniques, combined with urban and industrial growth, have seriously interfered with the availability of freshwater (UNEP, 2007: 133–5). Climate disruption, largely through its impact on the oceans, will affect rainfall patterns that will compound the effects of human activity, with rainfall becoming increasingly erratic, even where it is increasing (Parry *et al.*, 2007: 177–178, 183, 186–187, 190, 192–193; UNEP, 2007: 125–127). Arid regions will become wider and drier, while water management infrastructure will become effectively obsolete (Parry *et al.*, 2007: 175, 178–179, 185, 193–5, 223, 225–6, 249, 435, 439, 447–9, 451, 472, 477–8, 583, 585, 590, 596, 606–7). The melting of glaciers and the mountain snowpack will destroy these immense reservoirs of fresh water that provide the base flows of innumerable rivers during the dry months of the year, depriving vast regions of their summer water supplies (Parry *et al.*, 2007: 175–7, 179, 184, 187, 194, 337–83, 814–22; UNEP, 2007: 127–8).

Climate disruption also causes the spread of diseases into regions where formerly the disease agents could not survive (UNEP, 2007, p127). In general, developing countries were found to be more vulnerable to the effects of climate disruption than were more developed countries (Parry *et al.*, 2007: 48–64), particularly because impacts on unmanaged systems (often more characteristic of developing countries) are more likely to be impacted than are managed systems (often characteristic of developed countries) (ibid.: 48). Critical to this analysis is that the future vulnerability of communities or societies will depend on the developmental pathway each community or society follows (ibid.: 75–6) – which brings us back to the scenarios. These scenarios necessarily cover a good deal more than just water resources (ibid: 146–61).

Governance options

The several scenarios adduced above describe plausible approaches to water governance problems likely to emerge in the next 50–100 years, providing templates for how to respond to the challenges of global climate disruption and other stresses affecting the management or use of water resources. These templates exist on a grid that ranges from governmental to non-governmental and from formal to informal. Most attention thus far has gone to governance options at the national or sub-national level that would be suitable to the challenges to water governance over the next 50–100 years. From such studies, the Intergovernmental Panel on Climate Change created a short list of issues that must be resolved in order to respond effectively to the coming challenges (McCarthy *et al.*, 2001: 222–3; see also Solanes and Jouravlev, 2006; UNEP, 2007: 141–2):

1. *The capacity of water-related institutions*, consisting of water agencies' authority to act, skilled personnel, the capability and authority to consider a wide range of alternatives (including but not limited to supply-side and demand-side interventions) in adapting to changed conditions, the capability and authority to use multi-objective planning and evaluation procedures in the assessment of policy alternatives, procedures for conflict resolution, and incentives to analyse policies and projects to learn what worked.
2. *The legal framework for water administration* that always constrains, for better and for worse, the options that are open to water management; while laws change as needs change, changes are slow and lag changing needs. In many countries, the legal framework for water management is moving toward increasing environmental protection (e.g., the European Union's habitats directive).
3. *The wealth of nations* in terms of natural resources and ecosystems, human-created capital (especially in the form of water control systems), and human capital (including trained personnel) that determines what nations can 'afford to commit' to adaptation, including, if necessary, the ability and willingness to transfer wealth among population groups and regions within a country and among nations.
4. *The state of technology* and the framework for the dissemination (or monopolization) of technology.
5. *The mobility of human populations* to change residential and work locations in response to severe climate events or climate change.
6. *The speed of climate disruption and the cumulative extent* of change affect the impacts on society in nonlinear fashions.

7. *The complexity of management arrangements* also may be a factor in response; in principle, the fewer agencies involved in water management, the easier it will be to implement an adaptation strategy (although the structure within the agencies will be very important), while If there are many stakeholders to involve – perhaps with conflicting requirements, management goals, and perceptions and each with some management control over part of the water system – it may be more difficult to adapt to changing circumstances.

8. *The ability of water managers to assess current resources and project future resources*, which requires continuing collection of data and the ability to use scenarios with hydrological models to estimate possible future conditions.

Drawing on the need to address these issues, the same report of the Intergovernmental Panel also described a set of tools required for successful adaptation to climate disruption (McCarthy *et al.*, 2001: 226):

1. *Data monitoring* – adaptive water management requires reliable data on which to make decisions, calibrate models, and develop projections for the future, data covering not just hydrological characteristics but also indicators of water use.

2. *Understanding patterns of variability* – important for medium- and long-term water management; in particular, the stability of the 'baseline' climate and recognition that even in the absence of climate disruption, the recent past may not be a reliable guide to the hydrological resource base of the near future.

3. *Analytical tools* – effective water management requires numerous tools to assess options and the future, including scenario analysis and risk analysis.

4. *Decision tools* – scenario and risk analysis must be supplemented with tools such as Bayesian and other decision-making tools to make decisions on the basis of the information provided.

5. *Management techniques* – techniques that are actually implemented to meet management objectives; a broad spectrum of techniques (such as building a reservoir or managing demand) is well known, but research is needed into specific aspects of many demand-side approaches, as well as into opportunities for seasonal flow forecasting and innovative water supply and treatment technologies (such as desalination) and to determine how to enhance the range of techniques considered by water managers.

Many of the issues are not yet being addressed effectively and the necessary tools may not exist in particular societies and communities. The scenarios, moreover, posit global governance responses that implicate global water governance and not just national or sub-national governance, yet global governance responses have received even less attention and implementation than governance at the national and sub-national level. In some respects, it is precisely at the global level that the differences between the several scenarios actually come into focus. While the following grid suggests some of the possibilities that need to be considered at all levels of governance, the remainder of this chapter will focus on the global or transnational approaches to water governance, with particular emphasis on the possible role of the United Nations or its organs.

Key governance options in relation to the scenarios

The ostensible goal of global water governance today could be described as 'water for all', which is set forth in the Millennium Development Goals supplemented by the growing recognition of a human right to water and sanitation (United Nations, 2000, 2010). And in today's world there are numerous transnational or international institutions for water governance that operate at the global or regional levels. These include highly formal institutions created under the auspices of the UN or other international organizations or by multilateral or bilateral treaties (Dellapenna, 1994; UNEP, 2007). They also include informal institutions created by water-oriented professional associations ('epistemic communities'), civil society groups, or market-place participants.

Existing institutions are relatively good at agenda setting, sharing inform-ation, mobilizing people, and, to a certain degree, in mobilizing resources. Yet although water has been on the agenda of many major summits (*e.g.* at the Millennium Summit or Johannesburg 2002), it is only loosely institution-alized at the global level. Recommendations produced at such gatherings are full of good intent and widely shared principles, maybe some overarching norms, but are much weaker concerning (legally) binding rules and procedures or the provision of resources to implement the recommendations. Whether anything more is required reflects in large measure which of the several possible scenarios is selected as most desirable or at least as most likely. This section focuses on five archetypal global governance options. The overarching questions of analysis will be: Who does what best at which level? And is one or another of these governance approaches conducive to moving towards one particular scenario or another?

A high-level advisory group

Perhaps the simplest governance option would be to provide a high-level advisory group. Such a group could be a public institution or a private epistemic community, but it must be located high up in the UN hierarchy or must have some source of authority. Either sort of group would serve to bring water governance functionaries together periodically to exchange information about water, water uses, and managerial practices. The group could operate globally, or within a particular region (such as a watershed), or between two nations. Examples would include the Global Water Partnership (Rana and Kelly, 2004) or any number of groups sponsor river basin action plans. Another example would be the UN Secretary-General's Advisory Board on Water and Sanitation (created in 2004). While the Global Water Partnership was founded in 1996 by the World Bank, the UN Development Programme, and the Swedish International Development Cooperation Agency, it is funded by Canada, Denmark, the EU, Finland, France, Germany, the Netherlands, Norway, Sweden, Spain, Switzerland, the United Kingdom and the United States. Wholly private or mixed public–private groups also exist, such as the various gatherings on a regular basis sponsored by one or another epistemic community. The Gates Foundation or other private philanthropic groups might help cover the limited administrative expenses of such a group. Such approaches open doors without threatening anybody because the group has no formal authority and no money to dispense. An advisory group can talk with UNICEF, the World Bank, and other global or regional water governance institutions, while promoting diplomatic exchanges were appropriate. The Secretary-General's Advisory Board meets twice a year, with board members serving without pay but receiving reimbursement for travel and lodging. The Board also needs money for publishing pamphlets and to maintain a secretariat of three persons.

Such approaches open doors without threatening anybody because the group has no formal authority and no money to dispense. An advisory group can talk with UNICEF, the World Bank, and other global or regional water governance institutions, while promoting diplomatic exchanges where appropriate. The Secretary-General's Advisory Board meets twice a year, with board members serving without pay but receiving reimbursement for travel and lodging. The Board also needs money for publishing pamphlets and to maintain a secretariat of three persons. Advisory groups are good at agenda setting. The UN Secretary-General's Advisory Board, for example, created the Hashimoto Action Plan (UNSGAB, 2006, 2010). The Plan is a compendium of actions necessary to finance, develop, and implement integrated water resources management. The Global Water Partnership similarly helps national and sub-national water governance institutions finance, develop, and implement water management programs (Rana and Kelly, 2004). The problem is that these agendas do not carry a legal commitment and provide no financial support for implementation of their agendas. Such groups also have been accused of being undemocratic.

Coordination agencies

A somewhat stronger option would be an institution charged with active coordination of the activities of operational institutions, whether bilaterally, regionally, or globally. Globally, the United Nations established an organization called UN-Water in 2003 precisely to do this, at least as far as the numerous UN agencies responsible for water issues are concerned (UN-Water, 2010). Today it coordinates the work of 31 cooperating agencies that in varying ways create or affect global water governance. It creates special task forces to address particular concerns, such as regional initiatives, the world water assessment program, the monitoring of sanitation and drinking water, gender and water, transboundary waters, and climate change and water.

Like the high-level advisory groups, UN Water or some other, hypothetical coordinating agency is not set up to make decisions or to set priorities. As a result, such an agency is unlikely to be able to cope with projected increased water stress or to respond effectively to a changing environment. One possible response would be to create or strengthen the regulatory function of this institutional arrangement – perhaps through a strong reading of the term 'coordination' in the UN-Water mandate. Some might question whether the problems are just too big and varied for a single coordinating agency to manage effectively. This argument gains strength in some scenarios relative to others. Some climate change issues are global and calls for a global response, which perhaps would justify stronger global coordination. Sanitation, on the other hand, is less of a global problem and perhaps would be better managed with minimal coordination. Pollution perhaps is somewhere in-between.

A framework water treaty

There already are a large number of framework water treaties or directives, ranging from bilateral to multilateral to global (Dellapenna, 1994). A framework treaty, as its name suggests, provides a broad set of principles around which interested nations or national legal systems can craft a specific legal regime to govern and constrain water management systems. In some ways, the most ambitious framework water treaty is the UN Convention on the Law of Non-Navigational Uses of International Watercourses (United Nations, 1997). The Convention has still obtained only 21 of the necessary 35 ratifications (Salman, 2007). The reasons for the slow pace of ratifications are open to debate, but may have to do with the relative inadequacy of the Convention. Its inadequacies are easily shown by comparing it to the International Law Association's Berlin Rules on Water Resources (ILA, 2004). The primary deficiencies are that the UN Convention addresses only transboundary issues and says rather little about concerns other than water sharing. While the Berlin Rules do address these and other issues neglected in the UN Convention, the Rules are unofficial and therefore do not have binding effect.

The European states have crafted two framework instruments that are much more comprehensive and detailed: the Helsinki Convention on the Protection and Use of Transboundary Watercourses and International Lakes

(UNECE, 1992); and the Water Framework Directive (EU, 2000). The Helsinki Convention suffers from being limited to transboundary issues, but is more comprehensive and detailed. It also has a permanent secretariat, a meeting of the parties to keep the Convention up-to-date, and provisions for continuing research – all lacking in the UN Convention. The Water Framework Directive is highly detailed and is administered by (and could be updated by) the European Union's organs, while also providing for continuing research. As frameworks, they still leave a considerable number to details to be worked out at the regional, national, or sub-national level.

Theoretically, the global community could replace the existing UN Convention (United Nations, 1997) with a more comprehensive and detailed treaty, replete with a conference of the parties, a standing body for scientific and technical advice and so on. Or we could add a protocol on water to the UN Framework Convention on Climate Change (United Nations, 1992). Too much detail at the global level, however, might actually be counterproductive if it prevented appropriate responses to local conditions. In any event, the governments of the world seem unwilling to commit to such a broad reaching alteration of global water governance given their reluctance thus far to ratify the less far-reaching UN Convention. That unwillingness might simply reflect a preference for a less centralized scenario.

A single water organization

Focusing on the reality that some water problems are global, the extreme of globalization of the response would be the creation of a single water organization that would address the full breadth and depth of at least some water problems. This is possibly even more hypothetical in nature that the idea of a new framework treaty or protocol. To do so would require the delineation of the functions is should address, the possible trade-offs that would be necessary to put it into operation, and how to overcome the gap between such an arrangement and current global water governance.

Consider, for example, if UN-Water were to attempt to substantially extend its responsibilities and powers. If such a proposal were made, UN-Water would almost certain loose many of its members and their willingness to collaborate, but without any guarantee that the member states of the United Nations would agree to the propose extension or to adequate funding for the necessary functions. If the General Assembly would propose an Intergovernmental Negotiating Committee to deal with water as it did in 1990 to deal with climate change, this could lead to a series of steps in this direction.

Markets

One popular solution would be to rely on markets for water management (Griffin, 2006). After all, when people – even poor people – can see a real benefit from something, they are willing to pay for it. Consider, for example, how readily mobile phones have spread even into the poorest communities, will little or no government involvement. Public private cooperation in the area of water services became increasingly important in the 1990s and water as increasingly been seen as an economic good in line with the Dublin Declaration (1992). Experiences along these lines have been mixed at best. Increasing international arbitration on water (Schouten and Schwartz, 2006) and the difficulties in reconciling the newly adopted human right to water and sanitation within the General Assembly and the treatment of water as an economic good are raising questions about whether water resources are suitable for market solutions – a question that is hotly debated (Rothfeder, 2001). At best, markets can solve some water management problems on the small scale, but the will be of limited or no utility at the global scale (Dellapenna, 2008).

Comparative analysis – from governance options to water scenarios

If one wanted to select among the foregoing global governance options, one should first ask what scenario of a water future one would like to achieve. Then one can reason back and ask which option, or what mix of options, would be most conducive achieving the selected scenario. Space allows only a cursory consideration of that question.

Several scenarios emphasize the preservation of local identities or control. These include the Intergovernmental Panel's A2, the Millennium Environmental Assessment's Order through Strength, and perhaps the Global Environment Outlook. While those who prefer these scenarios cannot completely ignore the global dimensions of their water futures, they will prefer the less centralizing global governance options. These people are likely to prefer a high-level advisory group, or perhaps a fairly weak framework treaty such as the UN Convention on the Law of Non-Navigational Uses of International Watercourses (United Nations, 1997). They might also like markets to the extent that they can be made to serve, although one could go with the high-level advisory group or a framework treaty without recourse to markets.

Two of the Millennium Environmental Assessment scenarios specifically emphasize markets: Global Orchestration and Techno Garden. Predictably, those who prefer these scenarios will support the market option for global water governance. Even for those scenarios, however, something more will be required for markets cannot resolve all questions of global water governance. The people are also likely to select a high-level advisory body or a fairly weak framework treaty, although some might prefer a stronger coordinating body or a more strongly developed framework treaty. The precise choice would turn on the degree of one's confidence in the need for more or less regulation of the market.

Those who believe that our water future would be best served by strong global growth – whether in terms of industrial and agricultural production

(A1) or information services (B1) – would probably prefer the strongest option (a single global water agency), but might have to settle for a coordinating agency or a highly developed framework treaty. Markets could supplement this arrangement. Supporters of any of the Global Environment Outlook options except Markets First would probably also come out here.

Conclusion

Those considering developing governance strategies to respond to the emerging global water crises must first determine what sort of water future they would prefer. Then they must determine what sort of global governance option (or mix of options) would be most suitable for bringing about that future. Finally, they must pursue strategies that have a chance of bringing that option into effect. Strategies can include advocacy, arranging financing, law reform, and developing or supporting epistemic communities. Should they succeed in creating such institutions, they will need to follow through to see that they are properly implemented.

References

Dellapenna, J. W. (1994) 'Treaties as instruments for managing internationally shared waters: Restricted sovereignty vs. community of property', *Case Western Reserve Journal of International and Comparative Law*, 26 (3): 27–56.
Dellapenna, J. W. (2008) 'Climate disruption, the Washington consensus, and water law reform', *Temple Law Review*, 81 (3): 383–432.
Dublin Declaration (1992) 'Dublin Declaration on Water and Sustainable Development', available at www.gdrc.org/uem/water/dublin-statement.html (accessed 28 January 2013).
EU (2000) 'Water Framework Directive', EU Dir. 2000/60/EC, 43 OJ (L 327), European Union.
Griffin, R. C. (2006) *Water Resource Economics: The Analysis of Scarcity, Policies, and Projects*. Cambridge, MA: MIT Press.
ILA (2004) 'The Berlin Rules on Water Resources', in *Report of the Seventy-First Meeting of the International Law Association*, International Law Association, pp. 335–384.
IPCC (2007) *Working Group II Report: Impacts, Adaptation, and Vulnerability*, Intergovernmental Panel on Climate Change, Geneva, Switzerland, available at www.ipcc.ch/publications_and_data/publications_ipcc_fourth_assessment_report_wg2_report_impacts_adaptation_and_vulnerability.htm (accessed 28 January 2013).
McCarthy, J. J., Canziani, O. F., Leary, N. A., Dokken, D. J. and White, K. S. (eds) (2001) *Climate Change 2001: Impacts, Adaptation, and Vulnerability*. Cambridge: Cambridge University Press.
MEA (2005) 'Scenarios', in *Millennium Ecosystem Assessment, vol 2: Ecosystems and Human Well-Being*. , Washington, DC: World Resources Institute, ch. 8.
Parry, M., Canziani, O., Politukof, J., van der Linden, P., and Hanson, C. (2007) *Climate Change 2007: Impacts, Adaptation and Vulnerability*. Cambridge: Cambridge University Press.

Rana, S. and Kelly, L. (2004) *The Global Water Partnership – Addressing Challenges of Globalization: An Independent Evaluation of the World Bank's Approach to Global Programs.* Washington, DC: World Bank.

Rothfeder, J. (2001) *Every Drop for Sale: Our Desperate Battle over Water in a World about to Run Out.* New York: Tarcher/Penguin Books.

Salman, S. M. A. (2007) 'The UN watercourses convention ten years later: Why has its entry into force proven difficult?', *Water International*, 32 (1): 1–15.

Schouten, M. and Schwartz, K. (2006) 'Water as a political good: Implications for investment strategies', *International Environmental Agreements: Politics, Law and Economics*, 6 (3): 407–21.

Solanes, M. and Jouravlev, A. (2006) *Water Governance for Development and Sustainability*, Recursos naturales e infraestructura serie no. 111. Santiago, Chile: United Nations.

UNECE (1992) 'Convention on the Protection and Use of Transboundary Watercourses and International Lakes', adopted 17 March 1992, United Nations Economic Commission for Europe, available at www.unece.org/env/water/pdf/watercon.pdf (accessed 28 January 2013).

UNEP (2007) *Global Environment Outlook 4 (GEO-4): Environment for Development*, United Nations Environment Programme, Nairobi, Kenya, available at www.unep.org/geo/GEO4/report/GEO-4_Report_Full_en.pdf (accessed 28 January 2013).

United Nations (1992) 'Framework Convention on Climate Change', adopted 9 May 1992, available at http://unfccc.int/resource/docs/convkp/conveng.pdf (accessed 28 January 2013).

United Nations (1997) 'Convention on the Law of Non-Navigational Uses of International Watercourses', UNGA A/Res/51/229, adopted 21 May 1997, available at http://untreaty.un.org/ilc/texts/instruments/english/conventions/8_3_1997.pdf (accessed 28 January 2013).

United Nations (2000) 'United Nations Millennium Development Declaration', UNGA A/Res/55/2, adopted 18 September 2000, available at www.un.org/millennium/declaration/ares552e.pdf (accessed 28 January 2013).

United Nations (2010) 'The Human Right to Water and Sanitation', UNGA A/Res/64/292, adopted 28 July 2010, available at www.un.org/ga/search/view_doc.asp?symbol=A/RES/64/292 (accessed 28 January 2013).

UNSGAB (2006) *Hashimoto Action Plan*, United Nations Secretary-General's Advisory Board on Water and Sanitation, United Nations, New York, available at www.unsgab.org/docs/HAP_en.pdf (accessed 28 January 2013).

UNSGAB (2010) *Hashimoto Action Plan II*, United Nations Secretary-General's Advisory Board on Water and Sanitation, United Nations, New York, available at www.preventionweb.net/files/12657_HAPIIen.pdf (accessed 28 January 2013).

UN-Water (2010) *A Guide to UN Water*, United Nations, New York, NY, available at www.unwater.org/downloads/unw_brochure_en_webversion.pdf (accessed 28 January 2013).

10 How the UN agencies contribute to the needs of the world

Focus on gender

Yuliya Lyamzina

Introduction

In 2007 it was estimated that there were more than 29 armed conflicts occurring around the world involving 25 countries (Project Plowshares, 2007). Most armed conflicts take place in low-income countries. According to the World Health Organization (WHO) *World Report on Violence and Health*, 190 armed conflicts have occurred since the Second World War (WHO, 2002). Only a quarter of them were between states; the rest were within the states. Most of the conflicts were shorter than six months. Those that lasted longer went on for many years or are continuing (e.g. in Afghanistan, Angola, Colombia, Viet Nam, etc.). The total number of armed conflicts in progress was less than 20 in the 1950s, over 30 in both the 1960s and 1970s, and rose to over 50 during the late 1980s. After the 1980s, there was sharp increase of conflicts in Europe because of the collapse of communist regime in eastern Europe and the former Soviet Union. In general, the size and area of the conflict has changed radically in the past two centuries (WHO, 2002).

Due to the fact that armed conflicts very often take place within the country, civilians are usually the ones placed at the heart of the conflict, endangered not only because of the proximity of the conflict but also because they are becoming main targets. Sometimes civilians can become actively mobilized in fighting or can often be forced to choose sides and support fighters in different forms, for example by providing food, shelter or other services (Lindsay, 2001).

Gender

According to WHO, there are 3.3 billion women around the world, and only 15 per cent of the world's population lives in high-income countries. Most women in the world live in low- and middle-income countries and almost half of them are located in southeast Asia and western Pacific regions. One in every two children under nine years old lives in low-income countries. In contrast, one in three women over 60 years old live in high-income countries (WHO, 2009).

Already in 1996 the World Health Assembly in its 1996 resolution WHA49.25 (WHA, 1996) declared violence a leading public health problem. Nevertheless, violence against women continuingly occurs in every country and in different parts of society. In many countries, it is the norm, and or a part of historical and cultural practice, which is widely tolerated and supported.

A global study on homicide conducted by the United Nations Office on Drugs and Crime confirms that 'women are the most frequent victims of intimate partner violence and they are often killed by family members in all countries and across all cultures. Home is where women are most at risk of been killed, while men are more at risk in the street' (UNODC, 2011).

Data related to gender-based violence remains mostly hidden due to the problems related to measurements and the comparability of data on reported crime and/or type of crime that is measured. In terms of gender-based and sexually based violence we usually see only the tip of iceberg, while most of the data remain hidden due to all the above-mentioned problems.

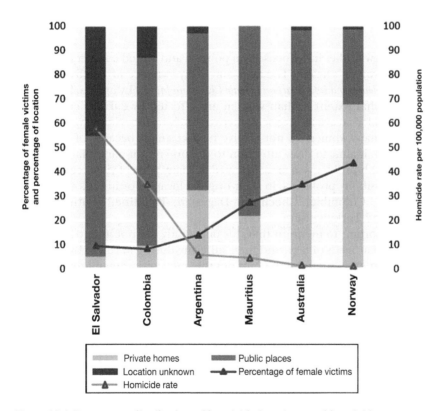

Figure 10.1 Percentage distribution of homicide locations and homicide rates, selected countries (2009 or latest available year)
Source: Me, A. (2012), Power Point Presentation, INEGI Conference 2012, Vienna, UNODC

134   *Yuliya Lyamzina*

Gender-based violence   Homicides

Figure 10.2 What is measured in gender-based violence, and the comparability of
data on reported crime depending on the type of crime

Source: A. Me, Power Point Presentation, INEGI Conference 2012, Vienna, UNODC

Only a few studies have focused on political and armed conflict as a determinant of women's health. The main aim of my own recently published book
Political Violence and its Impact on Female Civil Population (Lyamzina, 2011) was
to see to what extent civilian women are affected by current conflict or
violence and what are the consequences on their health. Nowadays, in many
countries many women do not receive respect simply because of their sex.
In addition, it aims to draw attention to the urgency of particular forms of
mental health problems in areas affected by many years of violence and with
acute accessibility problems, in their original location or in regions such as
Azerbaijan, Colombia, Chechnya, Dagestan, Palestine, South Sudan–
Ethiopia and Turkmenistan.

It is important to mention that this pilot study did not intend to negate
the particular needs of men and their suffering during wartime. By focusing
only on women it intended to point out that men and women are linked by
the impact of violence and armed conflict, because they belong to the same
community and/or family. That is why it is important to look at the impact
of violence through the prism of gender and to realize that the impact of war
on women is inevitably connected to the impact of war on men, and that
men often become targets through the women in their family or community
(Lindsey, 2001).

Results of the research

Data were obtained from populations in Azerbaijan (settled community),
Dagestan (settled community), Chechnya (settled community), Colombia

(settled community and temporary shelters of internally displaced persons, Palestine (settled community), South Sudan–Ethiopia (refugee camp). Tables 10.1–10.3 are related to political and security issues. In Table 10.1 women were asked whether they believe in their government, whether it can provide necessary security and whether they had some hope for help while experiencing traumatic events (for example, help from relatives abroad or international organizations in the region). High levels of distrust were expected in each country, with a total score of 64 per cent (n = 93). In addition, 70 per cent (n = 102) of women don't believe that the government can provide them with necessary security (Lyamzina, 2011).

Table 10.2 provides information how many women from our sample have received professional help after the incident and if not, how many of them did ask for it themselves. From the total sample (n = 146), only 15 per cent (n=22) of women received professional help, while 74 per cent (n = 108) did not get any. Only 17 per cent (n = 25) did ask the professional help and 77 per cent (n = 112) of women did not ask for psychological help after the incident.

From the total sample of 146 women, only 15 per cent of women have received help mostly from the Red Cross International! Table 10.3 summarizes the types of professional help received.

Main findings

Violence against women occurs in every country and in different parts of society. In many countries, it is the norm, and even worse, it is a part of historical and cultural practice that is widely tolerated and supported. We can see violence everywhere, not only during armed conflicts, where it is used as a weapon, but also during peacetime. Though problems occurring in situations of armed conflicts have been very well known for a long time, the problems experienced by women have received increased attention only in recent years. Every day we hear in the news about emergencies, natural disasters, new terrorist attacks and mass violence crimes, so the rise of mental and psychosocial problems is not surprising. However, scientific evidence regarding mental health and psychosocial support during emergencies and armed conflict is still scarce.

Civilian women are exposed to very high level of traumatic events due to the different types of violence. 74 per cent of the total sample (n = 134) have experienced military combat or being in a war zone; 23 per cent of the total sample of women have seen their husbands or sons killed in the conflict; 34 per cent of the total sample have experienced the life threat to the entire family. 81 per cent of the total sample is suffering from post-traumatic stress disorder (PTSD). 18 per cent have a severe level of depression according to the Beck Depression Inventory.

Primary prevention currently is very limited, because it is influenced by political, social, economic and environmental factors, which lead and influence armed conflicts and violence.

Table 10.1 Level of political trust

		Dagestan		Turkmenistan		Azerbaijan		Palestine		Colombia		South Sudan–Ethiopia		Chechnya		Total	
		n	%	n	%	n	%	n	%	n	%	n	%	n	%	n	%
Number of subjects		22	100.0	20	100.0	20	100.0	18	100.0	30	100.0	23	100.0	13	100.0	146	100.0
Do you believe in your government?	No	12	55.0	16	80.0	13	65.0	12	67.0	13	43.0	23	100.0	4	31.0	93	63.7
	Yes	8	36.0	4	20.0	7	35.0	1	6.0	17	57.0	0	0.0	3	23.0	40	27.4
Do you believe, that your government can help you / can provide you necessary security?	No	12	55.0	16	80.0	13	65.0	12	67.0	22	73.0	23	100.0	4	31.0	102	69.9
	Yes	7	32.0	4	20.0	7	35.0	1	6.0	8	27.0	0	0.0	2	15.0	29	19.9
Did you have hope for help?	No	13	59.0	14	70.0	10	50.0	6	33.0	5	17.0	23	100.0	2	15.0	73	50.0
	Yes	2	9.0	5	25.0	9	45.0	5	28.0	20	67.0	0	0.0	5	38.0	46	31.5

Table 10.2 Professional help provided to women

		Dagestan		Turkmenistan		Azerbaijan		Palestine		Colombia		South Sudan-Ethiopia		Chechnya		Total	
		n	%	n	%	n	%	n	%	n	%	n	%	n	%	n	%
Number of subjects		22	100.0	20	100.0	20	100.0	18	100.0	30	100.0	23	100.0	13	100.0	146	100.0
Did you get professional help from somebody after the incident?	No	16	73.0	13	65.0	18	90.0	9	50.0	23	77.0	23	100.0	6	46.0	108	74.0
	Yes	3	14.0	6	30.0	2	10.0	1	6.0	4	13.0	0	0.0	6	46.0	22	15.0
Did you ask for the professional help?	No	16	73.0	14	70.0	18	90.0	9	50.0	26	88.0	23	100.0	6	46.0	112	77.0
	Yes	4	18.0	6	30.0	2	10.0	3	17.0	3	10.0	0	0.0	7	54.0	25	17.0

Table 10.3 Types of professional help provided

	Dagestan		Turkmenistan		Azerbaijan		Palestine		Colombia		South Sudan-Ethiopia		Chechnya		Total	
	n	%	n	%	n	%	n	%	n	%	n	%	n	%	n	%
Number of subjects	22	100.0	20	100.0	20	100.0	18	100.0	30	100.0	23	100.0	13	100.0	146	100.0
After the incident																
I did not get any help	13	59.0	18	90.0	20	100.0	5	28.0	24	80.0	23	100.0	0	0.0	103	70.5
I had psychotherapy	0	0.0	0	0.0	0	0.0	1	6.0	2	7.0	0	0.0	0	0.0	3	2.1
I was visited by social worker	0	0.0	0	0.0	0	0.0	0	0.0	1	3.0	0	0.0	0	0.0	1	0.7

Further research should focus on new aetiological factors, influencing violence and prevalence of PTSD, paying more attention to the civilian population of the affected communities, and not focusing our attention solely on victims or survivors of direct violence.

UN and women

UN Women (www.unwomen.org) is the new UN body for gender equality and the empowerment of women. It formed from the merging of four of the world body's agencies and offices: the UN Development Fund for Women (UNIFEM), the Division for the Advancement of Women (DAW), the Office of the Special Adviser on Gender Issues, and the UN International Research and Training Institute for the Advancement of Women (UN-INSTRAW). UN Women became operational on 1 January 2011.

Some other UN and other agencies continue dealing with gender issues. These include FAO, GGCA, ILO, ICT, IUCN, OECD, OSCE, UNAIDS, UN DESA (UN Department of Economic and Social Affairs),UNDP, UNESCO, UNFPA, UNICEF, UN-HABITAT, UNHCR, UNODC, WEDO, WFP and WHO.

Main existing problems in the UN related to violence

The first and biggest problem is the lack of reliable and comparable data to assess the extent of the phenomenon, and therefore to find appropriate solutions. Despite the seriousness of the problem and existing wide range of instruments in national and regional levels, the question of violence against women and girls, and its effects on their health, still does not have the attention it deserves from the international community.

The UN remains a big, bureaucratic organization facing challenges of coordination and linking different entities. The United Nations itself is not the cause of the problem, but a part of it. The biggest challenge is to create social, political and economic systems within our countries and around the world so people themselves can participate in the decision-making process about their lives. A balanced approach should be used.

What can be done? Possible preventive measures

The main solution of the problem would be to conduct reliable and comparable surveys in order to produce data to assess the extent of the phenomenon and to find the appropriate solutions. Evidence needs to be provided by key stakeholders (policy makers, practitioners, NGOs) for the development of policies and other measures to combat violence against women. Informed, targeted polices to combat the violence need to be shaped. All states should be called upon to ratify and implement United Nations Security Council resolution 1325 (2000) on Women, Peace and Security. Women need to be allowed to participate in the peacekeeping and peacebuilding processes, and their contribution in the decision-making process should be recognized. All these measures will help to bridge the gap between knowledge and existing policies on gender-specific issues.

It is also necessary to establish a better exchange of information and cooperation among all actors involved in emergency and conflict-related work in order to prevent the duplicate work and gaps in research, documentation. Technical expertise based on local women's knowledge and experience must be developed, as only they know what is best for them and what their needs are!

In terms of gender-based and sexually based violence, work to educate people at all levels (local, national, regional, international, global) and involving all actors (especially men) is necessary to promote the end of violence. We must train researchers, health workers and emergency workers experienced in conflict settings, taking into account all ethical considerations, logistics and the security situation. It is essential to establish post-conflict programmes that will target women, men and children alike. It is equally necessary to include gender-related issues with a special focus on mental health needs.

Conclusion

In order to achieve an effective strategy, communities must be involved in its preparation, as only local people know what is best for them and what their real needs are. This will save time and avoid the production of another document which relies on needs-based research, instead taking into account real needs of people.

It is necessary to confront the international efforts, programmes, declarations and other instruments of the United Nations, to follow the effectiveness of international activities and face the fact that certain activities and assistance riches very limited number of people. For example a better exchange of information and cooperation among different actors involved in emergency and conflict related work would prevent from duplicated work and gaps in research and documentation. Technical expertise based on local women's knowledge and experience would help to produce detailed and problem focused guidelines, policies and programmes and legislation which would fit the real needs of women.

It is obvious that no single organization or government can ensure all this planning, research and implementation itself; that is why international collaboration is vital to achieve real progress. Violence is preventable, displacement is preventable, and so all forms of mental and social diseases are preventable; but in order to achieve this prevention we need better data, deeper analysis and improved policies. Only when violence against women is properly brought to light together with the available data – only then they can be used to influence policy and programmes to respond to and prevent violence.

References

Lindsey, C. (2001) 'Executive summary', in *Women Facing War*, Study on the Impact of Armed Conflict on Women, International Committee of the Red Cross (ICRC), Geneva, Switzerland

Lyamzina, Y. (2011) *Political Violence and its Impact on Female Civil Population: Prevention of Health Damage as a Result of Terrorism, Political Violence and its Impact on Civil Population, with Special Focus on Women.* Saarbrücken, Germany: Lambert Academic Publishing.

Me, A. (2012). The impact of statistics on decision making related to law enforcement and crime prevention. Power Point Presentation, INEGI Conference 2012, Vienna, UNODC.

Project Plowshares (2007) 'Summary', in *Project Plowshares Armed Conflicts Report*. Waterloo, Canada.

United Nations Security Council resolution 1325 (2000) on Women, Peace and Security.

UN Women (2012). www.unwomen.org, accessed 02 June 2012.

UNODC (2011) *Global Study on Homicide, United Nations Office on Drugs and Crime*. Vienna, Austria: United Nations Office on Drugs and Crime.

WHA (1996) 'Prevention of violence: a public health priority', WHA49.25, World Health Assembly, Geneva, Switzerland, available at www.who.int/violence_injury_prevention/resources/publications/en/WHA4925_eng.pdf (accessed 28 January 2013).

WHO (2002) *The World Report on Violence and Health*, World Health Organization, Geneva, Switzerland, available at www.who.int/violence_injury_prevention/violence/world_report/en (accessed 28 January 2013).

WHO (2009) *Women and Health: Today's Evidence, Tomorrow's Agenda.* Geneva, Switzerland: World Health Organization.

Part III
From disintegrity to ethical concern
Cases and issues

Introduction

Prue Taylor

It has so often been said that we only appreciate what we have once we have lost it. In this age, in which we are now confronting collapse, we have moved from a phase of presaging and warning of great harm to observing it unfold. How will we respond? How *must* we respond?

The concept of ecological integrity provides us with critical guidance in this next phase of human–nature relations. First and foremost, it reminds us that our value system is at the core of our problems and therefore must be the lodestar of our solutions. Laura Westra has defined the principle of integrity, as a first order moral principle, in these terms: 'The first moral principle is that nothing can be moral that is in conflict with the physical realities of our existence or cannot be seen to fit within the natural laws of our environment in order to support the primacy of integrity' (Westra, 1998: 11). Second, the moral principle of integrity must drive the design of policy and law. It cannot be compromised or traded off in favour of political, economic or other presumed advantage.

> If integrity is an ultimate value and if the principle of morality based upon it is not open to trade-offs or negotiations because of its fundamental connection to life and life support, then we need to design second-order principles following upon it, so that we can use the principle of integrity in personal morality and in public policy.
>
> (Ibid.: 12)

The chapters in Part III reflect upon the moral basis for disintegrity and offer insights into how we can, and should, move beyond this state. Out of various instances of ecological degradation comes the prospect of learning how to do things very differently; to re-chart our moral course and redesign our public policy and law, and stick with it. Experience will now be our best teacher.

In Chapter 11, János I. Tóth uses the largest ecological disaster in Hungarian history (the 'red sludge disaster' of 2010) as a case study for clarifying the underlying reasons for these events. By examining pre- and post-disaster behaviour of key actors, he demonstrates how the drive for profit justifies the externalization of the costs of social and environmental protection. While this is not a new observation, the case study cogently demonstrates how the state (and its agencies) openly prefer the interests of the corporate sector over those of communities and the environment. The closeness of this relationship between the state and the market, together with new harmful technologies expose us to ecological harms of vastly increased spatial and temporal dimensions. Tóth observes that we cannot presume that the corporate sector or the state will act in a morally responsible manner. Thus, disasters of this kind are simply waiting to happen! In Hungry, at least, the disaster seems to have spurred an appropriate response. A new government has imposed harsh penalties and passed a new law to prevent state agencies from favouring corporations.

In Chapter 12, Janice Gray traces the history of water management (in the Murray–Darling river basin of Australia) through the use of tradable water permits and an increasingly complex co-management regime. She questions whether, from a number of perspectives, this approach to environmental regulation could be consistent with attaining ecological integrity. She demonstrates how the values that underpin market mechanisms and the property rights that they give rise to may threaten ecological integrity. Gray argues that we have an important opportunity to learn from the experience of water trading in Australia – that it should not be adopted in other water catchments without a more comprehensive analysis and understanding of its implications. Interestingly, the normative inadequacies of water trading can assist us in better appreciating the strengths of communal property regimes. Gray's chapter opens the door to the growing literature on commons governance and Earth jurisprudence.

Reference

Westra, L. (1998) *Living in Integrity*. Lanham, MD: Rowman Littlefield.

11 Key actors of the red sludge disaster in Hungary

János I. Tóth

Introduction

The case study refers first to the concrete, specific and single case, but science is also interested in the abstract and general character (Flyvbjerg, 2011). The difference between the single and concrete case and general character means an old philosophical problem. A case study allows the following type of generalization: 'If it *is* valid for this case, it *may be* valid for all (or many) cases.' So the case study says what *is* true for a mining company *may be* true for all mining companies that caused some kind of environmental pollution. I think that the method of the case study is a very productive and heuristic method which leads to interesting hypotheses, but, of course, not theses. These hypotheses are needed for further research to confirm.

All industrial accidents (e.g. the Bhopal gas tragedy in 1984, the Exxon Valdez oil spill in 1989, the Baia Mare cyanide spill in 2000) have common actors: the *polluter*, the *victims* and the *environmental protection agency*. In this chapter I will study the behaviour of these three key actors of the red sludge disaster in Hungary. This disaster occurred on 4 October 2010 when a reservoir burst at the huge Ajka Timföldgyár Zrt. aluminium plant, located around 165 kilometres southwest of Budapest. The Ajka alumina factory was taken over by Hungarian Aluminium Production and Trade Company (MAL Co. Ltd).

We expect the company to be liable, and the agency to be working fairly. Theoretically just or fair government agency should balance the interests of the company and the local residents (potential victims). The case of toxic sludge catastrophe in Hungary shows that the company (MAL) worked negligently and the authority was permissive to the company. The government agency prefers the interests of the big company to the local residents (potential victims). In my opinion, these problems are not only characteristic of the MAL, but usually of the big companies and their regulating authorities, as well.

International outlook

Aluminium is produced from bauxite in two stages. Stage 1 is converting bauxite to alumina by Bayer process. Stage 2 is converting alumina to aluminium by the Hall–Heroult process. Bauxite is one of the (not very common) components of the Earth's crust. It is produced by surface mining. The world's three top bauxite producer countries are Australia, China and Brazil. In 2003, Hungary was ranked as sixteenth largest bauxite producer in the world, with about half a million tonnes a year. Later this value dropped by half since then, as today, only MAL produced bauxite in Hungary (Jávor and Hargitai, 2011: 124–5).

Bauxite contains a mix of minerals, including aluminium, iron oxides and titanium dioxides. It is dug out of the ground and washed with hot sodium hydroxide as part of the Bayer process, invented in the nineteenth century. This extracts the aluminium oxide, or alumina, from the ore that is subsequently used to produce pure aluminium. The waste, known as *red mud*, is a mix of solid impurities, heavy metals such as cadmium, cobalt and lead, and the processing chemicals. The caustic mixture can burn skin on prolonged contact and is an environmental liability, and is difficult to store (Jha, 2010). During the production of four tonnes of bauxite, four tonnes of red mud is formed, while only one tonne of aluminium can be produced.[1]

The biggest challenge for every alumina producer is the proper red mud storage. Presently this by-product cannot be processed or recycled in an economic and efficient way. Some countries, such as France, Greece and Japan, still dispose washed red mud slurry into the sea, saying that alkali contents of red slurry is neutralized by certain components of seawater. This solution is not allowed by EU laws; however, France has gained permission for sea disposal until 2015. According to data provided by Red Mud Project, today only seven of the world's 84 alumina plants dispose of red mud into the sea.[2]

Mainland storing technology depends on environmental conditions to some extent. Previously, only diluted red mud was pumped out and it was left to thicken and dry by itself, however, without proper protection towards the subsoil, it could easily result in the contamination of the environment, particularly of the ground water. That is why reservoirs with double, membrane polymer and clay isolation are widespread, as this way toxic materials cannot leak out to the environment.

During the thickening process, the alkaline fluid, which accumulates on the surface as a 'surplus', is normally driven back to the alumina plant. Dry red mud storing, which poses less environmental risk, is also becoming more and more common. For example, several Australian companies (Queensland Alumina Limited, Rio Tinto Alcan Gove Alumina Plant and Yarwun Plant) reduce alkalinity of red mud down to pH 9 by a relatively new process using seawater. In the three alumina plants of the United States (in Texas and Louisiana) they use more modern but expensive technology (Jávor and Hargitai, 2011: 127).

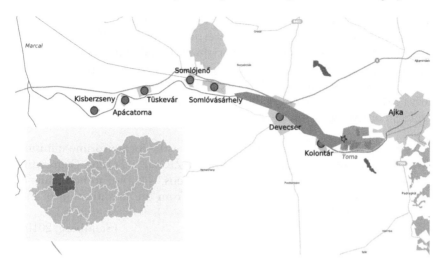

Figure 11.1 Maps about red sludge disaster

Source: © OpenStreetMap contributors, CC-BY-SA; Juhasz peter; G ambrus;
http://en.wikipedia.org/wiki/File:Ajkai_vörösiszap-katasztrófa_vázlat_2010-10-04.svg

A widespread drying method in the US is to settle red mud and remove water from the surface continuously. According to experts, in the United States an industrial disaster similar to the one happened in Hungary cannot occur even in case of a breach in the dam, as the dry material could not flow out. Besides the USA, dry storing is also widespread in some Australian and Brazilian alumina plants. In China, about 10 per cent of the red mud is reused they produce bricks out of it. In Japan, bauxite is enriched before the Bayer process in order to reduce the quantity of red mud produced at the end (Jávor and Hargitai, 2011: 128).

There has never been a similar accident to the Kolontar catastrophe in the world. Wet red mud reservoirs usually damage the environment with a leakage towards the subsoil. The Kolontár Report collected a few similar major industrial accidents (the Buffalo Creek flood; dioxin poisoning in Seveso; the tragedy in Bhopal; an oil disaster in the Gulf of Mexico; the accident of the Prestige crude oil tanker; the accident at Baia Mare and the cyanide contamination of the river Tisza; Jávor and Hargitai, 2011: 132–9).

Short description of the disaster by MAL

The Hungarian Aluminum Production and Trade Company (MAL Co. Ltd) is a significant player in Hungarian economy. It is one of the largest employers in the region, and together with its suppliers it provides jobs to 6,000 people. MAL is 100 per cent in Hungarian ownership. Its registered capital is €10 million (HUF3 billion).

The present ownership structure was established in a relatively complicated process under a socialist government (between 1995 and 1997). The Ajka alumina factory, which was originally founded in 1943, was taken over by MAL, a company set up in 1995 following the widespread privatisation of the industry in the 1990s. According to the Hungarian ecological party (LMP), 'guided privatization' occurred (Jávor and Hargitai, 2011: 21). Stefan Steinberg noted that:

> A key figure in the privatisation process was the former prime minister and leader of the social democratic MSZP party, Ferenc Gyurcsany. Gyurcsany, one of Hungary's richest citizens, is known to have gained part of his own huge personal fortune from the privatisation of the aluminium industry.
>
> (Steinberg, 2010)

MAL (similarly to other firms) produces alum earth by the Bayer technology. The MAL stored this mixed material (red mud and alkaloids) in various containment ponds. In the MAL factory 700,000 tonnes of red mud is formed every year, and in total 14.5 million tonnes of this material is stored from previous production. The disposal and neutralizing of this quantity would cost an enormous amount of money, and the company did not even put any effort towards trying it. This hazardous waste is a constant and growing threat on the surroundings.

On 4 October 2010, at 12:05pm, one of the reservoir walls ruptured and a lot of toxic sludge was released. About 1.8 million m^3 of strongly alkaline (pH 13) liquid red sludge flooded out to cover nearby settlements and 4,000 hectares (40 km^2, or 15 square miles) in area. This section of reservoir (measuring 300m × 500m) belongs to MAL Co. Ltd. In this section the amount of alkaline above the red mud with the depth of 6–7 metres was 1 million tonnes. The waste reservoir is at a height of 50–60 metres above the village. The toxic wave reached the first village, Kolontar in five minutes where 8 people drowned in the 2 metre high liquid. In the meantime the death of 2 people and other injuries was caused by the caustic effect of the alkali. If the rupture of the dam had happened at night, the catastrophe would have been more serious.[3]

Ten people lost their lives in the disaster and 406 needed medical care, of which 120 were seriously injured. More than 300 families (731 people) lost their homes. The settlements of Kolontár, Devecser and Somlóvásárhely were the worst affected by the disaster. The flood swept away everything – cars, tractors, fences. The damage to agriculture and the environment was also significant because red sludge flooded the Torna brook; thus it covered nearby settlements and 4000 hectares, including 1,036 hectares of agricultural land.[4] Hungarian authorities report that a total of 7,000 people have been affected. It was Hungary's largest ever industrial and environmental catastrophe.

Key players of industrial catastrophe

All industrial accidents have common actors, which are briefly summarized as follows: the *polluter* (or company causing damage, in this case MAL); *victims*, which are usually neighbouring inhabitants and other companies, maybe future generations and non-human beings); *environmental protection agencies* (governmental organizations, which may be local, regional, national or global); and also disaster management agencies, courts, environmental organizations (non-governmental organizations), media, insurance companies and banks. First, I am examining the behaviour of the top three players before and after the disaster. Then I will try to outline some morals of it. From the facts investigated, a strong hypothesis can be formulated considering MAL, while only a weak one can be formulated considering the other companies.

Behaviour of MAL before the pollution

Seven empirical facts in relation to the behaviour of MAL before the pollution:

1. As for waste disposal, MAL's technology operation was not sustainable. It constantly produced extreme alkaline red mud sludge. At least the alkali recycling should have been resolved. During the handling of the waste, the MAL did not use the best available technology (the so called dry technology; Report, 2011: 20).
2. Concerning the highly alkaline sludge disposal, MAL did not comply with its own rules. Approximately 6 metres of liquid alkali base was on the solid red mud, while a maximum thickness of 1 metre was allowed. Less fluid would cause less damage (Jávor and Hargitai, 2011: 53).
3. The MAL previously reached an agreement with the authorities, which stated that the red mud pond should *not be considered hazardous* waste reservoir.
4. The subsequent analysis of the available satellite images showed that the north-western wall of the reservoir was moving steadily: a centimetre per year. Such examinations could have been performed even before the tragedy. However, before the disaster neither the management nor the inspection of authorities examined these images (Jávor and Hargitai, 2011: 30–1).
5. MAL had not prepared a reserve safety barrier which would have stopped the movement of alkaline sludge.
6. There were warning signs that the company ignored. The day before the red sludge broke out the MAL safety instruments showed abnormal readings. These instruments gave the alarm warning half an hour before the accident occurred.
7. MAL liability insurance did not cover the victims that are the insurer was not paying anyone.

There are strong hypotheses in relation to the behaviour of MAL before the pollution. Steinberg averred that 'The cause of the catastrophe was the drive for profit' (Steinberg, 2010). MAL wanted to solve environmental safety at the lowest possible cost:

> Dumping the red sludge costs virtually nothing: the toxic slurry is stored in a reservoir whose walls are made out of slag, ashes, or soil, and is occasionally covered with sewage-sludge or other, also harmful waste under the pretext of recultivation.
>
> (ibid.)

Because of lower costs, MAL's profits increase; on the other hand, it enhances the firm's competitiveness. The behaviour of MAL is not characterized by corporate social responsibility (CSR). MAL follows up the practice of the 'private profit and social risk (and cost)'.

There are weak hypotheses in relation to polluters, such as that all (mining) companies caused some kind of environmental pollution wanted to solve environmental safety at the lowest possible cost. We know this behaviour has characterized several companies (e.g. BP wanted to solve environmental safety at the lowest possible cost, and this arguably resulted in the Deepwater Horizon oil spill). So this weak (or working) hypothesis can be verified (or not) by the further research. Environmentalists remind us that it is often cheaper for these companies to take risks than to invest into environment protection, this being a form of socialization of risks and privatization of benefits.

No doubt firms in a competitive market should continue to reduce their costs and thus the environmental security-related costs will be reduced. Under the capitalist system many experts consider the issue of environmental protection hopeless. So, some radical environmentalist movements (e.g. deep ecology, social ecology, bioregionalism) refuse the capitalist system itself. I consider this problem more sophisticated. I think the market competition has a dual effect on the environment. The reduction in costs in general increases the environmental efficiency, and this is *good and useful*. On the other hand, reduction in 'environmental costs' (that is in environmental security-related costs) is *harmful and bad*. For example, MAL should have built an emergency dike (barrier), which increases the (environmental) cost of production, but it would be necessary from an environmental point of view.

Environmental protection should *support* market competition in general, but it should *prevent* market competition in certain domains (related to 'environmental costs'). So we must accept that there are environmental costs where the logic of free market should not be used. (Modern capitalism has recognized that the *labour cost* as a special cost, where the market considerations have limitations.)

From the point of view of the economy, the pollution caused by MAL was a *negative externality*. The concept of an externality is central issue for environmental economics. We can speak about externality if the economic activity in question involves participants (third parties or stakeholders) who do not take part in the market transaction. In this case we are faced with the danger that advantages arising from (direct) market activities are enjoyed exclusively by market actors (e.g. owners, managements, workers, consumers), while the disadvantages are suffered by indirect or non-market actors (particularly local residents).

Economic experts think that direct advantages (i.e. profit of the owners) or indirect advantages (i.e. creation of jobs or satisfaction of consumers' needs) always exceed the negative effects of an enterprise in which local residents are involved mainly. The issue of externality is regarded implicitly as of secondary importance in the current economic practice. Liberal economists often assume that the positive and negative externalities are balancing each other on social level, and that externalities in the private economy are insignificant. Laissez-fare economists such as Friedrich Hayek and Milton Friedman refer to externalities as the 'neighbourhood effect'. In the past this opinion might have been be true. Externalities may, however, be neither small nor localized.

A new situation has developed with the modern technology, as several authors emphasized (Ellul, 1964; Jonas, 1984; Daly, 1999). The effective potential of technology is increasing remarkably and is affecting people who live far away in space (in the other countries) and in time (the next generations). Because of this, society has to pay more and more attention to these negative effects which exist through non-market mediation. Society, of course, has numerous ways to force these firms to obey environment protection laws: the proper formulation of rules, the harsh punishment of rule-breakers, and so on.

The behaviour of MAL after the pollution

Three empirical facts in relation to the behaviour of MAL after the pollution:

1. After the pollution, MAL claimed that the red mud is not hazardous. Because of the redness, everyone thought that the main composition of the sewage material is red mud. It is true that the red mud is not dangerous in itself, but the effluent sludge (pH 13) was dangerous (Report, 2011: 4).
2. MAL claimed that only a minimal amount of pollutants was leaked. According to MAL, 300,000 m^3 of red mud spilled from the reservoir. The expert that was cited by the ad hoc parliamentary committee stated that the amount of spilled material was 1,644,000 m^3 (ibid.: 4). It is worth mentioning that this amount is much more than the 780,000 m^3 of crude oil released in the Deepwater Horizon oil spill in 2010. Furthermore, at the cyanide pollution of Baia Mare in Romania in year 2000, about

100,000 m³ of material burst out from the containment pond. So in the case of Kolontár there was a substantially bigger amount of pollution.

3. MAL claimed that the company's pollution did not occur due to their fault, but the accident was caused by unforeseen consequences of natural processes and due to faulty government decisions made in the past (i.e. the negative effects on soil stability of the western clay wall ordered to be built earlier, during the communist regime).

Three overall hypotheses about the polluters:

1. The polluting companies try to deny that they caused the pollution.
2. The polluter is always trying to reduce the amount of damage and denies his own responsibility.
3. In general, after environmental disasters you cannot count on the fact that the companies take on their responsibilities. Because of the '*polluter pays principle*', one of the key questions is to determine who is considered a polluter.

Behaviour of potential victims

The mostly poor population living near the reservoir was confident that the company and the agencies ensure environmental safety. The recession and restrictions before the disaster also ruined a number of non-governmental organizations (NGOs), and also governmental organizations (GOs). This weakened the NGOs, which are independent from authorities.

The victims first want rapid compensation from the polluter or the government. The victims are indifferent who will compensate them as long as somebody does. The reason of the catastrophe will turn out at court after a long time because of conflict of interest. During this time there will be no remediation, reconstruction and compensation, or if there is it will happen from public funds.

The polluter company will pay compensation only after a court ruling, and this may take several years. Victims often do not have much money reserve to wait for years for a court decision. Thus, they tend to settle with the polluter company out of court for the amount of compensation which is usually much *smaller* than the actual amount of damages. (It usually happens like this.) This solution is the best for the polluters and *worst for the victims*.

The government (state) can immediately *compensate* victims partially or completely. Therefore, it is best for the victims if the state compensates them immediately and later the state litigates with the polluter. (This happened after MAL's pollution.) This solution is the worst for the polluters, because in this case they are confronted with the state which is much stronger than them; and they are not confronted with the victims which are much weaker. The problem of this solution is that the government could give compensation to the victims from taxpayers' money.

One good solution to these problems would be if the hazardous plants would take out compulsory insurance for these types of risks. On one hand this ensures that victims are compensated immediately, on the other hand, the insurance company will monitor the hazardous company which in turn will increase the environmental safety. Introducing compulsory insurance could raise environmental security itself.

> Interesting security mechanisms are the Swedish and Finnish Environmental Damages Insurances (EDI)....Essential is that the EDI only provides compensation to third parties remaining uncompensated in the event of insolvency of the insured. It is not liability insurance. It can be analyzed as a direct (casualty) insurance take-out by the operator for the benefit of unnamed third parties. EDI does not protect the insured party against liability.
> (Intergovernmental Working Group on Civil Liability, 2002: 4)

Behavior of governmental agencies

Before the pollution

The local government agencies that were controlled by the previous socialist government (2002–2008) *were too lenient towards MAL.* The environmental protection central government agency *abolished the hazardous classification* of the MAL's red mud waste storage on 4 December 2003. Thus MAL's red mud storage facility was (officially) no longer considered hazardous waste reservoir.[5] This caused the inspecting powers of local environmental agency to be significantly reduced (Jávor and Hargitai, 2011: 105).

In addition, Hungarian authorities have never introduced the type of tax known as landfill tax, which is commonplace throughout Europe (Steinberg, 2010). A brief examination of the recent history of the Hungarian aluminium industry makes clear it was only a matter of time before such a disaster took place (ibid.).

The practical relationship of the three main players was that the Hungarian government agency being unjust and unfair prefers the MAL's interests to the local residents (potential victims). The government agency has many reasons to *be lenient towards large companies:*

1. A big company is a major tax payer and also a large employer. These things earn high respect for the company. It is therefore understandable that the agency also favours the company; as the popular slogan from the early 1950s had it, 'What's good for General Motors is good for the USA.' Similarly, certain banks and companies are 'too big to fail' (i.e. so large that their failure will be disastrous to the economy, and which therefore must be supported by government when they face difficulty).

2. Additionally, the companies can *support the political parties* and in return these parties will return favours later. Therefore the large companies could expect favourable treatment from authorities in general (political corruption).
3. Furthermore, several *multinational companies are often more significant economically than the government* wanting to control them, and in these cases it is particularly difficult for the agency to have control over the companies.

Therefore agencies often seek to relieve the companies from responsibility and obligation. One practical consequence of this practice is that big companies try to pass on the damage they have caused to another actors ('private profit and social cost'). So the above conclusion is generally true, because the government agencies prefer big companies to potential victims *in general.*

After the pollution

First, the Parliament set up an ad hoc parliamentary committee of inquiry with the aim of determining responsibility for this environmental disaster in 12 October 2010. According to the parliamentary committee, the directors of MAL and the regional environmental protection authorities were responsible for the tragedy (Report, 2011). The new *conservative government* (elected in 2010) *acted severely* against the MAL Ltd. These hard actions (arrests, nationalized operation, a huge penalties, etc.) shocked the leaders of MAL.

The company has received a record fine for infringement of waste management regulations of around €470 million (HUF135.14 billion). This fine is much higher than the damage (€118 million), and more than the fair value of the company (€10 million). MAL attacked the penalty in legal way.[6] Thus, the magnitude of the penalty and the payment date will be decided by the court. This penalty puts on a strong deterrent effect to all potential polluters.

Eight days after the tragedy (on 13 October) the new government put the activities of the privately-owned company under state supervision (nationalized operation) coordinated by a government commissioner. The plant started production again on 15 October 2010. State supervision was terminated on 30 June 2011.[7] This state supervision creates a strong deterrent effect to all potential polluters.

As a result of the 'pressure' of state supervision the plant introduced *dry technology* in February 2011. The by-product of aluminium production is not strong alkaline liquid red sludge; it is non-caustic material of a solid consistency. This is the best available technology (BAT). However, it produced a new problem: too much red dust in the air. The solution is covering the reservoir.

Since the catastrophe, more than 145,000 people have been working together for remediation and restoration. A more extensive environmental disaster – contamination of the Danube – was averted (by building a damn on the river Marcal, and by using a variety of techniques to neutralize the alkaline content in the water). Reinforcement of dam walls at Kolontár was done using state sources. These dam walls were built soon after the catastrophe, and relatively cheaply. So MAL could have built these earlier, thus avoiding the catastrophe. Later on, two safety barrier dam systems have been built for the reservoirs by the aluminium plant with multi-billion HUF investments. An integrated monitoring system measuring the airborne dust in the region is in operation.[8]

A total of more than 1 million m³ of pollutant material has been removed from central and outer areas, and placed in the designated storage reservoir. The government has allocated almost €118 million (US$157 million or HUF35 billion) to completely rebuild the stricken area. 112 houses were built with state support. Thus, a year after the catastrophe, life in the region was returning to its normal routine.[9]

The tragedy has called attention to a lack of regulatory precision. For example, the fact that the local agencies did not have complete freedom of action because the division of responsibilities was not clear. Therefore the Hungarian Parliament modified its law, and from December 2010 only mining authorities have been able to issue operating licenses for the operation of reservoirs similar to the one at Ajka. This will ensure firm authority, supervision and inspection.

In September 2011 the Hungarian Parliament adopted a new Disaster Management Act. Among other things this make the supervision of plants dealing with materials covered by the Disaster Management Act more effectively. It introduces fines for less serious offences extending the power of agencies to deal with such plants.[10] The Hungarian Parliament passed a law compelling industrial plants to have insurance in case in the course of their operations hazardous material may be released into the environment. The sum paid forms a fund for the insurance companies, and from this they can pay the reinstatement costs of an eventual disaster. The compulsory insurance extends to damage caused by the environment and private individuals.

The latest developments is that this case finally went to court in Veszprem in western Hungary on 24 September 2012. The first hearing was held in the criminal trial. On the first day, the indictment was presented and charges pressed against fifteen suspects in all, one of whom is Zoltan Bakonyi, managing director of the MAL. These individuals have gone on trial having been accused of negligence, waste management violations and damages to the environment due to the 2010 red mud spillage. All defendants were MAL employees at the time of the accident.[11] Many experts think that not only the staff of MAL, but the local authority was also at fault, and they should therefore be charged as well.[12]

MAL has serious difficulties with liquidity since the environmental disaster. Therefore, on 27 February 2013, one of the Hungarian courts ordered that the company be liquidated. A former Hungarian law provides that MAL should get gradually under *state ownership* during continuous production. A new state company is created, which takes over the factory together with the assets and workers.

Notes

1. See http://ozonenetwork.hu/ozonenetwork/20101005-maro-oxidkoktel-55-millio-tonna-vorosiszap-van-a-magyar-tarozokban.html (accessed 4 October 2012)
2. See www.redmud.org/Disposal.html (accessed 4 October 2012).
3. See www.kormany.hu/en/ministry-of-public-administration-and-justice/news/one-year-on-hungary-remembers-the-red-sludge-disaster (accessed 4 October 2012).
4. See www.kormany.hu/en/ministry-of-public-administration-and-justice/news/one-year-on-hungary-remembers-the-red-sludge-disaster (accessed 4 October 2012).
5. See www.europarl.europa.eu/sides/getDoc.do?pubRef=-//EP//TEXT+WQ+E-2010-011083+0+DOC+XML+V0//HU (accessed 4 October 2012).
6. See http://nol.hu/belfold/fellebbez_a_rekordbirsag_ellen_a_mal_zrt_ (accessed 4 October 2012).
7. See www.kormany.hu/en/ministry-of-public-administration-and-justice/news/one-year-on-hungary-remembers-the-red-sludge-disaster (accessed 4 October 2012).
8. See www.kormany.hu/en/ministry-of-public-administration-and-justice/news/one-year-on-hungary-remembers-the-red-sludge-disaster (accessed 4 October 2012).
9. See www.kormany.hu/en/ministry-of-public-administration-and-justice/news/one-year-on-hungary-remembers-the-red-sludge-disaster (accessed 4 October 2012).
10. See http://hvg.hu/itthon/20120328_katasztrofavedelem_bakondi# (accessed 4 October 2012).
11. See www.mnn.com/earth-matters/wilderness-resources/stories/plant-managers-on-trial-for-toxic-mud-spill-in-hungary (accessed 4 October 2012).
12. See http://magyarinfo.blog.hu/2012/09/28/vorosiszap_per_hol_az_allami_felelosseg?utm_source=ketrec&utm_medium=link&utm_content=2012_09_28&utm_campaign=index (accessed 4 October 2012).

References

Daly, H. (1999) 'Uneconomic growth in theory and in fact', First Annual Feasta Lecture, Trinity College, Dublin, 26 April, available at www.feasta.org/documents/feastareview/daly.htm (accessed 28 March 2008).

Ellul, J. (1964) *The Technological Society*. New York: Vintage Books.

Flyvbjerg, B. (2011) 'Case study', in N. K. Denzin and Y. S. Lincoln (eds), *The Sage Handbook of Qualitative Research*, 4th edn. Thousand Oaks, CA: Sage, pp. 301–16.

Intergovernmental Working Group on Civil Liability (2002) 'Economic Commission for Europe: Meeting of the parties to the convention on the protection and use of transboundary watercourses and international lakes', Geneva, 11–13 November, Working paper MP.WAT/AC.3/2002/WP.23, CP.TEIA/AC.1/2002/WP.23, available at www.unece.org/fileadmin/DAM/env/documents/2002/wat/ac3/ mp.wat.ac.3.2002.wp.23.e.pdf (accessed 28 January 2013).

Jávor, B. and Hargitai, M. (eds) (2011) *The Kolontár Report. Causes and Lessons from the Red Mud Disaster, Budapest,* March, p. 127, available at http://lehetmas.hu/ wp-content/uploads/2011/05/Kolontar-report.pdf (accessed 28 January 2013).

Jha, A. (2010) 'Hungary toxic sludge spill an "ecological catastrophe" says government', *The Guardian,* 5 October, www.guardian.co.uk/world/2010/oct/05/ hungary-toxic-sludge-spill (accessed 28 January 2013).

Jonas, H. (1984) *The Imperative of Responsibility: In Search of an Ethics for the Technological Age.* Chicago, IL: University of Chicago Press.

Report (2011) *Jelentés: A Kolontár melletti vörösiszap-tározó átszakadása miatt bekövetkezett környezeti katasztrófával kapcsolatos felel sség feltárását és a hasonló katasztrófák jöv beni megakadályozását célzó országgy lési vizsgálóbizottsága vizsgálatának eredményér l,* report of the Parliamentary Committee, available at www.parlament.hu/irom39/ 04795/04795.pdf (accessed 28 January 2013).

Steinberg, S. (2010) 'Toxic sludge catastrophe in Hungary', *World Socialist Web Site,* 8 October, available at www.wsws.org/articles/2010/oct2010/hung-o08.shtml (accessed 28 January 2013).

12 Dollars and dreams

Legal aspirations and report cards in the Murray–Darling Basin of Australia

Janice Gray

Introduction

By at least the 1980s, it was well recognized that Australia's terrestrial water resources were in trouble. A mix of natural and human pressures had led to their degradation (NWC, 2011c; COAG, 2012). The decade-long drought of the twenty-first century and a developing understanding of climate change later heightened the sense of crisis in water management, law and policy.

In response to the increasing pressures on water, new water legislation was introduced across Australian State and Territory jurisdictions from the late 1980s onwards. One of the key tools it used was trading. The dream was that ultimately the dollar, through the market, would help remedy water management problems by reallocating water resources more efficiently. Simultaneously eco-system health would improve and ecologically sustainable outcomes would be achieved. Water would be moved from low-value to high-value use because users, driven by efficiency concerns, would trade their water access rights under a cap and trade scheme, thus reallocating resources (COAG, 1994). Profligate use would diminish, judicious use would triumph and terrestrial water health would improve. Heavily water-dependent crops would not be grown because it would be uneconomical to do so.

When it emerged that the State- and Territory-based legal and regulatory reforms alone could not adequately solve scarcity sharing problems, nor effectively address related environmental concerns (such as blue-green algal blooms; NWC, 2011b), a sense of urgency escalated. A piecemeal State and Territory approach to protecting the culturally and environmentally significant Murray–Darling Basin (MDB) was not enough; a 'whole of government' approach was necessary. Progressively, the Commonwealth extended its role, and in 2007 it passed the Water Act 2007 (Cth), which, given the constitutional position in Australia whereby water is a States' matter, marked a significant turning point in co-operative management. The Act, like the various State and Territory Acts with which it interdependently operates, also relies on water trading as a tool of management.

This chapter evaluates the MDB governance model by reference to the trading mechanism and in keeping with the theme of this book explores the viability of ecological integrity under this market model. The chapter makes four main points:

1. despite the current romance with water trading as a tool of water management, the rationale for its introduction was inadequately interrogated, meaning that market-based mechanisms were insufficiently thought through prior to implementation;
2. the complexities of the multi-layered governance regime in the MDB pose problems although their objectives are praiseworthy;
3. the effectiveness of the water trading regime may, in operation, be more problematic than is commonly thought; and
4. in conclusion, caution and circumspection are to be encouraged regarding the adoption of water markets. Water trading may depend on values that are incompatible with wider social, environmental and policy goals and market values may threaten rather than serve, ecological integrity.

Background

In order to highlight the significance of the MDB this section provides some background details.

The MDB is Australia's food bowl. It starts in Queensland and stretches across New South Wales, Victoria and South Australia. It covers over one million square kilometres and accounts for 65 per cent of Australia's irrigated land. The Basin is economically and socially significant, generating approximately 40 per cent of the national income derived from agricultural production (MDBA, undated a). Over two million people live in the MDB including approximately 30 Aboriginal nations who have had spiritual and other connections to its land and water for thousands of years (MDBA, undated b; CSIRO, 2008).

Much of the MDB is listed under the Ramsar Convention while its birdlife is recognized under international migratory bird agreements (for example, the Republic of Korea–Australia Migratory Bird Agreement, or ROKAMBA, of 2007). Using a traditional ecosystem services typology, the Basin potentially provides a high level of services across all four categories of: provisioning; regulating; supporting and; cultural but to fulfil that potential it needs to receive greater volumes of environmental water and lose less to abstractions (CSIRO, 2012, tables 1.2 and 3.1).

Why water trading?

From about 1994 onwards the view that the market would be better equipped than the pre-existing system of public administration to deal with the

158   *Janice Gray*

severe environmental problems threatening water resources, gained currency. The development of a legal framework that facilitated the sharing of water scarcity through the trading of water access rights became a priority (Gardner *et al.*, 2009: 511).

The shift in favour of trading did not, however, occur in isolation. A broader international trend towards neo-liberalism was underway. Market deregulation, state decentralization and reduced state intervention into economic affairs, all neo-liberal tropes, had won favour (Lash and Urry, 1987; Harvey, 2005; Chomsky, 1999) and a more conservative monetarist discourse linked to rational expectation theories emerged (Heilbroner and Milberg, 1995).

Australia was not immune from these developments (Quiggan, 1999) and institutional change embracing neoliberalism (and privatization) became evident in sectors such as banking and telecommunications. Governments' willingness to fund large-scale (water) infrastructure development also declined. Both globally and domestically, faith in the power of the market increased. Markets were fashionable. Meanwhile, environmentalists and key policy makers worldwide had begun to argue that water management needed serious re-thinking. Global demand had begun to outstrip supply and water stress was evident. Water availability was being mooted as the new flashpoint.

The genealogy of environmentally water-focused calls for change may be seen internationally in:

- the United Nations (UN) 1972 Stockholm Conference which drew the connection between economic development and degraded physical environments;
- the UN's 1987 Brundtland Report which argued for sustainable development over simple economic growth;
- the 1992 Dublin Principles which set out four principles to help address over-consumption, pollution and other threats arising from water use;
- the 1992 Rio Earth Summit, which affirmed a commitment to environmental sustainability in Agenda 21 where the importance of 'the holistic management of freshwater…and the integration of sectoral water plans and programmes within the framework of national economic and social policy' was supported;
- the series of World Water Forums commencing in Marrakech in 1996 which highlighted the depletion of potable water supplies; and
- The Hague Declaration on Water Security, which argued that 'business as usual' was not an option if there was to be water security in the twenty-first century (Gardner *et al.*, 2009: 519–21).

But how, in the 1990s and beyond, was environmentally sustainable water development to be achieved and what type of reform was needed in Australia? The answer which received the most strident support was that the market and trading would provide the panacea. Water reform was married to market economics, creating a new model of water governance in which water access rights were separated from rights in land so the former could be-fashioned as independent property rights (COAG, 1994). The process reflected the trend towards 'unbundling', the phenomenon whereby rights are broken down into their component parts.

Yet despite the obvious shift towards a market-based approach to water governance, it was notable that the policy documents of the time did not clearly enunciate the reason *why* such an approach should be favoured over others. Policy documents tended simply to highlight the failings of previous water management approaches, outline the desired outcome (such as sustainable use and better water sharing) and then assert that trading would lead to improvements (Gardner *et al.*, 2009: 525). The rationale behind the introduction of water trading was treated as largely self-evident.

Accordingly, scholars have been left to comb the literature in search of what might amount to a rationale. The literature noted that markets: moved water from low-value to high-value use; benefitted irrigators financially; facilitated flexibility of operations; and encouraged sustainable irrigation production, for example (MDBC, 2008). Yet this list comprises potential *outcomes* rather than a *rationale* and whether these outcomes may be attributed to trade alone is contestable. Some of the above benefits would appear to arise from the movement of water itself, not necessarily from trading (Gardner *et al.*, 2009: 526). Similarly, key water instruments such as the NWI Agreement (NWI, 2004), focused on the *methods* by which water management would be achieved rather than articulating a rationale.

Without clear articulation of the justifications for the introduction of trading it is difficult to establish why trading, rather than another model, would produce better results.

> Conventional sustainability thinking provides ways of talking about the environment as an important policy issue, or about key actors within the world system. It does not suggest the need for any fundamental change to that system.
>
> (Adams and Jeanrenaud, 2008: 31)

Why, then, was the justification for water trading not further interrogated and what is the likely impact of not doing so?

Arguably, desperation drove the dream that terrestrial water health could be restored through a legal regime dependent on financial arrangements, trading and markets. Perhaps a 'yearning for a regulatory imaginary' (Szersynksi, 2012) dominated the agenda because the stark realities of water mismanagement appeared so insurmountable. That aspiration for a new way forward in the face of a seemingly bleak water future was arguably so powerful that the market was enthusiastically embraced by policy makers, the parliament and the public alike without sufficiently thorough, balanced and specific investigation. The market represented hope in desperate times but in retrospect, was perhaps only old laissez-faire principles dressed up as a 'new salvation' (Winterson, 2012) and tempered with some regulation. Enthusiastic adoption of the market arguably reflected frustration and an eagerness to 'do' something but a better path may have been first to consider how the disconnection between environmental markets and ecological sustainability would impact on outcomes. Given that water trading was to be underpinned by the legal concept of property rights, it may also have been prudent to analyse more carefully whether property rights in their present (or recast) form, are actually capable of supporting trading and simultaneously fostering sustainability (Taylor and Grinlinton, 2011: 5).

Depending on trading as an innovative water management tool also raises a methodological dilemma, evident in the bioscience and bio-technology spheres, and known as Collingridge's dilemma. The dilemma is that 'when change is easy, the need for it cannot be foreseen; when the need for change is apparent, change has become expensive, difficult and time consuming' (Collingridge, 1980; Marris and Rose, 2010). The dilemma concerns the issue of control and recognizes that although it is ideal to build in safeguards at the initial stages of innovation, it is very difficult to incorporate them when we do not know and cannot easily predict what problems may exist, until the technology has been extensively adopted. At the beginning of a project, (for example, the reconceptualization stage of new water governance) there is usually quite a deal of flexibility but the paths ultimately become set by the implementation and flexibility falls away. If Collingridge's dilemma is applicable to water trading, it may mean that negative environmental impacts from trading will not necessarily be protected against. It may also mean that the state will find it difficult to redistribute water entitlements because it has become 'hollowed-out', managing water indirectly through a system of signals and semaphores that link to the market (Gunningham and Grabosky, 1998; 2009: 4; Black, 2007: 58; Levi-Faur, 2005; Gray, J., 2011). Such results may not have been foreseen at a time when change was possible. There may have been significant unknown unknowns which even tools such as public participation or extended research, for example, cannot readily later address.

The solution is not to avoid all innovation, but rather to weigh carefully the reason for the introduction of the innovation against the possible ill-effects of inadequate safeguards. If, on balance, the risk is worth taking, then it should be taken. Without a clearly articulated and interrogated rationale for water trading such an assessment could not easily be made.

Complex governance

We now turn to the MDB water trading governance framework in order to evaluate its capacity and performance for the report card, observing that its complexity may inhibit environmentally sustainable outcomes.

In the post-NWI era a complex, multi-layered and multi-jurisdictional system of participatory governance and regulation developed. It operates at Federal, Basin State, regional and localized zone levels. Its backbone is a series of State-based frameworks entwined with a newer, over-arching Commonwealth framework. Potential inconsistencies exist between those frameworks leaving the governance structure difficult to negotiate and open to accusations of unwieldiness (Gray, J., 2012: 338).

The MDB trading framework includes the Commonwealth Water Act 2007 (Cth) (including the MDB Agreement, the MDB Plan and associated Trading and Market Rules); State water legislation; water resource plans under the Commonwealth Act and State legislation (including additional specific trading rules); water rights under State water legislation; and relevant international agreements. Many instruments are highly dependent on mandatory consultation and advice ranging from local statutorily created planning groups through to the Australian Consumer and Competition Council (ACCC) (Tan, 2006; Fisher, 2010; Gray, J., 2012). However, it has proved difficult to protect environmental concerns when the governance instruments permit decision-makers themselves to decide on the weight to be given to the environment and competing economic and social factors (Fisher, 2006). Usually the environment loses out (Bonyhady, 2012).

The key tradeable water rights are 'entitlements' and 'allocations'. They may be traded in and between the eighteen MDB trading zones existing for management purposes. An entitlement is the generic term to describe a perpetual share in a variable consumptive pool of water while an allocation describes the actual amount of water credited to a holder's account in any given water year (NWC, 2011b: 2). As the volume in the consumptive pool varies according to the annual water determination, the allocation is variable. Other rights which are potentially tradeable include extraction components, delivery and irrigation rights, options contracts and spill reliability allocations (Gray, J., 2012: 332).

In creating a plethora of tradeable rights (commonly upheld as a positive thing), the unbundling process has arguably led to a tyranny of choice, causing vendors and purchasers to incur additional expense investigating: (a) the range of water products available for transfer; and (b) the multi-stepped procedures to effectuate such transfers (ACCC, 2010). With the use of intermediaries, such as brokers (largely unregulated) and lawyers, trans-actional costs have increased, obscuring some of the alleged benefits of trading (NWC, 2011a: 117–25).

The complexity of the legislation along with the mandatory, consultative and approval processes, advice and plan requirements places enormous stress on the trading framework to produce improved water outcomes. The weight of consultation, approvals and compliance requirements is heavy. One criticism of the preceding public administration system was that the supporting bureaucracy was cumbersome. It would be ironic if the requirements for a regulated market proved similarly unwieldy and retarded positive environmental outcomes.

The report card: perceptions and reality

The common impression of the legal and regulatory framework for water trading is the panegyrized one, often provided by State and Federal agencies who, for example, refer to trading as 'a major success story in water policy reform' (NWC, 2011c: xi) or conclude that 'the ability to trade has delivered real benefits to individual water users, water-dependent industries and the environment' (NWC, 2011a, web introduction). However, it is worth interrogating the veracity of such claims through an examination of barriers to trade, trading figures, the normative value of trading, property rights and Earth jurisprudence.

Barriers to trade

Barriers to trade represent a source of dissatisfaction on both sides of the trading divide (NWC, 2012: xiv). The requirement that an approval to trade be dependent on the holding of associated rights is seen by some, for example, as (at best) a precaution to help maintain integrated water/catchment management, while to others it is a restriction inhibiting the flexibility that unbundling arguably provides.

The inadequacy of metering represents a very practical barrier to trade (ACCC, 2010: iii). One obvious consequence is that it is difficult to account accurately and water theft may go unnoticed, reducing the need to acquire water by trading and consequently skewing market outcomes. If the market is by-passed, it is hard to see how it can even begin to deliver promised environmental outcomes.

Interpreting the trading figures

Although trading has influenced water use at regional and local levels 'reductions in regional water use due to trading comprised less than 10% of total water use' between 1998–1999 and 2008–2009 (NWC, 2010: vii). Drought accounted for more reductions and while reports laud the fact 'that water trading has become an essential business tool for irrigators responding to drought and market fluctuations' those same reports fail to emphasize that irrigators no longer have alternative options (NWC, 2011c: 120). The old governance structure has been dismantled and replaced with the new trade-based one.

A breakdown of the trading figures is perhaps useful in assembling the MDB report card. In 2010–2011, there was a drop in entitlement trade of 38 per cent compared with the previous water year. By contrast, water allocation trades increased by 40 per cent in 2010–2011. However, the total value of trades in the Australian market is estimated to have fallen by half from around $3 billion in 2009–2010 to approximately $1.5 billion in 2010–2011 (Gray, J., 2012).

How should these figures be interpreted in relation to economic and environmental goals? It is possible that the allocation figures are, in part, explicable by above average rainfalls following the drought, leading to cheaper water prices because of plentiful supply (NWC, 2011b: x). When water prices fall and transaction costs increase, trade tends to decrease unless the increased transactional costs can be absorbed by the cheaper prices. If they can, cheap water prices may result in large volumes of water being traded into districts for additional crop production (NWC, 2011b: 18), but this may not be ecologically sustainable. The well-watered land on which the crops are grown may be degraded by over-use. Land needs to be nurtured and whether the market and trading paradigm will permit adequate nurturing is highly contestable. Trading is based on exploitation and 'a tension exists between the objectives of sustainability as a concept and its implementation through environmental markets' (Graham, 2011: 158). Further, the oddity of linking 'simultaneous calls for amoral market efficiency alongside calls for caring management' (Shepheard and Martin, 2010) is not really challenged when the focus of water policy and regulation remains one of *balancing* disparate objectives rather than setting environmental standards or embedding responsibilities. When the finite nature of natural resources is treated as infinite and when the environment is regarded as being able to support a continuous growth economy, there is little chance that ecological sustainability will be achieved. The propositions are simply incompatible.

The normative question: is water trading a good thing?

Markets may be effective tools for the distribution and management of many commodities such as cars and houses but whether they are also 'good' for the management of environmental resources, remains contestable (Kuttner, 1997; Gunningham and Grabosky, 1998). According to Graham, the kind of 'instrumentalism and entitlement that characterizes the unsustainable economy also characterizes environmental markets', making markets incapable of delivering sustainable 'people–place' relations (Graham, 2011). It follows that water markets lack the ecological integrity which supports sustainable development.

Yet trading is commonly portrayed as an end in itself where the goal becomes creating ideal market conditions. However, trading is not sacred (Hare, 2009). It is only worthwhile if it contributes to society's well-being. Hence the impact of the market itself and the decisions made to generate ideal conditions need to be assessed. Will market operation and the preparatory decisions supporting it have deleterious effects on other aspects of life? What will be the full effect of separating rights in land from rights in water to facilitate trade? Will it lead to a disconnection between land and water whereby the significance of place is overlooked (Gray, J., 2011: 787; Graham, 2011)? Will moving water from one location to another in order to serve anthropocentric ends permit sensitive responses to the differing biota in each location? Water that is diverted from its usual function in helping to nourish flood plains for example, may not necessarily provide equally valuable benefits in its new location. All water and all land are not the same.

In order to avoid compromising the specific relationship between particular land and water (a relationship possibly threatened by unbundling), modern governance relies on compliance with water plans for trading approval. However, much of the human element supporting environmental memory of the particular, has been diminished by approvals processes which increasingly rely on reduced localism and in which intimate knowledge of the inter-connectedness between people, land and water is less emphasised. Instead markets operate more efficiently without exceptions or discretion for the particular or the local. Flawed as the prior system of public administration may have been, the loss of accreted local knowledge is significant. Introducing the opportunity for greater water anonymity and sameness, increases the risk of marginalizing water's role in specific ecosystems and communities, potentially harming the environment.

Property rights, trading and markets

The subject of trade is usually private property. However, whether tradeable water entitlements and allocations constitute property remains an open question in Australia. The key case in the area, *ICM*, did not decide the matter (Gray, J., 2012). Nevertheless, water rights continue to be traded despite legal uncertainty. Only once the propertization issue is decided will the full range of ramifications emerge, perhaps highlighting Collingwood's dilemma once again.

Basing water trading on (albeit yet to be established) property rights raises at least two questions:

- is there an incompatibility between property rights and sustainability goals?; and
- could property rights be re-fashioned, better to serve environmentally sustainable outcomes?

The acceptance of 'dephysicalized' notions of property (whereby property is understood to be about the relationships between people concerning 'things' rather than rooted in the concrete and physical nature of the thing itself), may assist trading but not necessarily enhance ecological integrity. Permitting property to be conceptualized as an abstract bundle of (severable) rights or as an abstract exclusionary right, may simultaneously 'feed' unsustainable outcomes because the significance of 'people–place' relations is lost

(Graham, 2011: 151–4). If that is so, there would seem to be a fundamental inconsistency between private property and sustainability outcomes.

Further, if property is defined in terms of rights rather than responsibilities and if ownership of property includes the *jus utendi et abutendi*, the property paradigm is unlikely to promote ecological integrity. Why? Because as a Rembrandt could be deliberately abused by a piercing dart, the environment could be abused by the misuse of private property rights in water (Sax, 2001). If property law embraces the right to abuse, environmental harm potentially increases.

Arguably, owners of property can only legitimize the extensive ambit of the impact of the exercise of their property rights (affecting third parties and the environment), if they act on behalf of all humankind; a characterization only possible, it has been suggested, if the *reasons* for property owners' actions are taken into account (Katz, 2012). Yet what constitutes the common good is difficult to define. Given that 'private property allocates power over nature to individual owners' (Freyfogle, 2011: 44) and nature includes water, it becomes necessary either to find ways of reconceptualizing property so that power is not abused or alternatively dispensing altogether with the private property paradigm in relation to water.

Reconceptualization by way of creating new property categories may prove difficult if the *numerus clausus* doctrine (Swadling, 2000), which applies to real property, also applies to water. However, the creation of 'regulatory property' (Gray, K., 2010) perhaps suggests that the law has the capacity to craft new forms of property in relation to water. Yet this may be unnecessary. Another (and perhaps better) alternative is to organize access to water around pre-existing multi-layered, communal property notions; notions commonly rooted in indigenous traditions which emphasize the environment rather than people. Communal property regimes generally have the advantage of being more supportive of values promoting stewardship, the common good and common heritage. They may also reflect greater respect for the finite nature of ecological resources exactly because (rather than in spite of) those resources being part of a common pool (Godden, 2011).

An alternative way forward?

Under the present MDB water governance framework, which relies on trading and traditional concepts of private property, the physical environment needs taming. Engineering, regulatory and legal tools are employed to bring it into submission yet still yield its bounty. The aim is to ensure potentially large volumes of water are captured, moved to places of human priority and exploited. Yet this is environmentally unsympathetic and the Barmah Choke represents an attempt by nature to fight back. The choke in the river prevents application of the trading model to the extent that water simply cannot physically be transferred downstream from the upper reaches of the River Murray in Victoria (NWC, 2011c).

This capacity of nature to resist, assert itself and re-establish its dignity in the face of human interventions is captured in the emerging environmental philosophy of Earth jurisprudence which focuses on an eco-centric concept of an Earth community where living and non-living entities are equally valued. Much pre-existing water law reflects the antithesis of this philosophy as the debate around the MDB Plan indicates (MDBA, 2012). Where the environment is portrayed as a necessary servant to both the economy and society its instrinsic value goes unrecognized as does the importance of the ecological integrity of nature (Burdon, 2012). If MDB water management is adjudged through the lens of Earth jurisprudence, the report card is not positive. Water trading represents an attempt to conquer nature (by moving water from one location to another) rather than co-existing with it in a democratic and holistic way. But how realistic is it to rely on this developing jurisprudence? To many mainstream legal scholars it is risible. The idea that water, for example, might have standing is ludicrous. Yet perhaps change is afoot. In New Zealand, a country renowned for environmental leadership (Taylor and Grinlinton, 2011: 3), under a 2012 preliminary agreement between Whanganui River iwi[1] and the Crown, the Whanganui River will become a legal entity and have a legal voice. The river will be recognized as a person 'in the same way a company is, which will give [it] rights and interests' (Shuttleworth, 2012).

Conclusion: caution and circumspection

This chapter counsels others against adopting the MDB water management model until it has been better analysed and evaluated from a range of perspectives, particularly those beyond government. Although aspects of the model, such as participatory decision making, are positive because they seek to engage communities, policy makers and irrigators, other aspects are more problematic for various reasons. The complex web of legislation and institutional arrangements that is needed to support trans-jurisdictional governance has led to potential inconsistencies between State and Commonwealth law and is unwieldy and expensive to negotiate. The key Commonwealth legislation has been the subject of potential constitutional challenge (Byrne, 2012). The extensive trading approval, compliance and reporting mechanisms are noble in aim, but arguably onerous in application. The volume of water moved under *allocation* trades is relatively high, but is not high under *entitlement* trades which arguably have greater long term impacts and the extensive primary research on trading's impact on communities and the environment (NWC, 2012) needs further unpacking by scholars.

Further, although the water market is presently operational, there is not yet clarification on the legal nature of the entity being traded. Should tradeable water rights prove not to be property, the fiscal ramifications could be far-reaching. Such rights are already the subject of mortgage securities, superannuation portfolios and wills, for example. If tradeble water rights prove not to be property and hence do not attract an extensive sphere of enforceability, they may be devalued. Meanwhile, irrigator traders have been left with few alternatives to trading because the pre-existing water management regime was decommissioned before the property issue was resolved.

Yet there is also strong reason to think that the private property paradigm for water trading and management is not necessarily a good fit. It embraces the values of individualism, exploitation and profit that are arguably antithetical to the protection of the common heritage of humankind and ecological integrity. Perhaps communal property rights that call on ancient (indigenous) histories of stewardship offer an alternative and more effective model for water management in the MDB and elsewhere. They would seem to align more readily with the tenets of Earth jurisprudence and its focus on an eco-centred community which respects human interconnectedness and nature and which a growing field of scholarship sees as foundational to our legal system if the environment is to be well protected for future generations. Accordingly, the MDB report card should perhaps conclude that there is 'room for improvement'.

Note

1. Iwi is the largest social unit in Maori culture. Its meaning is akin to tribe, peoples or nations. See A Ballara, *Iwi: the dynamics of Maori tribal organisations from c 1769–c 1945*, Wellington, NZ, Victoria University Press.

References

ACCC (2010) 'Water trading rules final advice, 2010', Australian Consumer and Competition Council, available at www.accc.gov.au/content/index.phtml/itemId/862714 (accessed 16 October 2012).
Adams, W. M. and Jeanrenaud, S. J. (2008) *Transition to Sustainability: Towards a Humane and Diverse World*. Gland, Switzerland: IUCN.
Black, J. (2007) 'Tensions in the regulatory state' *Public Law*, 58–73.
Bonyhady, T. (2012) 'Putting the environment first?' *Environmental Planning and Law Journal*, 316.
Burdon, P. (2012) 'Earth jurisprudence and the Murray Darling Basin', available at http://ssrn.com/abstract=2067995 (accessed 29 January 2013).
Byrne, E. (2012) 'High Court Rejects Irrigators, Constitutional Challenge' ABC News, 29 November, available at www.abc.net.au/news/2012-11-29/high-court-rejects-irrigators-constitutional-challenge/4398824 Accessed 5 February, 2013.
Chomsky, N. (1999) *Profit Over People: Neoliberalism and the Global Order*. New York: Seven Stories Press.
COAG (1994) 'Water reform framework', Communique from the Meeting of 25 February, Council of Australian Governments, available at www.environment.gov.au/water/publications/action/pubs/policyframework.pdf (accessed 30 October 2012).
COAG (2012) 'Water Climate Change and the Environment', Council of Australian Governments, available at www.coag.gov.au/water_climate_change_and_the_environment (accessed 9 October 2012)

Collingridge, D. (1980) *The Social Control of Technology*. Basingstoke: Palgrave Macmillan.

CSIRO (2012) *Multiple Benefits of the Basin Plan Project*, Commonwealth Scientific and Industrial Research Organisation, available at www.csiro.au/en/Organisation-Structure/Flagships/Water-for-a-Healthy-Country-Flagship/MDB-Multiple-Benefits-Project.aspx (accessed 27 April 2012).

CSIRO (2008) *Water Availability in the Murray-Darling Basin: A Report to the Australian Government from the CSIRO Murray-Darling Basin Sustainable Yields Project*, Commonwealth Scientific and Industrial Research Organisation, available at www.clw.csiro.au/publications/waterforahealthycountry/mdbsy/pdf/Murray-Report.pdf (accessed 10 October 2012).

Fisher, D. E. (2006) 'Markets, water rights and sustainable development', *EPLJ*, 23, 100.

Fisher, D. E. (2010) 'Murray–Darling basin governance: the focus of the law', *The Journal of Water Law*, 21 (4): 145.

Freyfogle, E. (2011) 'Taking property seriously' in D. Grinlinton and P. Taylor (eds) *Property Rights and Sustainability: Toward a New Vision of Property*. Netherlands: Martinus Nijhoff, pp. 43–63.

Gardner, A., Bartlett, R. and Gray, J. (2009) *Water Resources Law*. Sydney, Australia: Lexis Nexis.

Godden, L. C. (2011) 'Communal governance of land resources as a sustainable property institution', in D. Grinlinton and P. Taylor (eds) *Property Rights and Sustainability: Toward a New Vision of Property*. Netherlands: Martinus Nijhoff, pp. 249–72.

Graham, N. (2011) 'The mythology of markets', in D. Grinlinton and P. Taylor (eds) *Property Rights and Sustainability: Toward a New Vision of Property*. Netherlands: Martinus Nijhoff, pp. 149–66.

Gray, J. (2011) 'Water Trading and Regulation in Australia', in A. Saddy and M. Aurilivi Linares (eds), *Derecho de las Infraestructuras: un studio de los distintos mercados regulados [Infrastructure Law: a study of regulated markets]*. Brazil: Lumen Juris.

Gray, J. (2012) 'The legal framework for water trading in the Murray Darling Basin: An overwhelming success?' *Environmental Planning and Law Journal*, 29 (4): 328.

Gray K. (2010) 'Regulatory property and the jurisprudence of quasi trust', *Sydney Law Review*, 32, 237.

Gunningham, N. and Grabosky, P. (1998) *Smart Regulation: Designing Environmental Policy*. Oxford: Oxford University Press.

Gunningham, N. (2009) 'The new collaborative environmental governance: the localization of regulation', *Journal of Law and Society*, 36 (1): 145

Hare, D. (2009) *The Power of Yes*. London: Faber and Faber.

Harvey, D. (2005) *A Brief History of Neoliberalism*. Oxford: Oxford University Press.

Heilbroner, R. and Milberg, W. (1995) *The Crisis of Vision in Modern Economic Thought*. New York: Cambridge University Press.

Katz, L. (2012) 'Spite and extortion: a principle of abuse of (property) rights', *Yale Law Journal*, 122, 100.

Kuttner, R. (1997) *Everything for Sale: The Virtues and Limits of Markets*. New York: Alfred A Knopf.

Lash, J. and Urry, J. (1987) *The End of Organised Capitalism*. Madison, WI: University of Wisconsin Press.

Levi-Faur, D. (2005) 'Regulatory capitalism: the dynamics of change beyond telecoms and electricity', *Governance*, 19 (3): 497–525.

Marris, C. and Rose, N. (2010) 'Open engagement: exploring public participation in the biosciences', *PLoS Biol*, 8 (11), available at www.plosbiology.org/article/info%3Adoi%2F10.1371%2Fjournal.pbio.1000549 (accessed 15 October 2012).

MDBA (undated a) 'About the Basin', Murray Darling Basin Authority, Australian Government, available at www.mdba.gov.au/water/about_basin (accessed 8 October 2011).

MDBA (undated b) 'Explore the Basin', Murray Darling Basin Authority, Australian Government, available at www.mdba.gov.au/explore-the-basin (accessed 9 October 2012).

MDBC (2008) *Brief Assessment of the Merits of Purchasing Water Entitlements During a Time of Low Water*, Murray–Darling Basin Council, available at www2.mdbc.gov.au/__data/page/1327/SERPadvice_water_purchases.pdf (accessed 14 October 2012).

NWC (2010) *The Impacts of Water Trading in the Southern Murray Darling Basin: An Economical, Social and Environmental Assessment Report*, National Water Commission.

NWC (2011a) 'Strengthening Australia's water markets', National Water Commission, available at www.nwc.gov.au/__data/assets/pdf_file/0019/10783/681-NWC_ImpactsofTrade_web.pdf (accessed 12 February 2013).

NWC (2011b) 'Water markets in Australia: trends and drivers 2010–2011, National Water Commission', available at http://apo.org.au/research/australian-water-markets-trends-and-drivers-2007-08-2009-10 (accessed 31 October 2012).

NWC (2011c) 'Water markets in Australia: a short history', National Water Commission, available at http://archive.nwc.gov.au/library/topic/markets/water-markets-in-australia-a-short-history (accessed 24 October 2012).

NWC (2012) 'Impacts of water trading in the southern Murray Darling Basin between 2006–07 and 2010–11', National Water Commission, available at http://archive.nwc.gov.au/site-search?search=1&queries_search_query=Impacts+of+Water+Trading+in+the+Southern+Murray+Darling+Basin+between+2006-07+and+2010-11&submit_button=Search (accessed 27 October 2012).

NWI (2004) 'Intergovernmental Agreement on a National Water Initiative', available at www.nwc.gov.au/reform/nwi (accessed 9 October 2012).

Quiggan, J. (1999) 'Globalisation, neoliberalism and inequality in Australia', *The Economic and Labour Relations Review*, 10 (2): 240.

Sax, J. (2001) 'Playing darts with a Rembrandt', *Public and Private Rights in Cultural Treasures*. Michigan University Press, Michigan, USA.

Shepheard, M. and Martin, P. (2010) 'The political discourse of land stewardship, reframed as a statutory duty', in K. Rubinstein and B. Jessup (eds) *Environmental Discourses in International and Public Law*. Cambridge: Cambridge University Press, pp. 71–95.

Shuttleworth, K. (2012) 'Voice for river in historic signing', *New Zealand Herald*, 31 October, p. 2.

Swadling, S. (2000) 'Opening the numerus clausus', *Law Quarterly Review*, 116, 354

Szersynski, B. (2012) 'Who builds regulatory imagination?', presentation, Centre for Socio-Legal Studies. Oxford: University of Oxford, 13 June

Tan, P.-L. (2006) 'Legislating for adequate public participation in allocation of water in Australia', *Water International*, 31, 21.

Taylor, P. and Grinlinton, D. (2011) in D. Grinlinton and P. Taylor (eds) *Property Rights and Sustainability: Toward a New Vision of Property*. Leiden, Netherlands: Martinus Nijhoff, pp. 1–20.

Winterson, J. (2012) *Why Be Happy When You Could Be Normal?* London: Random House.

Part IV
Integrity and economy

Introduction

Prue Taylor

The direct relationship between monetary policy, economic activity and growing ecological disintegrity has long been a major focus of GEIG. More recently, the global financial crisis has created the opportunity to reconsider the role of the global financial sector in facilitating large-scale ecological and social harm. With crisis comes the opportunity to re-evaluate and make fundamental changes for the better. But crisis also brings the risk of repeating the patterns of the past.

Chapter 13 by Giovanni Ferri discusses the causes of and responses to the global financial and economic crisis of 2007–2009. He demonstrates that beneath the dream of permanent high economic growth lay the reality of a massive debt crisis. The extent of our human hubris is evident in the three inter-related causes that Ferri describes. Further analysis reveals that 'reckless behaviour and a lack of responsibility' drew these factors together with devastating consequences. In the absence of strong leadership, we seem to be on course to experience further economic collapse. Ferri argues that the regulatory response has been too light handed to require and enforce responsible behaviour by the banking and finance sectors. More significantly, he notes that a comprehensive response will require limits to the much vaulted ideal of the free market economy in the form of 'deglobalization'.

Michelle Gallant's chapter follows on from Ferri's by suggesting that a response to the economic recession needs to look beyond the re-regulation of conventional banks. Her chapter considers the role of credit unions and other co-operative financial institutions in creating more financial and economic stability. Gallant argues that their governance principles and structures, based on an ethic of co-operation with community, offer considerable potential. However, in a world dominated by the pursuit of profit, remaining true to the ideals of co-operative governance is proving difficult. Ultimately their continued co-existence with the global financial sector is questionable. In a damning irony, Gallant suggests that they may be, or become, victims of their own success.

Chapter 15, by Geoff Garver, approaches the fundamental issue of living within planetary boundaries by introducing readers to the concept of 'degrowth'. The essence of degrowth is not that a growth economy is impossible because of Earth's biophysical limits – rather, it is that the economy has already exceeded those limits. It is already too big and must therefore 'degrow'. Garver explores the 'degrowth' movement primarily from the perspective of ecological limits to the human economy. A key issue for the nascent movement is that of scale. Global ecological pressures and drivers are a manifestation of diverse cultural and ecological contexts. Consequently, governance responsibilities must be a balance of global and local initiatives. This chapter ends on a positive note with the observation that 'degrowth' may contribute to a profound change in thinking; that we should be growing those things that deliver benefit to all – ecological integrity, respect for life and compassion.

Chapter 16 by Noémie Candiago also addresses the discourse on 'degrowth' and directly applies it to the concept of 'ecological debt' and the search for primary obligation in international law. She argues that drawing upon both could solve the failure of international environmental law, to penetrate and respond to the structural causes of ecological harm and human poverty. Her chapter makes interesting reading for international lawyers concerned that the law still does not articulate a primary obligation (or responsibility) to not harm ecological systems and the associated autonomy of local economic, social and political systems of governance.

The final chapter in this part approaches the topic of economic activity from a totally different scale – international trade in tobacco. Valentina Vadi's chapter demonstrates how tobacco control, for the purpose of protecting public health, is coming under increasing attack with state and non-state actors. They resist legal reform, which they perceive as restricting their freedom. A particular focus for current legal action is investment treaties. Companies argue that national measures for tobacco control violate their legal protections and entitle them to compensation. The outcomes of these cases contain lessons for the future, should states show an increased willingness to regulate to protect ecological integrity within national jurisdictions. Corporate interests will respond by looking to their legal remedies under investment treaties and other trade agreements. The terms of these treaties, particularly dispute resolution provisions, must be carefully crafted to prevent global economic interests from trumping the values of public health and ecological integrity.

13 How regulation of finance got it wrong and how it still does

Giovanni Ferri

Introduction and premise of the great crisis

While we were told that the world had entered the epoch of the 'Great Moderation' – a kind of new Eldorado in which permanently high growth was coupled with low inflation and unemployment (Bernanke, 2004) – an unsustainable debt overhang was accumulating at the global level. That was the result of several causes: global imbalances, excessively lenient monetary policy by the Federal Reserve and the downside of deregulation/liberalization of finance. I will first look at the first two of these causes in order, leaving the third for the rest of the chapter.

Global imbalances

Using the IMF's Direction of Trade Statistics (Table 13.1), we can see that the main source of the imbalance was the USA, having a merchandise deficit equal to 1.56 per cent of world gross domestic product (GDP) in the years leading to the crisis. The main issue here lies with the linkages between finance and the build-up of the global imbalances. To this end, one needs to recall that – to close the accounting equivalence of the balance of payments – any deficit of the current account finds an equivalent surplus in terms of net capital inflows. In other words, when the USA was running its huge current account deficit (up to 6.5% of its GDP in 2006), the counterpart of it was that the surplus countries acquired additional assets on the USA, by granting it credit or through other forms of capital such as FDI and portfolio investments flowing in to the USA.

Nevertheless, beyond the truth of this accounting equivalence there were additional key ingredients in the academic and policy debate. On the one hand, the US authorities often rebuked those who accused their external imbalance was building a major threat to global stability that the problem was not in the USA but in the surplus countries, largely in China. This line of reasoning may be epitomized as the 'global saving glut' view (Bernanke, 2005). According to it, the problem was not the excessive absorption by the USA but the fact that the surplus countries – particularly China – were

Table 13.1 Bilateral and global merchandise imbalances: underlying world merchandise trade flows as a percentage of world gross domestic product

Importer	USA	Japan	Euro Area	Emerging Asia	Latin America	Emerging Europe	Rest of the World	Total imports
USA	–	0.27	0.50	1.04	0.57	0.04	1.26	3.68
Japan	0.11	–	0.09	0.44	0.04	0.01	0.43	1.14
Euro area	0.33	0.14	–	0.76	0.18	0.59	1.74	3.74
Emerging Asia	0.41	0.61	0.43	–	0.15	0.05	1.36	3.15
Latin America	0.42	0.06	0.15	0.18	–	0.01	0.16	1.07
Emerging Europe	0.03	0.03	0.74	0.16	0.01	–	0.41	1.40
Rest of the World	0.82	0.20	1.88	1.02	0.17	0.34	–	4.38
Total exports	2.12	1.31	3.78	3.36	1.06	1.04	4.66	–

Source: IMF (2009)

exceedingly parsimonious, with Chinese household saving rate in the order of 40 per cent of disposable income. Various reasons were cited to account for this very high saving rate. Some authors blamed China for keeping an artificially undervalued exchange rate, following a mercantilist approach, which would not only boost exports but also discourage imports and consumption (Dooley *et al.*, 2004; Goldstein and Lardy, 2006). Other pundits focused on a portfolio approach; namely, following rapid financial innovation the USA host the most developed and sophisticated financial markets in the world while, on the contrary, the surplus countries feature pervasive financial under-development. Thus, surplus countries demand (dollar-denominated) assets in the USA as a result of their optimal portfolio strategy and this is consistent with the recycling of their surpluses (Caballero and Krishnamurthy, 2003; Kose *et al.*, 2006; Lockhart, 2008).

Other experts claim that China faces a financial challenge (McKinnon and Schnabl, 2009). This arises from its large trade (saving) surplus resulting in a currency mismatch because it is an immature creditor that cannot lend in its own currency, thus foreign currency claims (largely dollars) build up within domestic financial institutions and the consequent attempt by the Peoples' Bank of China to sterilize the abundant liquidity is increasingly difficult posing inflationary threats that would demand a newly stable exchange rate parity.[1]

Also, emerging countries' ballooning reserve accumulation should be put in the context of an increasingly crisis-prone international monetary and financial system following the various emerging countries' systemic crises of the 1990s. We must recall that the East Asian crisis of 1997–1998 represented a serious escalation in financial instability in as much as – differently from Latin America where countries had lower reputation – this time the crisis hit the poster boys of economic development and industrial catch up, quickly going from the east Asian miracle (World Bank, 1996) to the east Asian debacle. This induced many banks, corporations and governments from emerging economies to deeply reassess their dependence on international capital inflows: if that dependence had burned the model countries any country could be hit any time. Thereafter, emerging economies ran for the exit from their net debt positions to become net capital exporters since 2003. In crisis-hit countries the adjustment – to reduce their exposure to shocks originating from the international capital markets – took two paths: (i) corporate external de-leveraging aimed at reducing exposure to currency risk, and (ii) accumulation of net foreign assets by the private sector of emerging economies; later on, there was also (iii) accumulation of currency reserves by these countries' central banks. Taken as a ratio to total external debt, for the main emerging countries reserves have indeed scaled up from some 20 per cent by the mid-1990s to beyond 100 per cent by 2006.

This transformation was at odds with the conventional wisdom that postulates capital flows going from rich to emerging countries and necessarily requires a more detailed explanation (Rajan, 2008). Indeed, we may think of these as precautionary savings made by emerging economies to avoid further financial crises. Nevertheless, an excess of foreign reserves may have its costs. In fact, the accumulation of excess reserves can generate excess liquidity – which may induce inappropriately permissive credit policies – or cause costly sterilizations (Edison, 2003). For his part, Rodrik (2006) estimates that earnings equivalent to around 1 per cent of developing countries' GDP are lost due to excessively high currency reserve balances. So, if we believe the precautionary saving view, to insure themselves against capital flights emerging economies are paying a high price.

Excessively lenient monetary policy by the Federal Reserve

The second determinant of the crisis was the overly easy monetary policy by the Fed to remedy the burst of the stock market bubble of the 'new economy' in 2000. Between January 2001 and June 2003, the target value for the fed funds rate was lowered from 6 to 1 per cent, and was kept so low until mid-2004. This encouraged households to borrow more to finance real estate holdings. The US household sector's debt grew, as a ratio to GDP, from 71 per cent in 2000 to 100 per cent in 2007, while house prices almost doubled between 2000 and 2006.

Real estate valuations were inflated by two circular mechanisms feeding the housing bubble. First, rising real estate prices increased its value as collateral and allowed households to get more credit, which in turn inflated house prices even more. Second, the rising real estate prices increased the value of the financial assets originated via the (increasingly used) securitization of mortgages, in turn allowing financial intermediaries to raise additional funds to be channelled to the primary market for new mortgages. Regulatory loopholes and the authorities' failure to fully understand the perils of excessive indebtedness allowed a generalized deterioration in the lending standards. Mortgages were offered even to low-creditworthy individuals (i.e. the subprime customers). It was generally known *ex ante* that the subprime customers would be able to repay their mortgages only if the real estate kept appreciating and they could refinance their existing mortgages.[2]

Between June 2004 and June 2006 the target Fed fund rate escalated from 1 per cent to 5.25 per cent, causing a significant increase in the cost of servicing adjustable rate mortgages (ARMs).[3] In addition, the increase in commodity prices also played an important role (e.g. by 2006 energy prices were about twice their 2003 level), making it more difficult for households to pay the instalments on their mortgages. Defaults increased – reaching 16 per cent by spring 2007 in the subprime segment – the housing demand cooled down and real estate prices started dropping.

Soon the difficulties in the subprime segment contaminated financial markets, as defaulting mortgages stopped the flow of payments on the collateralized debt obligations (CDOs) subscribed by many international investors. Between June and July, following several downgrades announced by the rating agencies, financial markets lost faith in the effective ability of the ratings to class the probability of default of CDOs. Suddenly, markets realized they had insufficient information to correctly evaluate the risk of these securities.

On 9 August 2007 the crisis became global: three European investment funds were frozen as it had become impossible to establish the value of their subprime-related assets. Panic spread on international financial markets. Investors tended to repudiate the whole of structured finance – beside its subprime-related segments – that was generally opaque (mostly unregulated, over the counter, markets) as well. In several market segments liquidity disappeared, prices collapsed, interest rate spreads (the premium over risk free interest rates) ballooned and stock markets experienced mounting losses. The responsibility of monetary policy is quite clear.

In the rest of the chapter, the following section starts with the bold announcements of the April 2009 London meeting of the G20 in terms of re-regulating finance, which, by and large, were not followed by the consequent actions in terms of the enforcement of a stiffer regulation. We then analyse what, in our opinion, were the deep mistakes of the 'light touch' regulation of finance, heightening the downside of deregulation/ liberalization of finance. In the subsequent section I argue that the current re-regulation provides more of the same and I would need to cater for diversity also in banking and finance. From there I devote a section to discussing what caused the slow motion of financial re-regulation, before outlining the political–economic cycle of finance, a concept describing long-run swings in regulation/liberalization of finance and of the economy at large. I end with some concluding remarks.

Emergency room and the lack of new rule enforcement

When the great leaders of the world gathered in London for the 2 April 2009 meeting of the G20, what they had in mind was the fourth phase of the crisis, as represented in Figure 13.1.

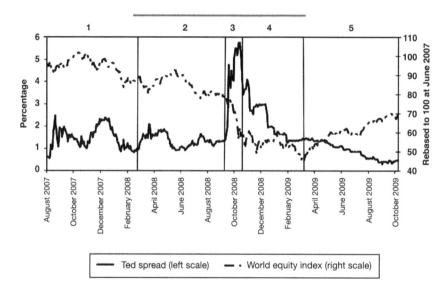

Figure 13.1 The five phases of the 2007–2009 crisis

Source: author's calculations on data from Bloomberg

The figure reports on the right-hand vertical axis the trend of the world stock exchange index taken as being equal to 100 as of 9 August 2007 and on the left hand vertical axis the Ted spread, computed as the difference between the 3-month Libor rate and the rate on three-month US Treasury bills – where this spread measures the risk perception on the interbank market. In the first phase of the crisis – going from August 2007 to March 2008, when the bankruptcy of Bear Stearns (the first investment bank to face distress) is avoided via a subsidized merger with JP Morgan – the Ted spread fluctuates around 1 percentage point (p.p.), twice its pre-crisis level, and shares drop to 90. In the second phase – from the rescue of Bear Stearns to the beginning of September 2008 – the Ted spread is less volatile but never goes down to its initial level, while stocks fall to around 80. The situation becomes dramatic in the third phase – approximately for one month following the bankruptcy of Lehman Brothers of 15 September – with the Ted spread approaching 6 p.p. and stocks plunging to 60. In the fourth phase – spanning between mid-October 2008 and the end of March 2009 – the Ted spread drops gradually back to 1 p.p., but shares keep dropping to below 50. In the fifth phase – after March 2009 – the Ted spread slowly goes back to its pre-crisis level while stocks rebound to 70 by November 2009.

So, when the world leaders met in London on 2 April, it was not exactly normality, since the crisis was then hitting the real economy and shedding jobs, but the financial round of the crisis was being overcome. Yet the leaders did not know that, as what they had in mind was the third and, most vividly, the fourth phase of the financial crisis. Therefore, they took a strong stance announcing stiff measures to re-regulate finance. Among the proposed measures the ones key to our discussion are:

- scaling up IMF resources for crisis prevention and assistance;
- establishing the Financial Stability Board to provide early warning of and address macroeconomic/financial risks;
- reshaping regulatory systems to identify and take account of macro-prudential risks;
- extending regulation and oversight to all systemically important financial institutions, instruments and markets, for the first time including systemically important hedge funds;
- endorsing and implementing tough new principles on pay and compensation and supporting sustainable compensation schemes and the corporate social responsibility of all firms;
- taking action, once recovery is assured, to improve the quality, quantity, and international consistency of banks' capital. In future, regulation should prevent excessive leverage and require buffers of resources to be built up in good times;
- taking action against non-cooperative jurisdictions, including tax havens, standing ready to deploy sanctions to protect members' public finances and financial systems;
- calling on the accounting standard setters to work urgently with supervisors and regulators to improve standards on valuation and provisioning and achieve a single set of high-quality global accounting standards;
- extending regulatory oversight and registration to Credit Rating Agencies to ensure they meet the international code of good practice, particularly to prevent unacceptable conflicts of interest.

The outcome of the 25 September 2009 meeting of the G20 at Pittsburgh suggested that the leaders' attention was still focused on restoring financial stability via sounder regulation/supervision. The communiqué at the end of the meeting stressed that 'reckless behaviour and a lack of responsibility led to crisis, we will not allow a return to banking as usual'.

However, unfortunately, finance seemed to be heading exactly to business as usual, and most of what was promised at the London meeting was not delivered. And even the rules that were introduced (e.g. the Dodd–Frank Act) appeared to be lagging and seemed largely ineffective.

The deep mistakes of the 'light touch' regulation of finance

Bank lending standards became lower (i.e. more loans go to less worthy customers) because many banks moved away from their traditional business model. Indeed, securitizations drastically changed the banking model, from the 'originate to hold' (OTH) to the 'originate to distribute' (OTD) model (Figure 13.2). In the OTH model the loan is a simple operation between the bank and the borrower. On the contrary, in the OTD model the loan origination is a complex operation (like a multistage production process) involving various subjects and hinging on financial markets. While OTD promotes risk diversification, it jeopardizes the two fundamental activities – screening and monitoring – performed by the banks to reduce the risk of granting loans to unworthy borrowers.

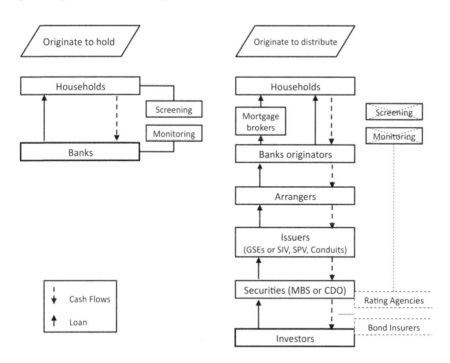

Figure 13.2 The bank business model: from 'originate to hold' to 'originate to distribute'

Apart from the unfavourable transformation from OTH to OTD, a further contribution to worsen lending standards in the US was given by the flourishing of a parallel, unregulated banking system, the so-called 'shadow banking system'. The importance of the shadow banking system, which was virtually nil until the late 1970s, started increasing thereafter, thanks to financial deregulation and liberalization. By the mid-1990s the total liabilities of the shadow banking system outran those of the regulated banking system. Ten years later, before the start of the crisis, the total liabilities of the shadow banking system approached US$20 trillion, dwarfing the US$13 trillion of the regulated banking system.

Those transformations – reducing the risk-control efficacy of the regulated banks and letting the new breed of shadow banks take the lead – heightened systemic risk (i.e. the risk of collapse of the entire financial system) and emerged to a large extent because of a misconceived approach to regulating finance. In this regard, the dominating approach followed the 'evolutionary view' of finance. Following the early promotion of Goldsmith (1966, 1969), the evolutionary view postulated that financial markets be more efficient than banks at managing risks. Thus, as suggested forcefully by Bryan (1988), banks should move from the old model (lend and keep the loans, OTH) to the new model (lend and sell the loans, via securitization, OTD).

Regrettably, banks' role as certifiers of loan quality was neglected, but that role was there only with the OTH model and not with the OTD model. As we already noticed, granting loans to sell them rather than to keep them endangered banks' incentives to perform in depth screening and monitoring of the borrowers, so that lending standards rapidly deteriorated. The evaluation of the creditworthiness of the loans underlying securitizations fell back on the rating agencies who founded such evaluation on past historical default rates, but these rates were based on the OTH model, and thus the agencies systematically gave overly optimistic ratings.

In more general terms, for too long we had a 'crossed-eyed' theory of finance. In fact, on one hand, the theory of financial markets is based on the assumption of complete markets and of investors holding perfect information. But, on the other hand, the theory behind the existence of financial intermediaries assumes the fundamental role of asymmetric information – the lender knows less than the borrower about the true quality of the latter – and of delegated monitoring – whereby depositors entrust banks to screen out and monitor those who will be granted credit. When, with liberalization, financial markets became dominating banks' practice and even regulatory principles (e.g. IAS, Basel 2) moved toward financial market type activities while weakening banks' credit function. In a sense, we applied to banks the theory, which, if adequate to financial markets, is certainly inappropriate to banks. There is a clear lesson here: it's wrong subordinating banks to financial markets (and also the opposite would be a mistake). Rather, we need to build on the bank–market complementarity, as suggested by Allen and Gale (2000).

The current re-regulation provides more of the same and need to cater for diversity

The current re-regulation (e.g. Basel 3) just requires more capital for banks, following the past approach of 'mechanical quantification' of risks. Alas, we know that current measures of risk, such as the Capital Asset Pricing Model (CAPM) or the Value at Risk (VaR), are probably misleading as they are based on untenable assumptions such as the often hypothesis of normality in the distribution of risks.

Let's consider the case of the CAPM, which assumes orthogonality between sovereign risk and private risk (i.e. lack of correlation between the former and the latter). This assumption is deeply questioned by the EU sovereign debt crises. Orthogonality would require that sovereign risk (typically hypothesized to be zero) be uncorrelated with private risk. This is the way we can derive the CAPM fundamental formula:

$$ER_i = r + \beta_i \, (ER^m - r)$$

where ER_i is the equilibrium expected return on risky asset i, r is the risk-free rate (proxied by treasury bond returns), ER^m is the equilibrium expected return on the diversified portfolio and the coefficient $\beta_i = \text{cov}(R_i, R^m)/\text{var}(R^m)$. The fallacy of the orthogonality of risks assumption is evident when governments save distressed banks: then the credit default swap (CDS)[4] spreads drop for banks and rise for sovereigns.

It seems that the right way to go about that would be to acknowledge that we need to revise risk pricing models. Instead, the authorities use stress testing. In the aftermath of the crisis, various authorities such as the Financial Services Authority for the UK, the European Banking Authority for the EU and the International Monetary Fund at the global level calculated stress tests.

In a stress test the authority looks at how robust a financial instrument is in certain crashes, a form of scenario analysis. However, this scenario analysis is calculated around the risk measures provided by the traditional instruments. As such, though potentially useful, stress tests make neither a sufficient nor a necessary condition. If the risk is overestimated (underestimated) by the traditional measures, stress testing it is not a sufficient (necessary) condition.

More generally, we should acknowledge the difference between financial risks vs. bank credit risks. Following the recalled assumptions of the theory of financial markets, financial risk management may well exhibit benefits of diversification (i.e. since the underlying risks are 'objective' and observable, the suggestion 'don't put all your eggs in just one basket' seems cogent). On the contrary, given the assumptions of the theory of financial intermediaries, bank credit risk management could feature benefits of specialization (i.e. as the underlying risks are 'subjective' and hard to observe, this seems to imply that it would be efficient for each intermediary to specialize in overcoming asymmetric information about specific customers rather than diversify their lending across borrowers they know less about).

If we accept the reasoning we just proposed of the benefits of specialization in lending, then we could also contemplate the possibility that different bank business models will deliver different abilities to manage bank credit risks. Thus, it would appear crucial to distinguish investment banks and wholesale commercial banks – likely to be better equipped to manage financial risks – from retail commercial banks and cooperative banks – probably more prepared to deal with true bank credit risks.

The reasoning just outlined would have obvious consequences in terms of separating financial market risks – and the intermediaries specialized in dealing with these risks – and bank credit risks – together with the intermediaries having a vocation to deal with these risks. Not surprisingly, this issue was key both in the Volker rule – a ban on the speculative 'proprietary' trading for commercial banks – embodied in the Dodd–Frank Act and in the Vickers' Report, introducing the principle of ring-fencing between commercial banking and investment banking.

What caused the 'lento pede' of financial re-regulation?

The obvious question is: why financial re-regulation is advancing so slowly? To put it another way, using Latin, why is it walking with such a *lento pede*? To answer this question we can gain important insights looking at what supported the re-regulation of the 1930s. Many observers give credit to the 'Pecora Commission' as being the key driver of that re-regulation. Thus, since the working of that Commission had been long neglected, it is worthwhile to recall the basics of it.

The Pecora Investigation was an inquiry begun on 4 March 1932 by the United States Senate Committee on Banking and Currency to investigate the causes of the Wall Street Crash of 1929. The name refers to the fourth and final chief counsel for the investigation, Ferdinand Pecora.

Born in Sicily and having migrated to the US in his early childhood, Ferdinand Pecora (6 January 1882 to 7 December 1971) was a lawyer and judge who became famous in the 1930s as Chief Counsel to the United States Senate Committee on Banking and Currency during its investigation of Wall Street banking and stock brokerage practices.

A member of the New York bar since 1911, Pecora was assistant district attorney in New York City (1918–1929), earning a reputation as an honest and talented prosecutor who helped shut down more than 100 bucket shops. Because of his tough reputation, Pecora was not appointed District Attorney. He left the district attorney's office for private practice, where he remained until 1933.

Ferdinand Pecora was appointed Chief Counsel to the US Senate's Committee on Banking and Currency in January 1933, the last months of the Herbert Hoover presidency, by its outgoing Republican chairman, Peter Norbeck, and continued under Democratic chairman Duncan Fletcher, following the 1932 election that swept Franklin D. Roosevelt into the US presidency and gave the Democratic Party control of the Senate.

Pecora's investigation unearthed evidence of irregular practices in the financial markets that benefited the rich at the expense of ordinary investors, including exposure of Morgan's 'preferred list' by which the bank's influential friends (including Calvin Coolidge, the former president, and Owen J. Roberts, a justice of Supreme Court of the United States) participated in stock offerings at steeply discounted rates. Spurred by these revelations, the United States Congress enacted the Glass–Steagall Act, the Securities Act of 1933 and the Securities Exchange Act of 1934.

Why, again, was there no substantive action after the London G20 meeting of early April 2009? How do we explain the differences with respect to the 1930s? Indeed, this time we lacked a Ferdinand Pecora to disclose the (often difficult to confess) sins of the late phase of financial capitalism. However, the Pecora Commissions don't come out of the blue. And, perhaps, this time the conditions on the ground were not favourable. First of all, there was a fundamental weakness of the Obama administration, which placed a high bet on health insurance reform and could not deal with many fronts at the same time. Perhaps even more important, expansionary economic policies – suddenly contradicting the deep credo of the free market ideology – avoided that recession turn into depression. So, the lessons of John Maynard Keynes made it more difficult to build the momentum for reform.

The concept of the political–economic cycle of finance

In our view, capitalism alternates phases in which free markets expand (e.g. globalization) and deepen (e.g. the emergence of new sectors as a result of innovation) with phases characterized by more regulated markets when rules and/or state intervention in the economy tend to be more pervasive. Over the decades, this alternation may be represented as a political–economic cycle of finance. This allegory helps read the events of finance between the 1930s and the present day.

Indeed, financial instability tends to intensify with the extent of the unfettered free market economy. By and large, freer markets sooner or later build imbalances and inefficiencies in price setting mechanisms and, consequently, in the allocation of resources. This occurs when excessively optimistic expectations about future developments evolve and the financial system fuels such misplaced assumptions, leading to excessive indebtedness in the economy. As a result, a speculative bubble – that is usually identified as such in retrospect – is formed. Eventually, this triggers an epochal systemic crisis, which marks a turning point to change direction towards stricter regulation of the marketplace. In our interpretation, this represents the end of one cycle and the start of a new one.

In fact, solving the crisis requires, in general, two types of actions. The first one consists in the intervention by the state that – fully or partly – takes on itself the losses suffered by the financial institutions in a way to rebuild the trust in them by individual investors and savers and to restore the functionality of the financial system. This action may even require (some) nationalization of the banks. The second action entails stiffening regulation and supervision of finance, assembling a framework consistent with pursuing the stability of the financial system. At the international level, the new set-up for financial stability may be crowned by the emergence of a new monetary order centred on the economic power that has come out in hegemonic position from the crisis, whose currency will become thereafter the reference for international exchanges. More generally, solving the crisis implies imposing limits on the free market, beyond the financial system, thereby often swinging the balance from the global to the national dimension of economic processes. This scenario is similar to what is usually known as de-globalization.

However, over the long run (it may take decades), the regulatory framework tends to lose its consistency and the economic system begins to operate again in an uncontrolled financial environment. Three main factors push in this direction. First, the financial system on its own tends to breed innovations. Alas, the financial innovations – though generally beneficial – short-circuit the logic and the substance of the stability controls set up with re-regulation and may undermine the functioning of the international monetary order. Second, the process of market extension – to exploit the international opportunities – and of market deepening – with the start of new business segments, often linked to innovations – needs the support of finance in new forms, different with respect to those consistent with the extant regulatory/supervisory framework securing stability. This further promotes the spread of financial innovations. Third, there is a swing in ideology, whereby free market visions tend to dominate and become increasingly entrenched. Then, economic theory and the policy debate excessively lean towards stressing the negative consequences of the failure by public intervention in the economy while advocating the benefits of letting the markets free (Leijonhufvud, 2009). This calls for deregulation and liberalization of the financial system.

The mix of these three factors leads once more to the formation of overly optimistic expectations – as Hyman Minsky (1975) reminded us – and this triggers excess indebtedness, misallocation of resources and the build-up of a new speculative bubble. At this point, it is only a matter of time and a new major systemic crisis will arrive, thus completing this political–economic cycle of finance that, as I described, embraces the path from one structure-breaking systemic financial crisis to the next one. To be sure, such a systemic crisis drawing the political–economic cycle of finance to a close is not a single, stand-alone episode, but rather it is the epilogue of a series of specific crises whose frequency and gravity tend to aggravate as we move on along the sequence. In fact, when the economic system is already operating within a generalized speculative bubble, even the well-meant interventions to stabilize the financial system after the initial instability events are likely, quite paradoxically, to have destabilizing effects. This happens because, in some way, the interventions to salvage the imperilled financial intermediaries cover their speculative losses and – unless a new consistent regulatory framework is quickly put in place – this strengthens speculation as the expectation becomes more widespread that also in the future new interventions to cover speculative losses will be offered. Accordingly, stabilizations turn out to be destabilizing because, in solving the instability of individual financial intermediaries, it amplifies systemic risk. Otherwise stated, in line with Charles P. Kindleberger (1978), if the lending of last resort (LOLR) is heavily used to bail out financial institutions in a systemic crisis, this will backfire in terms of augmenting exponentially the moral hazard of the financial intermediaries and building the foundations of a new bigger crisis down the line.

In a sense, financial liberalization is a driver for economic growth but over time the perils of instability may outweigh those benefits. The history of financial capitalism takes the form of various repeated political–economic cycles. The financial crises of the recent decades will possibly conclude this political–economic cycle of finance originated by the return to stricter regulation of the marketplace as a remedy to the major instability of the 1930s (Figure 13.3; see also D'Apice and Ferri, 2010). Already in the mid-1930s,

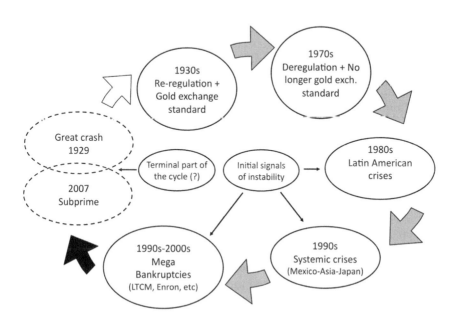

Figure 13.3 The political–economic cycle of finance

countries had developed a consistent regulatory framework to achieve domestic financial stability. Only after World War II was the framework finalized at the international level, with the definition of a new monetary order centred on the US dollar. However, after the abandonment of the gold exchange standard (in August 1971), financial innovation, deregulation and globalization have progressively generated inconsistencies in the original regulatory framework, providing the background factor of previous crises as well as of the most recent one. By and large, as already stressed, the stabilization interventions to cope with the crises may themselves turn destabilizing when the financial system is operating under an inconsistent regulatory/supervisory framework. A case in point was the rescue in 1998 of the speculative hedge fund long-term capital management (and also the abrupt drop of the Fed funds rate after the dotcom bubble burst in 2000–2001) that, in the absence of re-regulation, was a keystone laid for the Great Crisis that started ten years later in 2007.

The triumph of excessively one-sided ideology-driven free market views contributed to build exaggerated trust in the markets and in their ability to self-regulate, motivating policy choices. On the contrary, the progress made by other economics schools – such as Joseph E. Stiglitz and several other scientists moving on that track – in terms of the analysis of the failures of the market was largely disregarded.

The epochal crisis ignited in 2007 by the turmoil in the subprime mortgage market could suggest this political–economic cycle of finance is ready to come to a close. Indeed, this crisis implies an escalation in terms of its depth and geographical extension and also of the fact that it started at the centre of the financial system and not at its peripheries, as had happened with the previous systemic financial crises of the 1990s and the beginning of the new millennium. The authorities' call for stricter regulation might mark the start of a new cycle. However, re-regulation appears to have lost momentum. In fact, if the pronouncements by the leaders of the G20 in their London meeting of spring 2009 were bold about re-regulation, their statements at the following Pittsburgh meeting in the autumn of the same year had become much more timid. At the same time, parliamentary actions on both sides of the Atlantic did not seem to move ahead as fast as earlier announced.

Will this mean an even bigger crisis is waiting for us in the future, as the European sovereign debt crisis could suggest? This would be a terrible event also in view of the fact that the public finances of many advanced countries have been exhausted by the interventions to salvage finance from its instability.

There is a further problem. Nowadays, what was once the debate on the decline of Europe has transmuted into one in which, due to the difficulties encountered by the US, the danger of decline refers to the entire Western model. Various considerations ignite this debate but, perhaps, the most striking of all descends from observing that the on-going global crisis distressing the world economy and society originated from global imbalances and excessive indebtedness having the focus in the US (the 2007–2009 bout of the crisis) and later on found a second epicentre in the imbalances of Europe (since 2010). Though against that possible sunset of the Western leadership no practical alternative is yet in sight, undoubtedly the world's gravity seems to be moving from West to East, where two countries counting a combined population of approximately 2.5 billion (plus an additional 0.8 billion in the Association of Southeast Asian Nations – ASEAN) of the world's 7 billion total have come back to play a strong role.

Based on Maddison (2007), it is evident from Figure 13.4 that the Western model – as represented by western Europe and the US – gained its world economic leadership only after the Industrial Revolution. Before that, in 1820, the West approached 25 per cent of world GDP while the sum of ASEAN + 3 + India[5] accounted for 56 per cent. The ranking was already reversed by 1870, when the West was 42 per cent compared with 35 per cent for the east and south Asia aggregation – and in 1950 the disparity reached its maximum (close to 54% vs. 15%). However, since then the ASEAN + 3 + India has vividly rebounded. By 1973, at the time of the first oil shock, it approached 19 per cent – with the West at 48 per cent – owing mostly to the economic miracle of Japan and of the Asian Tigers. But the rebound intensified later on, with the inclusion of China and India, bringing the east and south Asia aggregation to 36 per cent (vs. 37% for the sum of western Europe and the US) in 2006. By 2010, four years into the crisis, the shift had further accelerated putting the two areas, respectively at 42 and 34 per cent.

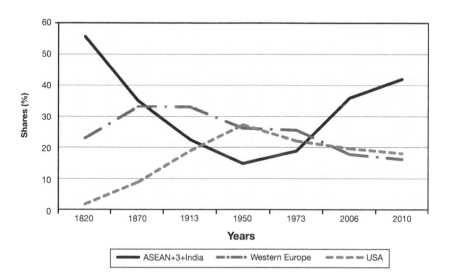

Figure 13.4 Distribution of world gross domestic product shares between 1820 and 2010: Western model vs. Asia

Source: author's calculations on data from Maddison (2007) and updates from IMF data

If we were to take at face value the GDP shares projected by Mold (2010), by 2030 the balance between the two areas could go back to a situation more similar to the pre-Industrial Revolution set up than to anything we have seen there since. Indeed, those projections forecast above 55 per cent for the ASEAN + 3 + India – with most of the gain for China – and just about 25 per cent for the sum of western Europe and the US.

Obviously, Mold's projections could be exaggerated because they are not adjusted for purchasing power parity. Besides, Mold simply projects the past trends to the future neglecting that all economic miracles have ended sooner or later. Furthermore, given the challenges posed by the current organization of production along the global value chains, the national accounts might overstate the extent of the Western decline as a large fraction of the value added created in the emerging economies still flows back to rich countries' investors. And, even accepting Mold's figures, that would imply a much milder decline of the West in terms of per capita GDP, due to divergent trends in population between the two areas. In spite of these and other possible corrections to its magnitude, the shift from the Western model to the east and south Asia aggregation is a reality. Shadows of possible decline of the West materialize also if one considers the conditions of public finances through Europe and the US.[6] There would be several other aspects to be pondered, but this West to East shift in the balance of economic power is most likely to be the single most important determinant around which to reshape the global economic governance.

Specific issues might arise with the above scenario. We will mention just two. The first issue is that of a possibly multipolar global set up, where evidently the East and South Asia aggregation is not a single entity. Still using Mold's 2030 projections, the largest economy would be China (accounting for 28% of the world GDP), followed by the US (14%) and then by India and western Europe (separately, both at about 11%). The other economies would follow at considerable distance. The apparent implication seems that a complex world economic architecture would be required to ensure smooth global governance. The second issue stems from the fact that some of the countries – most notably China – performing as main drivers in the West to East shift are structured as hybrid economic systems, with the State playing a pervasive role. Thus, it is not entirely clear how to interpret the functioning of the apparently vibrant market economy in those countries. And, even disregarding that, some of the emerging economic powers do not function as Western democracy, so raising questions about the respect of individual freedom.

Conclusions

We argued that the Great Crisis had three main causes: (i) the global imbalances, particularly between the US and China; (ii) the excessively lenient monetary policy by the Federal Reserve; and (iii) the downside of deregulation/liberalization of finance. The joint effect of the three factors was that of generating a debt overhang in the US.

When the financial round of the crisis broke out at the beginning of August 2007, and particularly after its escalation with the bankruptcy of Lehman Brothers in September 2008, the global scale contagion caused pervasive government intervention to salvage the endangered banks. Against this background, at the early April 2009 meeting of the G20 the chief leaders of the world made bold announcements to stiffen regulation in a way to bring back financial stability. However, those promises were largely not fulfilled.

Next we discussed the deep mistakes of the 'light touch' regulation of finance through which commercial banks were subjugated to financial market friendly rules. In addition, we claimed that the current re-regulation provides more of the same and does not cater enough for diversity within the banking system.

Regarding the slow advancement of the financial re-regulation, we argued that the lack of a strong prosecutor such as Ferdinand Pecora in 1933 made the progress of the reform more difficult. In any case, we asserted that a serious re-regulation is the only way out to restore financial stability, as the allegory of the political–economic cycle of finance helped us outline. Appropriate leadership will be needed to secure a reasonably rapid and smooth transition. Lacking that, the sustainability of finance risks being permanently endangered and the stability of the world could also be at stake.

Notes

1. The authors call this situation a conundrum. They believe that even strong real appreciation of the renminbi would not cancel the trade surplus since the high saving rate depends to a large extent on domestic structural factors, such as little social security. According to them, countries that are 'virtuous' by having a high saving rate (like China but unlike the US) tend to run surpluses in the current account of their international balance of payments (i.e. lend to foreigners). But because their domestic currencies are generally not used for international lending, these foreign claims are denominated largely in dollars. With the passage of time two things happen. First, as the stock of liquid dollar claims cumulates, domestic holders of dollar assets worry more about an appreciation of the domestic currency. Second, foreigners start complaining that the country's ongoing flow of trade surpluses is unfair – and threaten trade sanctions unless the currency is appreciated. Because of the destabilizing properties of open-ended currency appreciation, the virtuous country becomes conflicted. Whence conflicted virtue.

2. Hyman Minsky's approach (see e.g. Minsky, 1993) distinguishes three borrower types: hedge units (little leveraged and able to repay both their loan interest and principal), speculative units (able to pay interest on their loans but needing highly liquid markets to renew their debt) and Ponzi units (extremely highly leveraged unable to even pay interest on their loans unless the constant increase in the value of their collateral assets allows them to refinance their loans). In Minsky's terms, the subprime borrowers are Ponzi units.

3. Servicing loans became heavier also because of the reset clauses. US mortgages (particularly the subprime ones) often featured an initial teaser rate. At the end of the first two years the reset clause would bring the rate in line with market rates.
4. The CDS price can be considered as a proxy of the risk premium because these derivatives protect against the risk of default of a company or sovereign issue.
5. ASEAN comprises Brunei, Cambodia, Indonesia, Laos, Malaysia, Myanmar, Philippines, Singapore, Thailand and Vietnam, while the +3 means China, Japan and Korea.
6. In his long-run historical perspective, Kennedy (1987) argues that the great powers almost invariably decline after fiscal imbalances emerge.

References

Allen, F. and Gale, D. (2000) *Comparing Financial Systems*. Cambridge, MA: MIT Press.
Bernanke, B. S. (2004) 'The great moderation', Federal Reserve Board, speech at the meetings of the Eastern Economic Association, Washington, DC.
Bernanke, B. S. (2005) 'The global saving glut and the US current account deficit', remarks at the Sandridge Lecture. Richmond, VA: Virginia Association of Economics, 10 March.
Bryan, L. L. (1988) *Breaking Up the Bank: Rethinking an Industry under Siege*. Homewood, IL: Dow Jones-Irwin.
Caballero, R. J. and Krishnamurthy, A. (2003) 'Excessive dollar debt: financial development and underinsurance', *Journal of Finance*, 58, 867–94.
D'Apice, V. and Ferri, G. (2010) *Financial Instability: Toolkit and Perspectives up to the Current Crisis*. Basingstoke: Palgrave Macmillan.
Dooley, M. P., Folkerts-Landau, D. and Garber, P. (2004) 'An essay on the revived Bretton-Woods-system', *International Journal of Finance and Economics*, 4, 307–13.
Edison, H. (2003) 'Are foreign exchange reserves in Asia too high?', in *World Economic Outlook*. Washington, DC: International Monetary Fund, September
Goldsmith, R. W. (1966) *The Determinants of Financial Structure*. Paris, France: OECD.
Goldsmith, R. W. (1969) *Financial Structure and Development*. New Haven, CT: Yale University Press.
Goldstein, M. and Lardy, N. (2006) 'China's exchange rate policy dilemma', *American Economic Review*, 96 (2) May: 422–6.
IMF (2009) *World Economic Outlook: Crisis and Recovery*. Washington, DC: International Monetary Fund, April.
Kennedy, P. (1987) *The Rise and Fall of the Great Powers*. New York: Random House.
Kindleberger, C. P. (1978) *Manias, Panics, and Crashes: A History of Financial Crises*. Chichester: John Wiley.
Kose, M. A., Prasad, E., Rogoff, K. and Wei, S. J. (2006) *Financial Globalization: A Reappraisal*, working paper no 12484. Cambridge, MA: National Bureau of Economic Research.
Leijonhufvud, A. (2009) *Macroeconomics and the Crisis: A Personal Appraisal*, Policy Insight no 41. Washington, DC: Center for Economic and Policy Research.
Lockhart, D. P. (2008) 'Current financial stresses and persistent global imbalances', remarks by the President and CEO of the Federal Reserve Bank of Atlanta. Atlanta, GA: Southern Center for International Studies, 8 February.
Maddison, A. (2007) *Contours of the World Economy 1–2030: Essays in Macro-Economic History*. Oxford: Oxford University Press.

McKinnon, R. and Schnabl, G. (2009) *China's Financial Conundrum and Global Imbalances*, BIS working paper no 277, Monetary and Economic Department, Bank for International Settlements, March, available at www.bis.org/publ/work277.htm (accessed 1 February 2013).

Minsky, H. P. (1975) *John Maynard Keynes*. Cambridge: Cambridge University Press.

Minsky, H. P. (1993) 'The financial instability hypothesis', in P. Arestis and M. Sawyer (eds), *Handbook of Radical Political Economy*. Aldershot: Edward Elgar.

Mold, A. (2010) 'Maddison's forecasts revisited: what will the world look like in 2030?', 24 October, available at www.voxeu.org/article/what-will-world-look-2030-maddison-s-forecasts-revisited (accessed 1 February 2013).

Rajan, R. G. (2008) 'Global imbalances, or why are the poor financing the rich?', *De Economist*, 156 (1): 3–24.

Rodrik, D. (2006) 'The social cost of foreign exchange reserves', *International Economic Journal* (Korean International Economic Association), 20 (3) September: 253–66.

World Bank (1996) *The East Asian Miracle*. Washington, DC: World Bank.

14 Enhancing global regulation
Exploring alternative financial machinery

Michelle Gallant

With the behaviour of financial institutions perceived as instrumental in causing the recent global economic troubles, much of the remedial discourse focuses on the reform of banking regulation. Ignored in the corrective discourse is any consideration of alternative vehicles of financial intermediation, the increased reliance upon which would displace the centrality of conventional banks to securing a reasonably stable economic environment.

Credit unions, derivatives of the cooperatives movement, provide financial services and can, in practice, be indistinguishable from banks. Significantly different principles, however, underpin their operations, principles that yield a unique organizational governance framework. It is a distinctiveness that has made, and continues to make, the credit union model of financial services superior to that of the traditional banking model. And unlike banks, debates about credit union governance tend to centre on how best to preserve their remarkable organizational strengths rather than the reform of any fundamental flaws.

This chapter offers an appraisal of the credit union governance framework in contradistinction to the corporate bank-based model. While the core structural features of governance assure its identification as the preferred economic model, undercutting that preference are the latter-day forces of competition and the realization of financial success. In gently nudging towards a brighter tomorrow, the credit union alternative needs to assume a greater presence in the financial services industry.

Alternative financial machinery

A contemporary definition provides that credit unions are member-owned, not-for-profit financial cooperatives whose membership is based on a common bond, or shared linkage among savers and borrowers in which members pool their savings and deposits and finance their own loans rather than rely on outside capital (World Council of Credit Unions, undated a).

Aspects of this definition apply to all credit unions although not all institutions possess all these characteristics. American credit unions are largely non-profit entities while Canadian institutions are not.[1] Some contemporary cooperatives actively solicit external investment. In others, the shared linkage may be nothing more than the holding of accounts at the same institution. In addition, not all financial cooperatives are necessarily known as credit unions. Peoples' banks, building societies, and popular banks constitute variations on the cooperatives theme. Notably, any thematic similarities help to distinguish alternative financial service providers from shareholder-owned, for-profit banks.

The nature and size of credit unions varies widely. While tiny operations offer micro-finance to developing country farmers, massive European and American institutions control millions in loans and deposits. Statistics on the global dimensions of the credit union movement can also vary widely and can be heavily dependent upon the particular definition of cooperative financial institutions. Some reasonably reliable estimates of credit union membership place global numbers at upwards of 190 million. The value of assets under the control of financial cooperatives may lie somewhere between 1.3 and 1.5 trillion US dollars (World Council of Credit Unions, undated b). However imprecise any estimates of the size of the industry may be, they are decidedly modest when contrasted with size of conventional banks. The US Bank of America alone has an asset value of over US$2 trillion, as does JP Morgan (National Information Center, 2012). The domination of the financial services sphere by traditional banking entities is a reflection of the enormous wealth under their collective control. Credit unions are relegated to the ranks of 'alternative' financial service providers due to the relatively modest scale of their enterprises.

Currently, these alternative financial entities can be found in all parts of world. While the range of ventures clustered under the credit union umbrella is diverse, a particular philosophy, a common business ethic, animates their work. That ethic derives from, and is synonymous with, the cooperatives movement.

The cooperative movement

Credit unions are co-extensive with the cooperative movement, a partly social, partly political, partly economic organizational form often described as anti-capitalist. Most locate the geneses of the movement in the wealthy industrialist Robert Owen's experiment in social utopianism in New Lanark, Scotland. In the early 1800s, Owen attempted to build a community in which the profits of industrial activity were retained and reinvested in communal services such as healthcare and education (Fairbairn, 1994). While his ideal, a prosperous society attentive to the needs of workers, foundered upon his death, it inspired a group of craftsmen in Rochdale, England. In the hopes of resisting the impoverishing forces of industrialization, the craftsmen sought to harness their collective power through the establishment of a cooperative. By pooling their resources they founded their own store through which they were able to purchase wares at discount prices and pass any savings directly to their members. To define their association and to formalize the nature of their collectivity, the craftsmen articulated a series of premises of cooperation. These defining conditions of association became known as the Rochdale principles, the fundamental canon of the credit union alternative (Axworthy, 1977).

Cooperative institutions swiftly spread across the channel and onto the continent. In 1846 in Germany Hermann Schulze, later known as Schulze-Delitzsch, mobilized craftsmen and shopkeepers to create a cooperative purchasing society. He subsequently created a separate credit cooperative to enable the making of low-cost loans to members. Founded on the ideals of open membership and the democratic principle of one member one vote, the Schulze-Delitzsch model grew to be known as people's banks (Moody and Fite, 1971a; Guinnane, 2003). Imitating Hermann Schulze's aspirations, the Raiffeisen credit organizations were conceived to assist farmers rather than craftsmen. Similar to Owen's labourers, and to the English and the German craftsmen and shopkeepers, farmers in mid-nineteenth-century Germany were trapped in a cycle of perpetual poverty. The exorbitant interest rates banks charged on farming loans meant farmers could not escape from mounting debt. Responding to this plight, Friedrich Raiffeisen established member-owned financial institutions through which member–farmers could obtain agricultural loans at reasonable rates (Peal, 1988).

The Schulze-Delitzsch and the Raiffeisen cooperative ideals took hold and spread throughout Europe, to Austria, Denmark, Belgium and elsewhere.[2] The initiatives were particularly influential in leading Luigi Luzzati to found the Luzzati's Peoples Bank in Italy in 1886 (Leonardi, 2006).[3] Despite the usual fertility of American soil for European ideas, the cooperative organizational form first crossed the Atlantic into Canada and later migrated south. Like his German predecessors, Alan Desjardins, a Quebecois native from a small town, was incensed by the excessive interest paid by local farmers on bank loans. In 1901, he founded the first North American cooperative, in Quebec, which later became known as Caisse Desjardins (LaMarche, 1985; Boyle, 1951; MacPherson, 2007). Desjardins helped develop the credit union concept in the United States through the industrialist Edward Filene, the creator of a chain of prosperous discount stores. Filene aspired to assist the working class through the provision of accessible credit (Moody and Fite, 1971b).

A principled approach to governance

From Owen's utopian vision to the Raiffeisen institutions through to their modern successors, financial cooperatives are born of necessity, the product of exclusion and economic exploitation. Mercantile banks grew prosperous from the nineteenth century expansion of trade and their role in facilitating international payments. That prosperity failed to translate into the provision of affordable credit for labourers, craftsman, and farmers. Rather, this class was either afforded loans at extortionate interest rates or denied access to credit altogether. To remedy the exploitation, to ground the new and necessary financial institution in a different, non-exploitative ethic, a specific set of credit unions principles was forged. These are commonly referred to as the Rochdale principles (Krishnaswami, 1968).

Adherence to some, or most, of these edicts supplies the organizational core of credit union governance. These both express methods of governance as well as reflect certain common values. To the extent that modern credit unions offer a vision of financial service delivery that differs from conventional financial service providers, largely banks, the vision derives from the extent to which these principles shape credit union practice. Axiomatically, significant deviation from these foundational tenets tends to blur those distinctions.

Modern iterations of the Rochdale rules identify voluntary and open membership as a core feature of credit union governance. Initially the voluntary aspect meant that the governing boards, executives or institutional officers of credit unions were not paid for their efforts although financial experts, professional persons, are now more prevalent. The quality of volunteerism brings its own merits, the generally higher social significance ascribed to those who donate their services in contrast to those whose skills are purchased in the marketplace. As a distinctive feature of governance, however, volunteerism helps to separate an institutional officer from the whims of the market and, to a degree, from the financial performance of the enterprise. Volunteerism unshackles individual performance from economic self-interest. To an extent, this frees an executive to take other interests into account in decision-making, for example, to prefer the interests of employees at the expense of a financial prerogative. Under the conventional governance framework applicable to banks and other corporate bodies, executive compensation is commonly tied to the economic performance of the firm. The intertwining of self-interest, compensation and performance can be problematic, at times the cause of significant financial loss (Sorkin, 2009).[4]

Arguably the fullest expression of ethical governance is embodied in two Rochdale tenets: democratic member control and member economic participation. Democratic member control means that each member has an equal right to participate in credit union decision-making and that all votes are of equal weight. There is no privileging of voting power or institutional control, either on the basis of size of deposits or loans or through some other ownership claim. Member control also describes a unique feature of financial cooperatives, one that introduces a curious tension into decision-making.

Under a member control model of governance, the users of financial services, or the customers, are also the owners of institution. Members are also the source of institutional capital. Investment is not solicited from external sources but is solicited internally. This has profound implications. There is no separation between the interests of the institution and the interests of anyone else: the users of the financial services are the owners of the service and the providers of the capital. Under a capitalist system, the owners of capital profit at the expense of non-owners. Exploitation occurs through the necessary separation of ownership and customer or ownership (of the means of production) and worker. Credit union governance fuses the relationship, disabling any potential alienation because those who control and own the institutions are also those who use the financial services. Members are not external to ownership but integral to ownership. By the same token, the owner-user identity introduces a healthy tension into credit union decision-making that is not present under a conventional corporate governance framework: any preference conferred on owners negatively affects user and vice versa. Any increase to interest on loans provides more revenues to owners yet simultaneously deleteriously affects those same owners as users. This tension limits the opportunities for exploitation. This fusion of interests is an unusual feature of governance. Generally, the owners of a financial institution are not simultaneously the primary users; the owners can profit at the expense of users without creating any tension. The aspirations of owner–shareholder governance are constrained by market forces, not by tensions internal to the organization itself. Jackson illustrates this internal dynamic in finding that banks change interest rates in order to maximize profit whereas credit unions change rates to keep a constant equilibrium between loans and savings (Jackson, 2006). It is the unique governance tension that causes that equilibrium.

Nor are credit unions beholden to external interests, or external investors. Member-owned cooperatives are not, under ordinary circumstances, obligated to anyone other than the cooperative constituency. Under a classic corporate control framework, the corporation, unless privately held, is subject to external influences. Corporations usually solicit investment in return for an equitable interest in the company or the issuance of debt instruments. Equitable interests, shares, can give the shareholder investors varying degrees of control over institutional decision-making.

A fourth Rochdale tenet heavily shapes the institutional differences between banks and credit unions as well as influences ethical identity: the principle of concern for community. Financial cooperatives acknowledge that they form integral parts of their communities and require that concern for community inform any institutional decision-making. In species, this commitment reflects the origins and the communitarian aspect of any cooperative. The institution does not merely serve, or profit from, the community but self-identifies as an incident of that community.

A community-oriented ethic can mean subordinating pure financial interests to other considerations and adopting strategies that have been clearly rejected by conventional financial service providers. When diminishing returns precipitate an exodus of banks from particular regions, credit unions often venture in, enticed not by profit but by service to a community (Assiniboine Credit Union, 2011). The subordination of financial interest can mean engaging in new forms of lending, arguably riskier lending, because the higher level of risk is justified as serving a purpose unique to a specific community (Mavenga, 2010).[5] Again, it is communal well-being, not profit, that motivates.

Along with democratic community-oriented member–owner governance, the credit union canon emphasizes autonomy, independence, and education. Financial cooperatives are autonomous, independent self-help organizations. This quality is evident in the origins of the unions, their emergence as a tool to solve collective difficulties. The raising of capital from internal sources (members) assures some measure of autonomy. A commitment to education once meant educating workers or craftsmen although modern understandings of this ethic tend to contemplate increasing financial literacy. A subtle aspect of governance, the commitment to education underscores the distinction between capitalism's chronic exploitation of human vulnerability and weakness. A significant factor in the recent collapse of the United States financial markets was 'toxic' mortgages fuelled by excessive borrowing (Lewis, 2010). Profits accrued, and the interests of the financial institutions were ultimately insured by US taxpayers while the burden of debt was carried by the poorly advised, or unwise, borrowers. Credit unions promise to increase, rather than exploit the absence of, financial literacy (Credit Union Central of Canada, 2010).

Finally, credit union governance expressly aspires to an ethic that contradicts the market-imbued ethic of competition: cooperation. Cooperatives do not perceive other cooperatives as competitors for financial services business. Rather, they acknowledge the effectiveness and strength of collective action, of reliance, for example, on common facilities and of the efficiency of working to enhance the collective welfare of cooperatives. A cooperative character, however, does not preclude competition with entities outside the group, notably with banking institutions.[6]

Incorporation of these values, of concern for community, democratic control, autonomy, education, cooperation and the member–owner constitution set credit unions apart from traditional banks. Presumptively, credit unions are not classic corporate incarnations and therefore not subject to the dictates of corporate law.

Corporate governance typically places the interests of shareholders, the owners of the corporate entity, at the centre of corporate decision-making. A decision in the best interests of a corporation, the guiding rule of corporate law, usually equates to the decision which best maximizes shareholder wealth. This seriously constrains an organization's ability to give preference to other interests. A strategic decision to protect the environment, for example, would normally be precluded from consideration unless consistent with the maximization of shareholder value.[7] Equally, a decision by a financial entity to reduce its workforce would, if undertaken to maximize shareholder value, be acceptable. It would also be acceptable to retain that workforce provided that decision maintained shareholder value. In either case, the maximization of wealth is the governing creed.

Under the credit union governance model, there is no discussion of preferring the wealth of owners in the decision-making process. The owners cannot be preferred at the expense of users since they are one and the same. And it is entirely legitimate to privilege sustaining the environment, or to privilege the protection of employees from unemployment, since concern for community is part of the set of principles that shapes credit union decision-making. Classically the ethical difference between credit unions and banks is simply framed as the one existing to serve members, the other to maximize corporate profits.

Cooperative governance under challenge

Constituted differently than the financial service providers at the helm of the latter-day economic collapses, credit unions exemplify a preferable mode of financial service delivery. It is preferable because, unlike the conventional corporate enterprise, it proposes an inclusive governance structure. There is no chasm between owners and users, or owners and labourers. It is not employees, or users of services, or purchasers of products that govern the activities of a corporation. Had the highly leveraged borrowers whose asset values vanished in the recent financial collapse been party to earlier institutional decision-making, the risky yet extraordinarily lucrative practice of packaging and re-selling mortgages might well have met a premature death.

The credit union governance model is preferable because it permits, or obligates, the taking of multiple interests into account in decision-making. Had banks actually been compelled to take into account the wider societal interests of ensuring the provision of stable credit markets, different decisions might have been made and the resulting complete attrition of lending, if not avoided, than perhaps been far less severe. Moreover, credit unions governance acknowledges that financial interests are never the only interests at stake. Adequate access to credit, without more, would not protect other important ingredients of social well-being. Access to credit would not, for instance, assure access to clean water. An ethical concern for community, however, might well translate into preferred terms for loans to entities with environmentally friendly business practices or lead to a refusal to lend to projects whose environmental impacts are notoriously brutal.

Finally, credit union governance is preferable since it acknowledges that competition is not the only ideology upon which to found the development and advance of society. Cooperation as a form of social interaction, including cooperation as a method for organizing economic relationships, has much value to offer. It is regularly squeezed from the discourse by the cacophony of the competitive market. Credit unions demonstrate that the fusion of economic and social development promotes welfare, demonstrate that collaborative organizational modalities can, and do, produce positive results.

Despite the advantages of credit unions, the cooperative instinct continues to inhabit a world dominated by capitalist institutions, a world ruled by financial institutions rewarded by the pursuit of profit, often to the exclusion of any other human value. In this global reality, those same forces buffet the preferred model of financial service delivery. Rather than witness territory being ceded to this alternative provider, credit unions appear to be morphing into their antithesis. Any rising prominence occurs at the expense of the foundational tenets, consequently blurring the differences between alternatives and banks.

Ferguson and McKillop (1997, 2000) organize the development of credit unions into three evolutionary stages: nascent, transition and mature. Each evolutionary stage is marked by a set of characteristics. Credit unions in the nascent stage tend to have small asset bases, to rely heavily on volunteers, to be organized around some common bond and provide very basic financial products. In the transition stage, they tend to have more professionalization, to rely less on volunteers, to offer a greater diversity of services and financial products, to be less defined by socio-economic connections, to operate under stronger, more definitive, regulatory structures and to place more emphasis on growth and efficiency. In the mature state, credit unions are typically managed by highly professional persons, tend to have very large assets bases, tend to offer a full range of highly diversified financial products, to show high levels of technology, to have a very loose common bond and to have in place a mechanism for insuring deposits. Sometimes McKillop adds a fourth stage: demutualization (McKillop and Wilson, 2010).

Nascent institutions occur principally in the developing world, small, grass-roots organizations, often synonymous with new-age micro-credit operations. These are new, largely organic, unions, forming and evolving in ways reminiscent of the early Owenites. Transition financial cooperatives inhabit the developed and the developing world. The transition stage captures more mature entities than the nascent, entities that are in the process of professionalizing, in the process of moving from the classic credit union principle of reliance on volunteers to reliance on paid officers. The attributes of mature credit unions describe institutions in Europe, in the United States and in Canada. Mature credit unions offer a full range of services, to a wide group of members who are not defined by any socio-economic, or other, bond and are highly professional. They solicit external investment and are no longer solely reliant upon the economic contributions of their members. In this latter stage of evolution, the credit unions are almost indistinguishable from banks.

In many ways, cooperative financial institutions stand as victims of their success (Axworthy, 1981). They become bank-like through the forces of growth, expansion and financial achievement. As member base expands, the bonds among members break, the socio-economic bonds replaced by mere associational bonds. Expansion requires new resources and sends credit unions looking for external investment. The member–owner governance principle contracts to accommodate that third party. Pressure on the communal-orientation principle happens as the community expands and is redefined. Geographic proximity, originally a defining characteristic of the credit union community, loses its meaning as successful credit unions seek greater yields through engagement with the global community. Retaining and realizing upon a commitment to a local community becomes difficult when the institutional stakeholders form part of a different, much larger community.

Demutualization, of course, signals the ultimate demise of a credit union. It connotes the conversion of a credit union into a corporation, the conversion of members into shareholders. Lost in that conversion is the entire ethos of credit union governance. Demutualization can yield significant gains to members, a reason that many would welcome the invitation to transform. In many respects, this latter development shows the ultimate surrender of Rochdale governance to the whims of a competitive market, and to capitalism's setting of financial rewards about all other considerations.

Whether credit union governance can co-exist with globalization is a very real question. Whatever their flaws or evolutionary future, cooperatives tended to fare somewhat better than banks in negotiating the market declines and volatility that have characterized the recent past (Ferri, 2012). They did not experience significant institutional collapse, nor did they share in the trillion-dollar financial bailouts (Restankis, 2010). That fact alone should be reason enough to consider placing much greater reliance on the cooperative form of financial service delivery. Conventional banks have failed contemporary society. So far, conventional credit unions have not.

Notes

1. Canadian credit unions lost the battle with Canadian banks for non-profit status; see Schroeder (1983).
2. The migration was not entirely successful; see Guinnane (1994) and Colvin and McLaughlin (2012).
3. As Leonardi demonstrates, there were clear philosophical differences between German and Italy credit cooperatives.
4. Notably, too, Nick Leeson rose to infamy for singularly destroying Barings Banks. Leeson's superiors chose not to monitor his activities too closely since he was apparently generating enormous returns (Leeson, 1996).
5. Notably, too, credit unions have been at the forefront of the provision of micro-credit, micro-finance, the modern offering of very small, typically business-oriented, loans in poorer rural and urban areas.
6. For an indication of the influence of credit unions on banks, see Emmons and Schmid (2000).
7. Canadian corporate law admits some consideration of the interests beyond shareholders: *Peoples Department Stores (Trustee of) v Wise*, (2004) Supreme Court of Canada 461. In American law, the equivalent is corporate constituency statutes

which permit directors to take some account of the interests of non-shareholders in decision-making; Minnesota Annotated Statutes, Minn. Stat. ss 302A.251 (2007).

References

Assiniboine Credit Union (2011) 'ACU announces North-End branch', available at www.assiniboine.mb.ca/News/ACU-Announces-North-End-Branch.aspx (accessed 21 October 2012).

Axworthy, C. (1977) 'Consumer co-operatives and the Rochdale Principles today', *Osgoode Hall Law Journal*, 15, 137–64.

Axworthy, C. (1981) 'Credit unions in Canada: the dilemma of success', *University of Toronto Law Journal*, 31, 72–116.

Boyle, G. (1951) *The Poor Man's Prayer: The Story of Credit Union Beginnings*. New York: Harper Brothers.

Colvin, C. and McLaughlin, E. (2012) *Raiffeisenism Abroad: Why Did German Microfinance Fail in Ireland but Prosper in the Netherlands?*, working paper no MWP 2-12/01, European University Institute, available at http://ssrn.com/sol3/papers.cfm?abstract_id=2006003 (accessed 22 October 2012).

Credit Union Central of Canada (2010) *Canadian Credit Union Scan of Financial Literacy Initiatives*. Toronto, Canada: Credit Union Central of Canada.

Emmons, W. and Schmid, F. A. (2000) 'Bank competition and concentration: do credit unions matter?', *Federal Reserve Bank of St Louis Review*, May/June, pp. 29–42.

Fairbairn, B. (1994) *The Meaning of Rochdale: the Rochdale Pioneers and the Co-operative Principles*. Saskatoon, Canada: Center for the Study of Cooperatives.

Ferguson, C. and McKillop, D. G. (1997) *The Strategic Development of Credit Unions*. Chichester: John Wiley.

Ferguson, C. and McKillop, D. G. (2000) 'Classifying credit union development in terms of mature, transition and nascent industry types', *Service Industries Journal*, 20, 103–20.

Ferri, G. (2012) *Credit Cooperatives: Challenges and Opportunities in the New Global Scenario*, working paper no 031/12. Trento, Italy: Euricse.

Guinnane, T. (1994) 'A failed institutional transplant: Raiffeisen's credit cooperatives in Ireland, 1894–1914', *Explorations in Economic History*, 31, 38–61.

Guinnane, T. (2003) 'A 'friend and advisor': external auditing and confidence in Germany's credit cooperatives, 1889–1914', *Business History Review*, 77, 235–64.

Jackson, W. (2006) *A Comparison of Deposit and Loan Pricing Behaviour of Credit Unions and Commercial Banks*. Madison, WI: Filene Research Institute.

Krishnaswami, O. (1968) 'The principles of co-operation – a historical survey and a review', *Annals of Public and Cooperative Economics*, 39, 587–605.

LaMarche, J. (1985) *La Saga des Caisses Populaires*. Ottawa, Canada: Les Editions de la Press.

Leeson, N. (1996) *Rogue Trader: How I Brought Down Barings Bank and Shook the Financial World*. Boston, MA: Little.

Leonardi, A. (2006) 'Italian credit cooperatives between expansion and retrenchment (1883–1945)'. Helsinki: XIV International Economic History Congress.

Lewis, M. (2010) *The Big Short: Inside the Doomsday Machine*. New York: W.W. Norton & Company.

MacPherson, I. (2007) *One Path to Co-operative Studies*. Victoria, Canada: New Rochdale Press.

Mavenga, F. (2010) 'Economic impact of credit unions on rural communities', MSc thesis. Saskatchewan, Canada: University of Saskatchewan.

McKillop, D. G. and Wilson, J. (2010) 'Credit unions: a theoretical and empirical overview', available at http://ssrn.com/abstract=1702782 (accessed 21 October 2012).

Moody, J. C. and Fite, G. (1971a) 'The origins of cooperative credit', in their *The Credit Union Movement: Origins and Development, 1850–1970*. Lincoln, NE: University of Nebraska Press.

Moody, J. C. and Fite, G. (1971b) 'The origins and early development of credit unions in the United States, 1908–15', in their *The Credit Union Movement: Origins and Development, 1850–1970*. Lincoln, NE: University of Nebraska Press.

National Information Center (2012) 'Top 50 HCs', available at www.ffiec.gov/nicpubweb/nicweb/Top50Form.aspx (accessed 21 October 2012).

Peal, D. (1988) 'Self-help and the state: rural cooperatives in imperial Germany', *Central European History*, 21, 244–66.

Restankis, J. (2010) *Humanizing the Economy: Co-operative in an Age of Capital*. Gabriola Island, Canada: New Society Publishers.

Schroeder, D. (1983) *Deposits Fully Guaranteed: A History of Saskatchewan's Credit Union Mutual Aid Board, 1953–1983*. Saskatchewan, Canada: Credit Union Central of Saskatchewan.

Sorkin, A. (2009) *Too Big To Fail: The Inside Story of How Wall Street and Washington Fought to Save the Financial System-and Themselves*. New York: Penguin Group.

World Council of Credit Unions (undated a) 'What is a credit union?', available at www.woccu.org/about/creditunion (accessed 30 October 2012).

World Council of Credit Unions (undated b) 'International credit union system', available at www.woccu.org/about/intlcusystem (accessed 21 October 2012).

15 Moving forward with planetary boundaries and degrowth

Geoffrey Garver

The degrowth movement is an emerging response to humanity living beyond its means. By suggesting the human enterprise is too big by some measure, such that it must downsize, degrowth implicitly suggests a limit on the size of the global economy. Indeed, limits are the essence of degrowth. Yet degrowth goes beyond ecological economics, sustainability and other expressions of the idea that humans must live within the Earth's means – and therefore that an infinitely growing economy is biophysically impossible – by explicitly incorporating the notion that the economy has already exceeded those limits. The unmistakable warning of the jolting term *degrowth*, which derives from the French word *décroissance,* is not that the economy can and might become too big, but rather that it already is too big and therefore must degrow.

Despite its core focus on limits, the full meaning of degrowth and the objectives of the degrowth movement remain fluid. What limits have been exceeded, and what needs to degrow? The overriding limits inherent in degrowth are the ecological limits within which human society must operate in order to thrive in successive generations. Other limits may be relevant as well – on the size or scope of enterprises or institutions, on capital accumulation, on incomes and individual and collective monetary wealth, on consumption, on work time. However, from the systems based perspective on which ecological economics is founded, the paramount normative boundaries that should contain the collective activities of humans are ecological and are tied to the throughput of material and energy in the economy.

This chapter explores the relevance of emerging metrics of ecological limits on the human economy to the degrowth discussion. First, the contours of degrowth are described and its core ideas summarized. The importance of the fundamental notion of limits in degrowth emerges from this analysis. Second, some key tensions that persist within the degrowth discussion are examined. Third, key systems-based indicators of ecological limits, such as planetary boundaries of safe operating space for humanity (Rockström *et al.*, 2009) and metrics of social metabolism, are situated within the degrowth discussion. Ecological integrity and resilience of the human–Earth relationship are fundamental to the ecological limits on which degrowth depends. Last, implications of the fundamental importance of ecological limits on the ongoing development of the degrowth idea and the degrowth movement are considered. In particular, the ecological limits that underlie degrowth are global in scale, and therefore the tendency of the degrowth movement to favor local autonomy and decentralization poses a potential problem. Because the diverse human activities that place pressures on global ecological limits are interrelated, and their effects accumulate and interact in systems that transcend local contexts, degrowth must balance local and global initiatives. Degrowth should embrace a perspective that builds from a systems-based understanding of global ecological pressures and their drivers, acknowledges the diverse cultural and ecological contexts for those pressures and drivers and distributes governance responsibilities from the global to the local level according to these understandings.

What is degrowth?

Degrowth (or 'sustainable degrowth') has been defined as 'a downscaling of production and consumption that increases human well-being and enhances ecological conditions and equity on the planet' (Research and Degrowth, 2012). The terms contraction, sustainability, anti-productivism, voluntary simplicity and downshifting sound many of the same chords that degrowth does (Latouche, 2006). Degrowth has roots both in the quest of ecological economics for a steady state economy that respects ecological limits and in the socio-cultural objections to wealth accumulation and bigness reflected in Schumacher's *Small is Beautiful* and the earlier work of French intellectuals who critiqued 'gigantism' (Martinez-Alier *et al.*, 2010).

Although the term *décroissance* can be traced back at least to the 1970s (ibid.), the current degrowth movement took root with the publication of special issues on *décroissance* of the French magazine *Silence* in February and March 2002. Its visibility increased with François Schneider's fourteen-month donkey trek through southern France in 2004 and 2005 to raise awareness of the need to downscale the economy. What began as a provocative word intended to shake loose the human imagination from the overwhelmingly dominant idea that the economy must grow for humanity to survive (Latouche, 2004; Martinez-Alier *et al.*, 2010) has evolved into a collaborative discussion and research agenda aimed at developing 'a framework for transformation to a lower and sustainable level of production and consumption' (Research and Degrowth, 2012). A plurality of diverse approaches to degrowth is appropriate in light of different challenges in different parts of the world. However, the degrowth community appears to accept that, although rich nations have been and continue to be the leading drivers of dangerous pressures on the global ecosystem, 'degrowth must apply to the South as much as to the North if there is to be any chance to stop Southern societies from rushing up the blind alley of growth economics' (Latouche, 2004).

The organization Research and Degrowth, established in 2006, has been maintaining the focus of the degrowth movement by spearheading and overseeing a series of degrowth conferences and maintaining a repository of information about degrowth that has emerged from conferences and other venues. As of October 2012, three main international conferences on degrowth have been held – Paris 2008, Barcelona 2010 and Venice 2012 – along with several regional degrowth conferences in Vancouver in 2010 and 2011, Montreal in 2012 and Berlin in 2012.

The reforms associated with degrowth 'emphasize redistribution (of work and leisure, natural resources and wealth), social security and gradual decentralization and relocalisation of the economy, as a way to reduce throughput and manage a stable adaptation to a smaller economy' (Kallis, 2011: 876). A key outcome of the Barcelona conference was a more fulsome outline of a core set of degrowth 'bullet points' that reflect core degrowth proposals developed during the Paris and Barcelona gatherings (Barcelona Conference, 2010), and those ideas have continued to evolve. The Barcelona bullet points begin with the overarching assertion that 'Degrowth of the size of the technological and economic system as well as economical, political, social and cultural structural changes are urgently needed.' The propositions are organized under the headings democracy, education, social economy, natural resources and demography. Across these categories, the bullet points emphasize community involvement, decommodification and decommercialization, with a focus on reorienting the economy toward local autonomy, equitable sharing, low-impact technologies, a more restricted view of private property, food sovereignty and floors and ceilings on income, as well as on monetary reform, trade reform, constraints on advertising and moratoria on harmful technologies. The overarching proposal with regard to natural resources is to reduce and then maintain the throughput of energy and materials within the Earth's life support capacity The bullet points support full reproductive rights while encouraging reductions in total population and population growth rates. They support as well the right to migrate while encouraging efforts to increase local resilience so as to reduce the incentives for people to seek better lives in new places.

The Barcelona document also recommends a program of research, for example on how to decouple the drivers of innovations that will support a degrowth economy from the profit motive, how to reconsider development categories and relationships between the global North and the global South, whether examples of flourishing non-growing economies exist and how they function, what metrics and indicators are appropriate for degrowth, and how reform of financial and monetary systems is relevant to degrowth. Another recent set of degrowth research questions includes the relationship of ecological crises to economic crises, analysis of the winners and losers associated with commodity frontiers, more rigorous examination of the roots of the growth fetish, more in depth research regarding population and degrowth, and a variety of questions regarding the experience and role of social movements associated with degrowth (Kallis *et al.*, 2012).

Key tensions within degrowth

The foregoing sections reveal the ongoing evolution of the degrowth idea – an evolution that still has not crystallized into a clear concept or philosophy of degrowth (Latouche, 2006; Martinez-Alier *et al.*, 2010). As part of this evolution, some tensions regarding the meaning and implications of degrowth are fostering a healthy debate within the community of academics and activists engaged in the degrowth movement. A key discussion relates to whether and how degrowth is compatible with capitalism and conventional economics. As the word itself makes clear, degrowth is a direct challenge to growth-insistent economics and to economism (Latouche, 2004). However, prominent leaders in degrowth thinking have proposed internalization of environmental costs through Pigovian taxes (Latouche, 2006) or a temporary phase of Green Keynesianism, with public-supported investment in green technologies and infrastructure en route to a low-carbon economy (Martinez-Alier, 2009), within the context of degrowth. These proposals have garnered criticism as being too beholden to conventional economics in light of the perceived inherent incompatibility between degrowth and capitalism (Foster, 2011). This critique supports 'a "co-revolutionary movement"…that will bring together the traditional working-class critique of capital, the critique of imperialism, the critiques of patriarchy and racism, and the critique of ecologically destructive growth (along with their respective mass movements)' (ibid.: 32).

The point of tension between degrowth and capitalism highlights the fact that degrowth is inherently transitional, in that the move towards downsizing from the current situation of ecological overshoot must start before the socio-economic system that gave rise to it can be completely transformed. A post-degrowth world might be considered indifferent to growth, or 'a-growth' (Latouche, 2004; van den Bergh, 2011). Meanwhile, degrowth cannot avoid subsuming the challenges of transition (Martinez-Alier *et al.*, 2010). It must confront the historical legacy on which the current predicament rests, loaded with a sweeping complex of fossil-fuelled anthropogenic material and energy flows, physical and institutional infrastructure, patterns of behaviour, investment-backed expectations, and ideological perspectives that as an integrated whole has enormous momentum and inertia. Degrowth must tackle these challenges but also maintain a post-degrowth vision, whether of steady-state ecological economics (ibid.) or something else. Thus, the call for Green Keynesianism as part of degrowth is qualified with a warning against 'persever[ing] in the faith of economic growth' (Martinez-Alier, 2009), and the call for Pigovian taxes and other measures that rigorously and honestly internalize costs is cast as a possible way to trigger the kind of revolution that will spur mass support for degrowth (Latouche, 2006).

Still, these qualifications are reminiscent of the problematic acquiescence of some ecological economists to monetary valuation of ecosystem services – roundly rejected within the degrowth movement (ibid.). Monetary valuation of ecosystem services is defended as offering a practical way to secure environmental protections in the current economic system (TEEB, 2010), despite cogent warnings that it will be difficult or impossible, as Wes Jackson put it, to control the metaphor (Gayer, 2010). Just as Keynes's prediction that growth would be needed only until the 'economic problem' was solved (Skidelsky and Skidelsky, 2012) now appears naive, calls for temporarily relying on the system that caused the current ecological predicament give rise to understandable concern. At the very least, any transitional aspects of degrowth that rely on the current dominant economic paradigm should be strictly cordoned off from the long-term vision of ecological and social integrity that is at its core – a vision best conceived without being constrained by capitalist market economy thinking. And, if degrowth ultimately is incompatible with capitalism as it now exists, the transitional aspects of degrowth should focus on what the current dominant economic system can do on its way out to promote ecological and social integrity.

Other discussions within the degrowth arena have to do with the appropriate balance in making policy from the local to the global level (discussed further below), the relative roles of individual and collective action, and whether existing institutions of governance should be maintained but reformed or completely discarded and replaced. In addition, although the appeal for 'real democracy' that is not controlled by a wealthy and powerful elite is strong within the degrowth movement, the degrowth community must nonetheless contend with problematic arguments that degrowth will only be possible with some form of benign eco-totalitarianism. One response – probably insufficient to quell this point of tension – has been that degrowth 'wagers on a stick-and-carrot combination: regulations designed to force change, plus the ideal of a convivial utopia, will add up to a decolonisation of minds and encourage enough virtuous behaviour to produce a reasonable solution: local ecological democracy' (Latouche, 2006). Because of a strong resistance within the degrowth movement to an insistence on a particular set of principles regarding these and other questions, the degrowth idea continues to evolve in an inclusive manner despite these tensions.[1]

Ecological limits as the core idea of degrowth

Ensuring well-being in an ecologically finite world means providing all present and future members of life's commonwealth 'bounded capabilities' to flourish, contingent on Earth's limited capacity to support life and on fair intragenerational, intergenerational and interspecies sharing of that capacity (Jackson, 2009: 45–7; Brown and Garver, 2009). The notion of *bounded* capabilities adds important nuance to Sen's notion of human capabilities to be well nourished, to live long lives and to engage meaningfully in society (Sen, 2005), by underscoring the need to condition capabilities and freedom on aggregate ecological limits (Jackson, 2009). In other words, the goal of enclosing the social and economic spheres within the Earth's ecological limits (Daly, 1996) must have primacy against other goals (Garver, 2012).

In his plenary remarks at the Venice degrowth conference in September 2012, François Schneider reaffirmed that this notion of limits with primary importance is a core concept underlying degrowth. At the same time, degrowth economics is ultimately based on energetics, and on challenging the false idea that real wealth can be created by running down ecosystems, and hence increasing entropy, at rates that outrun their solar-powered generation (Martinez-Alier, 2009). Taking these ideas together, it follows that metrics of global ecological limits and of social metabolism – that is, of the throughput and cycling of material and energy in human society – are highly relevant to degrowth. In particular, the comprehensive framework of planetary boundaries of safe operating space for humanity (Rockström *et al.*, 2009), supplemented with measures of social metabolism such as ecological footprint and human appropriation of net primary productivity (HANPP), can help shape governance in a degrowth context.

In the planetary boundaries framework, normative limits for key planetary variables are established at a 'safe' distance from systems thresholds in the global ecosystem, beyond which catastrophic ecological change occurs. According to planetary boundaries researchers, proposed boundaries for atmospheric carbon dioxide concentration, biodiversity loss, and anthropogenic additions of nitrogen and phosphorus to the global ecosystem have already been crossed (Rockström *et al.*, 2009; UNEP, 2009; Carpenter and Bennett, 2011). Similarly, ecological footprint research indicates that human use of global biocapacity has outpaced the replenishment of biocapacity since the 1970s (Ewing *et al.*, 2010).

The planetary boundaries framework's conceptual foundation aligns with degrowth, especially in this overshoot situation, because global ecological boundaries, not insistence on economic growth, constrain the socio-political and economic spheres; 'the thresholds in key Earth System processes exist irrespective of peoples' preferences, values or compromises based on political and socioeconomic feasibility' (Rockström *et al.*, 2009: 7). Despite the primacy of planetary boundaries, the 'operating space' they enclose allows 'humanity…the flexibility to choose a myriad of pathways for human well-being and development' (ibid.). This notion of limits opening up vast possibility (Berry, 2008) invites creativity in all domains. The potential for the degrowth movement to develop new ways for humans individually and collectively to achieve well-being lies within this creative space.

To develop 'novel and adaptive approaches to governance' (Rockström *et al.*, 2009: 28) and other cultural, political, social and economic aspects within the context of degrowth, ecological bounds on the aggregate scale of the economy can be used to frame additional constraints and possibilities focused more directly on the socio-political dimensions of the human sphere. Aggregate environmental impact is a function of the size of the human population, its affluence and its technology: the well-known $I = P \times A \times T$ (or $IPAT$) formulation, where I is impact, P is population, A is affluence or consumption and T is technology (Ehrlich and Holdren, 1972). Each of the planetary boundaries can be considered a fixed limit of the I variable, with each boundary value of I constraining the P, A and T variables; if P rises, A or T, or both, must drop. For example, suppose I represents the total carbon emissions that will safely keep the human enterprise in safe operating space, P is the human population, A is the consumption of material and energy per person, and T is the amount of carbon emitted per unit of material and energy consumed. As population rises, either per capita consumption (A) must decrease, the emissions per unit of consumption (T) must decrease, or both must decrease for total emissions (I) to remain unchanged. If I must decrease to return to safe conditions, as is now the case for several boundaries, the degrowth challenge becomes starker. An additional variable, ethics (E), may be introduced to this relationship to call attention to the role of ethics in making individual and collective choices regarding the other variables – making the framework $I = f(PATE)$ (Brown and Garver, 2009).

Accounting for material and energy stocks and flows is essential for maintaining the human enterprise within planetary boundaries of safe operating space. For example, HANPP is a useful tool in this regard. Net primary production (NPP), the amount of biomass energy that plants accumulate through photosynthesis in a given time period, is vital to essential ecosystem functions and to human needs. Spatially explicit information on HANPP and the flows of harvested biomass from the points of appropriation to consumption endpoints (Erb *et al.*, 2009b) is important for understanding the drivers and implications for sustainability of agriculture, timber harvest, forest fires, urbanization and other land use change, and other forms of biomass appropriation. These metrics of HANPP can help link social metabolism to pressures on planetary boundaries. For example, the impact of HANPP on species extinctions and other aspects of biodiversity has been a prominent question in HANPP research (Vitousek *et al.*, 1986; Wright, 1990; Haberl *et al.*, 2007; Erb *et al.*, 2009a). Tracking the movement of HANPP and other material and energy sources in the global economy at high resolution, in conjunction with geographically explicit data on the drivers and impacts related to climate change, biodiversity, biogeo-chemical fluxes and other key systems processes, will allow for better governance, at an ecosystem-specific scale, of difficult obstacles to sustainable degrowth. Ongoing extension of the analysis of HANPP can help in particular with challenges related to feeding a rising human population that is consuming more and more meat; deciding the future role of biofuels in the global energy picture; contending with the trend toward increasing metabolic rift in an increasingly globalized economy; and controlling the impacts of intensive biomass production that depends on fertilization, genetically modified organisms, pesticides and irrigation (Erb *et al.*, 2009a; Foley *et al.*, 2011; Bringezu *et al.*, 2012).

Reconciling planetary limits with the focus on local autonomy

Several tensions within the degrowth movement were noted above. In regard to how to deal collectively with aggregated pressures on global ecological limits that derive from geographically and temporally diverse sources, the question of the relationship between localities horizontally with each other and vertically with other levels of political order is particularly cogent. In general, the degrowth community tends to doubt the possibility of true democracy at higher levels of political organization, on the grounds that democracy 'can probably only function where the polis is small and firmly anchored to a set of values' (Latouche, 2006). Hence the proposition:

> The relationships between the polities within the global village could be regulated by a democracy of cultures, in what might be called a pluriver-salist vision. This would not be a world government, but merely an instance of minimal arbitration between sovereign polities with highly divergent systems.
>
> (Ibid.)

The problem is that the dynamics and interregional interdependencies of biogeochemical, geologic, hydrologic, climatic, atmospheric and other processes prevent any sub-global region or locality from being isolated from the rest of the integrated global ecosystem, as a study that detected finger-printed dioxins from sources in Mexico, the United States and southern Canada in mothers' milk and other receptors in Inuit communities in Nunavut illustrated starkly (Commoner *et al.*, 2000). Moreover, authoritarian rule and inequality in the weight of different voices can exist even at the local level, and retraction of society into largely autonomous but unavoidably interdependent communities could exacerbate, not alleviate, divisiveness and suspicion of the other.

How does a locality protect itself from impacts that arise outside of it, and what ensures that it will be responsible for impacts it causes that transcend its borders? A central challenge for degrowth is to develop legal and policy mechanisms, using tools such as HANPP, for distributing the responsibility to respect global ecological limits down to the local level. This architecture of distribution should also incorporate mechanisms for enabling all humans and other living beings to flourish, built on principles of intragenerational, intergenerational and interspecies fairness (Brown and Garver, 2009; Bosselmann, 2008). The European principle of subsidiarity provides a way to reconcile a preference for establishing policy at the local level with the reality that localities are never immune from impacts that arise from away or able to avoid causing impacts that reach other localities.

Subsidiarity favours intervention at the level at which it will be most effective for achieving policy objectives (Saunier and Meganck, 2009). The European Union treaties establish subsidiarity as a core principle of governance in the European Union. Thus, Article 5(3) of the Treaty on European Union provides that, consistent with the principle of subsidiarity, the EU 'shall act only if and in so far as the objectives of the proposed action cannot be sufficiently achieved by the Member States, either at central level or at regional and local level, but can rather, by reason of the scale or effects of the proposed action, be better achieved at Union level.' In the United States, the federalization of environmental law that took place starting in the late 1960s can be seen as an adjustment based on subsidiarity, given the ineffectiveness of state laws in regulating environmental problems.

The challenge in applying the subsidiarity principle is to account for a broad range of cultural, ecological and socio-political contexts, and a plurality in the way behaviour is made to conform to limits, in fashioning a predictable and consistent global system for implementing limits such as planetary boundaries. Subsidiarity should be implemented in recognition that global governance includes the participation of 'a long list of institutions including governments, businesses, nongovernmental organizations (NGOs), universities, research centers, and foundations [operating] inside and outside of government and across national and institutional boundaries' (Saunier and Meganck, 2009: 3–4). Although degrowth calls for significant reforms in these institutions, the principle of subsidiarity should nonetheless be useful for allocating governances roles among political orders at different scales.

Conclusion

The current global commitment to economic growth is hard to square with the strong historical correlation of economic growth with ecological degradation and persistent social injustice, and with the daunting challenge of sufficiently decoupling ecological degradation from growth in the future (Speth, 2008; Jackson, 2009). Sustainable development is growth-insistent, as defined at the 1992 Earth Summit in Rio and emphatically reaffirmed at the Rio + 20 conference in June 2012. Yet sustainable development has shown little sign of being capable of triggering the 'overarching policies and radical change of behaviour needed at individual and collective scales' (Martinez-Alier *et al.*, 2010: 1741) to curb the rampant consumerism that drives patterns of social metabolism that are undermining the capacity of the Earth's ecosystems to support human and other life. Degrowth is a forceful critique of and challenge to the growth-insistent sustainable development model (Martinez-Alier *et al.*, 2010; Kallis, 2011), and a more hopeful approach to a mutually enhancing human–Earth relationship over the long term. Planetary boundaries and metrics of social metabolism will help support governance in the context of degrowth.

If the degrowth movement succeeds, the very term degrowth may give way to a focus on maintaining the human enterprise within ecological boundaries, and on enhancing ecological and social integrity. Meanwhile, as a reaction to a perspective that insists on economic growth, degrowth assumes the language of growth-insistent economics and therefore takes on a negative connotation. Although good reasons exist for degrowth to jolt the imagination using the language of the system it seeks to undermine (Kallis, 2011), growth in fact causes many things to decline. In view of the future that the degrowth movement is working toward, degrowth should also be flipped around so as to promote the positive growth of things that decline as the economy grows: ecological integrity, biodiversity, cultural diversity, compassion, equity, respect for life, human solidarity, simplicity, vegetarianism – and ultimately, the prospect for all beings to live a good life.

Note

1.   The Research and Degrowth website lists areas of inquiry and invites people to edit the descriptions of evolving degrowth proposals. See www.degrowth.org/dimensions (accessed 31 October 2012).

References

Barcelona Conference (2010) '"Degrowth bullet points" from the Barcelona conference', Barcelona Conference on Economic Degrowth for Ecological Sustainability and Social Equity, available at www.montreal.degrowth.org/downloads/degrowth_barcelonabulletpoints.pdf (accessed 31 October 2012).

Berry, W. (2008) 'Faustian economics: hell hath no limits', *Harper's Magazine*, May, pp. 35–42.

Bosselmann, K. (2008) *The Principle of Sustainability: Transforming Law and Governance*. Burlington, VT: Ashgate.

Bringezu, S., O'Brien, M. and Schütz, H. (2012) 'Beyond biofuels: assessing global land use for domestic consumption of biomass: a conceptual and empirical contribution to sustainable management of global resources', *Land Use Policy*, 29, 224–32.

Brown, P. G. and Garver, G. (2009) *Right Relationship: Building a Whole Earth Economy*. San Francisco, CA: Berrett Koehler.

Carpenter, S. R. and Bennett, E. M. (2011) 'Reconsideration of the planetary boundary for phosphorus', *Environmental Research Letters*, 6, 1–12.

Commoner, B., Woods, P. W., Eisl, H. and Couchot, K. (2000) *Long-Range Air Transport of Dioxin from North American Sources to Ecologically Vulnerable Receptors in Nunavut, Arctic Canada*. Montreal, Canada: Commission for Environmental Cooperation.

Daly, H. E. (1996) *Beyond Growth*. Boston, MA: Beacon Press.

Ehrlich, P. R. and Holdren, J. P. (1972) 'Critique of *The Closing Circle*', *Bulletin of the Atomic Scientists*, May, pp. 16–27.

Erb, K.-H., Krausmann, F., Gaube, V., Gingrich, S., Bondeau, A., Fischer-Kowalski M. and Haberl, H. (2009a) 'Analyzing the global human appropriation of net primary production – processes, trajectories, implications: an introduction', *Ecological Economics*, 69, 250–9.

Erb, K.-H., Krausmann, F., Lucht, W. and Haberl, H. (2009b) 'Embodied HANPP: mapping the spatial disconnect between global biomass production and consumption', *Ecological Economics*, 69, 328–34.

Ewing, B., Moore, D., Goldfinger, S., Oursler, A., Reed, A. and Wackernagel, M. (2010) *The Ecological Footprint Atlas 2010*. Oakland, CA: Global Footprint Network.

Foley, J. A., Ramankutty, N. Brauman,K. A., Cassidy, E. S., Gerber, J. S., Johnston, M., Mueller, N. D., O'Connell, C., Ray, D. K., West, P. C., Balzer, C., Bennett, E. M., Carpenter, S. R., Hill, J., Monfreda, C., Polasky, S., Rockström, J., Sheehan, J., Siebert, S., Tilman D. and Zaks, D. P. M. (2011) 'Solutions for a cultivated planet', *Nature*, 478, 337–42.

Foster, J. B. (2011) 'Capitalism and degrowth: an impossibility theorem', *Monthly Review*, January, pp. 26–33.

Garver, G. (2012) 'Introducing the rule of ecological law', in Westra, L., Soskolne, C. L. and Spady, D. (eds), *Human Health and Ecological Integrity: Ethics, Law and Human Rights*. Abingdon: Routledge, pp. 322–44.

Gayer, D. E. (2010) 'Perennial thinking', Vermont Design Institute, available at www.vtdesigninstitute.blogspot.ca/2010/02/perennial-thinking.html (accessed 31 October 2012).

Haberl, H., Erb, K.-H., Krausmann, F., Gaube, V., Bondeau, A., Plutzar, C., Gingrich, S., Lucht, W. and Fischer-Kowalski, M. (2007) 'Quantifying and mapping the human appropriation of net primary production in earth's terrestrial ecosystems', *Proceedings of the National Academy of Science*, 104 (31): 12,942–12,947.

Jackson, T. (2009) *Prosperity Without Growth: Economics for a Finite Planet*. London: Earthscan.

Kallis, G. (2011) 'In defence of degrowth', *Ecological Economics*, 70, 873–80.

Kallis, G., Kerschner, C. and Martinez-Alier, J. (2012) 'The economics of degrowth', *Ecological Economics*, 84, 172–80.

Latouche, S. (2004) 'Degrowth economics', *Le Monde Diplomatique* (English edition), 14 November, available at www.mondediplo.com/2004/11/14latouche (accessed 31 October 2012).

Latouche, S. (2006) 'The globe downshifted', *Le Monde Diplomatique* (English edition), 13 January, available at www.mondediplo.com/2006/01/13degrowth (accessed 31 October 2012).

Martinez-Alier, J. (2009) 'Herman Daly festschrift: socially sustainable economic degrowth', in C. J. Cleveland (ed.) *Encyclopedia of Earth*. Washington, DC: Environmental Information Coalition, National Council for Science and the Environment, available at www.eoearth.org/article/Herman_Daly_Festschrift:_Socially_Sustainable_Economic_Degrowth (accessed 11 September 2012).

Martinez-Alier, J., Pascual, U., Vivien, F.-D. and Zaccai, E. (2010) 'Sustainable degrowth: mapping the context, criticisms and future prospects of an emergent paradigm', *Ecological Economics*, 69, 1741–7.

Research and Degrowth (2012) 'Definition', available at www.degrowth.org/definition-2 (accessed 31 October 2012).

Rockström, J., Steffen, W., Noone, K., Persson, Å., Chapin, F. S., Lambin, E., Lenton, T. M., Scheffer, M., Folke, C., Schellnhuber, H., Nykvist, B., De Wit, C. A., Hughes,

T., van der Leeuw, S., Rodhe, H., Sörlin, S., Snyder, P. K., Costanza, R., Svedin, U., Falkenmark, M., Karlberg, L., Corell, R. W., Fabry, V. J., Hansen, J., Walker, B., Liverman, D., Richardson, K., Crutzen, P. and Foley, J. (2009) 'Planetary boundaries: exploring the safe operating space for humanity', *Ecology and Society*, 14 (2), art 32, available at www.ecologyandsociety.org/vol14/iss2/art32 (accessed 29 August 2011).

Saunier, R. E. and Meganck, R. A. (2009) *Dictionary and Introduction to Global Environmental Governance*, 2nd edn, Earthscan, London.

Sen, A. (2005) 'Human Rights and Capabilities', *Journal of Human Development*, 6 (2): 151–66.

Skidelsky, R. and Skidelsky, E. (2012) *How Much Is Enough? Money and the Good Life*. New York: Other Press.

Speth, J. G. (2008) *The Bridge at the Edge of the World*. New Haven, CT: Yale University Press.

TEEB (2010) *Mainstreaming the Economics of Nature: A Synthesis of the Approach, Conclusions and Recommendations of TEEB*, The Economics of Ecosystems and Biodiversity, Geneva, Switzerland, available at www.teebweb.org/teeb-study-and-reports/main-reports/synthesis-report (accessed 1 February 2013).

UNEP (2009) *Climate Change Science Compendium*. Nairobi, Kenya: United Nations Environment Programme.

van den Bergh, J. C. J. M. (2011) 'Environment versus growth – A criticism of "degrowth" and a plea for "a-growth"', *Ecological Economics*, 70, 881–90.

Vitousek, P. M., Ehrlich, P. R., Ehrlich, A. H. and Matson P. A. (1986) 'Human appropriation of the products of photosynthesis', *BioScience*, 36 (6): 368–73.

Wright, D. H (1990) 'Human impacts on energy flow through natural ecosystems, and implications for species endangerment', *Ambio*, 19 (4): 189–94.

16 The virtuous circle of degrowth and ecological debt

A new paradigm for public international law?

Noémie Candiago

The seventh G20 was hosted by Mexico in Los Cabos on 18–19 June 2012. After the USA, the UK, France and South Korea all rated as 'developed', 'high-income' countries, it was for the first time a developing country's turn to direct the Leader's Summit. However, the resulting response put forward as an answer to the global world issues remained unchanged and univocal: growth, growth, growth.[1] The mainstream discourse of international politics is fostering merchandising, markets, finance, competition, which could all be regarded as basically capitalistic values, hoping that the magic trickle-down effect is going to raise standards of living everywhere and for everybody. Public international law is no exception to this trend. What has been called 'development law' since the 1960s , specifically applicable to 'underdeveloped countries', is an illustration of this evolution towards a global capitalist order always seeking to produce and consume more. Its ideology rests on Rostow's take-off theory, according to which every country should follow the great path of evolution of 'first world' countries and 'grow' towards a society of mass consumption and productivism – what we would call a 'growth society' or 'society of growth' (Rostow, 1960).

But growth is not the only paradigm for international law. The *jus gentium* also acknowledges humans should live free, in a decent environment, in good health. The Universal Declaration of Human Rights states that everyone has the right to a standard of living adequate for the health and well-being of himself and of his family. In many (but sometimes oblique) ways, international law is calling for an actual 'degrowth' of production and consumption. The best example is the Kyoto Protocol, which obliges states to achieve their 'limitation and reduction commitments' of 'anthropogenic carbon dioxide equivalent emissions of the greenhouse gases'.[2] In this second paradigm, law becomes synonymic to equity, and its fundamental aim to allow each citizen to enjoy what belongs to him only because of his existence.

The fact that the 'growth paradigm' embraced by international law is the outcome of a self-serving 'transnational capitalist class' (Al Attat and Thompson, 2011) has been shown particularly by the TWAILers (Third World Approaches to International Law), whose central insight is to bring the problematic of colonialism and imperialism to the centre of

216 *Noémie Candiago*

international law structure.³ As Andrew Simms argues in his book on ecological debt, there is always a clear reason why some people get something, and why others do not (Simms, 2005). But it seems that this duality no longer much depends (if it ever did) on a North–South opposition, as the Mexican declaration tends to show, but rather on a governor–governed breach, where laws, norms and policies are used to serve particular interests undermining the common well-being.

We would like to argue here that environmental and social justice is condemned to be defeated by the 'right to growth', inherently allowing some to take what belongs to others. Thus, one of the solutions to reverse the vicious circle of growth could be the recognition of ecological debt carried through an ethic of degrowth.⁴

The concept of ecological debt was born in the early 1990s in South America. It was originally thought to be a counterargument to a plundering financial debt. As southern countries were considered to be debtors, they started arguing that from a different perspective and under different criteria, they might actually be creditors of a much more consequential ecological debt. In twenty years, the idea has come a long way, as it is now understood almost commonly. Academics started working on it, and links were made between ecological debt, environmental and social justice.

On a more institutional level, it would not be honest to say that it has had no legal recognition (at least, not as a global principle). The term 'ecological debt' does not appear in any legally binding instrument. But everything in the concept of ecological debt raises extremely accurate and quite fundamental issues for the discipline of international law. The concept of ecological debt emerged in a 'bottom-up' dynamic. It was expressed and put forward by civil society, in the local communities where the problems it tried to resolve were actually felt. Another element that ought to be empasized is that its criticism is structurally oriented. It seeks to undermine the structural causes of poverty and environmental damages. The way it emerged, from what and from whom, what it looks for and how it could be achieved, everything in the concept of ecological debt points out to a shift in the way we think, and consequently in international law.

We will start with an overview of the concept in which we will define the harms constituting the ecological debt followed by an analysis of the relationship between ecological debt and state sovereignty. We will draw a line from harm to debt to responsibility. Then, we will show what is lacking in the way international law captures the issues of ecological debt. We will conclude our presentation by proposing a convergence between ecological debt and degrowth.

What is ecological debt and where does it come from?

We are first going to define the concept of ecological debt and qualify it in terms of facts before giving it some resonance in law. The first way to describe ecological debt is to do it in a very simplistic way as the responsibility that have industrialized Northern countries for gradually spoiling and damaging the ecosystem of Southern countries. We are going to first ask ourselves what the ecological debt is made of.

In their effort to define ecological debt, NGOs tried to divide it into different components that are today quite commonly accepted (Colectivo de Difusión de la Deuda Ecológica, 2003):

- the carbon debt, resulting from greenhouse gas emissions;
- the waste debt, which refers to exportation in the South of hazardous waste produced in industrialized countries and then send to poorer countries to be recycled or even just stored;
- the biopiracy debt, following the spoliation of knowledge and biological resources of local and indigenous populations by private companies through intellectual property appropriation;[5]
- the alimentary debt, subsequent of the loss of food sovereignty itself stemming from land grabbing and monoculture directed towards exportation; and
- the corporate debt, made of environmental and social cost of private companies activities.

In order to clarify the concept, we suggest starting by thinking of these elements more as harms, as prejudice, rather than as actual 'debts'. In 2004, the University of Ghent finalized a report called *Elaboration of the Concept of ecological debt*, in which the concept was analysed through scientific methods in an academic way. The ecological debt of a country A was then defined as:

1. The ecological damage caused over time by country A in other countries or in an area under jurisdiction of another country through its production and consumption patterns; and/or
2. The ecological damage caused over time by country A to ecosystems beyond national jurisdiction through its consumption and production patterns; and/or
3. The exploitation or use of ecosystems and ecosystem goods and services over time by country A, at the expense of the equitable rights to these ecosystems and ecosystem goods and services by other countries or individuals.

(Centre for Sustainable Development, 2004)

Let us now move on to a second interrogation: where does ecological debt come from? Or perhaps we should ask: what is/are the cause(s) of the previously outlined harms? The activists as well as the academic response seem quite clear. Ecological debt comes from 'production and consumption patterns…characteristic of the present development model'.[6] Unfortunately, it appears conceptually difficult to look at these patterns as an accurate legal fault or tort. Nevertheless the characterization of these production and consumption patterns leads to outlining two constant drivers – capitalism and neo-liberalism – and an obvious marker: economic growth. We can try to define these mindsets by focusing on their alleged consequences in the view of ecological debt proponents.[7]

Capitalism generates a commodification of the ecosystem, and therefore an increasing use of its services. This process of increasing social metabolism (Martinez-Alier, 2012), inherently produces loss and degradation of natural resources.

Ecological degradations are also very constantly linked to environmental and social conflicts.[8] This raises awareness on a more political or societal content in the claim for ecological debt recognition. This issue has more to do with neo-liberalism, whose response to scarcity and basic needs lies in free-trade and market mechanisms rather than in popular sovereignty. Hence, local population feel dispossessed of their capability to manage natural resources and ecosystem because of mechanisms such as concessions granting or lands sales to multinational companies (often refers to as 'land grabbing' by scholars). They also often claim to be deprived of their right and responsibility to sustain their own needs with their own resources, as what they actually produced is mostly exported to foreign developed countries. We could call this phenomenon a loss of the capacity to use natural resources.

To conclude this section, we outlined two different types of damages constituting the ecological debt. We have the ecological damages, understood in an environmentally centred way relating to the natural resources depletion and degradation. Then, ecological debt is also made of political and social damages stemming from the disempowerment of sovereign citizenry regarding the management and use of their natural resources.

Ecological debt and state sovereignty

The concept of ecological debt is a slogan used as a catchphrase in order to express political claims. So, if we want to truly understand it, we have to get over the words and redefine them in an international legal way. When we hear 'ecological debt', we first think of a financial obligation resulting from an infringement on a property right or on an environmental right. That would be a normal definition in the language of the dominant discourse of international law. But it would be logically opposite to the one in which the concept of ecological debt was originally thought.

The ethic of debt lays on a temporal ethic of awareness of 'what led us to where we are'. The ethic of ecological debt would be to make people grateful for what they got in the past in order to act right in the future. It is a dynamic concept that cannot be reduced to a pecuniary liability; debt rather has to be thought in a metabolic vision of material and immaterial flow analysis

between states and people, even more probably in term of power distribution among them. That 'state-centred' approach is a natural consequence
of our field of study, public international law; but it also reflects the
geopolitical logic of the concept of ecological debt, based on a dual reading
of international relations within a North–South opposition, or a centre–
periphery vision. But we will see that this state-centredness is not an end in
itself.

The concept of ecological debt clearly challenges the concepts of state
sovereignty and 'sovereignty over natural resources'. In international law,
the concept of sovereignty can be understood in two different ways. The
external side of sovereignty refers to the fact that all States are equal among
them, in their relationships and interactions. But a State is also internally
sovereign because there is no superior power inside itself. Going back to
ecological debt, the ecological damages as defined above can be seen as an
infringement in a classical property right approach where the ecosystem,
the property of a state, is 'injured' by another state; this can be related to a
matter of external sovereignty. Damaging another state's environment is
clearly forbidden by international law and has been recognized as a
customary principle of international law for over a hundred years;[9] this is
acknowledged in the Principle 21 of the Stockholm Declaration:

> States have, in accordance with the Charter of the United Nations and
> principles of international law, the sovereign right to exploit their own
> resources pursuant to their own environmental policies, and the respon-
> sibility to ensure that activities within their jurisdiction and control do
> not cause damage to the environment or other areas beyond the limits
> of national jurisdiction.[10]

Behind this matter, we observed another prejudice encompassed in the
notion of ecological debt: the disempowerment of the right and responsibility of people to use their natural resources. Since people do not truly
benefit from the use and enjoyment of their natural resources, we could
plead something like an infringement on the people's usufruct right on
natural resources,[11] or, to put it another way, a violation of the intrinsic
components of sovereignty. We are in this case facing a matter related to the
internal side of sovereignty, the side of sovereignty according to which a state
has the right to be in control of its country and not subordinate to any other
entity.

From ecological debt to ecosystemic responsibility

In law, a debt is an obligation bonding a debtor to a creditor. In international law, the word 'debt' refers almost exclusively to a financial obligation.
As noted above, one of the biggest concerns that keeps on being expressed
about ecological debt is that it cannot be subsumed into a financial relation.

Therefore, if we want to be loyal to the South discourse, we will need to find another legal qualification.

We know that a debt in law is an obligation characterizing a binding relationship between two or more entities. But where does an obligation come from? Well, obligation comes from responsibility; we are obliged when we can be held responsible. But again, what brings responsibility in international law? Responsibility can refer to an obligation to repair, such as 'the state's responsibility for internationally wrongful acts', or even 'responsibility for transboundary harm'. But responsibility can also refer to a charge, a duty, as in 'responsibility to protect'. We have two types of responsibility: a liability and a duty. To differentiate this dual meaning in international law, we talk about primary obligations, defining the content of a substantial rule, and secondary obligations, defining the consequences of the non-observance of a substantial rule.

Then, an 'ecological debt' understood as an 'ecological responsibility' could refer to:

• the secondary obligation to repair ecological and social damages;
• the primary obligation to preserve not only the ecosystem, but also people's capabilities and capacities to manage it.

Both of these obligations have to be temporally conceptualized, as we said, the idea of debt in itself seeks to acknowledge a time-lined responsibility in order to insure that duties were and are well balanced within a society. If this equilibrium appears not to have been respected, then it generates a liability, which could be criminal or, more frequently, civil.

In the sphere of ecological debt, the purpose of secondary obligations would clearly be to act a past, historical responsibility of industrialized countries in today's environmental and social issues. Then, the ethic of its primary obligations would certainly be to enforce people's sovereignty on their natural resources. At a political level, some kind of historical responsibility has been recognized through the principle of common but differentiated responsibilities.[12] However, legally, it was never considered to acknowledge a historical liability. It was even used in a future-orientated way, as it appears clearly in the Kyoto Protocol within the Clean Development Mechanism. This mechanism allows industrialized countries to get 'Certified Emission Reductions' to reach their own reduction commitments, by investing in emission reduction projects in developing countries in order to facilitate their sustainable development. So, to acknowledge a responsibility due to the fact that an ecosystem was damaged because it had not been properly managed by an entity non-sovereign on this ecosystem, the Kyoto Protocol suggests having that ecosystem still managed by a non-sovereign entity, but, properly this time, allowing at the same time that entity to cash some real money and its home state to appear as it had actually lowered its CO_2 emissions. What is this mechanism, if not a continuation of disempowerment of developing countries?[13] Lessons from historical perspective are not learned and therefore not linked to a possibly different management of our natural resources. We hardly find any traces of clear and coherent primary obligations, mostly because of the supremacy of trade law and market values that characterize international law.

Ecological debt: what are states' responsibilities?

International law is often presented as being divided into sections working almost in an autonomous way within what is called 'self-contained regimes'. Nevertheless, the trade law regime often seems to supplant all the others. If it does not have any superior legal force than any other field, it surely is the most effective and has the most developed jurisdictional system with both the World Trade Organization (WTO)'s dispute settlement body and the International Centre for Settlement of Investment Disputes (ICSID). Those judges and arbitrators have the sense of the superiority of trade law very much in mind since it is by definition the one they are ruling on. As an example, the WTO's appellate body concluded in a 1998 report that whatever the status of the precautionary principle was 'under international environmental law', it had not become binding in international trade law.[14] Of course, the principle of sustainable development was thought to resolve this paradox by creating a bridge between social, environmental and economic concerns, just as was the idea of a green economy. It is not my point to go into this debate today, but it has been shown by many scholars that these pretty words were translating little more than a rhetorical change. In fact, this 'change' is constantly focusing on dealing with secondary obligations. This logic can be found today in most approaches of international environmental law, and its best example lays in the 'polluter pays' principle, known to be one of the greatest achievements of environmental law. It only deals with the consequences of trade and its 'externalities'. It uses market mechanisms as tools and 'cost-effectiveness' as standard. Principle 16 of the 1992 Rio Declaration reads:

> National authorities should endeavor to promote the internalization of environmental costs and the use of economic instruments, taking into account the approach that the polluter should, in principle, bear the cost of pollution, with due regard to the public interest and without distorting international trade and investment.[15]

Therefore, environmental law has become tort law, and its purpose to ensure that 'those who suffer harm or loss as a result of such incidents involving hazardous activities are not left to carry those losses and are able to obtain prompt and adequate compensation.'[16] The encompassing and sacred primary principle remains untouchable: natural resources are to be used for the benefits of the one who has the money to pay for them.

When environmental law is not focusing on secondary obligations, it is to create never-ending lists of *policies* assorted with *compliance mechanisms*. Yet the policies seem to be seldom implemented. We need to look for primary obligations concerning the actual management and use of natural resources.

ecological debt calls for a recognition of newly thought primary obligations that would respect the basic requirements of the coherence principle. Instead of thinking of environmental law as a palliative way to frame trade law and repair damages, advocates of ecological debt ask for a structural change in our production and consumption patterns. But then we are facing a huge challenge: how can we prove the legal existence of something like an 'ecosystemic responsibility', which is to say a local responsibility–duty of population on their ecosystem? Or, put another way, can we legally demonstrate that capitalistic patterns of consumption and production are wrong?

In conclusion: degrowth and autonomy to move forward?

In order to find a State ecosystemic responsibility in international law, we have to understand – and use – the discourse of international law and demonstrate that there are positive dynamic relations between the concept of ecological debt and international law. We need to establish that these two spheres of thinking are appealing, and maybe even generating each other. For Professor Martti Koskenniemi, law should be found 'in a narrow space between fixed textual understandings (positivism) on the one hand, and predetermined functional objectives (naturalism) on the other' (Koskenniemi, 2007). For him, we can no more structure our legal comprehension on strict positivism; we have to read law with some predefined values in mind. In other words, law has to be built on an explicit theory of justice. Behind this assumption lies the idea that, anyway, law is always the result of a political discourse, it is never purely neutral (Koskenniemi, 2011). Applying Koskenniemi's methodology on the idea of ecological debt, we could show that positive international law features elements favouring the recognition of ecological debt, but also that the ecological debt philosophy is relevant in terms of international law justice foundations.

In trying to find a just foundation of ecological debt, we realized this concept was a very accurate counterpart of a Northern doctrine called the degrowth theory,[17] which could work as a substantive base to formulate primary obligations regarding the management of our ecosystems.

We often describe degrowth as an actual decrease in gross domestic product. That would be reducing its true signification. If degrowth was primarily a criticism of our over-consumption and over-production, those patterns were found to be the results of another deeper problem: the lack of people's political and economic autonomy, stemming from a capitalistic and neo-liberal model of production. Hence, degrowth was making a clear link between ecological integrity and local communities responsibilities and capabilities. Its basic idea is that citizens free of 'imaginary colonization' and financial constraints have the ability to use their natural resources sparely and efficiently, in a way that would sustain their needs while not endangering the fulfilment of the needs of other people and species. That assumption has been verified by the work of Elinor Ostrom and her research team (Ostrom, 2012).

In France and Spain, there seems to be a growing consensus around the notion of autonomy as a key tool of degrowth. Autonomy is viewed as an efficient way of framing one community's impact on Earth. Learning to do with what was given to us by the nature around us would not only free us from depending on global mechanisms and contingency, but also radically limit our exploitative and dominative potentiality on other humans and non-humans.

Autonomy derives from *auto* ('self') and *nomos* ('custom, law'). It refers to the capacity of an entity to make a decision about its actions without the involvement of another entity. Autonomy is a concept that drives away from free-trade but which has nothing to do with autarky. The ethic of free trade depends on a liberal approach in which the key right would be *freedom*, but this freedom is accepted as being granted by a supra-entity holding the capital. In the ethic of autarky, the primary feature would be *self-sufficiency*, where a community stands by itself, excluding exchanges. Within those two political systems, the given options are to move in chain or to stand alone. *Autonomy* attempts to make communities move alone. It could then be the primary feature of a system of 'open localism' where individuals and communities consciously build their own rules while cooperating with each other's. It could in fact relate to the concept of sovereignty, as used, for example, in the concept of 'food sovereignty' developed by Via Campesina.[18] We chose not to use this word because of the state-centred vision it generates in our mind today. The notion of autonomy aspires to be applied to individuals, or local communities. Then, it could be a state's responsibility–duty to ensure that communities are autonomous and that individuals are free in their decision-making processes. This relates to a new way of thinking of the rule of law, not only as being ruled by the law (the 'rule *by* law') but as having the capacity to take part in the making of the law and in decisions concerning our livelihood.

Finally, if degrowth severely scratches the state power, it does not necessarily lead to its abolition. It rather seeks to redefine it as a neutral structure responsible for power distribution among its citizenry in order to avoid exploitation of human and natural resources.

Notes

1. As an anecdotal but yet eloquent fact, we noted 55 occurrences of the word *crecimiento* (growth) in the final Spanish declaration (see www.g20mexico.org/images/stories/docs/g20/conclu/declaracionlideresg20.pdf).
2. Article 3 of the Kyoto Protocol to the United Nations Framework Convention on Climate Change 11/12/1997, A-30822.

3. See, for example, Anghie (2006); see also Gathi (2011) and Chemni (2006).
4. We have chosen to write both ecological debt and degrowth with capitals to refer to them as specific concepts differentiated from their common meanings.
5. See, for example, Shiva (1997).
6. Quoting the NGO Acción Ecológica's definition.
7. We use the word mindset in the sense that was given by Professor Koskenniemi in Koskenniemi (2008).
8. See the EJOLT database at www.ejolt.org for more information on environmental conflicts.
9. *Trail Smelter Arbitration*, UNRIAA, vol. III, p1905 at p1965 stated: 'under the principles of international law,…no State has the right to use or permit the use of its territory in such a manner as to cause injury by fumes in or to the territory of other or the properties or persons therein, when the case is of serious consequences and the injury is established by clear and convincing evidence.'
10. Declaration of the United Nations Conference on the Human Environment, Stockholm, 116/06/972.
11. The usufruct, in roman civil law, is the right to enjoy the use and the fruits of a good without damaging the substance of the thing.
12. Article 3 of the United Nations Framework Convention on Climate Change, conclusion 09/05/1992, entry into force 21/03/1994, registration number I-30822.
13. For a strong criticism of those mechanisms, see Bond *et al.* (2012).
14. WTO Report of the Appellate Body, European Communities – EC Measures Concerning Meat and Meat Products (Hormones), 16/01/1998, WT/DS48/AB/R.
15. Rio Declaration on Environment and Development, 13/06/1992.
16. Draft Principles on the Allocation of Loss in the Case of Transboundary Harm Arising out of Hazardous Activities, International Law Commission, 2006.
17. For an introduction, see Latouche (2009).
18. La Via Campesina describes itself as 'the international movement which brings together millions of peasants, small and medium-size farmers, landless people, women farmers, indigenous people, migrants and agricultural workers from around the world. It defends small-scale sustainable agriculture as a way to promote social justice and dignity. It strongly opposes corporate driven agriculture and transnational companies that are destroying people and nature.'

References

Al Attat, M. and Thompson, R. (2011) 'How the multi-level democratization of international law-making can effect popular aspirations towards self-determination', *Trade Law and Development*, 3 (1): 65–102.

Anghie, A. (2006) *Imperialism, Sovereignty and the Making of International Law.* Cambridge: Cambridge University Press.

Bond, P. *et al.* (2012) *The CDM in Africa Cannot Deliver the Money*, report, Centre for Civil Society, University of KwaZulu–Natal with Dartmouth College Climate Justice Research Project, available at http://climateandcapitalism.com/files/2012/04/CDM-Africa-Cannot-Deliver.pdf (accessed 1 February 2013).

Centre for Sustainable Development (2004) *Elaboration of the Concept of ecological debt*, report. Ghent, Belgium: University of Ghent.

Chemni, B. (2006) 'Third world approaches to international law: a manifesto', *International Community Law Review*, 8, 3–27.

Colectivo de Difusión de la Deuda Ecológica (2003) *Deuda ecológica: ¿Quien debe a quien?* Barcelona, Spain: Colección Contraargumentos.

Gathi, J. T. (2011) 'TWAIL: a brief history of its origins, its decentralized network, and a tentative bibliography', *Trade Law and Development*, 3 (1): 26–64.

Koskenniemi, M. (2007) 'International law: constitutionalism, managerialism and the ethos of legal education', *European Journal of Legal Studies*, 1, 1–18.

Koskenniemi, M. (2008) 'Constitutionalism as mindset: reflections on Kantian themes about international law and globalization', *Theoretical Inquiries in Law*, 8 (1): 9–36.

Koskenniemi, M. (2011) *The Politics of International Law*. Oxford: Hart Publishing.

Latouche, S. (2009) *Farewell to Growth*. Cambridge: Polity.

Martinez-Alier, J. (2012) 'Environmental justice and economic degrowth: an alliance between two movements', *Capitalism Nature Socialism*, 3 (1): 51–73.

Ostrom, E. (2012) 'Par-delà les marchés et les États: la gouvernance polycentrique des systèmes économiques complexes, conférence Nobel', *Revue de l'OFCE*, 120, 15–72.

Rostow, W. W. (1960), *The Stages of Economic Growth: A Non-Communist Manifesto*. Cambridge: Cambridge University Press.

Shiva, V. (1997) *Biopiracy: The Plunder of Nature and Knowledge*. Boston, MA: South End Press.

Simms, A. (2005) *ecological debt*. London: Pluto Press.

17 Tobacco wars, analogies and standards of review in international investment arbitration

Valentina Vadi

Introduction

Tobacco use causes the death of more than five million people a year, and this figure could rise to more than ten million by 2020 unless measures are taken to control the tobacco epidemic (WHO, 2004). Against this background, tobacco control has become an essential aspect of contemporary public health governance (Vadi, 2012b: 94). At the national level, countries have adopted measures to control and restrict the tobacco use thereby reducing the mortality it causes. Tobacco control measures include interventions such as mass media campaigns, increased cigarette excise taxes, restrictions on smoke in public places, restrictions on the advertising, promotion, and marketing or packaging of cigarettes, among others. Analogously, at the regional level, regional economic organizations such as the European Union have adopted a number of regulatory initiatives relating to different aspects of tobacco control (Duina and Kurzer, 2004; McNeill *et al.*, 2012). At the international level, countries have massively adhered to the World Health Organization Framework Convention on Tobacco Control (FCTC),[1] which has established a 'cognitive and normative consensus' for promoting global public health through tobacco control (Meier, 2005: 160–1).

As countries are gradually implementing tobacco control measures, a number of disputes has arisen with regard to these regulations before national, regional and international courts and tribunals. As Fidler puts it, 'States and non-State actors resist governance reforms that would restrict their freedom of action' (Fidler, 2007). While states have claimed that tobacco control measures are in breach of international trade law,[2] tobacco companies have challenged the constitutionality of tobacco control measures before national courts,[3] the legitimacy of such measures before regional courts and tribunals,[4] and their compatibility with the relevant bilateral investment treaties before investment treaty tribunals (Vadi, 2009). As a consequence, tobacco control disputes have made headlines (Rushe, 2011; Thompson, 2012) and tobacco control has come to the forefront of legal debate; illustrating the difficulty for states to address the tobacco pandemics and testing the multilevel system of public health governance.

Tobacco control-related investment treaty arbitrations are the most recent articulation of the culture clash between the regulatory power of states and the economic interests of (affected) tobacco companies. At the same time, these disputes epitomize the more general tension between public health measures interfering with foreign investments and investment treaty provisions. Under most investment treaties, States have waived their sovereign immunity, and have agreed to give arbitrators a comprehensive jurisdiction over what are essentially regulatory disputes. As investment treaties provide foreign investors with direct access to investment arbitration, foreign investors can directly challenge national measures aimed at tobacco control and can seek compensation for the impact of such regulation on their business. Some scholars and practitioners have expressed concern regarding the magnitude of decision-making power allocated to investment treaty tribunals (Van Harten, 2007). Indeed, many of the recent arbitral awards have concerned the determination of the appropriate boundary between two conflicting values: the legitimate sphere for state regulation in the pursuit of public goods on the one hand, and the protection of foreign private property from state interference on the other.

Several questions arise in this context. Is investor-state arbitration a suitable forum to protect public interests? How can arbitrators adjudicate such difficult cases? The argument will proceed in two parts. After examining some pending arbitrations, this chapter will focus on the relevant standards of review. Some preliminary conclusions will follow.

The 'tobacco wars': case studies in international investment law

As countries are gradually implementing tobacco control measures, a number of investment arbitrations have arisen before arbitral tribunals with regard to these regulations. In particular, affected trademark owners have argued that labelling regulations by imposing the use of certain warning phrases or images infringe their trademark. Trademark owners have also alleged violation of the fair and equitable treatment standard and the prohibition of unreasonable measures.

In *PMI v. Uruguay*, three subsidiaries of Philip Morris International (hereinafter PMI) have recently filed an arbitration claim against the Republic of Uruguay, alleging, *inter alia*, expropriation of their intellectual property rights under the Switzerland-Uruguay BIT.[5] Presidential Decree no. 287/2009 required that at least 80 per cent of each side of cigarette boxes be covered by graphic images of the possible detrimental effects of smoking, and extended the prohibition on the use of deceptive product names (such as 'light' and 'mild'), to restrict the use of different shades or colours on tobacco packaging.[6] To implement the decree, the Ministry of Public Health issued Ordinance 514 which required each cigarette brand to have a single presentation and prohibited different packaging for cigarettes sold under a given brand.[7]

Admittedly, the claimants did not contest the governmental right to promote and protect public health, but claimed that in the alleged furtherance of public health goals, the state could not 'abuse that right'.[8] According to the claimants, the enacted regulations amounted to an indirect expropriation.[9] First, by illustrating the adverse health effects of smoking, the images would undermine the good will associated with PMI protected trademarks 'depriving them of their commercial value'.[10] Second, according to the claimants, the size of the health warning would jeopardize the right of the claimants to use the trademarks.[11] Third, the claimants held that Ordinance 514 forced them to remove from the market seven of the twelve cigarette products they previously sold, allegedly wiping out the commercial value of the intellectual property rights.[12] Thus, the companies sought both compensation for losses in relation to their investments in Uruguay and suspension of the application of Uruguay's recent regulatory measures (Peterson, 2010).

More recently, as Australia announced its legislation requiring 'plain packaging' for cigarettes,[13] Philip Morris filed an investor-state arbitration against the Federal Government under the Hong Kong Australia BIT (Kenny, 2011). Plain packaging means that 'trademarks, graphics and logos are removed from cigarette packs with the exception of the brand name which is displayed in a standard font' (Alemanno and Bonadio, 2010: 268). Plain packaging aims to reduce tobacco consumption by making cigarette packs less attractive. The company contended that plain packaging will encroach on its trademark rights, constituting an indirect expropriation. Furthermore, the company contested the case for plain packaging, as this policy could ease trade in counterfeit cigarettes.

With regard to the investment claims concerning fair and equitable treatment, in *PMI v. Uruguay*, the claimants contended that the host state 'failed to maintain a stable and predictable framework consistent with [the claimants] expectations'.[14] According to the claimants, not only did the host state fail to respect private property,[15] but it also adopted measures incompatible with obligations under the Trade Related Aspects of Intellectual Property Rights Agreement,[16] as well as the Paris Convention for the Protection of Industrial Property.[17]

Likewise, in *PMA v. Australia*, the company argues that plain packaging would be in violation of the fair and equitable treatment given the alleged 'substantial impairment' of the given investment, 'the lack of credible evidence that the measure will contribute to the achievement of the legislation's stated objectives, the availability of effective alternative means of reducing smoking prevalence, and the contravention of Australia's international obligations' under the TRIPS Agreement, the Paris Convention and the Agreement on Technical Barriers to Trade.[18]

Finally, with regard to the prohibition of unreasonable measures under the BIT, in *PMI v. Uruguay*, the claimants contended that the prohibition of the use of colours to identify and differentiate brand packs constitutes an unreasonable measure.[19] According to the claimants, the protection of public health could have been achieved with a narrower and more tailored measure and the images selected for the health warnings were 'neither necessary nor justified to warn consumers of the health risks associated with smoking'.[20] Analogously, in *PMA v Australia*, the investor alleges that 'plain packaging legislation will also constitute an unreasonable impairment to the investments'.[21]

Standards of review and analogies in investment treaty arbitration

In the clash between investment protection and the pursuit of public interest objectives by the host state, the standards of review play a fundamental role because the degree of deference given by arbitral tribunals in reviewing a given decision of the relevant authorities influences the outcome of the proceedings. Appropriate standards of review can enhance the legitimacy of investment treaty arbitration and 'may mitigate some elements of the frequently asserted "legitimacy crisis" of, and "blacklash" against, investment arbitration' (Von Staden, 2012: 3). The standards of review can range from full deference, where the determinations of the decision makers are not questioned, to *de novo* review, which amounts to a new trial, where the reviewing body reprocesses and revaluates the evidence, and takes the decision anew (Schill, 2012: 6). Given the fact that investment treaties tend to be silent on the issue of standards of review, what criteria are used (and should be used) by arbitral tribunals when adjudicating investment disputes and reviewing state conduct?

This section explores the reasons why arbitral tribunals have adopted different standards of review in adjudicating investment disputes; namely it will illustrate the hybrid nature of investment treaty arbitration highlighting the different features which make it analogous to different legal systems, including commercial arbitration, administrative review and public international law adjudication. Depending on the selected analogy, the standards of review adopted by investment treaty tribunals have varied. This section concludes that while a complete deference would render investment arbitration meaningless diluting the substance of investment treaty guarantees (ibid.), arbitrators should not second-guess the regulatory choices of the relevant authorities. In this sense, investment treaty arbitration has a public law dimension that should not be neglected in favour of purely economic considerations.

Analogies in investment treaty arbitration

Given its hybrid features, investment treaty law and arbitration has been analogized to different legal systems. First, given the fact that under most investment treaties, states have waived their sovereign immunity, and have agreed to give arbitrators a comprehensive jurisdiction over what are essentially regulatory disputes, such an investment review has been compared to a sort of administrative review. Van Harten and Loughlin claim that investment arbitration can be analogized to domestic administrative review since investment disputes arise from the exercise of public authority by the state and arbitral tribunals are given the power to review and control such an exercise of public authority (Van Harten and Loughlin, 2007). Second, because of the procedural rules which govern it, investor-state arbitration has been analogized to commercial arbitration. Arbitrators are selected by the parties and or an appointing institution and the hearings are held *in camera*. However, the distinction between investment treaty arbitration and international commercial arbitration is clear: while international commercial arbitration generally involves private parties and concerns disputes of a commercial nature, investment arbitration involves states and private actors (Blackaby, 2006). Third, arbitral tribunals have been analogized to other public international law tribunals because bilateral investment treaties are international treaties. Compelling arguments stand in favour of assimilating arbitrators to international judges. From a historical perspective, adjudication traces its roots to arbitration. From a functional perspective, like judges, arbitrators are asked to safeguard vital community interests.

Standards of review in investment treaty arbitration

Analogies and comparisons are not neutral (Vadi, 2010). In fact, depending on the selected perspective, the outcomes can be different. If one deems investment arbitration analogous to commercial arbitration, the principle of equality of the parties requires that no deference whatsoever be paid to the state (Roberts, 2013). Commercial arbitration presupposes a contract-based horizontal relationship between the parties; and its structure does not take into account the public dimension of certain investment disputes (Schill, 2012: 9). As Schill aptly puts it, 'Party equality would thus translate into a "no deference"-paradigm' (ibid.: 10). However, a powerful argument runs against assimilating investment arbitration to commercial arbitration: investment arbitration deals with public law matters.

On the other hand, if one duly conceives arbitral tribunals as creatures of public international law and adopts a public international law paradigm, a qualified level of deference does play a role. According to such paradigm, the standard of review should 'strike an appropriate balance between state autonomy and the need for compliance with international obligations' (Henckels, 2012: 10). Under international law, a state 'may not invoke the provisions of its internal law as justification for its failure to perform a treaty';[22] rather, it has the duty to bring internal law into conformity with international law (Brownlie, 2008: 35). When dealing with national laws and regulations, international courts and tribunals often judge on the question whether or not in applying those measures, the state is acting in conformity with its obligations under international law.[23] However, an overly intrusive review would not be appropriate as they lack legislative mandate.

The same applies if one analogizes investment treaty arbitration to human rights and trade law adjudication. On the one hand, with regard to human rights adjudication, the European Court of Human Rights has elaborated the margin of appreciation doctrine to grant qualified deference to state conduct. Such doctrine secures some latitude for the host state to define and adopt public interest policies. According to the margin of appreciation doctrine, states maintain a space for manoeuvring in fulfilling their international law obligations due to their social, cultural and historic features (Benvenisti, 1999: 843) and 'their direct and continuous contact with the vital forces of their countries'.[24] Therefore, such doctrine grants qualified deference to governmental regulations adopted on the basis of scientific evidence and reduces the risk of arbitral tribunals second guessing democratic authorities (Orellana, 2007: 675). The margin of appreciation doctrine would apply specifically to the risk management, where value judgments and other public considerations apply. On the other hand, in the trade law context, one can identify a 'middle level of review that d[oes] not amount to either *de novo* review…or total deference' (Roberts, 2013: 36).

Finally, if one conceives investment treaty tribunals as 'substitutes for domestic courts in reviewing government conduct', then the standard of review 'should be framed as a public law concept connected to the separation of powers doctrine' (Schill, 2012: 4). In this context, the standard of review reflects 'the allocation of authority between a legal system's primary decision-makers and its adjudicators and shape the balance of power within a legal system' (Henckels, 2012: 9). Under this model, the state is divided into three branches –executive, legislative and judiciary – each with separate powers and areas of responsibility so that no branch has more power than the other branches. As Henckels puts it, 'decisions about what is in the public interest are primarily political decisions' (Henckels, 2012: 20) and adjudicators should not become law-makers. After all, arbitrators do not have enough time, resources or even qualifications to undergo *de novo* review in particular in those cases involving complex scientific issues (Chen, 2012: 29).

Different approaches

So far, arbitral tribunals have adopted different approaches. Some arbitral tribunals have shown a low degree of deference, finding liability with regard to host state measures taken in the public interest.[25] Other tribunals have shown a higher degree of deference.[26] Legitimacy concerns arise where arbitral tribunals find the host state in breach of international investment law because of a strict scrutiny of host state measures (Henckels, 2012: 10).

With regard to public policy-related disputes, authors have suggested the adoption of a 'qualified deference' (Orellana, 2007: 723; Vadi, 2012a: 155–8). Like other international adjudicative bodies,[27] arbitral tribunals are not to undertake a *de novo* review of the evidence once brought before the national authorities, merely repeating the fact-finding conducted by the latter. It is not appropriate for arbitral tribunals to decide on the validity of the scientific findings underlying public policy measures.[28] For instance, the *Chemtura* tribunal noted at the outset that 'the rule of a Chapter 11 Tribunal is not to second-guess the correctness of the science-based decision-making of highly specialized national regulatory agencies'.[29] In the *Glamis Gold* case, the arbitral tribunal accorded deference to the federal and state legislative measures. The arbitral tribunal recognized that: 'It is not the role of this Tribunal or any international tribunal, to supplant its own judgment of underlying factual material and support for that of qualified domestic agency' and held that 'the sole inquiry for the tribunal…is whether or not there was a manifest lack of reasons for the legislation'.[30] Finally the *Lemire* tribunal acknowledged that a breach of a treaty provision does not occur where a national authority 'makes a decision which is different from the one the arbitrators would have made if they were the regulators. The arbitrators are not superior regulators; they do not substitute their judgment for that of national bodies applying national laws.'[31]

On the other hand, arbitral tribunals, like other international tribunals, should not be deterred to scrutinize the given national measures and their compliance with the host state investment law obligations. Thus, arbitral tribunals are not to pay a total deference before national measures, simply accepting the determinations of the relevant national authorities as final. Rather, they must objectively assess whether the competent authorities complied with their international investment law obligations in making their determinations. As the *Chemtura* tribunal stated the review 'must be conducted *in concreto*', and taking into account 'all the circumstances, including the fact that certain agencies manage highly specialized domains involving scientific and public policy determinations'.[32] Analogously, in *Tecmed v. Mexico*, the tribunal noted that 'the analysis starts at the due deference owing to the State when defining the issues that affect its public policy or the interests of society as a whole'.[33] However, the tribunal held that such starting point 'does not prevent the Arbitral Tribunal…from examining…whether such measures are reasonable with respect to their goals, the deprivation of economic rights and the legitimate expectations of who suffered such deprivation'.[34]

Thus, it will be important for the states to show that their regulations are aimed at achieving legitimate public goals and that they follow due process of law. As an arbitral tribunal held:

> 'public interest' requires some genuine interest of the public. If mere reference to 'public interest' can magically put such interest in existence and therefore satisfy this requirement, then this requirement would be rendered meaningless since the Tribunal can imagine no situation where this requirement would not have been met.[35]

Similarly Wälde and Kolo argue that 'such controls can be seen as a desirable constraint over the domestic political process' as 'investor-state litigation rights are a step towards good governance in international economic relations' (Wälde and Kolo, 2001: 846).

Conclusions

Tobacco control has come to the forefront of legal debate. Investment treaty arbitration constitutes the last frontier of a long stream of 'tobacco wars' brought by tobacco companies before a variety of courts, including national courts, regional tribunals and international economic law *fora*. By analysing two pending investment arbitrations this article illustrated the clash of cultures between international economic governance and national health policies, and stressed that investment treaty arbitration should not be analogized to commercial arbitration; rather it should be interpreted as a dispute settlement mechanisms analogous to other forms of international public law adjudication. Therefore, qualified deference to national measures should be adopted by arbitral tribunals.

By analysing other public health-related cases, it becomes evident that although arbitral tribunals have not articulated standard of review *expressis verbis*, when dealing with public health related cases, they have increasingly shown a high degree of deference for national measures adopted in good faith for pursuing legitimate public health objectives (Vadi, 2013). The paper concludes arguing that: (i) the protection of public health is intrinsic to state's regulatory powers; and (ii) in recent public health related arbitrations arbitral tribunals have adopted a high level of deference. Accordingly, one might argue that innovative tobacco control measures can be adopted insofar they do not discriminate against foreign property, are not manifestly unreasonable and/or do not violate the legitimate expectations of foreign companies. With regard to the legitimate expectations of foreign companies, it would be difficult for the companies to argue that they have a *legitimate* expectation that the legal framework will not change in such a sensitive field as tobacco control, which has increasingly been regulated in the past decades. In conclusion, tobacco control-related disputes epitomize the conflict between private and public interests, testing the capacity of international law to protect the commonweal and embody principles of 'what Aristotle considers to be *eunomia*: good laws well obeyed' (Westra, 2010: 9–10).

Acknowledgements

The author wishes to thank Professor Laura Westra for her comments. The author holds a fellowship granted by the European Commission for conducting research in the area of international investment law (grant agreement no 273063). The chapter reflects the author's views only and the usual disclaimer applies.

Notes

1 WHO Framework Convention on Tobacco Control, 27 February 2005, 2302 UNTS 166, www.who.int/fctc/signatories parties/en/index.html (hereinafter FCTC).

2 Disputes relating to tobacco control measures have been adjudicated before the World Trade Organization (WTO) dispute settlement mechanism. For instance, in the recent *US-Clove Cigarettes* dispute, a Panel and the Appellate Body of the WTO addressed the question as to whether the US ban of flavoured cigarettes exempting those containing menthol (most of which are produced in the US) was an overly trade-restrictive or discriminatory measure contrary to international trade law. Appellate Body Report, *United States –Measures Affecting the Production and Sale of Clove Cigarettes*, WT/DS/406ABR, adopted 24 April 2012. More recently, after requesting WTO consultations with Australia regarding the plain packaging legislation, Ukraine has filed a request for the establishment of a WTO panel. At its meeting on 28 September 2012, the WTO Dispute Settlement Body established a panel. *Australia – Certain Measures Concerning Trademarks and Other Plain Packaging Requirements Applicable to Tobacco Products and Packaging*, dispute DS 434, www.wto.org/english/tratop_e/dispu_e/cases_e/ds434_e.htm, accessed 7 November 2012.

3 See, e.g. *JT International SA v. Commonwealth of Australia* [2012] HCA 43, 5 October 2012.

4 Case C – 491/01, *The Queen v. Secretary of State for Health (ex parte British American Tobacco Investments Ltd and Imperial Tobacco Ltd)* [2002] ECR I – 11453 (hereinafter *Tobacco Products Judgment*) and Cases C – 210/03 and C – 434/02, *Swedish Match AB, Swedish Match UK Ltd v. Secretary of State for Health* [2003] ECR I – 11893.

5 *FTR Holding S.A. (Switzerland), Philip Morris Products S.A. (Switzerland) and Abal Hermanos S.A. (Uruguay) v. Oriental Republic of Uruguay (PMI v. Uruguay)*, ICSID Case No. ARB/10/7, Request for Arbitration, 19 February 2010, available at http://ita.law.uvic.ca/documents/PMI-UruguayNoA.pdf (accessed 6 November 2012). The case was registered on 26 March 2010.

6 Presidential Decree no 287/009, promulgated on 15 June 2009 and entered into force on 12 December 2009, Article 12. *PMI v. Uruguay*, Request for Arbitration, §21.

7 Ministry of Public Health Ordinance no 514, issued on 18 August 2009 and entered into force on 14 February 2010.

8 *PMI v. Uruguay*, Request for Arbitration, §7.

9 Ibid., §82.

10 Ibid., §48.

11 Ibid., §47.

12 Ibid., §44.

13 Australia, *Tobacco Plain Packaging Act*, Act no 148 of 2011, www.comlaw.gov.au/Details/C2011A00148, accessed 6 November 2012.

14 *PMI v. Uruguay*, Request for Arbitration, §84.

15 Ibid., §84.

16 Marrakech Agreement Establishing the World Trade Organization ('WTO Agreement'), Annex 1C, Agreement on Trade-Related Aspects of Intellectual Property Rights ('TRIPS Agreement'), 33 ILM 81 (1994).

17 *PMI v. Uruguay*, Request for Arbitration, §84.

18 Written Notification of Claim by Philip Morris Asia Limited to the Commonwealth of Australia, at §10b.

19 *PMI v. Uruguay*, Request for Arbitration, §78.

20 Ibid., §81.

21 Written Notification of Claim by Philip Morris Asia Limited to the Commonwealth of Australia, at §10c.
22 Vienna Convention on the Law of Treaties, Vienna Convention on the Law of Treaties, Vienna, 22 May 1969, entered into force on 27 January 1980, 1155 UNTS p331, Article 27.
23 See e.g. *Certain German Interests in Polish Upper Silesia*, PCIJ, Ser. A, No. 7, p19.
24 ECtHR, *Wingrove v. United Kingdom*, 25 November 1996, Reports of Judgments and Decisions, 1996-V ¶58.
25 See generally the long stream of investment arbitrations against Argentina relating to the measures the host state had adopted vis-à-vis the economic crisis of 2001–2002.
26 See e.g. *Continental Casualty Company v. Argentine Republic*, ICSID Case No. ARB/03/09, 5 September 2008, at ¶181, http://italaw.com/documents/ ContinentalCasualtyAward.pdf (accessed 6 November 2012).
27 See e.g, DSU, Article 11. Understanding on Rules and Procedures Governing the Settlement of Disputes 15 April 1994, Marrakesh Agreements Establishing the World Trade Organization, Annex 2, 33 ILM 1226 (1994).
28 For instance, in *EC Measures Affecting Asbestos and Asbestos Containing Products*, the WTO panel pointed out that 'in relation to the scientific information submitted by the parties and the experts…it is not its function to settle a scientific debate, not being composed of experts in the field of the possible human health risks posed by asbestos. Consequently, the Panel does not intend to set itself up as an arbiter of the opinions expressed by the scientific community.' *European Communities- Measures Affecting Asbestos and Asbestos Containing Products*, Panel Report, Doc. WT/DS135/R, 18 September 2000, ¶8.181, www.worldtradelaw.net/reports/wtopanelsfull/ec-asbestos(panel)(full).pdf (accessed 6 November 2012).
29 *Chemtura Corp. (formerly Crompton Corp.) v. Government of Canada*, Award, 2 August 2010, http://italaw.com/documents/ChemturaAward.pdf (accessed 6 November 2012), ¶134.
30 *Glamis Gold Ldt v. United States of America*, ICSID Award, 8 June 2009, available at www.state.gov/s/l/c10986.htm (accessed 6 November 2012, ¶¶779 and 805.
31 Joseph Charles *Lemire v* Ukraine, ICSID Case No. ARB/06/18, decision on Jurisdiction and Liability, 14 January 2010), http://italaw.com/sites/default/ files/case-documents/ita0453.pdf (accessed 6 November 2012), ¶283.
32 *Chemtura* Award, ¶123.
33 *Tecnicas Medioambientales Tecmed SA v. The United Mexican States*, ICSID Case No. ARB(AF)/00/2, Award, 29 May 2003, https://icsid.worldbank.org/ICSID/ FrontServlet?requestType=CasesRH&actionVal=showDoc&docId=DC602_ En&caseId=C186 (accessed 6 November 2012), ¶122.
34 Ibid.
35 *ADC Affiliate Limited and ADC & ADMC Management Limited v Republic of Hungary*, ICSID Case ARB/03/16, Award 2 October 2006, https://icsid.worldbank.org/ ICSID/FrontServlet?requestType=CasesRH&actionVal=showDoc&docId=DC648 _En&caseId=C231 (accessed 6 November 2012), ¶432.

References

Alemanno, A. and Bonadio, E. (2010) 'The case of plain packaging of cigarettes', *European Journal of Risk Regulation*, pp. 268–70.
Benvenisti, E. (1999) 'Margin of appreciation, consensus and universal standards', *New York University Journal of International Law and Politics*, 31, 843–54.

Blackaby, N. (2006) 'Investment arbitration and commercial arbitration (or the tale of the dolphin and the shark' in J. Lew and L. Mistelis (eds) *Pervasive Problems in International Arbitration*. The Hague, The Netherlands: Kluwer Law International.

Brownlie, I. (2008) *Principles of Public International Law*. Oxford: Oxford University Press.

Chen, T.F. (2012) 'The standard of review and the roles of ICSID arbitral tribunals in investor–state dispute settlement', *Contemporary Asia Arbitration Journal*, 5 (1): 23–43.

Duina, F. and Kurzer, P. (2004) 'Smoke in your eyes: the struggle over tobacco control in the European Union', *Journal of European Public Policy*, 11 (1): 57–77.

Fidler, D. (2007) 'Architecture amidst anarchy: global health's quest for governance', *Global Health Governance*, 1, 1–17.

Henckels, C. (2012) 'Proportionality and the standard of review in fair and equitable treatment claims: balancing stability and consistency with the public interest', *SIEL Working Paper* No. 27/2012, available at http://papers.ssrn.com/sol3/papers.cfm?abstract_id=2091474 (accessed 6 November 2012).

Kenny, C. (2011) 'Big Tobacco ignites legal war', *The Australian*, 27 June.

McNeill, A. *et al.* (2012) 'Tobacco control in Europe: a deadly lack of progress', *European Journal of Public Health*, 1–3.

Meier, B.M. (2005) 'Breathing life into the Framework Convention on Tobacco Control: smoking cessation and the right to health', *Yale Journal of Health Policy Law and Ethics*, 5, 137–92.

Orellana, M. (2007) 'Science, risk and uncertainty: public health measures and investment disciplines', in P. Kahn and T. Wälde (eds) *New Aspects of International Investment Law*. Leiden, The Netherlands: Martinus Nijhoff.

Peterson, L.E. (2010) 'Philip Morris files first-known investment treaty claim against tobacco regulations', *Investment Arbitration Reporter*, 3 March.

Roberts, A. (2013) 'Clash of paradigms: actors and analogies shaping the investment treaty system', *American Journal of International Law*, 107, available at http://papers.ssrn.com/sol3/papers.cfm?abstract_id=2033167 (accessed 6 November 2012).

Rushe, D. (2011) 'Philip Morris to sue if Australia puts all cigarettes in plain green wrappers', *Guardian*, 27 June.

Schill, S.W. (2012) 'Deference in investment treaty arbitration: re-conceptualizing the standard of review through comparative public law', *SIEL Working Paper*, no 33/2012, available at http://papers.ssrn.com/sol3/papers.cfm?abstract_id=2095334&rec=1&srcabs=2091474&alg=1&pos=1 (accessed 6 November 2012).

Thompson, C. (2012) 'Smoking: Big Tobacco's market place battle', *Financial Times*, 27 September.

Vadi, V. (2010) 'Critical comparisons: the role of comparative law in investment treaty arbitration', *Denver Journal of International Law & Policy*, 39 (1): 67–100.

Vadi, V. (2012a) *Public Health in International Investment Law and Arbitration*. London: Routledge.

Vadi, V. (2012b) 'Global health governance at a crossroads: trademark protection v. tobacco control in international investment law', *Stanford Journal of International Law*, 48, 93–130.

Vadi, V. (2013) 'Foreign investment in the energy sector and public health' in E. De Brabandere and T. Gazzini (eds.) *Foreign Investment in the Energy Sector: Balancing Private and Public Interests*. Leiden, The Netherlands: Brill.

Vadi, V. (2009) 'Trademark protection, public health and international Investment Law: Strains and Paradoxes', *European Journal of International Law*, 20 (3): 773–803.

Van Harten, G. (2007) *Investment Treaty Arbitration and Public Law*. Oxford: Oxford University Press.

Van Harten, G. and Loughlin, M. 'Investment treaty arbitration as a species of global administrative law', *European Journal of International Law*, 17, 121–50.

Von Staden, A. (2012) 'Deference or no deference, that is the question: legitimacy and standards of review in investor-state arbitration', *Investment Treaty News*, 4 (2): 3–4.

Wälde, T. and Kolo, A. (2001) 'Environmental regulation, investment protection and "regulatory taking" in international law' *International and Comparative Law Quarterly*, 50, 811–48.

Westra, L. (2010) 'Ecology and the law: democracy, globalization and the Greek roots of ecological problems' in J. R. Engel, L. Westra and K. Bosselmann (eds) *Democracy, Ecological Integrity and International Law*. Newcastle upon Tyne: Cambridge Scholars Publishing.

World Health Organization (2004) 'Why is tobacco a public health priority', available at www.who.int (accessed 7 November 2012).

Part V

Moving forward

New approaches and concluding thoughts

Introduction: beyond collapse: claiming the holistic integrity of planet Earth

J. Ronald Engel

Every form of human endeavour seeks a way to deal successfully with the problem of the one and the many, the universal and the particular, the same and the different, the global and the local, which greets us in all of our encounters with the world. This problem has now been raised to an unprecedented level of importance and urgency by the globalization of one particular and highly exploitative way of life as the governing paradigm for human existence in the Anthropocene. The imperial dogma that we can sustain the trajectory of global expansion indefinitely and increase our quantitative levels of production, consumption, and population without regard for the basic human rights of those at the base of the sacrificial pyramid or for planetary biophysical limits is now driving the world toward collapse. The question of the one and the many must be addressed anew if we are to move beyond the impending collapse of the biosphere and our precarious planetary civilization.

This way of organizing humans and nature has never gone unchallenged by other myths and ways of life that viewed the world in more pluralistic and relational terms. There has been the dream of human liberty enjoyed within the context of a mutually shared, nurtured and stewarded commons, a story (in its Atlantic revolutionary phase) perhaps best told by Peter Linebaugh in *The Magna Carta Manifesto: Liberties and Commons for All* (University of California Press, 2008), wherein the civil and political rights of the English 1215 Magna Carta are founded in the rights and obligations of the Forest Charter that governs the relations of humans and nature on the commons.

The flashpoint where these two contending paradigms of the one and the many are most decisively confronting one another today is in the relationship between the global and the local. Will globalization mean the ever-greater increase of empire, whether ruled by one nation (such as the United States), or an oligarchy of corporate and government superpowers, bringing every locality of the planet under its heel? Or will it be resisted and transformed by movements with the capacity to realize the potential of humankind for interdependent local and global Earth citizenship? Will we in this generation see the final and absolute 'enclosure' of the commons of the planet, its land, water and atmosphere, as well as the space beyond, as the images of 'star wars' portend, or will we find the way to 'perpetual peace,' as Immanuel Kant dreamed, by reconstituting the world order as a confederation of semi-autonomous self-governing republics, each living, as Alexander von Humboldt hoped, within the carrying capacity of its bioregion and all together living in harmony with the biosphere as a whole?

Global ecological integrity calls for a relational model of the global and the local, whereby the global is constituted by the unique character of each of its diverse member localities and the relationships they have to one another and to the Earth as a whole. So stated, ecological integrity provides the standard, the base line for planetary civilization, at global, multi-lateral (including bilateral), and local scales. It is descriptive of the fundamental character of a healthy and sustainable civilization and biosphere, and it is prescriptive for the ethics and governance policies we need to adopt if we are to achieve a healthy, sustainable civilization and biosphere.

Ecological integrity presents a threefold ethical demand:

- the value of autonomy, the value of each entity and locality for itself;
- the value of relationality, the value of diverse entities and localities of the world for each other;
- the value of global Earth community, the systemic value of the world as the objective totality of the activities and relationships of all entities and localities and as the necessary supportive matrix for all of them.

The upshot is that if we are to achieve a relationship between the global and the local that claims and restores ecological integrity, we must act simultaneously at local, lateral (bi and multilateral), and global scales. As the papers in this volume attest this requires mobilizing both the intellectual and organizational power to engage the ideas and institutions that govern each of these several interlocking spheres.

Human civilization faces an unprecedented situation. While no previous complex human society of significant size has ever achieved sustainability, the consequences of that failure were geographically limited. Failure resulted in either the collapse of that society or a successful attempt to postpone collapse by exploitation of new resources on the frontier. Today there are no significant new frontiers apart from the ocean floor and the poles, and what has become a global empire has nowhere, delusionary dreams of space exploration aside, to go. We must move to maintain and restore ecological integrity if we are to survive and flourish, and the transformation in economic, political and cultural relationships required must constitute, in the admonition of Peter Brown in the Foreword to this volume, a new 'holistic framework' that engages all interdependent spheres of planetary governance: local bottom-up self-governance; multi-lateral cooperation; and internationally institutionalized global norms.

Different persons and schools of thought have different judgments regarding whether the local, bilateral and multi-lateral, or global is the most effective point of leverage for this worldwide transition at this historical juncture. Members of the Global Ecological Integrity Group are likewise divided on this question. No one, however, is ready to argue that work at one or another of these spheres is alone sufficient to achieve the transformations in the relationships between local and global that are needed today. All three are necessary and because feedback occurs between them at every point the challenge is to orchestrate the work undertaken in each. A primary mission of the Global Ecological Integrity Group and its partner organizations going forward will be to help provide that orchestration.

Against this background of the problem of the one and the many as we encounter it in the struggle between commons and empire in the twenty-first century, what do our authors in this concluding section argue are the ideas and organizational pre-requisites necessary to claim the holistic integrity of global and local and move the world beyond collapse?

To begin at the end, in Chapter 22, William E. Rees, 2012 recipient of the Blue Planet Prize, which recognizes outstanding efforts in scientific research that contribute to solving global environmental problems, joins other ecological economists in arguing that our modern 'neoliberal (expansionist) worldview' is deeply flawed in the way it organizes the one and the many. Its model of the 'whole' tends to be 'simple, linear, deterministic, and single equilibrium-oriented.' At the core of the model is a faulty conception of the economy as an ever-expanding independent system that is abstracted from the dynamics and constraints of the energy and material flows that constitute the ecosphere – the foundation of all life on Earth. In effect, the 'neoliberal economy' has become our holistic framework for the relationships between the global and the local. Rees is well known as the originator of 'ecological footprint' analysis which quantifies the ways local centres of economic power such as the world's cities depend upon appropriations of ecosystems beyond their biophysical boundaries. We will never reach sustainability, in Rees's view, until we replace this view with a 'steady-state worldview' in which each locality accommodates itself to the carrying capacity of its regional ecosystem, and the relations between localities are so governed as to enable the global economy to function as a 'fully contained, dependent, integral sub-system' of the ecosphere.

In Chapter 19, Joan Gibb Engel, in her critique of the film *Journey of the Universe*, while expressing her appreciation for the grandeur of the film's pictorial presentation of the evolutionary saga of the Earth and the cosmos, questions its adequacy as a holistic framework for understanding our experience and responsibilities on the planet today. Since this film, and the worldview of Teilhard de Chardin and Thomas Berry on which it is based, are influential in circles of scholarly and public opinion concerned for avoiding collapse by affirming a holistic naturalistic understanding of human existence, in principle a viewpoint she strongly endorses, Engel believes it is essential to point out the dangers of a Gaian model of the one and the many, especially one, as in this case, that effectively identifies one species among the many, the 'human,' with cosmic creativity itself, so that we become the Incarnational point at which the 'universe becomes conscious of itself.' Engel argues for the importance of attending to difference as well as continuity in the holistic framework of the global and the local that we adopt and brings her point home by showing how the film fails to attend to the concrete reality of its local empirical setting, the island of Samos.

Sheila Collins (Chapter 20) seconds Engel's insistence on attending to the particular, different and local as essential to any holistic framework that can claim the integrity of the global and the local. But her reason for doing so comes not so much from the need to recognize the irreducible immediacy of our different locations in the world as from the need to understand the promise of local movements as significant agents of global change. The 'Occupy Wall Street' movement in New York City in the autumn of 2011 is a stunning example, in her view, of the power of a class-based analysis of the relation between the many and the one (99% vs. the 1%) to challenge the very centre of the corporate empire that is driving us to collapse. Occupy Wall Street came to life in a tiny public space at a particular time in the history of the United States, yet it encompassed a wide diversity of persons, issues, and approaches to revolutionize our collective way of interacting with each other and with the earth, and came to represent in the minds of many a prefigurement of the just, sustainable, participatory, spiritually fulfilling global civilization to which increasing numbers of persons worldwide aspire. Its message might be summarized in the admonition: 'to change the system we must start everywhere at once.'

Peter D. Burdon (Chapter 18) and Klaus Bosselmann (Chapter 21) give the same name to the holistic framework they advocate: Earth Democracy. Building on the work of Rudolph Bahro and Vandana Shiva, among others seeking to show that ecological issues cannot be understood apart from social and economic analysis and sustainability achieved without social justice, they both seek to bring 'democracy' and 'ecology' together in a unified vision. By 'Earth Democracy' they mean a much more substantive and comprehensive vision of democracy than that which informs the reigning liberal or 'state capitalist' system. Earth Democracy includes not only the traditional liberal freedoms, but strong social support for the practices of deliberative or public reason, substantive as well as procedural equality, and principled commitment to living within the constraints of the biosphere and providing everyone with the necessary means to sustain life. What they are seeking to conceptualize is a holistic framework for global governance that captures the positive understanding of the integrity of global and local provided by the root concept of ecological integrity as we have described it above. Burdon and Bosselmann both find in the Earth Charter's integration of the principles of ecological integrity, social and economic justice, and peace within a comprehensive vision of Earth community a landmark expression of the meaning of Earth Democracy.

Burdon and Bosselmann are both professors of environmental law and share a common interest in reconstituting domestic and international law in ways that align it with the vision of Earth Democracy. In their essays for this volume they draw upon different intellectual sources for this task, and address different dimensions of their shared project. Burdon is indebted to seminal figures in the anarchist and libertarian socialist tradition of Marxist thought such as Murray Bookchin as he seeks to build a set of constructive proposals regarding how we can effectively move toward a global confederation of democratically governed bioregions. Arguing that the state capitalist system will not voluntarily relinquish power, Burdon, like Sheila Collins, finds hope in the prefigurative politics of non-violent resistance movements, especially those such as Occupy Wall Street, claiming what he calls the 'right to the city.'

Bosselmann raises the stakes on Burdon's analysis by addressing the challenge of global ecological integrity from the perspective of Rio + 20 and the real life, real time, real on the ground fact that democratically elected governments neither have the will, or apparently the capacity, to address collapsing ecological, social, economic and financial systems. Bosselmann attended Rio + 20 in June 2012. His sober judgement: 'More than anything, Rio + 20 demonstrated just how ill-equipped the state-centred model of global governance is to meet the challenges of the 21st century.' States are now subservient to the logic of the market and seek their own competitive advantage at the cost of global decline.

Where then is there hope for Earth Democracy? Bosselmann, like Collins and Burdon looks to those civil society groups and movements that are seeking to carry forward the vision of the Earth Charter and resist the enclosure of the local and global commons. Recognizing, appreciating, organizing the local and global commons is no doubt one of the greatest needs and challenges of our century. One movement in which Bosselmann is personally investing much thought and energy, and which he represented at the Rio+20 stakeholder forum, is the movement to draft and institutionalize a World Environment Organization that would constitute a primary component in the holistic legal framework necessary for the people of the world to claim the holistic integrity of the planet and make good on their claim to be its rightful rulers.

18 The project of Earth Democracy

Peter D. Burdon

In this chapter I develop a conceptual analysis pertaining to the project of
Earth Democracy. This project is a continuation of the International Union
for the Conservation of Nature (IUCN) Governance for Sustainability
Project and was officially launched in 2009 at a symposium at the European
Institute in Florence, Italy (Engel *et al.*, 2010). A subsequent conference was
co-organized in 2011 by the Global Ecological Integrity Group (GEIG) at
Charles University in Prague, Czech Republic (Westra *et al.*, 2011).

To develop my analysis I will first introduce the idea of Earth Democracy
and comment briefly on the meaning of the term 'Earth'. Following this, I
will spend the majority of this chapter problematizing the term 'Democracy'
and consider whether democratic institutions are a barrier or a prerequisite
for a sustainable further society. I also want to make clear my own point in
advance, so that the reader can better evaluate and judge my analysis. I argue
that the contemporary version of democracy that dominates global
governance structures – namely state capitalism – is a highly inadequate
social theory and is a barrier to ecological protection. However, rather than
embracing totalitarian governance, I contend that the *idea* of democracy
needs to be reclaimed and that civil society must play a far greater role in
decisions that affect social relationships and our relationships with nature.
This represents a shift away from private interests in the pursuit of short-
term growth and toward notions of the comprehensive common good. To
bring this about, I argue that civil society must engage in nonviolent acts of
resistance and that the city is the most appropriate venue for this action.

The idea of Earth Democracy

The project of Earth Democracy is an attempt to fuse ecocentric ethics with
participatory democracy. Vandana Shiva describes the idea as follows:

> We are all members of the earth family, interconnected through the
> planet's fragile web of life. We all have a duty to live in a manner that
> protects the earth's ecological processes, and rights and welfare of all
> species and all people. No humans have the right to encroach on the

ecological space of other species and other people, or to treat them with cruelty and violence.

(Shiva, 2005: 9)

In describing this idea, Shiva draws a parallel between human exploitation of the environment and the way that human beings exploit one another. This comprehensive perspective recognizes that ecological problems cannot be understood, let alone solved, without a careful understanding of our existing society and the economic, ethnic, cultural, and gender conflicts that dominate it. Social ecologist Murray Bookchin (2007: 19) supports this point, noting that to separate ecological problems from social problems or even to play down or give token recognition to their relationship 'would be to grossly misconstrue the source of the growing environmental crisis'.

Consistent with this analysis, the project of Earth Democracy advocates recognition of an Earth community (as opposed to anthropocentrism or other hierarchical structures of domination and exploitation). Cultural Historian Thomas Berry describes the Earth community in the following terms: 'The universe is a communion of subjects and not a collection of objects' (Swimme and Berry, 1992: 243). This perspective and the ethic of responsibility is also eloquently captured in the preamble of the Earth Charter, which reads:

> To move forward we must recognise that in the midst of a magnificent diversity of cultures and life forms we are one human family and one Earth community with a common destiny. We must join together to bring forth a sustainable global society founded on respect for nature, universal human rights, economic justice and a culture of peace. We must join together to bring forth a sustainable global society founded on respect for nature, universal human rights, economic justice, and a culture of peace. Towards this end, it is imperative that we, the peoples of Earth, declare our responsibility to one another, to the greater community of life, and to future generations.[1]

As described in the Charter, democracy is not an end in itself – it is a means for achieving social and environmental goals. Thus, the Charters positive affirmation of democratic ideals should not be confused with a general endorsement for existing democratic states and geopolitical their machinations. Indeed, a brief examination of current State responses to the environmental crisis does not inspire confidence. As Klaus Bosselmann (2010: 92) notes: 'Any attempt to find an example of successful governance for sustainability among existing states must fail. It simply does not exist.' This is true despite the piecemeal greening of national constitutions that has occurred since the 1980's.

The failure of existing states to respond adequately to the environmental crisis highlights a fundamental dilemma for the project of Earth democracy. Is there an irreconcilable tension between the ideals of democracy and contemporary environmental imperatives? Or is democracy a prerequisite for sustainability? Theoretical arguments could be made to support either view. For example, in support of the former view, it has been suggested that a benevolent totalitarian regime might be better suited to implementing environmental regulations. Yet, recent forecasts for energy consumption in China would surely undermine this argument (International Energy Agency, 2012). Likewise, democratic societies might be more responsive to the voice of its citizens, but become beholden to economic power.

In considering the failure of western democracies to pass strict environmental regulations, one must question whether it is the *idea* of democracy or the limited existing version of democracy that is blocking environmental progress. I think the problem is unquestionably the latter. Indeed, I contend that it is not democracy that stands in the way, but the current arrangement of state capitalism. Bosselmann (2010: 92) makes this point as follows: 'As long as economic growth dictates the direction and extent of "sustainable development", we will not move forward. Like hamsters in their wheels, we will be running in circles.'

Further to this reasoning, before examining how democracy can be perceived and linked to environmental protection, I will first critique existing governance structures and consider why they have failed to protect the Earth community.

Democracy and its discontents

The existing form of government in Western countries is most aptly described as state capitalist. State capitalism is a regressive and highly inadequate social theory. To begin, capitalisms inherent thirst for short-term growth and self-expansion (Wallerstein, 1983: 14) is fundamentally opposed to environmental protection. Since its emergence in 1750, Capitalism has grown at a rate of 2.5 per cent per annum compound growth since 1750. In good years, growth is measured at an average of 3 per cent (at this percentage, the rate of growth doubles every 24 years). This is subject to uneven geographical development, particularly since the onset of neoliberal policies since the 1970s (Harvey, 2007). When capitalism was first constituted and material resources were abundant, 3 per cent compound growth was not considered a problem. However, this is no longer the case in the age of scarcity and resource wars (Klare, 2012). Indeed, the total economy in 1750 was approximately US$135 billion. It had grown to US$4 trillion by 1950 and US$40 trillion at the beginning of the new millennium. If the global economy doubles over the next decade, it will have grown to US$100 trillion and by 2030 will need to find US$3 trillion profitable opportunities for growth. There are limits to growth, and we have hit those limits, both environmentally and socially.

State capitalism is also inconsistent with basic principles of democracy. This can be explained by distinguishing two systems of power – the political system and the economic system. The political system consists of elected representatives who set public policy. In contrast, the economic system consists of private power, which is relatively free from public input and control. There are several immediate consequences of this organization of society. First, the range of decisions that are subject to democratic control is narrow. For example, it excludes decisions made within the commercial, industrial and financial system. Second, even within the narrow range of issues that are subject to public participation, the centres of private power exert an inordinately heavy influence through financial contributions, lobbying, media control/propaganda and by supplying the personal for the political system itself.

In short, contemporary democratic institutions function within a narrow range in a capitalist democracy and even within this narrow range, its function is inordinately weighted toward private power. Such is the concentration and influence of the private sphere that Noam Chomsky (2005: 48) argues: 'It is a truism, but one that must be constantly stressed, that capitalism and democracy are ultimately quite incompatible.'

A deeper investigation only confirms this argument. Today, the neo-liberal state views public participation as a potential threat to individual rights and constitutional liberties (Plant, 2012: 3). Neoliberals favour governance by elites. A strong preference exists for governance by executive order and by judicial decision rather than participatory decision-making (Harvey, 2007: 66). Neoliberalism has also entailed increased reliance on public-private partnership (a tool that often results in the transfer of public wealth into private hands). Further, corporate leaders not only collaborate intimately with government representatives, but even acquire a strong role in writing legislation, determining public policies, and setting regulatory frameworks. Perhaps the most striking recent example of this was documented by Paul Krugman and concerned the role of the American Legislative Exchange Council in providing the language for Florida's controversial Stand Your Ground laws (Krugman, 2012). These laws gained international headlines after the fatal shooting of African American teenager, Trayvon Martin.

From this perspective, state capitalism is best understood as a plutocracy (a rule by moneyed interests) in which some of the formal elements of democracy nonetheless remain. In ancient Greece, democracy was associated with the rule of *demos* the common people. In contrast, State capitalism has redefined democracy in economic terms where people simply vote periodically for 'political entrepreneurs, who seek out their vote much like commercial interests seek out dollars in the marketplace' (Magdoff and Foster, 2011: 13). Certainly, the idea of democracy is largely a sham when any form of autocratic elite controls the industrial system. Indeed, so long as a certain elite group is in power, it will make decisions that promote the interests that it serves. And so long as governance is tied to the imperative of economic growth, social and environmental justice will remain a distant concern. Martin Buber (1996: 127) stated the problem quite succinctly when he wrote: 'One cannot in the nature of things expect a little tree that has been turned into a club to put forth leaves.'

Reconceptualizing democracy

In conceptualizing the notion of Earth Democracy, I believe there is an important role for what is sometimes called 'blue sky thinking' or 'ideal forms'. My own belief is that the Project of Earth Democracy should ultimately be conceived with reference to a blend of libertarian socialist and bioregional principles. By this I mean a range of thinking that extends from left-wing Marxists such as Rosa Luxemburg and Anton Pannekoek, classic liberal writers such as Wilhelm von Humboldt, anarchists such as Murray Bookchin and bioregional thinkers such as Peter Berg. From this perspective, future societies would be organized within defined ecological boundaries and promote the free association of individuals without coercion by the state or other authoritarian institutions, in which human beings can create, inquire and achieve the highest development of their powers in covenant with one another.[2]

While limited, historical examples of societies driven to attain elements of this ideal form can be noted with the Paris commune, the spontaneous revolutionary activity in Germany and Italy after World War I, in Catalonia in 1936 and the Israeli kibbutzim. More recently, the late economist Eleanor Ostrom (2010) has ignited interested in common governance within a polycentric governance system. Further, Bookchin's confederation of libertarian municipalities might be considered the most sophisticated proposal to deal with the creation and collective use of the commons across a variety of scales (Bookchin, 1987).

Of course, such an ideal form would need to engage with many issues, which I do not have the capacity to explore in this paper. Of upmost importance is the issue of scale. Indeed, the possibilities for sensible ecological management of a common resource that exist at one scale (such as a shared water right between one hundred farmers in a small river basin) do not and cannot carry over to problems such as climate change. Further, whether municipal governance can occur on a large scale without some form of centralized governance (and thus hierarchy) is still a fruitful area of investigation. David Harvey (2012) has recently reopened this conversation. For Harvey, centralization is vital and might protect an otherwise decentralized social order from slipping into a radical form of neoliberal market based individualism. Other writers such as Bookchin would disagree. Whatever ones specific position, these are pressing questions for those engaged in developing an ideal form toward which the project of Earth Democracy can strive toward.

Deepening democracy

While I believe that conceptualizing ideal forms has an important role in the project of Earth Democracy, one must also keep at least one foot planted firmly on the ground. Mordecai Horton, mother of the radical American educator Myles Horton, made this point in the following terms: 'You can hitch your wagon to the stars, but you can't haul corn or hay in it if its wheels aren't on the ground' (Horton, 1997: xxii).

As this quotes illustrates, there must be some connection between a proposed ideal form of Earth Democracy and the daily life, experience and capacity of individuals operating within contemporary state capitalism. This was recognized by Saint Simon who argued that no social order could achieve changes that are not already latent within its existing conditions. For this reason, energy needs to be directed towards developing new social relationships and re-skilling citizens to occupy decision-making roles in their communities. The importance of prefigurative politics has been well documented in contemporary literature (Epstein, 1993; Hopkins, 2008; Bosselmann *et al.*, 2008).

Just what the prefigurative forms are is an open question and must be considered with reference to local conditions, politics and levels of expertise. Four pathways for deepening democracy deserve specific mention:[3]

- Participatory budgeting originated in Porto Alegre, Brazil and is a process of democratic deliberation and decision-making in which citizens decide on how to allocate funds of a municipal or council budget (Wampler, 2009).
- Communal councils have been established in Venezuela and seek to empower citizens to form neighbourhood-based elected councils that initiate and oversee local policies and projects for community development (Martinez *et al.*, 2010).
- Workers cooperatives represent one part of what Michael Albert (2003) calls 'participatory economics'. A worker cooperative is a cooperative owned and democratically managed by its worker-owners. While this model exists in all industrial countries, a particularly interesting case study is the Mondragon Corporation,[4] whose federation extends over the Basque region of Spain. In the 2012 European financial crisis, unemployment in the Basque region only rose to 6 per cent. This can be contrasted with the rest of Spain which simultaneously experienced unemployment levels at 25 per cent with youth unemployment at 50 per cent.
- The reclaiming of public space for community decision-making, which has been integral to the decentralized and open decision-making processes employed by the Occupy movement (Blumenkranz, 2011).

These and other examples intend to shift the power structure that dominates contemporary decision-making from private interests, to the collective. It is surely conceivable, perhaps even likely, that decisions made by the collective will reflect both community and ecological interests better than those made by corporate executives or members of parliament operating within the structure of state capitalism. Properly conceived, democracy is about securing the conditions that make it possible for ordinary people to better their lives by becoming political beings, or what Bosselmann (2010: 105) calls ecological citizens. What is at stake is whether citizens can become empowered to recognize that their concerns are best addressed and protected under a governance structure governed by principles of commonality, ecological integrity, equality and fairness; a governance model in which taking part in politics becomes a way of staking out and sharing in a common life and cultivating a deep respect and relationship with the broader Earth community.

The role of civil society

In considering pathways for deepening democracy, one must also confront the question: who is going to do it? Some commentators have argued that civil society must enact gradual reform at the ballot box. According to this view, Governments are elected by the *demos* (citizens) and it is only by virtue of their consent that government are able to reaffirm their commitment to state capitalism. For many reasons already discussed, I do not believe that the project of Earth Democracy should settle for this narrow analysis. As mentioned, the centres of private power enjoy an inordinately heavy influence on existing 'democratic' processes. There are also countless studies in the social sciences that illustrate that many of the top decision-makers in western States have come from the executive suites and law officers with close ties to the financial sector. Thus, Chomsky (2005: 50) contends: 'You can't vote the rascals out, because you never voted them in, in the first place. The corporate executives and corporations lawyers…remain in power no matter who you elect.'

It is also interesting to note that elements of this ruling elite are pretty clear about their social role. For example, in 2006 Warren Buffett (architect of the US Buffet Rule) was quoted in the *New York Times* as saying: 'There's class warfare alright, but it's my class, the rich class, that's making war, and we're winning' (Stein, 2006). The losers, obviously enough, are minorities, the poor and the environment.

Thus rather than confine ourselves to the very narrow opportunities of participation that are permitted under state capitalist regimes, I contend that we need to go 'beyond elections'. As a way to begin thinking about alternative options, we would do well to recall Henri Lefebvre's seminal essay, 'The right to the city' (1996: 167). This right was first a 'cry' in response to the withering away of the city and also a demand for citizens to re-imagine the use and occupation of public space. Importantly, Lefebvre did not etch in stone the form which an ideal urban life would take – such an approach would be contrary to the fundamental nature of the 'right' (which Lefebvre conceived in collective, rather than individualistic terms). Instead, Lefebvre understood the project as open, dynamic and fundamentally place-based. To have any meaning at all, the right necessitated public ownership and involvement.

Over the last decade, Lefebvre's idea of the 'right to the city' has undergone something of a renaissance (in both academic and activist circles). This is timely because for the first time in human history, over half of the world's people now live in cities. Further, nearly two billion new urban residents are expected in expanding cities such as Guangzhou and Mumbai in the next twenty years. With great perception, Lefebvre argued that the most fertile ground for building public participation from civil society, was not the factory – a position that put him at odds from the traditional left – but the urban population (Hardt and Negri, 2005). This, Lefebvre observed, is a very different kind of multitude. It is fragmented, dynamic, itinerant and multiple in its aim and needs. Others (like Bookchin) have supported this analysis and maintained that the city provides the best venue for restructuring society so that the people can play a meaningful role in the decisions that affect their lives. Thus for Bookchin (1987) the city provides the best venue 'to create face-to-face democracy.'

In considering this analysis, it should also be noted that the recent history of urban struggle is stunning (Mason, 2012). If we only look at the last ten years there have been significant rebellions in Latin American cities such as Cochabamba in 2000 and 2007; El Alto in 2003 and 2005; Bolivia and Buenos Aires in 2001–2002; and Santiago in 2006 and 2011. In 2003 the largest anti-war rally in human history took place in urban centres such as Rome, Madrid, London, Barcelona, Berlin, Athens, New York, Melbourne and over 200 cities in Asia. Note also the current youth movements from Cairo to Madrid, the 2011 street revolts in London, followed by the Occupy movement and Second Arab Revolt (or Arab Spring).[5]

In listing these significant acts of resistance, I am not seeking to romanticize or invent victories for people's movements. However, to paraphrase Howard Zinn (2010: 10–11), to think that legal and social analysis must simply 'recapitulate the failures that dominate the past' is to make us 'collaborators in an endless cycle of defeat.' Instead, if academic analysis is to be 'creative' and anticipate a possible future, without denying the past' then it should 'emphasize new possibilities by disclosing those episodes of the past when, even if in brief flashes, people showed their ability to resist, to join together, occasionally to win.'

Importantly, the collective right to the city is an empty signifier. Everything depends on how the right comes into existence. This in turn relates to who gets to fill the right with meaning. As is common today, the financiers and corporations can influence the political process so that their own interests are protected. But then, so can environmentalists, anti-capitalists and the homeless. We inevitably have to confront the question of whose rights are being identified, while recognizing, as Marx (1992: 344) puts it, that 'between equal rights force decides'. The definition and interpretation of the 'right' itself is an object of struggle – and that struggle has to proceed alongside the struggle to materialize it.

While important work has been done at the edges to curve the excesses of State capitalism, we must be clear that this model of governance will not voluntarily put appropriate measures in place to stop the exploitation of the environment. Their parasitic bonds with moneyed interests mean that the psychology of actors within state capitalism is focused on the augmentation of exchange-value and the accumulation of social power in limitless money-form. Politicians become mere cogs in a larger mechanism and those who speak up against State capitalism risk losing social standing and political power.[6] Harvey (2010: 260) eloquently captures this tension and the task before civil society: 'Capitalism will never fall on its own. It will have to be pushed. The accumulation of capital will never cease. It will have to be stopped. The capitalist class will never willingly surrender its power. It will have to be disposed.'

As ecological and social conditions deteriorate, it is increasingly important that communities engage in an intelligent dialogue about the need for transition and nonviolent acts of resistance to State capitalism (Sharp, 2005). This is, I contend, a precondition for establishing any kind of meaningful Earth democracy.

Concluding remarks

In this chapter, I have argued that contemporary forms of democracy have developed within the context of industrial civilization. Existing governance structures have relied upon the exploitation of people and the environment for material and political gain. According to the rhetoric of state capitalism, this exploitation is deemed legitimate on the debunked myth that private vices yield public benefits. Alongside this rhetoric, it has long been understood that a society that is based on infinite growth will destroy itself in time. It can only persist (with the suffering it entails) as long as it is possible to delude a population that the destructive forces approved by state capitalist regimes are limited and the environment is an infinite resource.

At this period of history, either one of two things is possible. Either the general principle will take back control of its own destiny and concern itself with community interests, guides by values such as Earth community, solidarity and concern for others (both human and non-human) or alternatively, there will be no destiny for anyone to control. As long as privileged elites are in control of governance, it will set policy in the special interests that is serves. However, the conditions of survival require rational social planning that takes seriously the needs of the compressive Earth community. As Chomsky (1992) observes:

The question in brief is whether democracy and freedom are values to be preserved or threats to be avoided. In this possibly terminal phase of human existence, democracy and freedom are more than values to be treasured, they may well be essential to survival.

Notes

1. Read the Earth Charter online at www.earthcharterinaction.org.
2. For analysis of the term 'covenant' and its implications for the Project of Earth Democracy, see Engel and Mackey (2011).
3. See the movie *Beyond Elections* (www.beyondelections.com).
4. For further information on the Mondragon Corporation see www.mondragon-corporation.com/language/en-US/ENG.aspx.
5. Immanuel Wallerstein argues quite persuasively that the term 'Second Arab Revolt' should be preferenced to 'Arab Spring'. See Wallerstein (2011).
6. The United States Supreme Court decision in *Citizens United v. Federal Election Commission*, 558 US 50 (2010) strengthens this point. For an analysis see http://blogs.adelaide.edu.au/public-law-rc/2012/07/05/citizens-united-and-the-crisis-of-democracy.

References

Albert, M. (2003) *Parecon: Life After Capitalism.* New York: Verso.

Blumenkranz, C. (2011) *Occupy! Scenes from Occupied America.* New York: Verso.

Bookchin, M. (1987) *The Rise of Urbanization and the Decline of Citizenship.* San Francisco, CA: Sierra Club Books.

Bookchin, M. (2007) *Social Ecology and Communalism.* Oakland, CA: AK Press.

Bosselmann, K. (2010) 'Earth Democracy: institutionalizing sustainability and ecological integrity', in J. R. Engel, L. Westra and K. Bosselmann (eds), *Democracy, Ecological Integrity and International Law.* Newcastle upon Tyne: Cambridge Scholars Publishing, pp. 99–115.

Bosselmann, K., Engel, R. and Taylor, P. (2008) *Governance for Sustainability: Issues, Challenges and Successes.* Gland, Switzerland. World Conservation Union.

Buber, M. (1996) *Paths in Utopia.* New York: Syracuse University Press.

Chomsky N. (1992) *Manufacturing Consent: Noam Chomsky and the Media.* Directed Archbar, M. and Wintonick, P. Zeitgeist Video.

Chomsky, N. (2005) *Government in the Future.* New York: Seven Stories Press.

Engel, J. R. and Mackey, B. (2011) 'The Earth Charter, covenants, and Earth jurisprudence', in P. Burdon (ed.), *Exploring Wild Law The Philosophy of Earth Jurisprudence.* Adelaide, Australia: Wakefield Press, pp. 313–23.

Engel, J. R., Westra, L. and Bosselmann, K. (2010) *Democracy, Ecological Integrity and International Law.* Newcastle upon Tyne: Cambridge Scholars Publishing.

Epstein, B. (1993) *Political Protest and Cultural Revolution: Nonviolent Direct Action in the 1970s and 1980s.* Berkeley, CA: University of California Press.

Hardt, M. and Negri, A. (2005) *Multitude: War and Democracy in the Age of Empire.* Sydney, Australia: Penguin Book.

Harvey, D. (2007) *A Brief History of Neoliberalism.* Oxford: Oxford University Press.

Harvey, D. (2010) *The Enigma of Capital.* Oxford: Oxford University Press.

Harvey, D. (2012) *Rebel Cities: From the Right to the City to the Urban Revolution.* New York: Verso.

Hopkins, R. (2008) *The Transition Handbook: From Oil Dependency to Local Resilience.* Totnes: Green Books.

Horton, M. (1997) *The Long Haul: An Autobiography.* New York: Teachers College Press.

International Energy Agency. (2012) *World Energy Outlook 2012.* Paris, France: International Energy Agency.

Klare, M. (2012) *The Race for What's Left: The Global Scramble for the World's Last Resources.* New York: Metropolitan Books.

Krugman, P. (2012) 'Lobbyists, guns and money', *The New York Times*, 25 March, available at www.nytimes.com/2012/03/26/opinion/krugman-lobbyists-guns-and-money.html (accessed 2 February 2013).

Lefebvre, H. (1996) 'The right to the city', in his *Writings on Cities.* Hoboken, NJ: Wiley-Blackwell, pp. 147–59.

Magdoff, F. and Foster, J. B. (2011) *What Every Environmentalist Needs to Know About Capitalim.* New York: Monthly Review Press.

Martinez, C., Fox, M. and Farrell, J. (2010) *Venezuela Speaks! Voices from the Grassroots.* Oakland, CA: PM Press.

Marx, K. (1992) *Capital: Volume 1: A Critique of Political Economy.* Sydney, Australia: Penguin Classics.

Mason, P. (2012) *Why It's Kicking Off Everywhere: The New Global Revolutions.* New York: Verso.

Ostrom, E. (2010) 'Beyond markets and states: polycentric governance of complex economic systems', *American Economic Review*, 100 (3): 641.

Plant, R. (2012) *The Neo-liberal State.* New York: Oxford University Press.

Sharp, J. (2005) *Waging Nonviolent Struggle: 20th Century Practice and 21st Century Potential.* New York: Porter Sargent Publishers.

Shiva, V. (2005) *Earth Democracy: Justice, Sustainability and Peace.* New York: Seven Stories Press.

Stein, B. (2006) 'In class warfare, guess which class is winning', *The New York Times*, 26 November, available at www.nytimes.com/2006/11/26/business/yourmoney/26every.html (accessed 2 February 2013).

Swimme, B. and Berry, T. (1992) *The Universe Story: From the Primordial Flaring Forth to the Ecozoic Era – A Celebration of the Unfolding of the Cosmos.* San Francisco, CA: Harper.

Wallerstein, I. (1983) *Historical Capitalism.* New York: Verso.

Wallerstein, I. (2011) 'The contradictions of the Arab Spring', *Al Jazeera*, last modified 14 November, available at www.aljazeera.com/indepth/opinion/2011/11/2011111110171539134.html (accessed 2 February 2013).

Wampler, B. (2009) *Participatory Budgeting in Brazil: Contestation, Cooperation, and Accountability.* University Park, PA: Penn State University Press.

Westra, L., Bosselmann, K. and Soskolne, C. (2011) *Globalisation and Ecological Integrity in Science and International Law.* Newcastle upon Tyne: Cambridge Scholars Publishing.

Zinn, H. (2010) *A People's History of the United States.* San Francisco, CA: Harper Perennial Modern Classics.

19 Dreaming the universe

Contending stories of our place in the cosmos

Joan Gibb Engel

I

It is entirely appropriate that we who are concerned for the integrity of life on planet Earth pause to contemplate the incredible journey that brought us here. In the words of T. S. Eliot, 'Time past and time present are contained in time future.' Duty to our children demands this effort.

The film *Journey of the Universe* by Mary Evelyn Tucker and Brian Swimme is a several-pronged endeavour that includes a book and material in the form of interviews with an array of educators who elucidate or comment on its features.[1] The book is a more explicitly philosophical exposure to the film's several themes, including the vast odds that the universe, the trillion galaxies, and the 'not too solid, not too liquid' Earth should arise amid a 'great flaring forth', and should continue to complexify despite powerful forces of dissolution.

Stardust as the essential matter of all known entities including the human body; the likeness of all living things as well as those things ordinarily considered not living such as the atmosphere; the possibility that the Earth is a self-organizing planet; the origin of awareness in the cellular membrane and its presence in all life; the key role of pattern and the mystical and essential role of death and suffering in evolutionary change; the universality of passion; the evolution of parental care; the possibility that humans evolved big brains due to the prolongation of childhood; the role of symbols in the evolution of consciousness; and the key role that humans play in the story of the universe and in the future of Earth – all these are treated with dramatic flair, spectacular photography and poetic phraseology using words such as 'bonding', 'entwinement' and 'communion' in the narration by Swimme on the island of Samos in the Aegean Sea.

Midway through the book version of these ideas, the authors write, 'We can have, at most, only a glimmer of the full significance of where our actions are leading us. We are enveloped in something like a dream.'

In viewing *Journey of the Universe* from our conference site in the French seaport city of La Rochelle on the Bay of Biscay we were also enveloped in something like a dream. The question is, what sort of a dream was it? Did we experience a pipe dream, a vision formed of baseless fabric, or was the film, as was the film-makers' intent, a substantial contribution to the flourishing of life on planet Earth? We need to pass the experience through the reticulum of a dreamcatcher, that Ojibway device for separating good dreams from bad.

For we are, in the words of Loren Eiseley, 'the dream animal'. In *The Immense Journey*, written in 1946, before Teilhard de Chardin's *Le Phénomène Humain*, before Thomas Berry's *The Dream of the Earth*, Eiseley described the evolution of the big-brained human in these words:

> He was becoming something the world had never seen before – a dream animal – living at least partially within a secret universe of his own creation and sharing that secret universe in his head with other, similar heads.
>
> (Eiseley, 1946: 129)

Thomas Berry, some forty years later, projecting the notion of humans as dreaming animals upon the universe as a whole, wrote that the 'fantastic variety of expression in shape, colour, scent, feeling, thought, and imagination' that constitutes the universe was itself a dreaming:

> In the beginning was the dream. Through the dream all things were made, and without the dream nothing was made that has been made.
>
> (Berry, 1988: 197)

Yet Berry had the wisdom to see that the secret universe in our heads evolved until it was 'a distorted dream experience' and 'a supreme pathology'. He said it had emerged from the millennial expectations of our scriptures and was, unfortunately, enshrined in our humanistic learning. 'The most powerful dream that has ever taken possession of human imagination', it went by the name of 'progress' (ibid.: 204–6).

II

Thomas Berry, theologian and cultural historian, and Teilhard de Chardin, priest, philosopher and palaeontologist, who along with Loren Eiseley, inspired Berry, are major influences on the authors of *Journey of the Universe*.

Mary Evelyn Tucker, after studying world religions with Berry, worked closely with him for thirty years until his death in 2009 at the age of 94. During that time she edited several of Berry's most important works (Tucker, 2012).

Brian Swimme left a teaching job in mathematics to study with Berry. As he tells it (Bridle, 2012b), the first thing Berry did was hand him a copy of *The Phenomenon of Man* (Teilhard, 1959). In 1984, Swimme published *The Universe is a Green Dragon*, a work popularizing the cosmic tradition of Berry and Teilhard. In 1992, Swimme and Berry coauthored *The Universe Story:*

From the Primordial Flaring Forth to the Ecozoic Era: A Celebration of the Unfolding of the Cosmos.

Behind the scenes for Tucker, Swimme and Berry is Teilhard. While Berry became less optimistic and far more critical of industrialization than Teilhard, he basically adopted Teilhard's view of a universe developing in irreversible stages of increasing complexity, composed of matter that has both a physical and a spiritual dimension. The subjective presence of things to one another, or in the words of Berry, the universe as a 'communion of subjects', was central for both (Berry, 1988: 45). They describe evolution as having purpose as well as direction, as being 'the onward and upward march towards greater consciousness' (Teilhard, 1959: 159). This process culminated in the symbolic consciousness of us thinking humans. Teilhard adopted Julian Huxley's expression: 'We are evolution become conscious of itself' (ibid.: 220), a phrase that Berry, then Swimme and Tucker, echo as 'We are the universe becoming conscious of itself.'

There are many important things about the film we had the pleasure of viewing: most especially its attempt to convey the awesome reality of time – time beyond our few generations of acquaintance, time we must gather into our beings as we find courage to overcome the desire to merely subsist.

Knowing that Tucker and Swimme tell their dream to save the Earth from further desecration, I hesitate to find fault. But that sentence wants to stick in the netting of my dreamcatcher:

> *We are the universe becoming conscious of itself.*

Is this the story of life that we should tell our children? Will it lead to Earth's flourishing? I think not.

IV

Partly, I believe, I'm reacting negatively to Swimme's and Tucker's very free use of personification, the universe 'becoming conscious' being one of many examples. They also say that a neutron and a proton 'bond' to create a quantum 'community', that in photosynthesis, Earth and Sun 'commune'. The charged nature of protons and electrons they call 'allurement'. These are huge metaphoric leaps. Human bonding is vastly different from whatever protons and neutrons do, communing between sun and plant in photosynthesis is poetic and yes, profound, but also markedly unlike the discourse between contemplative beings, and allurement, surely, has a seductive fringe of eyelashes that electrons lack.

The use of figurative language is, however, not the problem; we can scarcely communicate without analogies. But by making everything in the universe person-like, our filmmakers have, unwittingly perhaps, robbed the universe of radical difference. Two experiences, one from childhood, the other from some years later, may help explain what I mean.

V

When I was six years old, I used to be sent on errands into the basement of the row house we lived in, down where the laundry tubs were. Its unpainted walls were always damp. Only dim light came through the window. Unless I hurried, and even when I did, from a dark corner a water bug would dart out and cross the floor in front of me. Glossy black, maybe around an inch long, although to my eyes it appeared much bigger, it would pause in the middle of the cold floor.

We would both stop. Terrified, I could not run. I was made to stand still and listen while the beetle conveyed its ties to an immense journey and its inalienable right to life.

Fast forward to 2008. My three-year-old granddaughter and I are in Tucson at the zoo. It is feed-the-giraffe time. We mount a stairs, stand in line, pay the required special fee, and she is handed a rectangular biscuit to feed the long-necked, dusty orange 'G is for giraffe' animal. She holds the biscuit in her hand excitedly as we move to the front of the line. When it's her turn, the creature lowers its head and extends – oh great surprise – a twenty-inch blue–black tongue. My granddaughter turns away. 'Come on, Helene', I say, as startled as she is. 'The giraffe won't hurt you.' But she refuses and I do the job.

VI

When we see a lily, a mantis, a dog, a tree, it is not their likeness to us that we instantly apprehend or appreciate, though we may later make comparisons with ourselves. A lily is beautiful because it is not-me; I am relieved of the burden of achieving such smoothness and grace. We and beetles have reproduction and excretion in common but our commonality does nothing to explain a waterbug's terrible isness. Our love may be like a red, red rose but only after the rose has captured our souls with its unique perfume. The world is so full of a number of things – giant clams, swirling vortexes, multi-coloured rainbows – is our appreciation of these phenomena the end of a line to which they have been tending? Or is it not rather that we are amazing creatures, as are they, our consciousness a blue-black two-foot tongue, or one among hundreds of receptive rain drops?

I know that Swimme and Tucker are not claiming that humans are the most significant things in the universe. Elsewhere, Swimme says pointedly that, while humans are unique in their particular role, they are not superior to anything else, not to the moon or to phytoplankton or to spiders (Bridle, 2012b). Nor would I deny the reality of evolution and the somatic connectedness of unlike beings. Nevertheless, by seeing all creation as tending toward self-reflective consciousness, Swimme and Tucker foreground an exclusively human trait and give all of creation a human head to head for.

Swimme and Tucker must feel skittish about a possible anthropocentrism charge, for, while in both the book and the film they include a quote from 'the celebrated physicist' Freeman Dyson, in the book it is rendered as 'The more I examine the universe and study the details of its architecture, the more evidence I find that the universe in some sense must have known that we were coming' – an obvious reference, I thought, to humans being present from the get-go. In the film that quote is rendered as 'must have known that *life* was coming.'

I wondered about that until I got hold of a copy of Dyson's *Disturbing the Universe* and found out it *is* humanity that the celebrated physicist was referring to (Dyson, 1979: 250). Not only that; in this book from which the quote is taken, Dyson says that he believes that humans will get out of the mess we are making of Earth only by escaping into the universe. He says we will have to redesign ourselves to do it, grow a new kind of skin, perhaps. Whereas Swimme, echoing Berry, has said that the challenge before us, and the solution to the crisis of mass extinction is 'to reinvent ourselves at the species level...*by means of story and shared dream experience*', (Bridle, 2012a; emphasis added), Dyson thinks we will (and can) reinvent our very bodies. Not a new idea, he says quoting from a passage penned by the Soviet rocket scientist Konstantin Tsiolkovsky in whose *Dreams of Earth and Sky* the natives from one planet survive on another planet by growing glassy skin and green chlorophyll-containing wings (Dyson, 1979: 234–235).

There's a dream the Ojibway censor should have snagged.

Besides, I don't think it's necessarily true that our consciousness is so tuned to cosmic evolution.

When I repeat the sentence *we are evolution becoming conscious of itself* to the witch-hazel tree behind my study, the tree twitters its leaves, barely hiding a yawn. Is that because we humans took so long to notice that it didn't grow tall by eating its weight in soil, or because we still haven't got photosynthesis down pat? Is it because we have but the barest of ideas of all that a tree does in a day, in a year, in a lifetime?

Or does it turn in disbelief because as a species we humans have a decided tendency to become less and less involved with wild nature, less and less attentive to our natural surroundings, to prefer cities, to become addicted to cell phones, to purchase apps like 'leaf snap' for identifying trees so we need not touch or smell or feel?

VII

I was aware, watching the film and reading the book, of a frequent use of 'science' and 'scientists' to legitimate the text. No wonder. It is difficult not to be skeptical when cosmologists throw such large numbers about. In §1 of the educational series that supplements the book and film, 'The Emergence of the Universe, Earth, Life, and Humans', physicist Joel Primack says the initial period of cosmic inflation lasted perhaps 'ten to the minus thirty seconds'; he tells us that in the 'first three minutes' the elements formed, and that 'after the universe expands and cools for about 300,000 years' atoms form.

But if the science card seemed at times overplayed, the influence of organized religion on the producers was not brought out in either the film or the book. Yet Thomas Berry with whom both Tucker and Swimme were closely associated was a Jesuit priest, and both authors have been interpreters of religious thought – Swimme's first book, *Manifesto for a Global Civilization*, was written with the theologian Matthew Fox; among Tucker's many publications is *Worldly Wonder: Religions Enter Their Ecological Phase*, and she has devoted much of her work to gathering practitioners of the world's religions to discuss ecological issues. With her husband, John Grim, who helped produce the film, she founded the Forum on Religion and Ecology at Yale. Their lifelong interest in religious thought and theology adds depth to their elucidation of the universe story. But it is important for the reader or the film-goer to know, for the questions with which *Journey* deals are religious questions and have to do with the place of humans in the scheme of things. It would seem that Tucker's and Swimme's world view is a form of evolutionism, which the moral philosopher Mary Midgley describes as an escalator, carrying the human race to the top of the animal world and on to future greater glories. (Midgley, 1992: 145)

That's a ride we seem ill-prepared to take.

Recently I read a most insightful book recommended to me by our son-in-law Scott Saleska, who teaches at the Universe of Arizona. The book is *Dreaming the Biosphere* by Rebecca Reider, and it tells the story of Biosphere 2, that desert 'planet in a bottle' that began as a first step in the making of eco-colonies in space; was designed to include 'a miniature world' of rainforest, desert, ocean, savannah, marsh, and farm; that was heralded as a way to save the planet when eight men and women lived in its sealed, glass-enclosed structure for two years; but was deemed a failure by the time they emerged; and that has had a renaissance of sorts in its present use as a University of Arizona-based laboratory for climate-change modelling (Reider, 2009).

Despite the make-overs, the arrogance of its name remains: 'Biosphere 2.' As if.

Biosphere 2 has had a bad rap. Although two of its directors wrote that they felt they must 'assist the biosphere to evolve,' not all of the young people involved in its conception were looking for an alternative model from which to escape our distressed world. Indeed, to a person they were idealistic and concerned for the future. Some wanted to heal the Earth, others merely to learn how Earth works (ibid.: 121).

Nor was it the failure it has widely been perceived to have been, though we still need to ponder its lessons. Here, for instance, are a few of the things the biospherians discovered:

• that microbes, not humans, guided progress inside Biosphere 2;

- that they knew amazingly little about the species they included in their world;
- that physical and emotional connection to the tasks at hand, growing the food they needed, for instance, was what determined their survival, not intellectual abstraction; and
- that the least manageable factor of all is the human mind (ibid.: 188).

Nineteen of the twenty-five vertebrate species introduced into Biosphere 2 went extinct. All of the bees and butterflies died. Morning glory vines and an uninvited ant got completely out of control.

The biospherians split into factions so hateful that in one instance they spit in one another's faces. 'I just don't know how people can treat each other so poorly,' one of them wrote in her journal, 'people with such a strong and beautiful common dream' (ibid.: 263).

Are there lessons here for us? As a mellow Brian Swimme sails off under starry skies into the Aegean at the film's end, away from Samos after a day of exploration, after visiting the cave where Pythagoras is thought to have hid from his persecutors, after dining on tapas and being entertained by folk dancers, does he know he is entering a war zone? We know, because when GEIG met in Samos in 2006, we were told of the dispute between Greece and Turkey over national airspace and how every day F-16 jets would take off from the two countries and fly at each other in a dare that had led to casualties on both sides.

How can people treat each other so badly? And if the universe knew we were coming, did it also know about the hatred between Tutsi and Hutu? Between Israelites and Palestineans? Between eight educated men and women in a glass menagerie? If the universe knew we were coming, did it know about F-16s, thalidomide, refugees, oil spills, mountaintop removal? Did it know about wolf eradication, homophobia, infanticide?

Did it know about dreams deferred?

IX

Once we sang, 'Turn back oh man, forswear thy wicked ways.' Swimme and Tucker shy from suggesting that sin or wickedness in the form of greed or lust for power have anything to do with our predicament. We are in the mess we are in, Swimme says, because we wanted to make a better world and to provide for our future, only with our improved technology we did it too well.

This apolitical stance is a move away from the anti-industrial, anti-corporate one Berry took. It is based on a faith in powers not fully enumerated but flowing through descriptions of 'energy that is aware', of insightful, adaptive matter with the will to flourish', of a path beginning with a star. 'Perhaps the universe is enfolding towards some new destiny', Swimme suggests.

This approach is not without its appeal. Each generation grapples with fearful premonitions of war and pestilence, of starvation, fire and flood, but it is doubtful that any generation before ours has been as fearful of the cataclysm captured in Bill McKibben's phrase, 'the end of nature'. The market is glutted with films that depict an end to time.

Perhaps, as several of the teachers on the educational disks testify, learning this story helps transform despair into a sense of empowerment. But I am dubious. I don't believe a film, even a beautiful one such as Brian Swimme and Mary Evelyn Tucker have produced, can do much for us now. We are already far too awash in virtual reality depictions of the future, and no generation has had more reason to question their respective validities. In this regard, I remember Jerry Mander's insightful *Four Arguments for the Elimination of Television*, published ages ago but still relevant. Argument one, 'The Mediation of Experience':

> As humans have moved into totally artificial environments, our direct contact with and knowledge of the planet has been snapped. Disconnected, like astronauts floating in space, we cannot know up from down or truth from fiction. Conditions are appropriate for the implantation of arbitrary realities.
>
> (Mander, 1978: 51)

I just had a dispiriting example of the failure of film to make a difference. This fall, I attended the showing of an independent film based on Woody Guthrie's song, '1913 massacre':[2]

> Take a trip with me in nineteen thirteen To Calumet Michigan in the copper country...

We *were* in Calumet, Michigan, in the Copper Country; in fact we were in the very theatre where bodies of the 74 persons, 59 of them children, of striking miners attending a Christmas Eve party were brought after someone yelled 'fire' in the crowded hall and they piled up in a stairway and smothered trying to get out. (There was no fire.)

Sitting next to me was a local high school student and his girlfriend. The young man had been playing with his mobile phone prior to the lights going down, but he turned it off as requested for the performance. We were treated to a complex story, excellently told, replete with black and white stills from the period depicting the miners, the strikers, the town, the children, and the hall before it was torn down, and there were colourful scenes from the present of townspeople reflecting on the tragedy and their versions of what really happened. It had mystery, drama, sentiment, dance, and of course, the now-famous song sung in the film by Woody's son Arlo. Afterwards, I turned to the young man and asked what he thought of it. He answered in a voice completely devoid of colour: 'It was interesting.'

I don't think there's any way forward except to do what GEIG and its members have tried to do these past twenty years. Make a personal connection with some part of the Earth and help others do the same; work for social and ecological justice; fight for people and policies that matter to Earth's flourishing, get our hands dirty.

> It will be anything but easy. However, this is the real journey of the universe.

X

I had a dream while I was working on this talk. In the dream Ron and I were living in a rather exclusive community which had just been given the use of a professional movie camera. We could take footage of where we lived and send the resulting film around to our friends at Christmas. When I learned that it would cost one hundred dollars a minute to shoot the film, I was reluctant. But Ron, always the big spender, insisted we do it. The remainder of the dream was spent deciding what to take pictures of – the scuttling crabs in the marsh grass or the crashing waves on the beach. *What we actually spent our time photographing was the living room sofa.*

I am thankful for the stress on beauty and awe in Swimme and Tucker's *Journey* – the beauty of number and pattern, of the night sky with its million billion stars. So often, up to our eyeballs in red sludge, we forget beauty. I am thankful for the rescuing of awe from the trivial 'awesome, dude' to which it has fallen. Awe at the colours and shapes of flowers, the speed of rabbits and sharp talons of eagles, awe at the mating dances of birds and beasts, the sentience of a living cell.

'Wonder will guide us', Swimme says. I nod my head and cross my fingers. That twenty-inch tongue. The apprehension of a waterbug. May we stand in solidarity with the astounding world of difference. No dream we dreamers dream comes close.

Notes

1. The film, *Journey of the Universe*, produced in 2011, is written by Brian Thomas Swimme and Mary Evelyn Tucker, and directed by Patsy Northcutt and David Kennard. The book of the same title is published by Yale University Press (Swimme and Tucker, 2011). The twenty-part educational series on four CDs is hosted by Mary Evelyn Tucker, and produced, directed and edited by Adam Loften and Patsy Northcutt.
2. *1913 Massacre*, produced and directed by Ken Ross and Louis V. Galdieri, Dreamland Pictures, 1911. Woody Guthrie wrote the song on which the film is based around 1941.

References

Berry, T. (1988) *The Dream of the Earth*. San Francisco, CA: Sierra Club Books.
Bridle, S. (2012a) 'Comprehensive compassion: an interview with Brian Swimme', available at www.enlightennext.org/magazine/j19/swimme.asp?page=2 (accessed 27 April 2012).

Bridle, S. (2012b). 'The divinization of the cosmos: an interview with Brian Swimme on Pierre Teilhard de Chardin', www.enlightennext.org/magazine/j19/teilhard.asp (accessed 27 April 2012).

Dyson, F. (1979) *Disturbing the Universe*. New York: HarperCollins.

Eiseley, L. (1946) *The Immense Journey*. New York: Random House.

Mander, J. (1978) *Four Arguments for the Elimination of Television*. New York: Morrow Quill.

Midgley, M. (1992) *Science As Salvation: A Modern Myth and its Meaning*. New York: Routledge.

Reider, R. (2009) *Dreaming the Biosphere: The Theater of All Possibilities*. Albuquerque, NM: University of New Mexico Press.

Swimme, B. T. and Tucker, M. E. (2011) *Journey of the Universe*. New Haven, CT: Yale University Press.

Teilhard, P. de C. (1959) *The Phenomenon of Man*, translated by B. Wall with an introduction by J. Huxley. New York: Harper & Brothers (originally published in French as *Le Phénomène Humain*, 1950).

Tucker, M. E. (2012) 'Biography of Thomas Berry', available at www.thomasberry.org/Biography/tucker-bio.html (accessed 28 April 2012).

20 Occupy Wall Street

The origins and trajectory of a movement to make a new world possible

Sheila D. Collins

Occupy Wall Street (OWS) was a movement waiting to happen, yet to most people's surprise, it sprang up almost spontaneously in the heart of the world capitalist empire, the country with the most entrenched and politicized corporate and financial power, the largest military budget and presence around the world, the most effective corporate media propaganda machine, and a political culture that is deeply antagonistic to collective action and solidaristic public policies. Yet it is not so surprising that it happened in the United States. Since the early 1970s corporate power – especially financial power – had been growing exponentially, resulting in the ripping apart of the regulations that had kept it in check since the Great Depression. The result has been the growth of enormous inequality and deepening poverty, high unemployment, the purchase of democracy by the highest bidders, and a ravaging of the environment. It is precisely these conditions that gave rise to OWS.

The movement began in the summer of 2011, when a few people gathered in New York City at the suggestion of a Canadian online magazine, to plan an encampment in September that they would label 'Occupy Wall Street'. To the surprise of even its organizers, the encampment drew hundreds and then thousands of participants, spreading to over 80 cities across the country and bringing hope to millions of people that something could be done to confront the powers that were now ruining their world.

Unlike most of the social movements that had occurred in the United States since the 1930s – movements that seemed to focus on single issues, such as opposition to war, environmental protection, or civil rights for various groups – this movement emphasized class, but with a clever twist. Its slogan, 'the 99 percent versus the 1 percent', laid the blame for the conditions that confront America and the world squarely on the practices and values of those at the top of the economic ladder. By collectivizing the majority of the population into one great class, it suggested that all of the single issue movements that in the past had divided a potentially insurgent population were now interconnected and could feed one another instead of competing. This was indeed revolutionary and, perhaps, a reflection of an evolution in human consciousness. Its power derived from the fact that it is based in a structural reality. The twenty-first century has seen the rise of a global corporate oligarchy so powerful that its destructive effects can be felt in almost every area of life: in the privatization, commoditization and homogenization of daily life; in the erosion of democracy and the disappearance of public space; in the destruction of workers' collective bargaining power; in the increasing militarization of civic life; and in the poisoning of our food, air and water.

The origins of OWS

Was OWS the start of a global movement to revolutionize our collective way of interacting with each other and with the Earth? Or, now that it no longer has a permanent visible presence in the streets of dozens of cities, was it simply a flash in the pan – destined to go the way of every other social movement in history? Neither of these questions gets us to the historical significance of this phenomenon. To understand what happened in the fall and winter of 2011 we have to examine the events that led up to the emergence of OWS, for it didn't appear in a vacuum. For years before it erupted, a new consciousness was beginning to emerge among a significant sector of the world's population. Its first shoots could be discerned as early as 1967–1968 in the wave of student protests in Europe, the United States and Japan. A poster attached to the Sorbonne on 13 May of that year put this awakening this way:

> The revolution which is beginning will call in question not only capitalist society but industrial society. The consumer society is bound for a violent death. Social alienation must vanish from history. We are inventing a new and original world. Imagination is seizing power.
>
> (Kreis, 2009)

According to Tom Hayden, a leader of that youthful movement of the late 1960s, the underpinnings of OWS can be found in Students for a Democratic Society's (SDS) Port Huron Statement's call for a

> life and politics built on moral values as opposed to expedient politics; its condemnation of the cold war, echoed in today's questioning of the 'war on terror'; its grounding in social movements against racism and poverty; its first-ever identification of students as agents of social change; and its call to extend participatory democracy to the economic, community and foreign policy spheres.
>
> (Hayden, 2012)

However, this new sensibility among the youth of the industrialized world was nipped in the bud before it could take root among wider sectors of the population. Recognizing the threat the movements of the sixties posed to their entire modus operandi, the corporate business class and their allies in the state security apparatuses quickly mobilized.[1] Through police repression, attacks on labour unions, characterizations of the student radicals as misguided youth who were simply rebelling against authority as well as a well-orchestrated and well-funded campaign to re-socialize the public in the values of market fundamentalism, they were able to prevent this incipient rebellion from spreading to other sectors of society.

But by 1992, a growing body of people who worked at the international level, were recognizing that the students of the sixties had been prescient in their call for a radical reorientation of our collective life and values. The UN Earth Summit held in Rio that year established that there was an objective basis to the need to rethink the way we produce and consume. Quite simply, if we were to continue on the same trajectory of exponential growth in both population and consumption, human life would become unsustainable. That message – that nothing less than a transformation of our attitudes and behaviour would bring about the necessary changes – was transmitted by almost 10,000 on-site journalists and heard by millions around the world (UNCED, 1992).

During the 1990s, many more people – particularly in the global South – were signalling the dawn of a new global consciousness which recognized that we were nearing the end of a long period in which Western capital markets were beginning to cannibalize the very sources of their existence. South America, which was the first to experience the devastating effects of the neoliberal stage of capitalism, threw off the yoke of authoritarian governments and, with some exceptions, established a variety of democracies, based on premises that were often different from the model imposed by the imperial North. The response from civil society to this new structural reality was also noticed in the Mexican Zapatista uprising which began in 1994. While rooted in local experience, this indigenous peasant insurgency was more than just a local phenomenon. Rather, as Subcommandante Marcos, its leader, pointed out, it was a rebellion against the exploitative global entanglement of trade, investment and political domination by the powerful (Tuck, 2001). As French historian Jerome Baschet observed at a meeting to discuss anti-systemic movements on the eighteenth anniversary of the Zapatista uprising:

> The logic of capitalism is causing us to lose control of our lives and it is time to recuperate that control. The world movement has arisen as a crossroads of all struggles: the struggle against the looting of material goods, of land, of ways of life, of the capacity to decide. It is a movement that calls on everyone who feels dispossessed.
>
> (Cassani, 2012)

Making use of the new connectivity made possible by the Internet, the Zapatista movement marked not only the evolution of a new consciousness, but of a new way of helping people across races, cultures and levels of civilization to recognize their common connections. And it was also a movement that was not just articulating a new worldview, but actually providing a living demonstration of this worldview. Paulina Fernandez, a professor at the National University of Mexico observed that 'Despite efforts to silence them, hide them away, marginalize them and isolate the movement up in the mountains...the Zapatistas are building a real alternative process on a daily basis' (ibid.).

Anthropologist Mercedes Olivera observed that the Zapatista communities have developed outside the mercantilist logic, which can be a viable point of departure for

> men and women to dare to experience the construction of another civilization based on solidarity not exploitation, to try to recreate the human sense of existence, recover the vital sense of the land and the sustainability of production for consumption, to be able to practice new forms of using and caring for natural resources, and in this way we can change and reorient our strategies toward building a new paradigm of development and attempt a civilizing process based on life and not on destruction, like the Zapatistas do in their autonomy.
>
> (Ibid.)

The Zapatista uprising was followed in quick succession by a series of civil society uprisings across the globe, each focused on protesting a piece of the multi-tentacled system of corporate domination that was leading more people from diverse walks of life to recognize their common victimhood, to assert their collective agency, and to begin to envision the possibilities of a different world. Since 1999, when the 'Battle of Seattle' took place against the policies of the World Trade Organization, the world has witnessed massive global justice protests and alternative summits which have accompanied most meetings of the G8, World Trade Organization, International Monetary Fund, World Bank and World Economic Forum, as well as the growth of a global peasant farmer movement, La Via Campesina, which has protested against, among other things, the genetic modification of food and the corporate takeover of small farmer landholdings. These protests have occurred in both the global South and North, often enhanced by regional and local manifestations aimed at specific policies resulting from the corporate domination of the planet, such as the water wars in Bolivia and South Africa, the Ogoni protests against Shell Oil in Nigeria; the anti-dam movements in India and Brazil; and the indigenous struggle against big oil in Ecuador, to name just a few. In addition to protest movements there have been the world and regional social forums, gatherings of NGOs, advocacy campaigns and other formal and informal social movements starting in Porto Alegre, Brazil in 2001. These gatherings have deepened the connections between civil society struggles on different continents, have served as a forum for showcasing and sharing new ideas about how to reshape societies that are socially and economically just and ecologically sustainable and have been laboratories for the practice of participatory democracy. The result was the creation of a vast global network of networks that operated horizontally with no hierarchy and no central organizing authority, facilitated and enhanced by a new generation of digital media.

The global financial meltdown of 2007–2008 signalled not only just how interconnected the global economy had become, but also how irrational and amoral. Interestingly, the first major response to the global crisis took place in the Middle East, long a cauldron of discontent waiting to explode. The young organizers of the Tunisian and Egyptian uprisings are part of a generation that had become aware of the history I have been recounting through their use of the social media. The sense that they were not alone in the world and the digital, and in some cases, face-to-face connections they had made with activists from other countries, no doubt gave them the sense of hope and political efficacy that all successful social movements require in order to get started. While Western media have portrayed these uprisings as rebellions against authoritarian rule, they were much more complex than that. The factors driving unrest in these countries are a combination of extremely high youth unemployment, corrupt, non-responsive and repressive governments, environmental degradation, and the escalating cost of food, housing, and other basic necessities.

In the wake of the global financial meltdown of 2007 and 2008 came the imposition on the global North of the very structural adjustment programmes that had long been thrust on the global South. Greece, Spain, Ireland and Portugal were the first to experience its effects – privatizations, unemployment, the loss of welfare and pensions, assaults on public education, and accelerated environmental damage, accompanied by massive public protests; but it took three years from the time of the financial meltdown before the appearance of Occupy Wall Street in the United States. This was due partly to the fact that the US had not been reduced to conditions of desperation, such as Greece and Spain were experiencing; it was also the result of thirty or more years of right-wing propaganda that had permeated the political culture, so that the initial response came in the form of a libertarian populist movement – the Tea Party – that was quickly co-opted by large right-wing financial interests that were able to do a great deal of damage to the political system by the time OWS arrived.

In its initial stage, as public encampments, OWS caught the imagination of the world. The centrepiece was a small square in the heart of New York City's financial district adjacent to the empty hole that had been the World Trade Center. Zuccotti Park, or Liberty Square, as it came to be dubbed, became a floating signifier – a place that both symbolically and in a visible way, brought all of the single issue movements together and, through its strategic location, to pose as a counterpoint to the politics of exploitation.

To those who participated, it was an extraordinary experience – a window into a new world of possibilities. To be there was like being inside a living organism that was creating and recreating itself. What we saw at Liberty Park and in the hundreds of other Occupy movements that spread across the country and the world was an entire society in microcosm built, not through conquest or war, but from the bottom up and inside out, organically. Inside the cell's membrane were several 'departments', each focused on meeting a specific function needed by the body as a whole, just as each organ in the human body. There was a legal institution (where occupiers could get information on and help with legal issues from law students and practising attorneys; a medical unit staffed by doctors and nurses; a food kitchen serving up healthy and delicious food brought by individuals, donated by organizations, or ordered from nearby restaurants by sympathetic supporters across the country and across the world (orders were even phoned in from Egypt); an entertainment centre where performers drummed, danced and played other musical instruments; a meditation corner where people meditated around an altar made up of the sacred symbols from the worlds' religions; a press/communications department where on any given day, news about Occupy events around the world was sent digitally across continents via social media; a 'comfort' department where coats, pillows, blankets and other things necessary to occupying a square of concrete in cold and inhospitable weather were available, even to the permanently homeless; a clean-up/recycling department where brooms, mops, bleach and buckets indicated a concern to keep the area free of refuse and vermin; a library containing over 5,000 books all logged in an online card catalogue by professional librarians, open and free to anyone – and with no fines for late returns; and a security department to make sure that Occupy's ground rules – peacefulness, non-violence, respect for differences, were enforced through gentle persuasion.

The entire park had become one big university where teach-ins were held on money and finance, healthy eating and food security, the mortgage crisis, police brutality, renewable energy, alternative electoral systems, and any number of other topics necessary to the creation of a new world; and the park had become a giant workshop where 'guilds' of artists and other craftspersons taught others their trade. The park operated as a people's government where those who wished to participate learned about and debated the issues that confront the world, practiced participatory democratic decision making, and heard from experts who dropped by from time to time to learn, bring information and encouragement. On Sunday afternoons one end of the park was dominated at its centre by a *papier maché* golden calf (resembling the Wall Street bull) held aloft and labelled 'false idol', 'greed' and 'money'. The appearance of the golden calf signalled that this end of the park had become a church/synagogue/mosque/Hindu temple/ethical culture meeting house/Friends meeting house/Baha'i temple/Buddhist gathering as an ecumenical 'service' was led by people representing differing pathways to the transcendent, but all united on the ethical values that should guide the good society.

In form and shape, then, OWS was like none of the previous manifestations of social protest – those organized by identifiable organizations like the communist party, trade unions, or movements built around the grievances of distinct population or interest groups . Leaderless, amorphous and spontaneous, it was a unique adaption to an age in which the old hierarchies of race, class, ethnicity, gender, sexual orientation, and nationality and the orthodoxies of religious dogma and market fundamentalism no longer define the identifies of a younger generation. At a time when more and more of the world is beginning to suffer a future of joblessness and homelessness, the poisoning of our food, air and water and the imminent threat of climate catastrophe, the Occupiers modelled a way of surviving and adapting to reduced circumstances and of working to build a new world in the midst of the old dysfunctional order. Incredibly creative, they transformed long discarded modes of operating into new possibilities. Denied a sound system or even a bullhorn by the city's billionaire mayor, they created the 'people's mic', a unique restoration of the oral history tradition where each speaker's words are repeated by others so that the message gets transmitted throughout the crowd. When the police took away their generators, threatening the cut-off of lights, heat and communication with the outside world, they found a way to generate electricity with bicycles. At a time when the book industry is threatened with extinction they created a library of real books donated by bookstores, publishers, libraries and individuals. At a time when 535 people in the US Congress could not make one intelligent decision, they found a way to gain the consensus of as many as 3,000 people at a time. Without housing or public toilets they found a way of surviving outdoors, on hard cement in the midst of a freak October snowstorm that left hundreds of thousands of homes without power across the northeastern US. Starting with no money and no formal organizational backing, they attracted as much as half a million dollars to their cause, all the food they needed to eat, medical, legal and psychological assistance, and tents as colder and inclement weather approached. Using the power of nonviolence, risking comfort, security, their health, and some even their lives for the sake of a greater good, they demonstrated that creativity and selflessness, generosity and the longing for community still lie embedded in the human spirit despite a system that has sought to stifle them.

Calculating OWS's influence

This model, replicated in cities across the country and in several other countries around the world, could not be tolerated by the powerful. With calculated military precision and ruthlessness, all of the encampments were eventually shut down, their occupants scattered and arrested. With the loss of a visible space, the Occupy movement was thrown into turmoil, with many of those in power predicting its demise. Yet it had succeeded as had nothing to date in accomplishing something significant. It had forged the beginnings of a class consciousness in the most class-conscious averse nation in the world and thus changed the national discourse from one framed by economic and political elites around austerity, privatization and continued exploitation of the environment to one that focused on the values of justice, economic fairness, and environmental sustainability. It had also reclaimed – at least for a time – public space that had almost entirely been privatized, calling attention to the lack of a public *agora*. Within a month of its emergence, the movement had gained more public support, according to opinion polls, than Congress or corporations (Montopoli, 2011).[2] It also made it acceptable to name the system that was at the root of so many of the problems – neoliberal capitalism – and to valorize the much-demeaned term 'socialism' in a country that had banned it from public discourse. It also renewed attention to corporate accountability and the corrosive role of corporate money in politics and called for participatory democracy at every level (van den Heuvel, 2012).[3]

In more concrete terms, the movement led to over half a million people or more in the US pulling their money out of big banks and relocating it in small community banks or credit unions, and energized a movement for public banking that was just getting started. On the West coast, the movement shut down the largest port for two days and two ports for a day. In November 2011, a massive civil disobedience campaign in Washington, DC organized by 350.org and supported by OWS against the Keystone XL pipeline slated to bring oil from the Canadian tar sands to Texas refineries resulted in 1,200 arrests, but it succeeded in forcing the Obama administration to postpone a decision to approve the pipeline and called attention to the destructive effects of the heightened rush to exploit more difficult sources of oil. OWS helped create the political climate which halted a weak settlement between the Obama administration, state attorneys general and the Big Banks which would have prevented a full and fair investigation into mortgage foreclosure fraud; it forced the governor of New York State to impose a tax on millionaires that he had previously eschewed; it helped Ohioans to overturn a law that curbed collective bargaining rights for public-employee unions; and it forced several companies to withdraw their support from the American Legislative Exchange Council (ALEC) – an organization devoted to getting right wing legislation passed by state legislatures. The movement also motivated a US labour movement that had become all but moribund to take risks that it had heretofore shunned. Within weeks several unions adopted the 99 per cent versus the 1 per cent and started organizing actions under the Occupy banner. Union-affiliated organizers around the country say it has helped some workers win better contracts and bolstered labour reformers (Gupta, 2012). Hundreds of families across the country were assisted by OWS in resisting the foreclosure of their homes. By the time the 2012 presidential campaign was underway, President Barack Obama had adopted the populist language used by the OWS movement; and though it is not acknowledged publicly, OWS's lingering influence was probably instrumental in helping to re-elect Obama to a second term and increase the Democrats' representation in Congress despite massive Republican voter suppression efforts and an unprecedented outpouring of corporate money.

Those in charge of police power had attempted to halt the movement by evicting and scattering occupiers, intimidating potential protesters with the use of draconian crowd control tactics, tying protesters up in court cases, practicing 'preventive detention' of protest leaders, initiating a spate of entrapment operations designed to frame anarchists as 'terrorists', and setting onerous restrictions on public assembly. By the winter of 2012, public activity was certainly curtailed, but it was not halted. Most occupiers recognized that there would be setbacks but vowed that they were in for the long haul.

By the spring of 2012, even though the major media had lost interest in the movement and pundits were announcing its demise, Occupy Wall Street had become a slogan, beneath which other organizations and coalitions that had previously fought lonely struggles around a variety of single issues received legitimacy and partners. Hundreds – perhaps thousands – of protest campaigns have flowed from Occupy Wall Street including massive May Day marches in cities across the world; Occupy Student Debt, a national campaign among students in the US to refuse to pay their high student debts; marches on the big banks in New York City; powerful student movements in Chile and Quebec, and student strikes in 130 cities across the world on 6 June 2012; anti-hydrofracking campaigns across the US; bank occupations in Spain; and a pan-European general strike in November of 2012. The point is, as one occupier wrote:

> Whether or not the word 'Occupy' continues to be the word to describe this movement is not important. What is important is that there's a wide community of opposition being formed across many social barriers, and those who hold power are very afraid.

(Vitelli, 2012)

The future of the global movement to make a new world possible

Though it achieved a remarkable set of outcomes in its short public life, OWS did not result in an overthrow of the system of domination. But those who expected it to and who now take the lack of media coverage of the movement as evidence that it is dead are mistaken. Occupy Wall Street must be understood as a pivotal moment in a longer-term global revolution aimed at making a new world possible. As Paul Rogers has observed, the world is up against the failure of an economic system built on endless growth to deal with the coming resource constraints (Rogers, 2011). The Occupy movement, by giving voice to this truth might just make it a little more likely that real change will come before it is too late. The necessary revolution will take different forms in different places. It will ebb and flow, but like a living organism it will recreate itself to adapt to changing circumstances. Interviews with many of those who participated demonstrate that those who have been touched by it will never be the same. They see the present world with clearer eyes and the future with a set of different possibilities.

Having said this, the movement nevertheless faces internal and external obstacles. There is the still unresolved tension between anarchists who believe that any cooperation with state power is futile and those seeking to influence the direction of electoral politics. There is also a tension between those who insist on complete horizontalism and those who believe that one cannot change society without some form of authoritative decision making. As one occupier observed:

> Occupy claims to be 'leaderless', which has values such as being inclusive and de-centralized. But some activists seem anti-leader. They oppose authority, any kind of authority...They oppose structure, mistaking it for hierarchy...Occupy often lacks follow-through and discipline. Its guiding ideas can be stronger than their implementation.
>
> (Bliss, 2012)

Burn-out is another internal problem. Social movements traditionally rise, reach a peak and then burn out as people grow weary and return to jobs, family responsibilities or just the effort to survive. Another internal problem is dissension that arises as a movement passes the peak of its success and activists start to turn their frustration on one another rather than on the external focus of their anger. It would be dishonest to say that this hasn't been a problem.

Then there are the insuperable external problems. Political repression has curtailed many social movements in the past, and if the movement escalates, becoming a more formidable threat to the system, we can expect even more fierce opposition. The test of the movement will be whether it can develop the organizational, cultural and institutional forms to sustain a long term movement – measured not in years but in decades–while also maintaining its dynamism, horizontalism, direct democracy, creativity, activism and transformative vision (Lobel, 2011).

Whether or not we have the time to build a long-term movement for a better world is a question, given the imminent threat of climate change. The evolution of human consciousness occurs at a glacial pace compared with the evolutional of our technological capabilities. Yet there are signs of hope in the many concrete manifestations of an alternative order being built among the ruins of the old: communities devastated by economic and/or environmental collapse building alternative currencies, community banks and other forms of exchange; producer cooperatives; farmers' markets and community gardens; transition towns; and many more. In the wake of Hurricane Sandy, which devastated large swaths of the northeast coast of the United States in the autumn of 2012, OWS surfaced once again as an umbrella under which to gather people and material resources to help the most severely affected victims of the storm which, not surprisingly, turned out to be the poorest and most marginalized population groups. Although city, state and federal governments as well as hundreds of NGOs were involved in the 'rescue' effort, most observers credited OWS with doing the most effective job. It may be that global catastrophe on an unprecedented scale will bring us more quickly to our senses as a human community. If so, Occupy Wall Street and its many cognates will have shown us the way.

Notes

1. A seminal document in this mobilization was the memo written to the Director of the US Chamber of Commerce in 1971 by Lewis F. Powell, then a corporate lawyer and member of the boards of 11 corporations (later to become a Supreme Court justice). Powell states 'what now concerns us is quite new in the history of America. We are not dealing with sporadic or isolated attacks from a relatively few extremists or even from the minority socialist cadre. Rather, the assault on the enterprise system is broadly based and consistently pursued. It is gaining momentum and converts' (Powell, 1971). He then urges the Chamber to go on the offensive to organize a sustained counterattack to this threat to the free enterprise system. That counterattack consisted of the funding of dozens of new think tanks, legal institutions, and propaganda machines designed to turn the ideology of the country back to a commitment to *laissez-faire.*
2. In a CBS/New York Times poll taken in November 2012, 46 per cent of Americans said 'Occupy Wall Street' represents the views of most Americans, compared with 34 per cent who said it does not, and 43 per cent said they personally agreed with the views of Occupy Wall Street. Two in three said that wealth is not distributed as equitably as it should be, while just one in four said wealth is distributed fairly. See Montopoli (2011).
3. Signs of its success in changing the national discourse could be found in the fact that US newspapers published 409 stories with the word 'inequality' in October 2010. Through September 2011, the number of stories about 'inequality' remained roughly the same. But in October 2011, when OWS erupted across the country and overseas, the frequency skyrocketed to 1,269 stories. Between October 2010 and September 2011, 'greed' stories fluctuated between 452 and 728. But in October of that year newspapers stories on greed jumped to 2,285 (vanden Heuvel, 2012).

References

Bliss, S. (2012) 'Occupy's growing pains – reflections of an insider', *Portside* listserv, 15 March, available at http://lists.portside.org/cgi-bin/listserv/wa?A2= PORTSIDE;db085d25.1203C (accessed 17 March 2012).

Cassani, M.S. (2012) 'Zapatistas: 18 years of rebellion and resistance', *Counterpunch*, 5 January, available at www.counterpunch.org/2012/01/05/zapatistas-18-years-of-rebellion-and-resistance (accessed 6 June 2012).

Gupta, A. (2012) 'What Occupy taught the unions', *Salon.com*, 2 February, available at www.salon.com/2012/02/02/occupys_challenge_to_big_labor (accessed 9 March 2012).

Hayden, T. (2012) 'Participatory democracy: from the Port Huron statement to Occupy Wall Street', *The Nation*, 16 April, available at www.thenation.com/article/167079/participatory-democracy-port-huron-statement-occupy-wall-street (accessed 2 May 2012).

Kreis, S. (2009) '1968: the year of the barricades', *The History Guide: Lectures on Twentieth Century Europe*, lecture 15, available at www.historyguide.org/europe/lecture15.html (accessed 7 June 2012).

Lobel, J. (2011) 'The future of the Occupy movement', *Truthout*, 6 December, available at www.truth-out.org/future-occupy-movement/1323353901 (accessed 11 January 2012).

Montopoli, B. (2011) 'Poll: 43% agree with views of Occupy Wall St.', 25 October, available at www.cbsnews.com/8301-503544_162-20125515-503544/poll-43-percent-agree-with-views-of-occupy-wall-street (accessed 9 June 2012).

Powell, L. (1971) 'The Powell Memo (also known as the Powell Manifesto)', reprint available at http://reclaimdemocracy.org/powell_memo_lewis (accessed 10 October 2012).

Rogers, P. (2011) 'A world in protest', *openDemocracy*, 17 November, available at www.opendemocracy.net/paul-rogers/world-in-protest-1 (accessed 5 December 2011).

Tuck, J. (2001) 'Mexico's Zapatista movement – then and now', *Mexconnect*, 1 January, available at www.mexconnect.com/articles/2593-mexico-s-zapatista-movement-then-and-now (accessed 6 June 2012).

UNCED (1992) 'UN Conference on Environment and Development', available at www.un.org/geninfo/bp/enviro.html (accessed 5 June 2012).

Vanden Heuvel, K. (2012) 'The Occupy effect', *The Nation.com* blog, 26 January, available at www.thenation.com/blog/165883/occupy-effect (accessed 11 February 2012).

Vitelli, B. (2012) 'Reports of Occupy's death have been greatly exaggerated', *Nation of Change*, 11 June, available at www.nationofchange.org/reports-occupy-s-death-have-been-greatly-exaggerated-1339420172 (accessed 4 September 2012).

21 The legacy of Rio + 20

Saving the commons from the market

Klaus Bosselmann

Twenty years of despair and hope

What can you do when, twenty years after the Rio Earth Summit, the world is in dire straits? When, in twenty years, Brazil alone has decimated its rainforests by the size of France? When many thousands of species have vanished forever? When greenhouses gases have increased by about one quarter?

One option, of course, is to be concerned. In 1992, when the first Earth Summit took place, states expressed their concern in the form of a Climate Change Convention, a Biodiversity Convention and a plea for sustainable development. Some 50,000 delegates from civil society expressed their concern through demonstrations and actions such as alternative treaties and the Earth Charter. In 2012, at the second Rio Earth Summit 50,000 delegates again expressed concern. There was something comical about Rio + 20: participants twenty years older and the planet twenty per cent more in decline, but no sign of urgency on the part of governments. Rather, a non-committal list of vague declarations of intent called 'The future we want'. The gap between the future *we* (real people) want and the future *they* (governments and corporates) want could hardly be greater. At Rio + 20 it felt as if we live on different planets.

Yet we share one planet and cannot escape the answer to a question all humanity is facing: how to stop the erosion of the fundaments of life in a world of overwhelming market and corporate dominance? As corporate-controlled governments almost routinely follow corporate management practices, it falls upon civil society to promote genuine governance. We can no longer take for granted that democratically elected governments consider real political alternatives.[1]

More than anything, Rio + 20 demonstrated just how ill-equipped the state-centred model of global governance is to meet the challenges of the twenty-first century. But 2012 was also the year of celebrating twenty years of an alternative model.

During the 1992 NGO Global Forum, held in parallel to the Summit, NGOs from nineteen countries drafted an Earth Charter (Vilela and

Corcoran, 2005) and thereby started a process of worldwide cross-cultural consensus building that eventually gave global civil society its identity, platform and voice. Twenty years later, the Earth Charter is widely credited with providing the ethical framework for governance at all levels. It is also the closest thing to a global constitution (Bosselmann and Engel, 2010). Members of the Global Ecological Integrity Group (GEIG) played an active part in this process. Of course, GEIG itself celebrated its twentieth anniversary in 2012. Its exploration of ecological integrity helped shape the Earth Charter and the development of sustainability policies and laws in several parts of the world. The chapters of this book are vivid proof of the cross-disciplinary, ground-breaking and trend-setting nature of ecological integrity.

This chapter aims for further illustrating this. The legacy of Rio + 20 is clearly one of transformation, either by choice or by necessity. Unless we develop new and better forms of governance around human rights, sustainability and democracy, the forces of nature will forge transformation. In the current system of *international* ('between nations') governance, states are locked into a perverse logic: maximize your own relative position and create competitive advantages even at the cost of global decline. *Fiat pecunia et pereat mundi.* Concerns for ecological integrity have no real place here. They are secondary to market demands as so aptly expressed in the notion of the 'green economy' dominating the Rio + 20 Summit.[2]

The challenge is therefore to reverse the order. Protecting ecological integrity is more important than protecting markets. The market may be efficient for producing and disseminating goods, but is totally inefficient for protecting the natural conditions under which they can be produced in the first place. The market is ecologically blind, oblivious to protecting the commons such as the atmosphere, the oceans, water, soils and biodiversity. Hence, governance of the market needs to be distinguished from governance of the commons.

Reclaiming the commons is arguably the most pressing issue of our time, especially since governments have not even started to see this as their priority. In twenty years our elected decision-makers have only ever expressed 'concern' for the commons, nothing more. By definition, the commons belong to all – neither to governments nor to individuals – hence need to be guarded with a deep sense of responsibility and an ethos of cooperation.

Rising markets, declining commons

The last few decades have seen a remarkable turn towards democratic states. Some 120 sovereign states out of 192 are considered democratic, embracing 58 per cent of the world's population (Archibugi, 2002: 27). This turn to democracy has led political scientist Patrick Deneen to conclude that 'democracy is the only regime most living humans now deem worthy of serious consideration, exploration, clarification, articulation, exportation, importation, and finally faith' (Deneen, 2005: xvi). Yet simultaneous with democratization has been the advent of globalization that has had a marked impact on the ability of states, and the citizens they represent, to exercise control over their financial, social and environmental affairs. The globalization process has meant that the sheer scale of 'contemporary social and economic change appears to outstrip the capacity of national governments or citizens to control, contest or resist that change. The limits to national politics, in other words, are forcefully suggested by globalization (Held *et al.*, 1999: 1). Citizens in countries as diverse as Germany to New Zealand, to Samoa, feel that they are being swept up in a tide of change over which they have no control and no voice.

The declining power of states to regulate their affairs in large part can be attributed to the spread of neo-liberal economics. This is because neoliberal economic policies such as free trade and the liberalization of markets, whilst preached as being the key to nation states independence through increased prosperity, in reality serve to usurp power from governments. So-called free trade agreements 'deliberately close off the ideological and legal space for governments to give priority to social needs and the common good over "trade" commitments or even to respond to a disabling political crisis. States are relegated to a self-limiting and "enabling" role vis-a-vis capital' (Kelsey, 2008: 319). And citizens find themselves as mere recipients of trade arrangements, rather than as participants in making them.

The damaging effects of neo-liberal policies present themselves for everyone to see. Since 2008 the global financial system is heading for collapse due to the housing bubble, subprime mortgages, credit crisis, exploding debts of public and private sectors, bail-out of banks, lack of government regulation and declining living standards for most people. Greece, in particular, has fallen into an austerity trap with an economy contracted by 7 per cent in 2012, youth unemployment of over 50 per cent and prospects of severe social disintegration (Gatopoulos, 2012). In all this government seem mere by-standers rather than actors.

So, notwithstanding the remarkable turn to democracy that has occurred in the last twenty years, there is a massive democratic deficit both at national and international level. If democracy 'requires that citizens decide all issues that are politically decidable' (Wheatley, 2010: 2) then we have lost some of the key areas that democracy is concerned with.

It was Karl Marx who insisted that nature, not capital or labour is the ultimate source of all wealth. In 1875 he protested vehemently against the first sentence of the Gotha Programme, designed to unite antagonistic fractions of the German Workers' Party ('Labour is the source of all wealth and all culture'), by stating: 'Labour is *not the source* of all wealth. Nature is just as much the source of use values…as labour which itself is only the manifestation of a force of nature' (Marx, 2001: 12). Marx knew that the war of capital was not just against labour, but against nature. Had he lived today, he would not be surprised about the nearly complete instrumentalization and privatization of nature (Goldman, 1998). The struggle has always been for control over the 'commons'. For human populations, the commons (land, soils, forests water, oceans, biodiversity, atmosphere) represent the essence of livelihoods and life itself. They need to be protected accordingly. For capitalism, these things are mere commodities, either free to use or acquired as private property.

Rio + 20 has done nothing to change these dynamics and stop the enclosure of the commons. To the contrary, the summit's overall objective was to define the 'green economy' as a readily agreeable policy option, thereby encouraging 'business as usual'. Restructuring of the market was never an option. The key phrases of business as usual can all be found in the outcome document; for example, 'promoting sustained economic growth', 'creating greater opportunities for all', 'promoting integrated and sustainable management of natural resources and ecosystems that support economic, social and human development' (UNGA, 2012, para. 4). The 'green economy' is described as providing 'options for policymaking but should not be a rigid set of rules' (ibid., para. 56). And 'green economy policies' should 'be consistent with international law', 'respect each country's national sovereignty', 'promote sustained and inclusive economic growth' and 'not constitute a...restriction to international trade' (ibid., para. 58).

By contrast, the 2010 UN Secretary-General's report *Harmony with Nature* to the United Nations made some valid points:

> The present technological age has seen an impoverishment in the historical relationship between human beings and nature. Nature has been treated as a commodity that exists largely for the benefit of people, and all environmental problems as solvable with a technological fix. Loss of biodiversity, desertification, climate change and the disruption of a number of natural cycles are among the costs of our disregard for nature and the integrity of its ecosystems and life-supporting processes. As recent scientific work suggests, a number of planetary boundaries are being transgressed and others risk being so in a business-as-usual world.
> (UN, 2010, para. 101)

The key issue, the commodification of nature, is mentioned here, but not further discussed. Neither the report nor Rio + 20 made any attempt to relate this issue to the Summit's two key themes (i.e. green economy and institutional reform).

Saving the commons from the markets

Any such attempt would have to acknowledge that the commons cannot be sensibly privately owned and traded on markets. Fresh water, healthy soil and clean air, but also the oceans, the atmosphere and diversity of life, are essential conditions for human life and well-being. This takes good governance.

A governance regime that aims to prevent 'the tragedy of the commons' (Hardin, 1968) must succeed in coordinating norms of behaviour that preserve and enhance the commons. Private ownership is not the way in which to achieve this. While private ownership may be successful in securing investment in those narrowly delimited goods which offer immediate returns, if it is relied upon alone to govern the global commons it would result in underinvestment (Kaul *et al.*, 1999). The proposed approaches (based on neoclassical economic theory) for incorporating common goods into economic analyses include:

- privatization and commodification of some aspect of the good to create a real market where it is traded;
- the generation of a shadow price through an imaginary market and then sampling citizen's hypothetical 'willingness to pay'; and
- estimating the cost of substituting alternative production sources of the good.[3]

These approaches should be rejected outright for the following type of common good: those goods which by their nature defy commodification, goods for which there is no evidence that their integrity can be protected through market based instruments, where pressing issues of social and economic justice are present (as stated in Earth Charter, principles 9–12)[4] and goods already recognized by international norms, laws and institutions as having non-market value.

There is no question that major institutional reform is required to respond to the pressing environmental challenges the world faces today, but just what shape this reform will take is still very much in question. The approach favoured at Rio + 20 is the establishment of a 'universal intergovernmental high-level political forum' (UNGA, 2012, para. 84). This forum would provide a platform for leadership, continued dialogue, information sharing and system wide cooperation and coordination to advance the sustainable development agenda. The design of the forum is to be defined through an intergovernmental, transparent negotiation process under the UN General Assembly. Crucially, the need to promote intergenerational solidarity in order to achieve sustainable development will be considered, with the Secretary General being invited to present a report on the issue (ibid., para. 86).

If a truly 'green' economy is to be achieved the greatest challenge lies in reclaiming the commons. The concept of 'commons' has its roots in Roman law where *res communis* was separated from *res privatae*. This meant that there was a clear distinction between what could be privately owned and what belonged to all. The Justinian Institutes outline that 'By the law of nature these things are common to mankind – the air, running water, the sea, and consequently the shores of the sea' (Sanders, 1922: 90). Those things common to mankind were not to be owned, mankind was instead to assume a guardianship role over them.

Current international environmental law is far from protecting the global commons. It is 'essentially a regime for the protection of property rights rather than a regime for the protection of the environment *per se*' (Taylor, 1998: 118). To live up to its promise, law protecting the environment needs to enable guardianship over the commons either through existing or new institutions.

The state as a trustee

One option is to conceptualize the state as an environmental guardian or trustee. (Bosselmann, 2008: 149). This can be achieved in two steps. The first step is through the revival and recognition of the state holding a fiduciary duty as the 'trustee' of its people and the environment. The second step is to draft and implement legally binding treaties that will correctly address the main environmental issues regarding the sustainability and exploitation of the global commons.

The idea of the state as a trustee for its people and the environment is not a new concept. International law defines the state as holding the responsibility to act as the agent for its people. 'State sovereignty denotes the effective authority of a state to rule and represent a permanent population within a given territory' (Fox-Decent, 2011: 90). This provides the basis for a fiduciary relationship to arise between a state and its people.

There are three fundamental conditions from which a fiduciary relationship arises. First, the fiduciary holds 'administrative power over the beneficiary or certain of his or her interests'; second, 'the beneficiary is incapable of controlling the fiduciary's exercise of power' ('or of exercising the type of power held by the fiduciary'); and, third, 'the relevant interests of the beneficiary are capable of forming the subject matter of a fiduciary obligation' (Fox-Decent, 2011: 93).

Applying these three conditions, it follows that a state can hold a fiduciary relationship with its people. The fundamental purpose of a state is to protect and govern its peoples, which gives a state the responsibility of establishing and upholding laws to the benefit of its citizens, satisfying the first condition. The state is the only entity capable of law making. Its citizens, in lacking the ability to individually exercise this power, see the second fundamental condition met. The third condition is not so obviously satisfied; however, fiduciary relationships are not exhaustive, with many new categories having begun to emerge in recent times. One particularly significant example of this is the newly recognized fiduciary relationship in Canada's constitutional law between the crown and native peoples (Constitution Act 1982 s 35(1)). The fulfilment of these identified fundamental conditions of a fiduciary relationship confirms that such a relationship can indeed exist between a state and its people.

Furthermore, this fiduciary relationship is arguably premised on a presumption of trust. This means that 'even in the absence of pre-existing rights and prior consent, a presumption of trust and its attendant obligations can authorize the fiduciary to act on behalf of the beneficiary' (Fox-Decent, 2011: 105). A state can consequently be said to be acting as a trustee for its people.

The fiduciary relationship between the state and its peoples must focus on protecting not just social and economic wellbeing, but environmental well-being or the foundation of life itself. It must be recognized that without a sustainable environment human life will be unable to survive. Wilson J argues that fiduciary duties may apply to 'substantial and vital non-legal or practical interests where no pre-existing legal claims exist for the beneficiary' (*Frame v Smith* [1987] 2 SCR 99). This means it is possible for the state to act as a fiduciary for its people on a trust based relationship, and this may, and should, include the protection of interests such as environmental sustainability. By extension, this should encompass the global commons, with states assuming the role of guardian or trustee.

To enable states to assume the role of guardian or trustee of the global commons, a redefinition of territorial sovereignty is required. This redefinition needs to recognize that national territories, which include parts of the global commons, are not simply the property of a nation state, but form part of the global environment as a whole. States must restrict their use and exploitation of the environment within their national boundaries in recognition of the place they hold within the larger global environment (Bosselmann, 2008: 149). A state can only succeed in this approach if its role as a guardian or trustee is prioritized over the neoliberal economic agenda that currently dominates. This demands a reformation of the state's role, which will naturally lead to tensions between territorial sovereignty on the one hand, and the well-being of the global environment on the other. With this is mind there are two factors that have been identified for consideration regarding changing the role of the state.

The first factor is the conceptual problem that will arise with territorial reform. For example, environmental thinking 'centres around the global environment', whilst legal thinking 'centres on the states' (ibid.: 149). This becomes a problem for environmental protection as the state creates both international and domestic law. Within a state any environmental laws are in competition with domestic laws that are generally speaking conducive to unsustainable development. In the international sense environmental laws represent the 'lowest common denominator' among states, giving the states a choice as to whether or not they comply with them. This leaves the global environment in a vulnerable position.

The second factor is that functions and powers of the state are constantly changing due to socio-economic relations being in a continuous state of flux. For instance, economic globalization has restricted the exercise of states' sovereign powers, as too has international environmental law. The globalization of both the economy and ecology are perhaps the greatest challenges that modern state sovereignty has faced. While states have responded well to economic globalization, the same cannot be said for ecological globalization. The modern territorial state is in need of a new identity to effectively accommodate global commons protection.

Although both factors are in conflict, there are no reasons in principle why the definition of territorial sovereignty should not change, as long as a state's basic functions to govern and serve its peoples common interests are not in jeopardy. It is imperative therefore that current systems are readjusted to adapt to the ecological reality of the global environment (Bosselmann, 2008: 150).

There is no argument that state participation is required for the successful management and sustainability of the global environment. To redefine the role of the state as a trustee or guardian will necessitate states' participation in the creation and subsequent implementation of legally binding international laws. Perhaps the biggest failure of Rio + 20 was that states were not prepared to even discuss such prospects, though this was not for lack of proposals to do so.

Trusteeship for the global commons

One such proposed agreement was the Draft People's Sustainability Treaty (2012), designed to follow up on the recommendation of the 'Brundtland Commission Report' to create a charter articulating principles to guide nations in transitioning to sustainable development. Such a charter was initially proposed at the Earth Summit in 1992, but failed to be adopted.

The 2012 Draft Treaty is significant in that it embraces and recognizes the importance of established principles and declarations such as the Stockholm Declaration, the Rio Declaration, the Johannesburg Declaration, the Earth Charter, the One Planet Living Principles, the Green Economy Coalition, the TUC 'Just Transition' principles and the new Economics Foundation. Furthermore, it places a strong focus on the Earth Charter; for example, the preamble specifically outlines the recognition of the Earth's 'vitality, diversity and beauty as a sacred trust' (Earth Charter, 2000).

Although not expressed in the wording of the document, the foundations of the Draft Sustainability Treaty would facilitate a trusteeship role of states. This is outlined most strongly in principles 3 and 12, where the recognition of intergenerational equity and restoration of natural habitats are principles that can be directly expanded to implement binding trusteeship roles for the state.

To see these trusteeship principles entering discussions at UN level, a political body must be established with the purpose of monitoring and promoting international environmental agreements, such as the proposed Draft People's Sustainability Treaty (2012).

The creation of a 'high-level political forum' (UNGA, 2012, para. 84) is among the few concrete outcomes of Rio + 20. The forum is to replace the UN Commission on Sustainable Development and will be mandated by the General Assembly. The decision on format and organizational aspects of the forum allows for an 'open, transparent and inclusive negotiation process' and recognition of 'intergenerational solidarity' and 'needs of future generations' (ibid., para. 86). All this provides global civil society with new opportunities that should be followed through (Stakeholder Forum, undated).

One prominent proposal for the 'high-level political forum' is the creation of a 'World Environment Organization' (WEO), as proposed by the European Union and several of its member states. The WEO could be established in one of two ways: via a treaty, or by way of a UN General Assembly resolution. The main principle of this organisation would be to operate first and foremost with the interests of the global environment in mind, rather than states' interests taking precedence (Bosselmann and Schroeter, 2012: 49). It would ideally be given a mandate to act in a trusteeship function over the global commons, thereby preventing individuals or states from exploiting these areas for economic short-sightedness.

Within the authority of the WEO should be included those areas that are yet to have been claimed as territory by states, such as the seabed, subsurfaces and Antarctica (Kimball, 1993). In addition areas such as the atmosphere and the highs seas could be within the organization's jurisdiction (Barnes, 2006; Wood, 2013). Essentially the WEO would stand in the position of a legal guardian or trustee of the global environment and future generations (Bosselmann *et al.*, 2012). This is an extension of the principle that allows guardians to be designated as the legal voice of persons who are unable to speak for themselves. The environment, being voiceless, similarly deserves such legal representation to ensure its interests do not remain silenced (Stone, 1993: 34).

Conclusion

What will be the legacy of Rio + 20, twenty years from now? Will Rio + 40 call for more action, just as Rio + 20 did? This is unlikely, as the dynamics of our current crisis are not the same as they were in the past. We are quickly reaching a point of no return, making it impossible to merely build upon existing structures and trends. As the crisis unfolds, nothing will stay the same and a profound transformation is inevitable; the only choice we have is to passively endure it or try and be the masters of our destiny.

Perhaps the most likely scenario is that existing institutions of governance will continue to fail us (and future generations) while people both inside and outside these institutions will increasingly act for change. Our so-called leaders may not recognize or may not want to recognize these new leaders, but they are there and will take charge eventually. It may well happen too late, but this is a moot point. What really matters is the human spirit, the belief that we can, in fact, turn things around. The vast majority of participants at Rio + 20 shared this belief and represented the human spirit in a most extraordinary way. Is this the true legacy of Rio + 20?

Notes

1. Collapsing ecological, social, economic and financial systems are symptoms of a systemic crisis that governments (with their short-term, economic and national focus) have so far not been able to address. See, for example, Jackson (2012), Held (2006) and Bosselmann *et al.* (2008).
2. See, for example, www.uncsd2012.org/index.php?menu=62 and www.unep.org/greeneconomy.
3. See the discussion in TEEB (2010).
4. Earth Charter Principles 9–12: '9. Eradicate poverty as an ethical, social, and environmental imperative; 10. Ensure that economic activities and institutions at all levels promote human development in an equitable and sustainable manner; 11. Affirm gender equality and equity as prerequisites to sustainable development and ensure universal access to education, health care, and economic opportunity; 12. Uphold the right of all, without discrimination, to a natural and social environment supportive of human dignity, bodily health, and spiritual well-being, with special attention to the rights of indigenous peoples and minorities.'

References

Archibugi, D. (2002) 'Demos and cosmopolis', *New Left Review*, 13, pp. 24–38.

Barnes, P. (2006) *Capitalism 3.0: A Guide to Reclaiming the Commons.* San Francisco, CA: Berrett-Koehler.

Bosselmann, K. (2008) *The Principle of Sustainability.* Aldershot: Ashgate.

Bosselmann, K. and Engel, J. R. (2010) *The Earth Charter: A Framework for global governance.* Amsterdam, The Netherlands: KIT Publishers.

Bosselmann, K. and Schroeter, M. (2012) *Earth Democracy: Institutions of Governance for Sustainability*, draft White Paper for Rio + 20 (unpublished).

Bosselmann, K., Engel, R. and Taylor, P. (2008) *Governance for Sustainability.* Gland, Switzerland: IUCN.

Bosselmann, K., Brown, P. and Mackey, B. (2012) 'Enabling a flourishing Earth: challenges for the green economy, opportunities for global governance', *Review of European Community and International Environmental Law*, 21 (1): 20–38.

Deneen, P. J. (2005) *Democratic Faith.* Princeton, NJ: Princeton University Press.

Draft People's Sustainability Treaty (2012) 'Peoples' sustainability treaty on ethical and spiritual values (draft for Rio + 20)', available at http://sustainabilitytreaties.org/draft-treaties/ethical-and-spiritual-values (accessed 30 November 2012).

Earth Charter (2000) 'The Earth Charter initiative', available at www.earthcharterinaction.org/content/pages/read-the-charter.html (accessed 30 November 2012).

Fox-Decent, E. (2011) *Sovereignty's Promise: The State as Fiduciary.* New York: Oxford University Press.

Gatopoulos, D. (2012) 'Austerity protests descend into violence', *The Huffington Post*, www.huffingtonpost.com/news/greece-economy (accessed 25 November 2012).

Goldman, M. (ed.) (1998) *Privatizing Nature: Political Struggles for the Global Commons.* New Brunswick, NJ: Rutgers University Press.

Hardin, G. (1968) 'The tragedy of the commons', *Science,* 162 (3859): 1243–8.

Held, D. (2006) *Models of Democracy.* Pala Alto, CA: Stanford University Press.

Held, D., McGrew, A., Goldblatt, D. and Perraton J. (1999) *Global Transformations: Politics, Economics and Culture.* Stanford, CA: Stanford University Press.

Jackson, R. (2012) *Occupy World Street.* White River Junction, VT: Chelsea Green Publishing.

Kaul, I., Grunberg, I. and Stern, M. (1999) *Global Public Goods: International Cooperation in the 21st Century.* New York: Oxford University Press.

Kelsey, J. (2008) *Serving Whose Interests? The Political Economy of Trade in Services Agreements.* Abingdon: Routledge-Cavendish.

Kimball, L. (1993) 'Environmental law and policy in Antarctica', in P. Sands (ed.), *Greening International Law.* London: Earthscan, pp. 130–1.

Marx, K. (2001) *Critique of the Gotha Programme.* London: Electronic Book Company.

Sanders, T. C. (trans.) (1922) *The Institutes of Justinian.* Westport, CT: Greenwood Press.

Stakeholder Forum (undated) 'High level political forum', Sustainable Development 2015, available at www.sustainabledevelopment2015.org/index.php/get-involved/get-involved-initiatives (accessed 2 February 2013).

Stone, C. D. (1993) 'Defending the global commons', in P. Sands (ed), *Greening International Law.* London: Earthscan, pp. 34–71.

Taylor, P. (1998) *An Ecological Approach to International Law.* London: Routledge.

TEEB (2010) *Mainstreaming the Economics of Nature: A Synthesis of the Approach, Conclusions and Recommendations of TEEB,* The Economics of Ecosystems and Biodiversity, Geneva, Switzerland, available at www.teebweb.org/teeb-study-and-reports/main-reports/synthesis-report (accessed 1 February 2013).

UN (2010) *Harmony with Nature,* report of the UN Secretary-General, A/65/314. New York: United Nations.

UNGA (2012) 'The future we want', outcome document adopted at Rio + 20, United Nations General Assembly, available at www.uncsd2012.org/thefuturewewant.html (accessed 30 November 2012).

Vilela, M. and Corcoran, P. B. (2005) 'Building consensus on shared values: history and provenance of the Earth Charter', in P. B. Corcoran, M. Vilela and A. Roerink (eds), *The Earth Charter in Action.* Amsterdam, The Netherlands: KIT Publishers, pp. 17–22.

Wheatley, S. (2010) *The Democratic Legitimacy of International Law.* Portland, OR: Hart Publishing.

Wood, M. (2013) *Nature's Trust: Environmental Law in an Ecological Age.* Cambridge: Cambridge University Press.

22 Confronting collapse

Human cognition and the challenge for economics

William E. Rees

Prologue

Who can doubt that the world is in unprecedented ecological, economic, social and political crisis? Cities and regions all over the planet now regularly experience weather extremes so statistically improbable that they simply cannot be dismissed as 'normal variation' (see Hansen *et al.*, 2012). Climate science tells us that even if current mitigation strategies are implemented the world is headed for a catastrophic 4°C increase in mean global temperature by late century, an eventual several metres of sea level rise and even more extreme an hazardous weather events (Anderson and Bows, 2008; World Bank, 2012). This would gradually flood coastal plains destroying major cities and changing much of the rest of the world into uninhabitable desert – which would, in turn, generate hundreds of millions (or billions?) more climate refugees, all clamouring for access to the still liveable parts of the planet. Meanwhile, poverty is a persistent problem in much of the developing world and is increasing even in many industrialized nations as the rich-poor income gap increases, social tensions increase and population health deteriorates (Wilkinson and Pickett, 2009).

Just what is going on here? How has the self-proclaimed most advanced species on the planet got itself into this predicament? After all, on the surface, humans have all the resources, technology and motivation necessary to solve the global socio-ecological crisis. Morover, consider just the following intellectual and emotional qualities that distinguish *Homo sapiens* from other advanced vertebrates:

- an unparalleled capacity for evidence-based reasoning and logical analysis;
- a unique capacity to plan ahead, to shape our own future;
- the capacity for moral judgement;
- an extraordinary array of cooperative behaviours and institutions; and
- a sense of compassion for other individuals and other species.

Given such unique potential, it is fair to ask why the world community – particularly rich, economically and technologically competent nations – has failed utterly to reverse or even substantially slow the degradation of the ecosphere, narrow the income gap, reduce biodiversity loss, and so on. On the contrary, the worst impacts of global change are arguably the *result* of high intelligence. David Orr argues that the depletion and pollution of the planet 'is not the work of ignorant people. Rather it is largely the result of work by people with BAs, BSs, LLBs, MBAs and PhDs' (Orr, 1994).

The only politically acceptable solution to chronic poverty so far proposed is further economic growth, this despite the obvious role of steadily increasing fossil-fuelled material throughput as the principal driver of the global convulsions that are undermining civilization. This chapter addresses this conundrum head on. Why is modern society fixated on growth-as-solution, despite the accumulating evidence that further increases in global economic scale are counter-productive even fatally dangerous? Is there an option that might enable the entire human family to live together harmoniously within the carrying capacity of Earth? If so, why are we not adopting it? We begin by examining the origins and nature of the dominant growth-oriented economic model at work on the planet today.

Economic paradigms: social constructs all

> What the scientist's and the lunatic's theories have in common is that both belong to conjectural knowledge. But some conjectures are much better than others.
>
> (Popper, 1972)

> You may say, if you wish, that all 'reality' is a social construction, but you cannot deny that some constructions are 'truer' than others. They are not 'truer' because they are privileged, they [become] privileged because they are 'truer.'
>
> (Postman, 1999: 76)

All cultural narratives, worldviews, religious doctrines, political ideologies, and academic paradigms – including economic paradigms – are 'social constructs'. They are products of the human mind massaged or polished by social discourse and elevated to the status of *received wisdom* by agreement among members of the social group who are creating the construct (see Berger and Luckmann, 1966).

In some contexts, people more or less automatically and passively acquire their allegiance to important social constructs. For example, we gradually adopt the fundamental beliefs, values, assumptions, and behavioural norms of our 'tribe' or society simply by growing up in a particular cultural milieu. In other situations – in church or in school, for example – we are essentially the captives of social institutions that exist explicitly to indoctrinate their 'clients' with the accepted way of seeing the world. In any event, by the time most people have reached mature adulthood they will have accepted their culture's overall 'narrative' and will subscribe, consciously or not, to any number of subsidiary religious, political, social and disciplinary paradigms.

It is important to underscore that, although it masquerades as 'reality' in our consciousness, all formal 'knowledge' is, in fact, socially constructed. Some constructs are *entirely* made up – there is no corresponding structure in the natural world for 'civil rights' or 'communism', for example. These well-known concepts were birthed and given legs entirely through words and social discourse. Other socially-constructed frameworks have been erected specifically to describe corresponding real-world phenomena. For example, everyone here will agree that 'the economy' is that set of activities central to the production, distribution and consumption of goods and services in a specified region or country. Nevertheless, such activities exist in all societies whether or not the people have any formal concept of 'the economy'.

Will the real economy please stand up

As implied above, there are many different ways of conceiving the 'appropriate' structure and function of the economy. Each alternative reflects its followers' unique set of socially-constructed beliefs, values and assumptions about the structure of the economy, how it relates to other systems and how economic activities should be conducted and regulated to serve particular specified ends. Alternative economic paradigms may differ radically – entities or activities that are given prominence in one paradigm may be marginalized or omitted altogether from another. Things can get complicated – an economic paradigm is a socially constructed model that may contain other models that are themselves socially constructed!

Despite being mere constructs, ideologies and paradigms are extremely powerful. They are perceptual filters through which we interpret all new data and information; while essentially subjective, they constitute our perceived 'reality' and determine how people 'act out' in the real world. It is therefore important to emphasize that:

- no economic paradigm can ever be more than a partial representation of external reality; and
- while all paradigms belong in the domain of conjectural knowledge, not all conjectures are created equal. Some conjectures are demonstrably better than others, particularly in terms of how well they represent the real world.

> Conjectures are our trial balloons, and we test them by criticizing them and by trying to replace them, by trying to show that there can be better or worse conjectures, and that they can be improved upon…So long as a theory stands up to the severest tests we can design, it is accepted; if it does not, it is rejected.
>
> (Popper, 1972)

Table 22.1 contrasts two competing economic visions, the neo-liberal expansionist paradigm (a corrupted version of which prevails in the world today) and the emerging ecological economics vision which is struggling to emerge from the ongoing sustainability discourse. The table shows that from their epistemological roots to their policy prescriptions, these two 'pre-analytic visions' of the economy reflect vastly different perceptions of economic and biophysical reality, particularly in terms of how the economy functions in relation to the rest of the ecosphere.[1] As Coase (1997) has opined, 'Existing economics is a theoretical [meaning mathematical] system which floats in the air and which bears little relation to what happens in the real world.' Ecological economics was therefore born of necessity, a concerted effort by liberated economists, ecologists and political scientists to bring the economy back to solid ground.

Table 22.1 Comparing competing economic paradigms

Property or quality	Neoliberal (expansionist) worldview	Ecological economics (steady-state) worldview
Epistemological and scientific origins	Modern roots in the enlightenment and accompanying scientific revolution (Copernicus, Galileo, Bacon, Descartes, Newton) of sixteenth to eighteenth centuries; Newtonian analytic mechanics.	Derived from twentieth-century physics and biology; Prigoginian self-organization (dissipative structures), far-from-equilibrium thermodynamics, complex systems theory, deterministic chaos, and systems ecology.
Central scientific premise	Nature is knowable through reductionist analysis, observation and experimentation; the observer is separate from the observed; nature is thus objectified (the origin of 'objective' knowledge).	The behaviour of natural systems is unknowable (unpredictable) at the whole systems level;[2] uncertainty is large and irreducible within wide margins; holistic approaches provide the best understanding of global change but whatever our investigative stance, humankind is an integral part of the ecosphere; there is no truly objective knowledge.
Structure of analytic and management models	Foundational models tend to be simple, linear, deterministic, and single equilibrium-oriented; management strategies assume smooth change, complete reversibility and little risk.	Models are complex, non-linear, dynamic, and characterized by multiple equilibria; management strategies recognize abrupt discontinuities, dynamic boundary conditions, and potential irreversibilities, necessitating a cautious (risk-averse), boundary-oriented approach.

Table 22.1 continued

Property or quality	Neoliberal (expansionist) worldview	Ecological economics (steady-state) worldview
Attitude toward people and the future	Emphasis on the individual and immediate national interests; primary concern for the present generation; comfortable with time and space discounting.	Greater emphasis on community and collective interests generally; concerned about present and future generations; cautious about conventional discounting.
Perspectives on Nature	Humankind is the master of nature; people can adapt 'the environment' at will to serve their wants and needs; values nature mainly as a source of resources and sink for wastes.	Humanity lives in a state of obligate dependence on the ecosphere; resources ultimately control people; there are few examples of industrial 'man' successfully managing or controlling resource systems sustainably (e.g. fisheries, forests, agricultural soils). In addition to production value and exchange value, 'nature' has intrinsic worth, value for its own sake.
Economic paradigm and connectedness to ecosphere	Neoliberal (neoclassical) economics treats the economy as an growing, independent system; analytic models are generally inorganic and mechanical, lacking any physical representation of the material and energy transformations and the structural and time-dependent processes of complex systems (see Christensen, 1991).	Ecological economics sees the human economy as a fully contained, dependent, integral sub-system of the ecosphere; industrial metabolism should be analysed as a thermodynamic extension of human metabolism. Understanding the physical/material transformations that bind the economy and ecosystems, maintaining essential ecosystems functions, and recognizing the lags and thresholds characterizing ecosystems and socioeconomic systems behaviour is paramount to sustainability.
Starting point for analysis	The circular flows of exchange value between firms and households (with money as the metric).	The unidirectional and irreversible flows of low-entropy energy/matter from nature through the economy and back in degraded form.[3] (Physical measures of stocks and flows should at least supplement money as the metric.)

Table 22.1 continued

Property or quality	Neoliberal (expansionist) worldview	Ecological economics (steady-state) worldview
Role and ecological efficacy of markets	Free markets stimulate (through rising scarcity value and corresponding prices) both the conservation of depleteable assets and the search for technological substitutes; free markets and technology can therefore help decouple the economy from nature.	Markets 'work' for a limited range of familiar non-renewable resource commodities but prices for renewable flows are inadequate indicators of ecological scarcity. Market prices reveal only exchange value at the margin and do not reflect the size of remaining natural capital stocks, 'transparent' ecological functions, whether there are critical minimal levels below which stocks cannot recover, nor the ultimate contribution of such stocks to human existence or survival. There are no markets for many biophysical goods (e.g. the ozone layer) and essential life-support services (e.g. photosynthesis and waste assimilation) which have immeasurable positive economic value. Material decoupling is not occurring and is impossible.
On the substitutability of natural capital	Natural capital and manufactured capital are near-perfect substitutes. Human ingenuity and technology can make up for any depleting natural resource. Typical quote of proponents: 'Exhaustible resources do not pose a fundamental problem' (Dasgupta and Heal, 1979, p205).	Natural capital is complementary to and often prerequisite for human-made capital. Given the market failures noted above, the standard measures of scarcity (prices and costs) may fail absolutely to induce either the conservation of vital stocks or technological innovation. In any case, it is unlikely humans will devise technological substitutes for many ecospheric life support functions whose loss would be irreversible and potentially catastrophic.

Table 22.1 continued

Property or quality	Neoliberal (expansionist) worldview	Ecological economics (steady-state) worldview
Attitude toward economic growth *a) social role of growth*	Economic growth is strongly associated with human well-being. Growth in both rich and poor countries is essential as the only practical means available to alleviate human poverty within nations and to address material inequities between countries.	Beyond a measurable point, long past in most rich countries, neither objective nor subjective indicators of population health and individual well-being increase further with income growth. Any available ecological space for growth should therefore be allocated to developing countries. Perversely, growth under prevailing economic dynamics mainly accrues to the already rich (who don't need it) and cannot be relied upon as the means to relieve material poverty. Equity requires significant intra- and international redistribution of wealth and access to nature's services. Political, social, economic and institutional reforms are needed to facilitate the necessary behavioural, value and attitudinal changes. This in turn calls for sophisticated public education programs on sustainability issues.
b) ecological role of growth	Growth in the developed world will increase the market for the products of developing countries. This will enrich developing countries, helping to provide the surpluses needed for the rehabilitation and future sustainable use of natural capital. (This paradigm often sees depletion of natural capital and local pollution as a problem of developing countries.)	We cannot safely grow our way to sustainability, particularly in the developed countries – the global economy is already running a large hidden ecological deficit, attributable mostly to consumption in rich countries. Far from providing the surpluses needed to rehabilitate natural capital, material growth based on current economic assumptions and available technology depends on its further depletion, increasing the sustainability deficit and leading to accelerated ecological decline. Real wealth is measured by supportive social relationships, enduring cultural artefacts, dynamic socio-political institutions, growing natural capital stocks, and long-term ecological security.

Table 22.1 continued

Property or quality	Neoliberal (expansionist) worldview	Ecological economics (steady-state) worldview
c) Nature of limits	There are practical limits on human population, but no constraints on economic growth (i.e. on *per capita* GDP); technology can generally substitute for depleted natural capital and, over time, the economy can be 'dematerialized' by increases in economic and technological efficiency.	There are real biophysical constraints on both population and material throughput growth; humankind must live on the natural income generated by remaining stocks of natural capital. Total human impact or load is the product of population and average per capita material consumption (including waste output) and cannot be reduced below critical maximum safe levels in the foreseeable future by technology and efficiency gains alone. Ecological fiscal reform is necessary to ensure 'prices tell the truth.'
Stance on carrying capacity[4]	There are no significant limits to regional or global carrying capacity; trade can relieve any locally significant limiting factors and technological advances will alleviate more general scarcities (see above).	Carrying capacity is finite and declining and should become a fundamental component of demographic and planning analysis. Trade and technology appear to increase local carrying capacity, while actually accelerating the depletion of vital natural capital stocks on a global scale. With unregulated trade, all trading regions can exceed domestic territorial capacities, become dependent on imports of depleteable resources, and ultimately bump up against the same globally limiting factor(s). (At this stage, there are no further safety valves.)

Table 22.1 continued

Property or quality	Neoliberal (expansionist) worldview	Ecological economics (steady-state) worldview
On GDP as welfare indicator	GDP (or per capita GDP) is an imperfect indicator, but correlates well with standard measures of population health and remains the best overall measure we have of human welfare.	GDP is woefully inadequate as a measure of social and ecological welfare. It says nothing about the distribution of the benefits of growth – average *per capita* GDP can rise while the money income of poorer people falls in real terms. In high income countries, the relationship between rising incomes and subjective well-being may actually become *negative*. In any case, GDP typically includes the depreciation of manufactured capital, environmental health costs, and defensive expenditures against pollution and other forms of ecological decline as positive entries, and does not account for the depletion of natural capital. GDP can therefore continue to increase, creating the illusion of increasing well-being, while economic, ecological, and geopolitical security are all being eroded This describes Herman Daly's 'anti-economic growth' (i.e. growth that 'makes us poorer rather than richer'; Daly, 1990, p242).
Attitude toward globalization	Deregulation, global markets, and free trade enhance economic efficiency and contribute to greater social equity and international security through expansive growth in world product (GWP).	Deregulation, expanding markets, and free trade will indeed increase gross global product, but under prevailing assumptions and terms of trade they also increase income disparities and accelerate the depletion of natural capital thereby decreasing both ecological and geopolitical security. Intervention in markets (e.g. depletion and pollution charges, ecological fiscal reform) will be necessary for sustainability.

Source: adapted from Rees (1995)·

A sub-purpose of this chapter, then, is to make the case that the neo-liberal vision, always crude in its representation of both *Homo economicus* and the economic system itself, is not only failing on its own terms but has actually become an ecological hazard to the future of civilization. A sustainable alternative is needed. Canadian environmental journalist and author, Andrew Nikiforuk describes our dilemma this way:

> Let's face it: *Homo economicus* is one hell of an over-achiever. He has invaded more than three-quarters of the globe's surface and monopolized nearly half of all plant life to help make dinner. He has netted most of the ocean's fish and will soon eat his way through the world's last great apes. For good measure, he has fouled most of the world's rivers. And his gluttonous appetites have started a wave of extinctions that could trigger the demise of 25 percent of the world's creatures within 50 years. The more godlike he becomes the less godly *Homo economicus* behaves.
>
> (Nikiforuk, 2006)

A major problem with neoliberal economics that its foundational models are based on ideas borrowed from Newtonian analytic mechanics (an excellent paradigm for the design of automobile engines), have a naively constricted view of actual human economic and social behaviour, carry reductionist logic to extremes by all but excluding reference to the rest of biophysical reality and reflect arrogant certainty in their prescriptions. By contrast, while by no means perfect, ecological economics is explicitly grounded in complex systems theory and far-from-equilibrium thermody-namics (necessary to describe behaviour of real-world economic systems, social systems and ecosystems), adopts a much more generous view of human nature, perceives the economy as an integral component of the ecosphere and accepts the need to adapt the economy to irreducible systemic uncertainty (Table 22.1). Keep in mind that every economic system is, in effect, an experiment that necessarily tests its fundamental propositions against the reality within which it is embedded. When a model fails the 'severest tests we can design' it should be modified or rejected and replaced outright. Given the current scale of economic activity, a faulty economic paradigm has the potential not only to undermine the world economy but also to wreck the biophysical basis of its own existence. The question is, based on the evidence, should we be considering rejecting the neo-liberal 'conjecture' and replacing it with (at least for starters) something resembling the ecological economics framework?

The cultural roots of bio-economic failure

And what is the evidence that the growth paradigm is failing? As noted at the outset, he world community is facing an unprecedented global ecological crisis. Anthropogenic greenhouse gases are accumulating in the atmosphere and resultant climate change is a fact; 75 per cent of the world's fish stocks are over-exploited; ocean dead (anoxic) zones are spreading; deserts are expanding; tropical deforestation wreaks havoc with biodiversity; half the land area of Earth has been appropriated for human purposes; soil degradation and rising energy costs threaten future food production; water scarcity is an urgent and growing problem for millions of people, particularly in densely populated poor countries – the list goes on. While each of these 'problems' is serious in itself, all are merely symptoms of a greater systemic malaise – *gross human ecological dysfunction*. Like all other species, *H. sapiens* has an innate tendency to expand to occupy all accessible habitat and to use all available resources (in the case of humans, 'availability' is defined by technology; Rees, 2010). These natural predispositions are currently being reinforced by a cultural and economic narrative based on the myth of continuous progress and perpetual economic growth. The human enterprise is therefore breaching biophysical limits and destabilizing critical life-support systems on this finite planet (WWF, 2008, 2010; Rockström *et al.*, 2009). No individual symptom of the resultant dysfunction can be solved without addressing this overall syndrome.

One source of eco-dysfunction is techno-industrial society's social construction of man-in-nature. The citizens of modern nations tend to perceive 'the environment' as separate from the human enterprise, as a distant 'other' that serves primarily as resource trove and physical backdrop for human affairs.[5] Consistent with this perception, the ethical foundation for human relationships with 'the environment' in industrial societies is *utilitarian, anthropocentric* and *instrumentalist*. It is utilitarian in that other species matter only to the extent that people value them; anthropocentric in that humans are assigning the values; and instrumental in that all of nature is regarded as a resource trove that exists strictly for human satisfaction (Randall, 1988). Certainly there is nothing about the distant 'other' that might constrain human ambitions, including the myth of continuous economic growth.

Indeed, the divorce of humans from nature is virtually complete when it comes to the neo-liberal market economics that dominates global development thinking today. 'Something strange happened to economics about a century ago. In moving from classical to neo-classical economics...economists expunged land – or natural resources' from their theorizing (Wolf, 2010). Land and resources (read 'the ecosphere and natural processes') were quietly dropped from mainstream production functions as capital (including finance capital) and knowledge came to be perceived as the principal sources of wealth and drivers of growth.[6]

This cognitive fiction has been maintained historically because:

- the undervaluation of nature relative to other factors of production (no one pays the earth for the resources we extract) means that in

'advanced' economies land and resources *per se* often contribute only marginally to GDP; and
- technology has succeeded (until recently) both in keeping the costs of extracting raw materials low and in finding substitutes for some resources that have become scarce (e.g. coal substituted for wood as the primary fuel of the industrial revolution; fish-farms increasingly substitute for wild fish-stocks).

Bottom line? Most contemporary economic models still float free from biophysical reality, blind to the energy and material flows essential for human existence, to the state of vital natural capital stocks, and to the complex dynamics of the ecosystems that produce them (see Christensen, 1991).

The ethereal economy

All thinking about the world involves a degree of abstraction. Economics has taken this principle further than any other social science.

(Wolf, 2010)

This is no trivial perceptual lapse. The traditional starting point for neoliberal economic analysis is the 'circular flow of exchange value', typically portrayed in standard texts as 'a pendulum movement between production and consumption within a completely closed system' (Georgescu-Roegen, 1971a). This model is totally abstracted from biophysical context. Value embodied in goods and services flows from firms to households in exchange for spending by households (national product). A supposedly equal value, represented by factors of production (labour, knowledge, finance capital), flows back to firms from households in exchange for wages, rents, dividend, and so on (national income). Some economists describe this stripped-down economy as a form of perpetual motion machine that generates a 'flow of output that is circular, self-renewing, self-feeding' (Heilbroner and Thurow, 1981). Indeed, the circular flows model makes no reference whatever to the energy and resources required to produce the goods and to generate the income flows that the model does represent. Thus, in economists' minds, 'the circular flow is an isolated, self-renewing system with no inlets or outlets, no possible point of contact with anything outside itself' (Daly, 1991: 196). Such a model can neither anticipate nor explain resource scarcity or pollution problems. Considering the economic process as a circular flow without considering the unidirectional throughput of energy and matter is akin to studying physiology in terms of the circulatory system with no reference to the digestive track. One might as well ask engineering students to fathom how 'a car can run on its own exhaust' or biology students to accept that 'an organism can metabolize its own excreta' (ibid.: 197).

The emergence of major ecological problems in the 1960s forced economists to adapt their thinking and at least acknowledge the existence of something outside the economy. Figure 22.1 shows the still-prevailing vision of the economy–environment relationship from the perspective of mainstream *environmental* economics.[7] Note that there are still two separate systems. And while the economy may draw on the environmental 'other' for resources but this is not really a critical relationship – many economists believe that, abetted by free-market incentives, human ingenuity will find technological substitutes for any product of nature that humans may deplete.[8] Similarly, we can solve problems arising from pollution (the over-filling of waste sinks) by 'internalizing the externalities' – putting a market price on waste sink functions. (Consider contemporary efforts around the world to put an effective price on carbon emissions.)

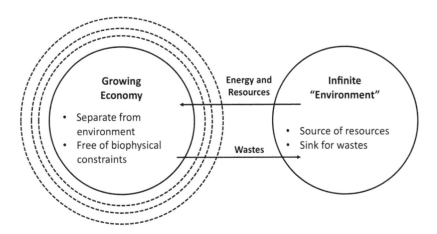

Figure 22.1 Growth-based neoliberal economics treats the economy as a separate, open, growing, quasi-independent system lacking any important connectedness to an inanimate 'environment'

Consistent with this perspective, some economists persist in their attempts to unshackle the economy from its annoying ties to the environment. Using abstract money-based models, they suggest that the human enterprise is actually 'dematerializing', that economic activities are 'decoupling' from the natural world.[9] The critical implication is that the human enterprise should be able to continue consuming and growing unaffected by resource depletion or changes in the state of the ecosphere. In effect, then, main-stream economic theory dissolves ecological constraints – or takes 'the environment' to be limitless – thus freeing the economy for perpetual growth (Figure 22.1). This is one reason why politicians and policy makers rarely hesitate to 'trade off' ecological concerns for economic gain (with a generally willing populace cheering from the bleachers). Economic growth has thus become the strongest plank in the policy platforms of most governments around the world for at least the last half century (see Victor, 2008).

Biophysical reality: The human enterprise as 'dissipative structure'

Any effort to articulate a 'truer' alternative construct of humankind–environment relationships must include a sound understanding of the biophysical laws underlying those relationships. One of the most fruitful ways of conceptually reconnecting people to nature starts with contemporary interpretations of 'far-from-equilibrium' thermodynamics. The starting point for this approach is the second law of thermodynamics, the entropy law.

In its simplest form, the second law states that any spontaneous change in an isolated system – a system that can exchange neither energy nor material with its environment – increases the system's 'entropy'. This is a technical way of stating that things naturally tend to wear out and run down. With each successive change, an isolated system loses potential – energy dissipates, concentrations disperse, gradients disappear. Eventually, the system reaches 'thermodynamic equilibrium', a state of maximum entropy in which no point is distinguishable from any other and nothing further can happen.

Of course, many systems in nature from new-born infants, through cities, to the entire ecosphere are hardly sliding toward equilibrium. The ecosphere, for example, is a highly-ordered self-organizing system of mind-boggling complexity, multi-layered structure and steep gradients represented by millions of distinct species, complex functional dynamics and accumulating biomass. Over geological time its internal diversity, structural/functional complexity, and energy/material flows have generally *increased* (i.e. the ecosphere has been moving ever *further* from the equilibrium state). Indeed, this phenomenon may well be the measure of life. As Prigogine (1997) asserts, 'distance from equilibrium becomes an essential parameter in describing nature, much like temperature [is] in [standard] equilibrium thermodynamics'.

Since living systems *gain* in structural mass and functional complexity over time, scientists and philosophers long thought they were exempt from the second law. This is not the case – all systems are subject to the same processes of entropic decay. (There are no known violations of the second law.) The paradox dissolves only when we recognize that all living systems, from cellular organelles to entire ecosystems and the ecosphere are *open* systems that freely exchange energy and matter with their host 'environments'.

Most critically, systems biologists have begun to emphasize that living systems, including the human enterprise, exist in overlapping nested hierarchies in which each component sub-system ('holon') is contained by the next level up and itself comprises a complex of linked sub-systems at lower levels. (Think of Russian 'nesting' dolls). This organizational form is the basis for 'SOHO' (self-organizing holarchic open) systems theory (see Kay and Regier, 2002). Within the hierarchy, each sub-system (or holon) grows and maintains itself using energy and material (negentropy) extracted from its 'environment' – its host system – one level up. It processes this energy/matter internally to produce and maintain its own structure/ function and exports the resultant degraded energy and material wastes (entropy) back into its host. In short, all living organisms produce and maintain their *local* organization as far-from-equilibrium-systems (i.e. they increase local negentropy) at the expense of increased *global* entropy, particularly the entropy of their immediate host systems (Schneider and Kay, 1994, 1995). Because all self-organizing systems survive by continuously degrading and dissipating available energy and matter they are called 'dissipative structures' (Prigogine, 1997).

SOHO thermodynamics should revolutionize economists' understanding of 'humans-in-nature'. Ecological economists argue that the entire human enterprise, like the ecosphere, is a self-organizing far-from-equilibrium dissipative structure. However, the human enterprise is also an open, growing, dependent *sub*-system of the materially closed, non-growing finite ecosphere (Table 22.1 and Figure 22.2). Thus, while the ecosphere evolves and maintains itself in a dynamic steady state by 'feeding' on an extra-terrestrial source of energy and by continuously recycling matter, the human sub-system continuously grows by 'feeding' on its supportive ecosystems and injecting its wastes back into them. From this perspective, the most important flows in the economy are not the circular flows of money values but rather the one-way, irreversible flows of energy and material. In effect, the growing increasingly consumption-based human enterprise is thermodynamically positioned to consume and dissipate the ecosphere from the inside out (Rees, 1999).[10]

Let's pause to ponder the socio-economic implications of this relationship.[11] Again, SOHO theory and far-from-equilibrium thermodynamics dictate that the human subsystem can grow and maintain its internal order *only* by degrading the ecosphere and increasing global entropy. The production of *anything* – an e-mail message, our own bodies, an ocean liner – requires the extraction and dissipation of useful energy and material and the ejection of useless waste. These are irreversible processes. The energy consumed is almost immediately permanently radiated off the planet and, while the material may remain in the system, it is often chemically transformed and widely dispersed into the air soils and water. Recapturing such dissipated material is economically impossible. Even recycling or reusing consolidated wastes (such as aluminium cans and glass bottles) invariably requires the consumption/dissipation of additional energy. To reiterate, *any* so-called 'productive' activity that raises the human system ever further from equilibrium is actually mostly a consumptive process that simultaneously degrades the ecosphere.

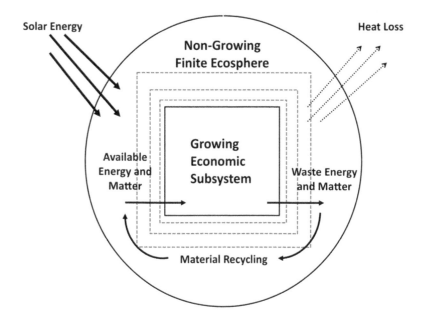

Figure 22.2 Ecological or steady-state economics sees the human enterprise as an open, fully contained, dependent subsystem of the living but non-growing ecosphere

All of which means that, contrary to popular belief, there is an inevitable and unavoidable conflict between *continuous* material economic growth and the maintenance of ecosystems integrity. Indeed, every so-called 'environmental problem' from fisheries collapses and deforestation (overexploitation) to marine dead zones and greenhouse gas accumulation (excess waste pollution) can be explained by reference to second law relationships. This in turn suggests two hard criteria for biophysical sustainability: The human enterprise must not on average consume more of 'nature's goods and services than ecosystems can produce nor discharge more wastes than ecosystems can assimilate or it risks descent into entropic chaos. And there is no escape from the grip of the second law. As physicist Sir Arthur Eddington famously observed, thermodynamics 'holds the supreme position among the laws of nature...If your theory is founded to be against the Second Law of Thermodynamics, I can give you no hope; there is nothing for it but to collapse in deepest humiliation' (Eddington, 1929).

The human ecological footprint

Consistent with the foregoing, the first questions of human ecology and sustainability economics should be:

- 'How much of Earth's biocapacity is required to sustain any specified human population?
- How does this compare with available supplies?

We can answer these questions using ecological footprint analysis (Wackernagel and Rees, 1996; Rees, 2006; WWF, 2008, 2010). As with other tools in ecological economics, the emphasis shifts to physical flows from money flows.

Ecological footprint analysis (EFA) starts from a series of inarguable premises:

- The human enterprise is an integral and fully dependent subsystem of the ecosphere;
- Most human impacts on ecosystems are associated with energy and material extraction and waste disposal (i.e. economic activities);
- We can convert many of these energy and material flows to a corresponding area of productive or assimilative ecosystems; and
- There is a finite area of productive land and water ecosystems on Earth.

We therefore formally define the ecological footprint of any specified population as:

The aggregate area of land and water ecosystems required on a continuous basis to produce the resources that the population consumes, and to assimilate (some of) the wastes that the population produces, wherever on Earth the relevant land/water may be located.

(Rees, 2006)

Population eco-footprints are based on final demand for goods and services. The area of the eco-footprint therefore depends on four factors: the population size, its average material standard of living, the average productivity of land/water ecosystems, and the efficiency of resource harvesting, processing, and use. Regardless of the relative importance of these factors and how they interact, *every population has an ecological footprint* and the productive land and water captured by EFA represents much of the 'natural capital' (productive natural resource base) required to meet that study population's consumptive demands.[12]

Note also that ecological footprints can be interpreted in terms of thermodynamic theory. The human enterprise is a 'dissipative structure' whose metabolic activities irreversibly dissipate useful energy and material (negentropy) and increase global entropy. It follows that, since the production of renewable resources is driven by solar energy, a population's ecological footprint is the area required, on a continuous basis, to regenerate photosynthetically the energy and biomass equivalent of the negentropy being consumed by that population. This rate of consumption is theoretically sustainable as long as adequate exclusive productive ecosystem area (biocapacity) is available.

The comparative eco-footprints of nations

Because consumption depends on income, per capita eco-footprints are strongly correlated with GDP per capita. Figure 22.3 shows the average per capita eco-footprints for a cross-section of countries. The citizens of rich countries like the United States and Canada need an average of 4–10 global average hectares (10–25 acres) to support their consumer lifestyles. Meanwhile, the chronically impoverished get by on less than half a hectare (one acre; WWF, 2008).

Unlike abstract sustainability indicators that have no theoretical limits (e.g. GDP per capita), EFA can be used to compare demand with available supply. Significantly, the data show that many (mostly rich) countries have eco-footprints several times larger than the area of their domestic productive landscapes and waterscapes. The Netherlands, for example, uses four times as much productive ecosystem area as is contained within its own borders; Japan's eco-footprint is *eight* times greater than the country's domestic

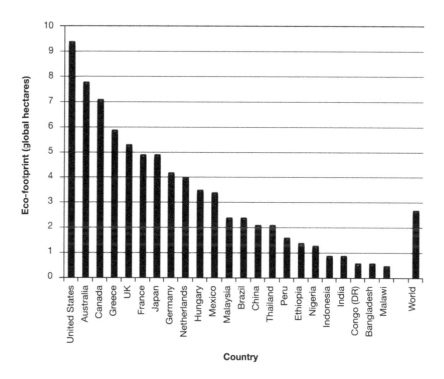

Figure 22.3 Per capita ecological footprints of selected countries

Source: 2005 data from WWF (2008)

biocapacity. Neither country could support more than a fraction of its present population on domestic biocapacity if cut off from external sources by climate change, energy shortages or geopolitical conflict.

Even if they have fiscal surpluses, all such countries are running ecological deficits with the rest of the world. This means that their populations survive mostly on biocapacity (both productive and assimilative capacity) appropriated from poorer countries, a few large relatively low-density countries such as Canada, and the global commons. Eco-footprinting thus reveals a hidden impact of global trade. The enormous purchasing power of the world's rich nations enables them to finance their ecological deficits by extending their ecological footprints deeply into exporting nations and the open ecosphere. Wealthy and powerful nations can now achieve through global commerce what used to require territorial occupation. From the ecological economics perspective, globalization has enabled an increasingly unsustainable entanglement of nations in which the world's moneyed elites gain market access to remaining pockets of productive natural capital, often at the expense of the poor. This relationship is clearly not sustainable under conditions of continuous growth.

Eco-footprints and global equity

Globalization creates additional problems. By separating production from consumption, globalisation blinds consumers to the fact that their survival may depend on the sustainable management of landscapes and waterscapes half a world away. Meanwhile, competition among commodity suppliers bids down world market prices and dissipate producer surpluses some of which might have gone toward maintaining productive natural capital. Long-distance exploitation therefore tends to accelerate the depletion of the foreign ecosystems upon which the importing populations now depend and risks the long-term sustainability of *both* trading partners (Kissinger and Rees, 2009).

Another obvious problem is that not all countries can run eco-deficits – for every sustainable deficit there must be a permanent surplus somewhere else. Unfortunately, the apparent 'surpluses' of the few large 'under-populated' countries such as Australia and Canada have already been absorbed into the eco-deficits of other countries. This means that there *is* no global eco-surplus. On the contrary, the average citizen of Earth had an eco-footprint of 2.7 global average hectares (Figure 22.3) while there are only ~1.8 ha of bio-productive land and water per person on the planet (WWF, 2010). Although half the population is still in poverty, the world is well into a state of ecological 'overshoot' – the human enterprise is using about 50 per cent more bio-productive and waste sink capacity annually than the ecosphere can regenerate. The world community is living, in part, by depleting natural capital and degrading ecosystems essential for survival – the very definition of unsustainability.[13]

Eco-footprint studies draw out another sobering socio-economic reality inaccessible to mainstream analysis. Extending the wealthy lifestyles of North Americans or Europe to the poor is wishful thinking. To raise just the present global population to North American material standards using existing technologies would require the biocapacity of four to five Earth-like planets. Since appropriate miracle technologies are not yet available, and we are unlikely to acquire the services of even one more Earth, we will probably have to do with the one we have. Perhaps we should get used to it!

Conclusions: strong sustainability, equity and the steady-state economy

A new scientific truth does not triumph by convincing its opponents and making them see the light, but rather because its opponents eventually die, and a new generation grows up that is familiar with it.

(Planck, 1949: 33)

Far-from-equilibrium thermodynamics and EFA underscore the fact that the human enterprise is fully imbedded in the ecosphere. Civilization remains dependent on natural capital and dematerialization is not taking place. Indeed, demand is increasing exponentially while supply is declining. These facts underscore the central place of the strong sustainability criterion in any global sustainability initiative:

A society is sustainable if and only if it maintains adequate *per capita* physical stocks of productive natural capital (biocapacity) from one accounting period to the next. (Manufactured capital should similarly be maintained, but in a separate account).

The world is currently in violation of this criterion; the human enterprise is in overshoot. Consumption increasingly exceeds sustainable (Hicksian) natural income on the global scale so that capital stocks (and therefore subsequent sustainable income) are in decline.

Can we 'socially construct' an alternative economic model and economy that better maps to reality? First we must acknowledge that because it is a global in scale, unsustainability is a collective problem requiring collective solutions. No person nor nation can become sustainable on his/its own. Perhaps for the first time in human history, *individual and national self-interest has converged with humanity's collective interests* (Rees, 2008).

In grasping this nettle, humanity must better exploit those qualities that make us unique: intelligence and reason; the capacity to plan ahead; the tendency to cooperate and the ability to extend compassion to others. How should such qualities be expressed to ensure the mutual sustainability of global society? Reason obviously dictates that both national and global policies for sustainability be consistent with the scientific evidence. We must therefore cooperate in a plan to restructure the global economy so that aggregate economic activity operates in a dynamic 'steady state' safely within the productive and assimilative limits of nature. To maintain adequate stocks of self-producing natural capital the world community should impose 'best science' quotas on harvests. Similarly, we should limit the exploitation of essential non-renewables and ensure investment of a sufficient portion of the proceeds in efficiency research or the search for alternatives. Once sustainable harvest and extraction rates have been set, auctions or other markets could be used to ensure the efficient allocation of available quotas among competing processors. Perverse subsidies that encourage over-exploitation and over-consumption must be phased out – market prices must reflect the true social costs of production.

Let's also assume that as good global citizens we acknowledge that today's levels of gross material disparity are intolerable. The richest 20 per cent of the world's population enjoy 76.6 per cent of private consumption the poorest 20 per cent subsist on 1.5 per cent. Almost half the human family remain in poverty living in degraded environments without basic services on less than US$2.50 per day (at purchasing power parity; Shah, 2010). Exercising their compassion for others, the wealthy should acknowledge that their historic levels of consumption are responsible for most ecological degradation to date and cannot be extended to the entire population. Basic equity considerations therefore require that rich countries initiate programs to *shrink* their national economies towards a viable energy/material steady state. North Americans, for example, would have to reduce their ecological footprints by approximately 78 per cent, from eight global average hectares *per capita* to an 'equitable Earth-share' of 1.8 global average hectares (data from WWF, 2010). Because humanity is already in overshoot, such contract-ion at the top is necessary to make room for needed growth in the developing world (Rees, 2008; Victor, 2008).

Giving up growth for sustainability-with-equity should actually not be difficult. Intelligent, well-informed citizens should be able to appreciate that in already rich countries further income growth produces no additional improvements in either population health or subjective well-being (Myers and Diener, 1995; Lane, 2000; Victor, 2008).[14] Average incomes in such countries are sometimes three to five times higher than necessary for optimal returns – further material growth merely degrades the 'enviroment' and appropriates ecological space needed for justifiable growth in low-income countries. Daly (1999) argues that the world may already entered a stage of 'uneconomic growth' in which the unaccounted social and ecological costs exceed the tangible benefits. This is growth that, in the aggregate, makes us poorer rather than richer. Unfortunately, the poor and weak suffer the costs while the rich and powerful reap the benefits (and have little incentive to change under the current paradigm).

There is another reason for sharing the wealth – greater equity is itself better for everyone. Wilkinson and Pickett (2009) show that today's widening income gap (more that poverty itself) is associated with declining population health and civil unrest and even encourages more competitive consumption. By contrast, social stability and sustainability are associated with reduced income disparity. Logic therefore dictates that even powerful nations should plan for greater equity – compassion aside, it is in their own long-term self-interest to do so. One can even find good news on the material side. Von Weizsäcker *et al.* (2009) show that the world already has the technology to enable the required 75–80 per cent reduction in energy and (some) material consumption while improving quality of life in both rich and poor countries.

Finally, we should have no fear of life in a steady-state economy. 'Steady state' simply implies that the 'throughput' of low entropy energy/matter reaches an optimum and then becomes more or less constant at the level required for maintenance and renewal. After an initial phase of growth, all healthy living systems including our own bodies, become steady-state systems. At the population and ecosystem levels, the innate propensity for further expansion constrained by negative feedback (e.g. incipient resource scarcity, predation, disease). Even the ecosphere as a whole is in an approximate steady state limited by the constant solar flux, the geographically variable availability of water and nutrients, and internal dynamics (including negative feedback). The economic sub-system has become the dominant subsystem of the ecosphere, and must increasingly conform to the operational dynamics of its host system if it is to survive. And the operational dynamics of its host are steady-state dynamics.

Note that a steady state is not to be confused with a static state. The economy needn't cease developing, it must merely stop growing. With luck and sound management it could hover indefinitely in the vicinity of its 'optimal scale' while human well-being steadily improves. There are no limits on the capacity of human ingenuity to better our quality of life, only on the quantity of throughput available to do it. And even within that constraint, new firms and even whole industrial sectors could both develop and grow even as their thermodynamic equivalents in obsolete or 'sunset' industries are phased out.

Epilogue

What is perhaps most intriguing in the evolution of human societies is the regularity with which the pattern of increasing complexity is interrupted by collapse.

(Tainter, 1995)

There is, of course, almost no possibility that the global community will opt voluntarily for anything like the sustainable steady-state-with-equity described above. It goes against the prevailing paradigmatic grain; instinct, emotion and habit regularly trump reason; society is in deep denial about the ecological crisis; humans rarely rise to their true potential in politics. According to historian Barbara Tuchman, sheer folly or 'wooden-headedness' often plays the dominant role in government. 'It consists in assessing a situation in terms of preconceived fixed notions [e.g. ideology] while ignoring any contrary signs. It is acting according to wish while not allowing oneself to be deflected by the facts' (Tuchman, 1984: 7).

Certainly, individual behavioural intransigence, combined with systemic institutional incompetence and organizational inadequacy, has played a significant role in the eventual implosion of seemingly successful human societies since the dawn of civilization (Tainter, 1988; Diamond, 2006). Thus, if history is any guide, rather than adopt a steady-state strategy, the world community is likely to further entrench the growth-bound, competitive, every-nation-for-itself *status quo* or some technologically engineered variant as the global standard. But if our best science is correct, the increasingly likely outcome of such a strategy on this crowded Earth is ecosystemic collapse, resource wars and geopolitical chaos. Not what one might expect from a *truly* intelligent, forward-looking, compassionate species.

There is a bigger problem. Previous societal collapses have been regional or otherwise of limited scale. There was always somewhere else or another time for civilization to rise and thrive again. But today's aggressive techno-industrial culture is a global consumption machine that spans the planet and still scours the earth in search of the resources needed to maintain its growth momentum. This is unprecedented in human history and has potentially unprecedented consequences. Astronomer Sir Fred Hoyle put the matter this way:

It has often been said that, if the human species fails to make a go of it…some other species will take over the running…this is not correct. We have or soon will have, exhausted the necessary physical pre-requisites so far as this planet is concerned. With coal gone, oil gone, high-grade metallic ores gone, no species however competent can make the long climb from primitive conditions to high-level technology. This is a one-shot affair. If we fail, this planetary system fails so far as intelligence is concerned. The same will be true of other planetary systems. On each of them there will be one chance, and one chance only.

(Hoyle, 1964)

There is one glimmering ray of hope in this otherwise gloomy story. The sweep and variety of modern communication technology is also unprece-dented; the real power of the internet has yet to be tested. It is conceivable that the cascade of dismal environmental data, that widespread knowledge of the chronic poverty and egregious social injustice (including a resurgence in human trafficking) that accompanies 'development' in much of the world, has begun to catalyse the emergence of a global consciousness around the modern predicament. Should this sense of shared unease foment sufficient popular unrest we may reach a critical tipping point (short of insurrection?) where public opinion forces effective political responses both within nations and by international agencies. The time will have come to forge a new, more adaptive, 'pre-analytic vision' for the economy and humanity. Subsequence success in establishing a truly new world order – living with economic security and greater equity within the means of nature – would at least extend the duration of modern humanity's 'one shot affair' on the only planet we are likely ever to know.

Acknowledgement

This chapter is revised from a presentation to the Institute for New Economic Thinking Annual Conference, Crisis and Renewal: International Political Economy at the Crossroads, Mount Washington Hotel, Bretton Woods, NH, 8–11 April 2011.

Notes

1. Economist Joseph Schumpeter famously observed that 'analytic effort is of necessity preceded by a pre-analytic cognitive act [vision] that supplies the raw material for the analytic effort' (Schumpeter, 1954). As such, one's 'pre-analytic vision' serves, albeit unconsciously, as a primary determinant of the outcome of the analysis.
2. Includes social and economic systems (i.e. any complex self-organizing system).
3. Even 100 per cent material recycling of the original good would consume additional net energy and ordered matter.
4. Carrying capacity is usually defined as the maximum sustainable population in a given area, but is better thought of as the maximum sustainable human 'load' (population × resource consumption/capita; Catton, 1986). This is the basis for ecological footprint analysis.
5. The psychological alienation of humans from nature has deep cultural roots traceable at least to ancient Greece; its modern expression flowered during the Enlightenment with the articulation of what we now know as 'Cartesian dualism'; and it has only recently found its most ebullient (and environmentally violent) expression in the ongoing scientific/industrial revolution.
6. This will seems odd to non-economists, because most people still participate in 'the economy' to acquire the material basis of their own existence.
7. *Environmental* economics is not to be confused with *ecological* economics. The former is simply an extension of the conventional analysis better to account for the costs, prices and trade-offs associated with so-called environmental goods and services. *Ecological* economics (see following section) more completely redefines the environment–economy relationship.
8. Nobel laureate economist Robert Solow put the case as follows: 'If it is very easy to substitute other factors for natural resources, then…The world can, in effect, get along without natural resources, so exhaustion is just an event, not a catastrophe' (Solow, 1974).
9. In some developed countries, GDP per capita is growing more rapidly than energy and material consumption suggesting that wealth creation is becoming less dependent on resources (i.e. production is becoming more efficient, resource productivity is increasing). Some analysts also believe that environmental problems abate as economies shift from resource exploitation and manufacturing to service industries. All such apparent 'decoupling' weakens if

we consider traded flows and actual material *consumption* (rather than dollar income) per capita.
10. Compare Figure 22.2 with Figure 22.1 and note how a simple change in structural relationships changes virtually everything else. In Figure 22.3, there is no separate 'environment' only the ecosphere and the latter *includes* the entire human enterprise. Instead of floating free from biophysical constraints, the economy is a fully contained by, and wholly dependent on, the ecosphere (see Daly, 1991). As such, it is potentially parasitic on its host (Rees, 1999).
11. Renegade economist Nicholas Georgescu-Roegen (1971a, 1971b) was among the first to understand the implications of the second law for the human economy. Since all economic activity must draw low entropy resources out of nature and dump useless high entropy waste back in, he reasoned first that 'in a finite space there can be only a finite amount of low entropy and, second, that low entropy continuously and irrevocably dwindles away'. He further speculated that since modern humans are unlikely to practice restraint in their use of resources, nature and human nature may combine to ensure that 'the destiny of man is to have a short but fiery, exciting, and extravagant life' (Georgescu-Roegan, 1975).
12. EFA is not intended to represent all human impacts, only those material demands that can readily be converted to a corresponding ecosystem area. Toxic wastes, for which there is no assimilative capacity, are not represented; similarly, such impacts as stratospheric ozone depletion are excluded because they cannot be converted into ecosystem area. We also err on the side of caution whenever data are sparse or conflicting. For all these reasons, EFA generates a *conservative* estimate of total human load.
13. The complementary empirical data include accumulating greenhouse gases, climate change, fisheries collapses, soil depletion, and so on – all are symptoms of general overshoot.
14. For example, the Canadian economy has grown by 130 per cent since 1976 and GDP per capita is 70 per cent higher. Nevertheless, there has been no change in the percentage of people in poverty or unemployed and the absolute numbers of both have increased (Victor, 2008). Meanwhile, subjective well-being is constant or declining.

References

Anderson, K. and Bows, A. (2008) 'Reframing the climate change challenge in light of post-2000 emission trends', *Philosophical Transactions of the Royal Society A*, 366 (1882): 3863–82.
Berger, P. L. and Luckmann, T. (1966) *The Social Construction of Reality*. Garden City, NY: Doubleday.
Catton, W. (1986) 'Carrying capacity and the limits to freedom', paper prepared for Social Ecology Session 1, XI World Congress of Sociology, New Delhi, India, 18 August.
Christensen, P. (1991) 'Driving forces, increasing returns, and ecological sustainability', in R. Costanza (ed.), *Ecological Economics: The Science and Management of Sustainability*. New York: Columbia University Press.
Coase, R. (1997) 'Interview with Ronald Coase', Inaugural Conference, International Society for New Institutional Economics, St Louis, MO: 17 September, available at www.coase.org/coaseinterview.htm (accessed 15 March 2011).
Daly, H. E. (1990) 'Sustainable development: from concept and theory towards operational principles', *Population and Development Review* (special issue).

Daly, H. E. (1991) *Steady-State Economics*, 2nd edn. Washington, DC: Island Press.
Daly, H. E. (1999) 'Uneconomic growth in theory and in fact', First Annual Feasta Lecture, Trinity College, Dublin, 26 April, available at www.feasta.org/documents/feastareview/daly.htm (accessed 10 March 2011).
Dasgupta, P. and Heal, D. (1979) *Economic Theory and Exhaustible Resources.* Cambridge: Cambridge University Press.
Diamond, J. (2006) *Collapse: How Societies Chose to Fail or Succeed.* New York: Viking Press.
Eddington, A. S. (1929) *The Nature of the Physical World.* New York: Macmillan, (republished by Kessinger Publishing, 2005).
Georgescu-Roegan, N. (1971a) *The Entropy Law and the Economic Problem*, Distinguished Lecture Series no 1, Department of Economics. Tuscaloosa, AL: University of Alabama.
Georgescu-Roegan, N. (1971b) *The Entropy Law and the Economic Process.* Cambridge, MA: Harvard University Press.
Georgescu-Roegen, N. (1975) 'Energy and economic myths', *Southern Economic Journal*, 41 (3).
Hansen, J., Sato, M. and Ruedy, R. (2012) 'Perception of climate change', *Proceedings of the National Academy of Sciences (USA)*, 109 (37): 14,726–14,727, available at www.pnas.org/content/109/37/E2415/1 (accessed 2 February 2013).
Heilbroner, R. and Thurow, L. (1981) *The Economic Problem.* New York: Prentice Hall.
Hoyle, F. (1964) *Of Men and Galaxies.* Seattle, WA: University of Washington Press.
Kay, J. and Regier, H. (2002) 'Uncertainty, complexity, and ecological integrity', in P. Crabbé, A. Holland, L. Ryszkowski and L. Westra (eds), *Implementing Ecological Integrity: Restoring Regional and Global Environment and Human Health*, NATO Science Series IV: Earth and Environmental Sciences, 1. Dordrecht, The Netherlands: Kluwer Academic Publishers, pp. 121–56.
Kissinger, M. and Rees, W. E. (2009) 'Footprints on the prairies: degradation and sustainability of Canadian agricultural land in a globalizing world', *Ecological Economics*, 68, pp. 2309–15.
Lane, R. (2000) *The Loss of Happiness in Market Democracies.* New Haven, CT: Yale University Press.
Myers, D. and Diener, E. (1995) 'Who is happy?', *Psychological Science*, 6 (1): 10–19.
Nikiforuk, A. (2006) 'At war with our planet', review of *The Weather Makers: How We Are Changing the Climate and What it Means for Life on Earth* by Tim Flannery (Harper Collins, 2006), *The Globe and Mail*, Toronto, 4 March, section D.
Orr, D. (1994) 'What is education for?', *In Context*, vol 27, available at (accessed 2 February 2013).
Planck, M. K. (1949) *Scientific Autobiography and Other Papers.* New York: Philosophical Library.
Popper, K. (1972) 'Conjectural knowledge: my solution of the problem of induction', in his *Objective Knowledge: An Evolutionary Approach.* Oxford: Oxford University Press.
Postman, N. (1999) *Building a Bridge to the 18th Century.* New York: Alfred Knopf.
Prigogine, I. (1997) *The End of Certainty: Time, Chaos and the New Laws of Nature.* New York: The Free Press.
Randall, A. (1988) 'What mainstream economists have to say about the value of biodiversity', in E. O. Wilson (ed.) *Biodiversity.* Washington, DC: National Academy Press, pp. 217–23.
Rees, W. E. (1995) 'Achieving sustainability: reform or transformation', *Journal of Planning Literature*, 9 (4): 343–61.

Rees, W. E. (1999) 'Consuming the Earth: the biophysics of sustainability', *Ecological Economics*, 29, 23–7.

Rees, W. E. (2006) 'Ecological footprints and bio-capacity: essential elements in sustainability assessment', in J. Dewulf and H. Van Langenhove (eds), *Renewables-Based Technology: Sustainability Assessment*. Chichester: Wiley.

Rees, W. E. (2008) 'Human nature, eco-footprints and environmental injustice', *Local Environment*, 13 (8): 685–701.

Rees, W. E. (2010) 'What's blocking sustainability: human nature, cognition and denial', *Sustainability: Science, Practice and Policy*, 6 (2), available at http://sspp.proquest.com/archives/vol6iss2/1001-012.rees.html (accessed 2 February 2013).

Rockström, J., Steffen, W., Noone, K., Persson, Å., Chapin, F. S., Lambin, E., Lenton, T. M., Scheffer, M., Folke, C., Schellnhuber, H., Nykvist, B., De Wit, C. A., Hughes, T., van der Leeuw, S., Rodhe, H., Sörlin, S., Snyder, P. K., Costanza, R., Svedin, U., Falkenmark, M., Karlberg, L., Corell, R. W., Fabry, V. J., Hansen, J., Walker, B., Liverman, D., Richardson, K., Crutzen, P. and Foley, J. (2009) 'A safe operating space for humanity', *Nature*, 461, 472–5.

Schneider, E. D and Kay, J. J. (1994) 'Complexity and thermodynamics: toward a new ecology', *Futures*, 26, 626–47.

Schneider, E. D and Kay, J. J. (1995) 'Order from disorder: the thermodynamics of complexity in biology', in M. P. Murphy and L. A. J. O'Neill (eds) *What is Life: The Next Fifty Years*. Cambridge: Cambridge University Press.

Schumpeter, J. (1954) *History of Economic Analysis*. Oxford: Oxford University Press.

Shah, A. (2010) 'Poverty facts and stats', 20 September, available at www.globalissues.org/article/26/poverty-facts-and-stats (accessed 13 March 2011)

Solow, R. (1974) 'The economics of resources or the resources of economics', *American Economics Review*, 64 (2): 1–14.

Tainter, J. (1988) *The Collapse of Complex Societies*, Cambridge: Cambridge University Press.

Tainter, J. (1995) 'Sustainability of complex societies', *Futures*, 27, 397–407.

Tuchman, B. (1984) *The March of Folly*. New York: Alfred A. Knopf.

Victor, P. (2008) *Managing Without Growth*. Cheltenham: Edward Elgar.

von Weizsäcker, E., Hargroves, K., Smith, M., Desha, C. and Stasinopoulos, P. (2009) *Factor 5: Transforming the Global Economy through an 80% Increase in Resource Productivity*. London: Earthscan.

Wackernagel, M. and Rees, W. (1995) *Our Ecological Footprint*. Gabriola Island, Canada: New Society Publishers.

Wilkinson, R. and Pickett, K. (2009) *The Spirit Level: Why Equality is Better for Everyone* London: Penguin Books.

Wolf, M. (2010) 'Why were resources expunged from economics?', *Financial Times*, available at http://blogs.ft.com/martin-wolf-exchange/2010/07/12/why-were-resources-expunged-from-neo-classical-economics (accessed 15 March 2011).

World Bank (2012) *Turn Down the Heat: Why a 4°C Warmer World Must be Avoided* Washington, DC: International Bank for Reconstruction and Development.

WWF (2008) *Living Planet Report 2008*. Gland, Switzerland: World Wide Fund for Nature.

WWF (2010) *Living Planet Report 2010*. Gland, Switzerland: World Wide Fund for Nature.

Index

For Product Safety Concerns and Information please contact our
EU representative GPSR@taylorandfrancis.com Taylor & Francis
Verlag GmbH, Kaufingerstraße 24, 80331 München, Germany